A Divided Life

A Divided Life

MEMOIRS

Bryan Forbes

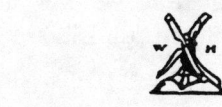

HEINEMANN : LONDON

William Heinemann Ltd
Michelin House, 81 Fulham Road, London SW3 6RB
LONDON   MELBOURNE   AUCKLAND

First published 1992

A CIP catalogue record for this book
is held by the British Library
ISBN 0 434 26828 3

Phototypeset by Wilmaset Ltd, Birkenhead, Wirral
Printed in Great Britain by
Mackays of Chatham PLC, Chatham, Kent

For Nanette with all my love

Writing is easy; all you do is sit
staring at a blank sheet of paper
until the drops of blood form on your forehead.

Gene Fowler

The life of every man is a diary
in which he means to write one story,
and writes another; and his humblest hour
is when he compares the volume as it is
with what he vowed to make it.

J. M. Barrie

ONE

I have always thought of myself as a writer who became an actor who became a screenwriter who became a film director and therefore much of my life over the past forty years has been occupied with such projects as Cyril Connolly castigated with his daunting admonition that 'all excursions into journalism, broadcasting, propaganda and writing for films, however grandiose, are doomed to disappointment. It is in the nature of such work not to last, so it should never be undertaken.' Occasionally all the various aspects of my life have overlapped, not always to my benefit, but my enduring passion has always been words. In the course of a chequered career I can recall having written some fifty-eight screenplays, seven published novels, three works of non-fiction, short stories and innumerable pieces of journalism. I list them not in order to boast, and in any case quantity does not signify quality, but to acknowledge my luck. And that list does not take any account of the stories never finished, the discarded novels, the ideas scribbled on the backs of envelopes which later, like odd telephone numbers, conveyed no sense at all. Then there are the screenplays that were subsequently tampered with and never reached the screen, and those I tampered with uncredited, for screenwriting was ever a cannibalistic pursuit. Nor must I forget the play that has been on the drawing board for ten years, with its brilliant opening I have never been able to complete but which periodically I take out from a drawer like a worthless family heirloom one is reluctant to dispose of. Added to all these are the journals which I have kept and which, when I have shuffled off into the wings and they can no longer give offence to the living, may see the light of day.

Early in my screenwriting career I was a contract script doctor, called in to perform emergency surgery on terminal cases. The most famous of these was an Alan Ladd epic called *The Black Knight*, the brain-child of half a dozen parents. One Saturday afternoon the producers rang me to say that they had reached an impasse. 'We've run out of pages,' they said, a cry not too far removed from the social embarrassment of finding oneself trapped in a strange loo without any paper (the analogy, as I quickly discovered, was valid). Could I come up with something by Monday morning? I was young and hungry, so with the misguided confidence which often goes with these two factors, I agreed and was shown footage of what had already been shot. I then set to work to make some sense of the plot.

And what was the plot? Let me try and remember.

England in the reign of King Arthur had been invaded by *Saracens disguised as Vikings* (rational minds came to a full stop right there). Meantime the 'Bishop' of Stonehenge – one of the more sublime inventions of a troubled brain – had just consecrated a new abbey at Camelot while Vestal Virgins, costumed like demented Tiller Girls, danced in celebration. Our hero, Alan Ladd, playing the simple village smithy with ambitions to become (a) a Knight of the Round Table and (b) a convert to Christianity, not necessarily in that order, was currently trapped within castle walls by the aforesaid heathen Saracens-unconvin-cingly-disguised-as-Vikings (or it could have been the other way around). In addition there was also a Fair Maiden, played by the delectable Patricia Medina, locked in an ivory tower and doubt-less desperate to contact her agent and find an escape clause in her contract. Memory blurs at this point, but I seem to recall that, inexplicably, she was imprisoned in a Spanish castle. My immediate brief was to devise a method whereby Mr Ladd could escape his captors to mumble dialogue of the Forsooth school and find God if not the nearest studio exit, meet up with the good Bishop and be handed a copy of the King James's version of the New Testament (this scene having already been shot), then with renewed vigour journey on to rescue Miss Medina. It would be fair to say that the plot anticipated and in certain respects surpassed the inventions of the *Blackadder* series.

I was handed one further problem and a final piece of advice. Sue Ladd, Alan's formidable wife, had script approval. Every word put into her husband's mouth had to be pronounced acceptable by her. 'Keep him monosyllabic,' I was instructed.

I wrestled with this madness over the weekend and arrived at the studio on the Monday morning with a few pages of dross. My answer to the problem was to have Alan dodge a few flaming arrows, then vault from the castle battlements into a conveniently placed wagon-load of hay, cut a couple of Saracens-née-Vikings in half with his trusty sword, seize the nearest horse and gallop across the rising drawbridge in the nick of time.

My pathetic efforts were duly handed to Mrs Ladd. She studied them and pronounced: 'Alan Ladd does not steal a horse, period.'

The assembled producers, director and acolytes looked around for an interpreter.

'Come again, Sue?' Irving Allen, the senior producer, asked.

'I'm telling you, Irving, Alan Ladd does not steal a horse. He steals a horse, we lose the Boy Scouts Association and The Daughters of the American Revolution, to say nothing of his fan club.'

Irving was equal to the occasion. To my amazement he not only understood what she was talking about, he had an answer. 'He's not *stealing* a horse, Sue, he's *borrowing* a horse. You know, like a Hertz car.'

'So show me the difference?'

'He's got to get out of the place, right? Otherwise the picture comes to a full stop.'

'Not on a stolen horse.'

'You want him to take a taxi?'

'Don't give me smart answers, Irving. I'm telling you the way it's gonna go. You keep the stolen horse, you start looking for another star because we're gonna be on the next plane.'

I became conscious that every head was now turned in my

direction. It was my moment to prove I was a genius. There comes a time in every screenwriter's life when he knows that he cannot kick against the pricks. I was inspired, almost certainly through sheer terror.

'How would it be,' I said, in a voice like a tape recorder run at the wrong speed, 'if we kept all the action up to the point where Mr Ladd disposes of the attacking Vikings, then runs to a sentry and says: "Is this the horse I ordered?" The sentry, taken off guard, or perhaps convinced that Mr Ladd will dispatch him too, nods in agreement. Mr Ladd jumps onto the horse and just manages to leap off the end of the drawbridge before it closes.'

What seemed like twenty-four hours elapsed before anybody spoke. All eyes were now focused on Mrs Ladd.

'Yeah, I'll buy that,' she said finally. 'It's never a waste of time to get things right.'

And in due course that is what they shot.

I offer that fragment of my apprenticeship to demonstrate early in this account that, in the film industry, everybody needs a little madness to survive.

All the same it is not given to many to realise even one ambition, and I have realised three while at the same time enjoying the infinite blessing of a happy marriage. That is the real triumph of my life, made possible by the extraordinary woman who has shared it with me and given me two ravishing daughters into the bargain. Nanette's worth to me can never be quantified and meeting her was the supreme piece of luck that ever came my way.

Fellow writers have remarked that the imagined lives we conjure in the small hours often seem more real than our own and I concur. Writing being one of the loneliest of pursuits, we work in isolation, striving to reduce the chaos of our experience to some sort of discernible pattern. Certainly anybody who elects to become a vendor of words seldom escapes from the country of the past where, as L.P. Hartley remarked with memorable effect, 'they do things differently there.' Hence, perhaps, the arrogance that triggers us to try and understand the thrust and meaning of our lives and to pay tribute to those who have influenced us.

My passion for the written word embraces authors of all hues – my taste is catholic, for there is something distasteful about literary snobbishness; books are there to be read and enjoyed, and I have always found it sad that Shakespeare is set for exams, for he was meant to be *acted* and enjoyed, not dissected in the classroom like some dead animal. From the moment when I began to earn my living and had a few spare shillings I became and have remained a manic collector to the extent that now this house resembles a vast library surrounded by small pockets of living space. (Twenty-two years ago, in the interests of self-preservation, I acquired my own bookshop. There is nothing like joining them if you can't lick them.) Obviously one's tastes change as the years go by, but I have always remained faithful to certain authors, returning again to those who illuminate the human condition. Ford Madox Ford, Graham Greene, A.E. Coppard, John O'Hara, Mauriac, the early Hemingway, H.E. Bates and an author now almost totally out of fashion, John P. Marquand, are numbered amongst my perennials. Other book-cases house a vast historical collection which starts at the time of the French revolution and continues to modern times. A third collection concentrates on films and theatre. My good friend, the composer Leslie Bricusse, shares my mania and our respective wives predict we will end our lives together in a shared house that contains no furniture, only books. Leslie once rang me from Los Angeles babbling with excitement. He had chanced across two complete sets of the original Limited Editions Club. Would I like one? I didn't hesitate: of course, count me in. A few months later I returned home from the studio one day to be greeted by, 'Were you expecting a few parcels today?' from Nanette. There was more than a hint of resignation in her voice.

'Parcels? What sort of parcels?'

'Look in the hall, if you can get into the hall, that is.'

I looked. Piled high were some forty or fifty packing cases. I felt as Howard Carter felt when he stumbled upon the tomb of Tutankhamun. The arrival of these treasures necessitated my building four new bookcases to house them, a minor consideration by comparison with Leslie who had to remodel his entire house.

The obsession began in Station Road, Forest Gate, in the East End of London, where I was born and where, until the outbreak of the thirty-nine war, I spent my early years. There, beside the long-vanished Splendide Cinema and within sight of the broken railway clock (a sort of depressed area's Grantchester timepiece signifying there was seldom honey for tea), stood the first bookshop I ever patronised. Its dismal exterior, grimed by years of the London and North Eastern Railway tank engines belching their slow progress to Liverpool Street, led one into a gloomy and disordered interior. The forbidding proprietor, whom I remember as having a perpetually angry expression, operated his dusty emporium on a barter system: you took in two magazines or books in exchange for one. How this enabled him to earn a living remains an unsolved mystery, but the shop endured until the Blitz when, together with the Splendide dream palace, it went the way of most of the East End of my childhood, including our own home.

The stock consisted mostly of magazines; the shelves were crammed with dog-eared copies of Sexton Blake, part-series of the Great War, comics such as *Film Fun* and *The Beano*, periodicals like *John Bull*, *Tit Bits*, and *Picturegoer* together with a well-thumbed selection of *La Vie Parisienne* which I now recognise catered for a more risqué taste. My favourites were the ever popular, peculiarly British sagas about public school life – *The Magnet* and *The Gem*. These bastions of our indestructible class system fascinated me and I continue to be amazed that they were the outpourings of one man, Frank Richards, a character few novelists would dare to invent for the sheer improbability of his life-style. Richards regurgitated variations of the same plot week after week, churning out in the course of a lifetime countless millions of words depicting the exploits of Billy Bunter, Harry Wharton, Bob Cherry et al, British to the core, and of course Vernon Smith, the 'Bounder of the Remove', the only one allowed a degree of venality in that he smoked and went 'down the towpath' to the local pub for an illicit beer. Strong stuff indeed! I devoured every word, believed every word, surrendering to a world I never expected to join. I think Richards' minor genius lay in the fact that he catered to young and old alike, for his countless fans remained faithful long beyond adolescence.

As a measure of Richards' influence, no less a figure than George Orwell felt compelled to do a politically slanted hatchet job in the pages of *Horizon* in which he expressed doubts that a series running for thirty years could possibly be the work of one man. Frank Richards was granted the right of reply and ably defended his unique talents and the unfounded accusation of plagiarism with style and wit. I felt he won the contest hands down.

One of Orwell's criticisms was the absence of sex in Richards' literary marathon. Rereading the article recently it struck me that Orwell was the victim of his own prejudices, for I doubt whether the fact that Harry Wharton and his merry band were denied any sexual contact with either boy or girl confused or troubled his innocent readers. Certainly I never detected any sense of sexual deprivation within my own circle of friends, avid followers of the stories like myself. We had all the normal urges and curiosities but there were few outlets for practical field studies in those halcyon pre-war days, for we did not grow up in an age sated with sex. Orwell also found the weekly descriptions of corporal punishment meted out by Richards' forbidding Mr Quelch profoundly disturbing, the implication being that such exposure was likely to steer an entire generation towards S and M. I have to report that I was frequently caned at my elementary and secondary schools, always with justification and never lastingly resented. My own nefarious exploits included tumbling through the skylight of the girls' changing rooms and riding an upright piano down an incline until it crashed straight through the door of the headmaster's study, there to disintegrate – two crimes that certainly merited six of the best. As I recall we were all cheerfully prepared to accept instant justice for such peccadilloes, rather than the imposition of a hundred lines and missing games. My form master was a Mr May. He caned us without discernible pleasure and was a very good teacher into the bargain whom we respected and to a degree loved. We knew exactly where we stood with him and where we were likely to cross his Rubicon of tolerance. Curiously I did not grow up into a child- or wife-beater as a result of these early experiences and as far as I can ascertain none of my school contemporaries, all of whom came from the same under-privileged backgrounds, went on to become serial killers.

Legend has it that Richards was paid a meagre sum for his weekly output, calculated on the number of words produced, and that when he had saved enough he then bicycled to the South of France where he promptly blew the lot at the roulette tables and despite his long career died a poor man. I would have loved to have met such a true eccentric, for he was the first author to cement my love of the printed word. To this day there is a continuing debate about the suitability of certain authors for children. Periodically literary papal bulls are issued by some self-appointed arbitress, signposting crimes that were never intended and which young readers would never suspect of their own accord. Every so often these crabbed (and I suspect childless) pundits fire a salvo in the direction of Enid Blyton; dark Freudian and racist undertones are unearthed for the unwary. The shot scatters, peppering the likes of A.A. Milne and Kenneth Grahame – the young, we are told, will be in danger of having their values corrupted for life by indiscriminate exposure to such wicked works. All balls, of course. Children of tender years are more likely to have their values distorted by a single day's viewing of television.

I did not come across the classic authors until later in life. For one thing we were never rich enough to afford books and, except for the occasional gift of an annual at Christmas, few hardbacks ever entered the house. I never saw my mother read a book until she was in her eighties when, like somebody coming off a starvation diet, she consumed three or four novels a week. For my part it wasn't until I became an evacuee billeted in the vicarage at Porthleven in Cornwall that the world of literature opened up for me. The Reverend Canon Gotto of Truro and his wife became my surrogate parents during my all-important formative years. The Canon had an eclectic taste in books. His personal preference was for detective stories – Agatha Christie, Dorothy L. Sayers, Margery Allingham figured large; he devoured them at one sitting, puffing away on his charred pipe in an ancient armchair that appeared to have been moulded to his exact shape. To live in a house that had a room called a library was amazing enough and to be given the run of it was unimaginable bliss. In addition to editions of Dickens, Thackeray and Trollope there was a complete set of *Punch* and it was from the latter that I derived a more accurate impression of what made Victorian and Edwardian England tick than from the stodgy history textbooks we studied at school.

I also found and read several volumes about the Christian martyrs which for sheer bestial horror took some beating. At an early age these confirmed in me a deep and lasting dislike for the trappings and rituals of organised Christianity, obsessed as it is with images of death rather than life, allied to the symbolic eating of flesh and the drinking of blood, accompanied by intoned mumblings that suggest a throwback to Medieval times. When I listen to the droning voice of the Church of England, I do not wish to deny the faithful their beliefs, I just feel sorry that they are denied joyousness. The Canon and his wife were truly good people and I never allowed them to suspect that I did not share their dedication, but I have never found sufficient cause to alter my opinion of Canterbury and Rome, for they have a lot to answer for in the sum total of human misery.

During this same period I was also fortunate in having a remarkable woman as my English teacher, the first person to encourage my embryonic literary talents. This was a Miss Bray, one of a large and dedicated staff at West Ham Secondary School, as it was then known, who sought to make our education embrace all aspects of the life ahead. The school now typifies a lost age in education as far as I can judge for it bears no relationship to what I read about modern comprehensives. I went to it on a scholarship when I was eleven, as callow as they come, not particularly bright, certainly innocent of most worldly ways, a very average schoolboy. But from the very first day I was cocooned within a

9

remarkable institution to which I owe much. We were taught elementary manners and disciplined if we forgot them by the inimitable Sergeant Pritchard. Ostensibly the PT instructor, he masqueraded as an unyielding martinet but in fact was a fair and inspiring old softie, spruce in his spotless whites, his moustache waxed like some stage-door masher, whose favourite expression, the one with which he invariably ended his homilies to us, was 'it simply isn't done'.

Although the school was co-ed, the good sergeant was solely responsible for instructing the boys, the only time when the sexes were segregated. I fell in love with monotonous regularity and there is nothing like an early unrequited passion to make one aspire to greater things. By some female alchemy Miss Bray not only decided that I might one day become a writer, she also discerned that I possessed hitherto hidden talents as an actor. Perhaps I was just the form show-off, the 'inky, grubby little boy' as Barrie described Ensign Blades in his play *Quality Street*, the role I played in the school dramatic society and the first time I tasted the heady brew of a live audience. Dame Edith Evans told me that she 'caught acting like the measles' and I can't improve on that, because it is an infection like no other which, once contracted, remains in the blood forever. Amazed by my success as Ensign Blades I went on to greater things, first stunning the school with a piece of vintage over-acting as the father in W.W. Jacob's melodrama *The Monkey's Paw*, and later straining the quality of everybody's mercy with my Shylock. Picture if you can (for happily no photographic evidence remains) a diminutive schoolboy wearing enough crêpe hair to stuff a mattress with, urging his unbroken voice into a parody of Tod Slaughter as Sweeny Todd. The local critic with remarkable charity (or total lack of grey matter) described me as 'possibly the finest fourteen-year-old Shylock of his generation', which conjures up a vision of an army of stunted little thespians competing for the title rather as Mel Brooks auditioned the singing Hitlers for his inspired comedy *The Producers*.

Upon leaving school and gaining a scholarship to the Royal Academy of Dramatic Art, alongside my acting training I immediately embarked on a series of turgid and mercifully unpublished novels. I think I can trace this urge to get into print to another unrequited love. During the war years RADA sported an abundance of nubile young ladies and very few young men. I believe the ratio was around twenty to one. One of my fellow students was an enchanting young actress called Pamela Brown who had already published a notable first novel, *The Swish of the Curtain*, which was a minor classic of its kind and deservedly remained in print for a long period. I was impressed and envious and determined to emulate her. First, heavily influenced by Aldous Huxley, I produced a four-hundred-page beast called *Awake and Wander* before entering my Hemingway period and what I fondly imagined would be the definitive war novel. Then I had a pastoral phase and slaved over something with the throat-slitting title *Nourished Is the Grass*, which was intended as my answer to *How Green Was My Valley*. Unfortunately a bucolic tale of life in the Lincolnshire fens was about as exciting as a sackful of dead mice. It wasn't until I was called up and commenced my war service in the army that I gained sufficient maturity and the necessary experience of life to write a number of short stories which were published as a collection after the war ended under the title *Truth Lies Sleeping*. A few of them contain some merit, but all are derivative, for by then I had discovered Saroyan and H.E. Bates. It was some twenty years before I commenced and finished another novel, and by then my life had changed out of all recognition.

What follows, then, is the story of that change and the many 'grandiose excursions' I have somehow survived. It will not be a cradle-to-grave account told in strict continuity, but rather tumbled recollections of a full life, a memoir of affection told in no particular order, since my life has always been subject to the winds of change. Looking back, I would not have had it otherwise.

TWO

The absurdities of my life have often been finely balanced against more sombre developments, and the trick has always been to try and reconcile them.

How, for instance, to come to terms, as I had to come to terms on the eve of my forty-ninth birthday, with the chilling verdict of a posse of doctors that I had MS, and balance this with appearing as Hitler at a charity dinner when the other male guests were in evening dress? The elements of potential tragedy in delicate juxtaposition with farce. Perhaps that is always the lot of the entertainer.

Let us leave the question of my health until later and begin with Hitler. Like most people in our profession, Nanette and I are frequently asked to lend our time and names to good causes. For several years we were invited to appear at a charity fancy dress dance. One particular year the invitation stated that the theme would be *The Spirit of the Thirties*. I was directing a film at the time and the question of what I would go as did not occupy my every waking hour. Nanette took herself off to Bermans, the estimable theatrical costumers, but I left it all too late. Returning from the studio on the evening of the event I was immediately thrown into a panic, bereft of any inspiration. In desperation I dressed myself as a gangster, but the result was pathetic. 'You can't go looking like that,' the family said, 'you look ridiculous.'

This justifiable comment threw me into a rage.

'Very well,' I said, 'I won't go at all.'

'You have to go,' Nanette cajoled. 'You're the guest of honour and you're making the speech.'

'Why don't you go as Hitler, Daddy?' our elder daughter Sarah said, trying to be helpful.

'Hitler?'

'Well, it's better than your choice.'

Finally persuaded, I dug out an old army uniform, some cowboy boots belonging to Elton John, and a large Lady Macbeth belt from an old costume of Nanette's. While she and Sarah hastily fashioned a swastika armband, I applied a quantity of brilliantine to my hair, plastered the famous forelock into position and cemented the whole with a lacquer spray. The final touch was to add the moustache with one of Nanette's indelible eyebrow pencils.

Thus disguised we rode out into a foggy November night in my storm-trooper-wagon which happened to be a Mercedes 600. Still in a bad mood, I lost our way in the fog.

'Go into that pub and ask the directions,' Nanette suggested.

'Don't be ridiculous! How can I go into a pub dressed as Hitler?'

We journeyed on through thickening fog and more by chance than design eventually reached our destination. By now we were disgracefully late and an anxious welcoming committee was waiting on the steps to greet us.

'Do you remember the name of our hosts?' I asked. Nanette didn't. For the first time since its arrival I took out the invitation card. With horror I read: THE SPIRIT OF THE THIRTIES, then in much smaller type, *Women fancy dress, Men black tie*.

There was nothing for it. Hitler got out of his Mercedes and advanced to meet our astonished hosts. They were all too polite or too stunned to pass comment on my appearance and we were escorted into the dining room where a further three hundred equally stunned guests awaited our journey to the top table. To cap it all it was primarily a Jewish charity. How I survived that evening I will never know. There was a point later on when I had to conduct the auction, and, in an agonised effort to make light of my predicament, I offered a signed copy of one of my own books with the words, 'What am I bid for *Mein Kampf*?' There were no takers. The episode still gives me recurring nightmares and needless to say we were never invited again.

I am a great believer that luck, good and bad, goes in cycles, and I suppose anybody who at an early age elects to become an actor has already settled for a life without security. At any given time the greater proportion of Equity members are out of work, or 'resting' as we prefer to call it. During various stages of my career, when I was primarily an actor, I have taken a variety of jobs to keep afloat. I have been a waiter in a café, served at the petrol pumps in a garage and helped out in a friend's bookshop – all grist to a writer's mill. There was a point early in our marriage when I had been without work of any kind for six months and of necessity I seriously entertained the offer of a partnership in a garage. While Nanette tried to argue me out of such a decision I set about convincing myself that there could be a life outside my cherished profession. I can remember we were lying on the bed in our minuscule East Sheen flat, Nanette in tears, having exhausted each other in endless discussions, when the phone rang.

It was a film producer named Aubrey Baring. Was I possibly free and available to accept a role in Carol Reed's new film, *The Key*, starring William Holden and Sophia Loren, which he was producing with Carl Foreman? I would be required for the entire fifteen weeks' schedule in one of the featured roles.

Galvanised into sitting bolt upright, I still managed to keep my wits about me. All actors have a built-in instinct for self-preservation, and rule one is never let anybody know you are desperate for work.

'That's wonderful,' I said, as calm as Jack Hawkins on the bridge during a naval battle. 'Say again when you would need me.'

'Starting July seventeenth.'

'The seventeenth?' I said, introducing a note of doubt. 'That could be tricky. Let me just look at my diary.'

I didn't possess a diary, but I rustled a copy of the newspaper close to the telephone mouthpiece.

'No, I'm working right up until the nineteenth,' I told him while Nanette regarded me with understandable horror.

'Oh, I don't think a couple of days presents any problem,' Aubrey replied. 'We can work round that.'

And so it was. My role was the First Mate to Bill Holden's Captain on a wartime ocean-going tug. The majority of the film was shot on location in Weymouth. Every day cast and crew sailed out on a pea-green boat and headed for what always seemed stormy waters beyond the Portland Race. Poor Carol Reed was a bad sailor and existed on a diet of cigarettes, Benzedrine and sea-sickness pills. I somehow managed to survive the fourteen queasy hours we spent afloat most days, though I confess that thoughts of the old heave-ho were never far distant.

At one point there was a long and difficult sequence involving a U-boat and a burning freighter. The Royal Navy provided a submarine, HMS *Trespasser*, to masquerade as the U-boat, and special-effects men went aboard the hired freighter to position their gas jets and explosive charges. Aiming for maximum realism, Carol had devised a stunning shot whereby we approached the burning ship and slid alongside it at close range. Fire at sea being every mariner's nightmare, every precaution was taken to ensure that the special effects were rigidly controlled, but there was still an element of danger. Filming from a moving ship is particularly difficult for the cameraman, since once he starts to shoot a sequence the camera boat must be continually manœuvred into the right position to ensure that the sun, his light source, remains in its original relationship to the actors. *Restive*, the ocean-going tug we used, was a survivor of the Atlantic convoy rescue service and not the easiest of craft to manipulate. From day one this frustrated Carol. A consummate technician, for my money the best director I ever worked with, he refused to accept that some of his instructions were impossible to carry out and remained convinced that the good tug *Restive* was fitted with disc brakes and that there was a conspiracy against him.

On this day Carol clutched the bridge rail with one hand and held the viewfinder to his eye in the best Nelson tradition.

'Ossie, how about if the U-boat surfaces exactly where it is now,' he said to our principal cameraman, Oswald Morris, 'then we pan over to hold Bill and Bryan in a tight two-shot as the tug stops and the Bofors gun starts firing? Do you buy that? Be a great shot, right?'

'The greatest,' Ossie agreed, who had learned not to raise any immediate objections to Carol's suggestions.

Carol aimed a loud-hailer towards the submarine and addressed the commander. 'Could you mark the spot where you are now, Commander, because that's where I want you to surface. Thank you.'

He turned to the *Restive*'s Captain, a taciturn character who by now was resigned to the fact that he was serving a collection of madmen.

'When we give you a cue, stop dead, will you?'

'Stop dead?'

'Yes, it's very important.'

'I'm not driving a bloody tram, you know. I've told you before, sir, this boat doesn't stop dead for you, me or God.' He looked around at the camera crew, appealing for support.

'It drifts, you see, Carol,' Ossie said, 'even when the engines are cut, it goes on moving.'

'But I don't want it to drift. I want it to stop. That's the shot. Don't let's waste time arguing about it.'

He turned back to the submarine as its commander answered him over his own loud-hailer system.

'*Trespasser* to *Restive*. Are you some sort of berk? If you think I can bring this thing up from the bottom on a sixpence, you've got another think coming. It'll be a bloody miracle if I surface within half a mile.'

'What's he saying?' Carol often feigned deafness when he did not want to hear bad news. He handed the loud-hailer to Ossie. 'You explain it to him, I've got to go below.' He left the bridge.

'Go on, Ossie,' Bill Holden said, enjoying the whole episode and certainly no stranger to the madness of filming. 'You heard Carol. It's quite simple. Have the boys row out and put some camera tape on the water to give him a mark. Then when he comes up, you pan to Bryan and me, and the Bofors gun which has never been fired since nineteen thirty-nine will let off a few rounds and with our luck blow us all out of the water. Carol gets a posthumous Academy Award, we get a burial at sea with full honours and Columbia goes out of business.'

Very wisely, Ossie didn't attempt any further instructions. Shortly afterwards the submarine commander headed back to Portsmouth in disgust, filming was wrapped for the day and Carol never got over it.

Bill Holden became a firm friend, and we kept in touch over the years although I never had the pleasure of working with him again. I did offer him a role in *Ménage à Trois* opposite David Niven and had he accepted it he might have been alive today. Although Bill liked the role, his agent persuaded him that the money was not enough. While we were on location in the South of France, alone in his Los Angeles home one weekend he suffered a fall and, unable to phone for help, bled to death. Except for Billy Wilder, I never felt that directors made use of his considerable talent at portraying callow opportunists. All too late he was 'rediscovered' in *Network*, but by then I felt he was a disillusioned man, too intelligent not to see through the phonies who chose to ignore him. He was the kindest and most generous of friends, and for many years he and I tried to secure the rights to Scott Fitzgerald's *Tender is the Night*, for he would have been the perfect Dick Diver. He had a streak of romanticism in him, allied to a sense of humour that was never cruel.

My luck held during and after *The Key* and while I was still in Weymouth Nanette moved into a derelict Seven Pines, the house which still remains our home. A strange example of Thirties' architecture which we unkindly refer to as Early Odeon Cinema style, it has had its outline softened over the years, for we have extended and rebuilt many parts of it. Again by luck and the good offices of an estate agent friend, we bought the house and eleven acres for what, even in the 1950s, was a song. That is not to say that we weren't hard pressed to find the reduced purchase price. Actors were not looked upon with favour by the banks and building societies and all my efforts to obtain a mortgage failed in the first instance. However, a close friend, Roger Machell, who had been our best man and who was later to be my editor at Hamish Hamilton, with typical generosity gave me a private mortgage at five per cent. Such a rate looks like manna in today's economic climate, but at that time it was often difficult to find the monthly payments.

Almost alone amongst our friends, Roger did not share the feeling that we were insane to take on a stately pile that had been derelict for seven years, many of the windows broken, no locks on the doors, the cellar under water, no heating, electricity or workable toilets. The fact that we lived for many years without security seems unreal in today's criminal climate when most people are forced to live with alarm systems and bars on the windows, but we never thought twice about it and slept soundly.

Now I am amazed that we had the courage to take it on. Perhaps I should qualify that and say that the real courage was Nanette's, for the major burden fell on her. Looking back I see that it was selfish of me, but the ruined house and overgrown garden had an enchantment I could not resist. I have always been attracted to castles and ruins, so I welcomed the challenge and accepted the struggle we had in those first years. Nanette was absurdly young for such responsibility and having spent most of her life in a small flat in Streatham, she was suddenly torn from our own modest apartment to become the chatelaine of a vast and virtual ruin where for the first six months we went to bed by candlelight and boiled buckets of water in order to take a bath. We often felt like revolutionaries occupying a pillaged palace. Our few pieces of furniture did not fill even one of the rooms, we used layers of newspaper on the bedroom floor in the absence of carpets and every spare penny I had was spent on restoring the basic utilities. Green to the ways of builders and decorators, we were frequently taken for a pair of suckers, which we undoubtedly were, and sometimes the lessons learned were painful in the extreme. Apart from the original builder, from all accounts an eccentrically wealthy individual who had used it as a weekend retreat, there had only been one other owner, a lady devoted to the demon gin, for we found hundreds of empty bottles strewn amongst the neglected flower beds. The local policeman and postmen described her as an occupational hazard who apparently was in the habit of greeting them stark naked, inebriated and often with desperate designs on their persons. She had also converted many of the smaller rooms into kennels where she bred Pekinese dogs, and their scatological memories lingered on. I spent every spare moment redecorating, often rising early to paint in my pyjamas before leaving for work. We recruited other actor friends during their 'resting' periods who in return for basic board and lodging lent a hand. On one occasion I spent the best part of a month painting the large circular hallway in what I fondly imagined was a stunning *House and Garden* green. When eventually I completed the task Nanette and I took stock of my handiwork. I looked at her, she looked at me.

'Shall I say it?' I said. 'It's an absolute pisser. I've managed to transform an ordinary hallway into a vast green municipal toilet.'

The next day I began again.

There were many such mistakes, even when our fortunes prospered and I was able to employ experts. We formed a friendship with two very engaging characters who ran an antique shop in nearby Ascot called The Clock House. Their names were Tony Flavell and Stanton Reddich, but they were affectionately known as Tick and Tock. From humble beginnings shampooing poodles, they had become upwardly mobile and moved into the rarefied world of antiques. They quickly prospered, for Stanton had a keen eye for business and Tony, scouring country auctions, bought wisely and on a heroic scale. My garden is graced with some major works of statuary thanks to them, together with a seventeenth-century ornamental pond and fountain which came to us in pieces and was lovingly assembled, like a jigsaw, by an ancient craftsman in their employ.

Their showrooms were crammed with treasures of every description and they liked nothing better than to buy something at ten o'clock in the morning and see it carried out of the shop by noon for a small profit. Their prices to us were always very reasonable although, being ignorant, we were over-enthusiastic and tended to acquire furniture and bric-à-brac from a variety of periods. Empire sofas and gilt chairs did not sit happily in a Thirties house, side by side with some modern horrors, for we were setting up home at a time when British design had yet to feel the impact of Terence Conran. Tick and Tock were ever obliging, cheerfully allowing us to exchange our major errors and, knowing our situation, giving us generous credit terms. As their own situation grew more affluent they moved into an enormous house on the outskirts of Windsor which became an annexe to their showrooms. When we went to dinner there we had only to admire a piece of furniture or china for Tony to remark: 'Turn it over, dear, the price is on the bottom.' We seldom left empty handed. They eventually made a modest fortune and, sadly for us, sold the business and retired abroad. I shall always be grateful to them for letting us learn and acquire taste with time to pay. We felt the loss keenly for they were honest and amusing and taught us a great deal.

Again lack of experience as much as lack of funds led me to make many mistakes in the garden. Until we acquired Seven Pines my knowledge of gardening was non-existent, I only knew that I felt a great affinity with the land, perhaps an inheritance from my mother who was a Lincolnshire farmer's daughter. Such scant credentials hardly prepared me for eleven acres of Bagshot sand with an iron pan stratum beneath producing what is known with masterly understatement as 'difficult soil'. When we purchased the house the grounds were a wilderness. The great rockery of Westmorland stone which borders the south aspect and pours down to what was then a stagnant stream was buried in undergrowth and had to be painstakingly excavated, rooting out the monstrous brambles and literally hundreds of birch and pine seedlings. In the course of clearing the rockery we unearthed and saved a variety of mature azaleas, together with several specimens of Japanese maple. By chance one of the original gardeners, a Mr Wallace, who had supervised most of the planting when the house was first built, still worked in the neighbouring Lake House. He proved an invaluable mentor, never mocking my grosser mistakes, but gently correcting them and setting me on

the right road. From him I learned to distinguish the dross –
those trees and plants that would never prosper no matter how
much time and effort was lavished on them. 'This ground's so
acid you could commit suicide with it,' he would say and indeed
anybody who has tried to produce a perfect lawn beneath giant
Scots pines will know what he means. I can admire the perfection
of other people's lawns, but to maintain them spells ruination
and I have settled for moss, daisies and dandelions.

I once allowed one of my fictional characters to distil my
cynical attitude towards the cultivation of our native soil. In *A
Song at Twilight* I gave this dialogue to a Mrs Van Norden
(borrowing the name from the dear lady who owned Lake House
all those years ago).

> Despite what everyone says, God never intended the English to
> have gardens. The moment anything buds we get out-of-season
> frosts; as soon as the blossom arrives He sends gale-force
> winds; and during the three days laughingly known as the
> English summer the whole place is infested with bugs, wasps
> and other creepies and crawlies. The whole thing seems
> absolutely pointless to me . . . It costs me a fortune to create
> an annual desert.

That isn't the whole truth and nothing but, of course. The
garden here at Seven Pines, despite the vicissitudes of Nature
and the frustrating vagaries of trees and plants, has given me
unalloyed pleasure as well as heartbreak. At times of stress and
disappointment I can always recharge my batteries in a few hours
by wandering lonely as a cloud by the lake and onto the island.
Periodically I embark on frenzied schemes, attacking the
encroaching bamboo and common rhododendrons which constantly threaten to take over the lower garden. Such efforts are
good for the waistline if nothing else. In the 1987 and 1990
hurricanes we suffered grievously, losing well over a hundred
huge mature trees which were plucked like teeth, one of them
falling to destroy a replica of the romantic Gothic aviary,
designed by Lord Snowdon, the original of which stands in Her
Majesty The Queen Mother's garden at Royal Lodge. After both

storms the garden has been left looking like a film set for the battle of the Somme and twice I have somehow found the energy, resolve and funds to begin again, planting replacement trees that I shall never live to see reach maturity. As a side issue I now have enough logs to last into the twenty-first century. So the dialogue I gave to my fictional character is not without some substance, a subconscious cry from the heart perhaps when thirty-six years of effort is destroyed overnight.

As well as the major setbacks I still find myself stymied by small mysteries, such as why do the raspberries and blackberries furthest from the sun ripen first? If nothing else, British gardeners are stoic. What pleases me most is the fact that, because of its wildness and lack of formality, the garden has become a minor wildlife sanctuary. We have woodpeckers, kingfishers, two amazingly intrepid magpies who chance their luck with our four cats every day, numerous foxes and two badger setts; swans nest most years, albeit without too much success – five cygnets were reared last year, but I suspect the parents didn't have too much grey matter for, tragically, the pike that lurks beneath the bridge to the island got them one by one. I have been fascinated to observe that the foxes and the cats, on the other hand, have come to an amicable arrangement; once the cats have finished eating, the urbanised fox emerges and carries their eating bowl a short distance away to polish off the remains and I have photographs to prove it. I suppose it is inevitable that natural predators abound: despite my efforts to save them, the heron gorged itself on my goldfish, the cats take their toll of small rodents and are also capable of killing squirrels which, unbelievably, they then eat. The idea of consuming raw squirrel is not something I wish to consider. My main battles are with an unwelcome family of fallow deer that devastate all the rose bushes the moment they are about to flower as well as mutilating every young tree I plant. Whenever this trio of Bambis appear I rush out and fire blanks at them, but they regard me with contempt, knowing that I would never have the heart actually to harm them. The only piece of advice I have been given is to ask Safari Park to provide a quantity of tiger manure to sprinkle around the perimeter; this is apparently guaranteed to keep deer at bay, but I suspect that it might also keep everybody else from visiting me.

It is difficult to encapsulate in print the atmosphere of a home that has been created over three decades. Nanette would, with hindsight, have preferred to live in a Georgian house (or better still a penthouse on top of Harrods) for she remains a resolute town creature, while I, despite Dr Johnson, have grown tired of cities and especially my native London which I have seen degenerate into an ugly architectural slum. We both admire the classic proportions of the Georgians, which to my mind have never been bettered, but we cast our lot for Seven Pines when we were both young and so much has happened to us both beneath this roof that, although on a number of occasions we have seriously entertained moving on, we always seem to find reasons to postpone the fateful decision.

In many ways it is a perfect house for us. Or to put it more accurately, Nanette has made it so. Despite the somewhat forbidding exterior, which we have tried to soften with Virginia creeper and shutters, the interior layout has been adapted over the years to our special needs and whenever I return from a long sojourn abroad I never fail to be enchanted by it. I suppose it represents so many things: the birth of children, family Christmases, chapters of heartbreak and triumph. I have the feeling that the original owner designed the interior and then said, 'Brick it up.' Obviously he designed it to provide the maximum comfort for two adults and from all accounts was possessed of a sense of humour. There used to be a concealed wall in the dining room which could be activated to rise from the cellar. This had a disconcerting and dramatic effect on unsuspecting guests, especially if they had been plied with drinks, and for many years until the machinery conked out it proved a great after-dinner diversion. He also installed what, in 1933, must have been a heating system well in advance of its time: a gigantic boiler circulated hot water in the walls and ceilings, a technical variation on the Roman method. Money being no object for him apparently, he even carried electricity and an early hi-fi system to the island, well over half a mile away, which had long since ceased to function by the time we moved in.

How well I remember the first time we walked up the overgrown drive. It was Springtime and the tangled lawns housed a mass of wild flowers. To me it was like coming across a haunted Xanadu. Some sort of madness infected me as we wandered through the empty, pillaged rooms. Against all reason, I knew I had somehow to find the ways and means to own it. I dreamed of nothing else and, in the three months or so it took me to raise the money, we used to revisit and picnic in the grounds where the grass, gone to reed, was certainly as high as an elephant's eye. I gave little thought to the enormity of the task of putting it into working order again for I was gripped with a sort of madness that allowed of no argument. Perhaps our joint ignorance gave us the necessary courage to weather those first perilous years when I teetered on the edge of bankruptcy every day, but somehow our luck held.

THREE

If one earns a living through the arts it is often difficult to discern any pattern. Luck, as I have said, plays a compelling role, for there is no guarantee of justice – the talented are passed over as often as the mediocre are exalted. Failure follows success with depressing regularity. I remember how amazed I was to read Noel Coward's diaries. I had always fondly imagined that the Master's career was one unbroken triumph, yet the reverse was true; despite his many talents Noel was no stranger to the slings and arrows.

That is why it is rewarding to nourish talent if one is in a position of influence. A film director has to assume many roles during the course of business. As well as knowing his own job he is required to be a wet-nurse, psychiatrist, liar, flatterer and a benevolent dictator. I have always found the pre-production casting sessions the most depressing aspect of my craft. Having been an actor myself I know only too well the hopes that are raised when the call comes to attend an interview, and I have never been a believer in screen tests, other than to judge costumes and character make-ups once an actor has been cast. Otherwise all one is testing are varying degrees of fear, never a reliable yardstick. I suspect that many directors test from a sense of inferiority or else wish to indulge their sense of power.

I had an old friend, alas now dead, who started life as a crowd extra. His name was George Hillsden, a lovely man whom I first employed on my directorial début for *Whistle Down the Wind* in which he played a non-speaking role as a policeman. I used him on all my British films thereafter, gradually giving him bigger and bigger roles which he always handled expertly, for although he had no training he was a natural. When I was suddenly thrust into directing *The Madwoman of Chaillot* in the South of France, I inherited the all-star cast headed by Katharine Hepburn, Yul Brynner, Danny Kaye and Charles Boyer, but in the short time allotted to me I still had to fill half a dozen of the featured roles. There happened to be a small, but effective, role of a waiter who had two or three scenes with Hepburn. I immediately thought of George.

'Who's George Hillsden?' the American producer queried. 'I've never heard of him.'

'Oh, he's one of the most sought-after character actors in England,' I lied. 'We'd be lucky to get him.'

'Well, let's get onto him if he's that good.'

George, a Cockney like myself, still lived in the East End of London. I rang him. His wife answered.

'Is George there?'

'No, he's down at the Labour Exchange drawing the dole,' she said.

I gave her my number in Nice. 'Tell him to ring me as soon as he gets in. I've got some good news. He's going to be spending the summer in the South of France.'

I negotiated his contract myself, made sure he had his own dressing room, and for the first time in his life he was accorded 'star' status. When he arrived he sat in his hotel room and cried. I let Kate in on the secret, which she thought was a gas, and she befriended him throughout the shooting period. Because we were caught in the middle of the French revolution of 1968, the schedule was protracted and George saved enough money to be able to buy the freehold of his house. He acquitted himself well in the film and on other occasions I took him with me to Spain for *Deadfall* and to Bordeaux for *The Sunday Lovers*. In many ways he became my talisman. Gradually his fame spread and he was given bigger roles on television. Towards the end of his life he shot a lucrative commercial for British Telecom for which he received several thousand pounds. 'Like winning the pools,' George said. I never knew him to be depressed and he was a great asset on my sets, willing to turn his hand to whatever was required. The last time he worked for me was on *International Velvet*, but he was taken ill while we were shooting in the North of England and unable to finish the film. He died the same week as Romy Schneider and, while the world press rightly headlined her sad end, George's death passed unnoticed except for those of us who knew and loved him.

As a memorial to our long friendship, when I came to write *The Endless Game*, I called the principal character, played by Albert Finney in the film, Hillsden. George would have enjoyed that and I like to think it kept his name alive.

Casting does not always go so smoothly. I remember that during the preparations for *The Stepford Wives*, which I shot in New York and Connecticut, I had a producer who constantly came up with new ideas for the leading lady. It would be discourteous of me to list the many famous names who were first considered and then, for one reason or another, discarded. I spent many frustrating weeks getting nowhere until he decided that his choice would be Diane Keaton. This was fine by me, I admire her extravagantly and looked forward to working with her. We duly met and spent a pleasant afternoon together going over the script. When we said goodbye I fondly imagined that our quest was finally over. However the following morning she rang me and said that, sadly, she had changed her mind.

'What happened between last night and this morning?' I asked.

'My analyst read the script and got very bad vibes from it,' she said.

That was the first and only time I have been rejected by an analyst.

I am often asked how I found the extraordinary collection of small children for *Whistle Down the Wind* and the answer is, it was surprisingly easy. Most children are natural actors who give instinctive reactions to dramatic situations providing they are not allowed to get bored. A greater part of filming involves a high degree of boredom for the players, and if, like children, they don't possess any technique to surmount the inevitable repetition, a director has to make it into a game for them.

My partner, Richard Attenborough, and I decided that, with the exception of Hayley Mills, who was then the number one box office star, we would only cast unknown children. So I journeyed to Clitheroe and got permission to sit in the classrooms of the local schools, the better to observe a number of children. Hayley's younger brother and sister were two vital roles that had to be cast and after a week of taking stock my critical eye fell on a remarkable little boy called Alan Barnes who was aged seven going on thirty-seven.

Choosing my moment, I got chatting with him, and then finally said, 'Would you like to be in my film?'

'I'm not bothered,' he said, fixing me with a beady eye, and I knew I had found my leading man.

Together with Diane Holgate, the young girl who played his sister, he proved to be a scene stealer, giving a quite remarkable performance for somebody of such tender years. (Shades of W.C. Fields here, whose advice to the players was, 'Never act with animals or children.') Of course I had to resort to bribes on occasion, but my method of avoiding the boredom factor was, with the exception of Hayley, never to let any of the children see an actual script. Since the plot revolved round a group of children mistaking a murderer on the run for Jesus, I was determined that none of my small cast started 'acting' a religious fable. I was tiptoeing across the thin ice of sentimentality throughout and scared of allowing the film to sink into bathos. So instead I fed them small pieces of the story at a time, always careful to give them a parallel situation they could relate to. We never had any long rehearsals, though as they became more accustomed to the demands of filming, both Diane and Alan proved capable of conveying great subtleties and sustaining lengthy dialogue scenes. In fact all the children were superb and never cost me any lost time. The only thing they all hated was still having to attend school for a number of hours a day. In order to comply with the law we built a wooden school hut on the location and employed several teachers. Losing part of the cast every few hours made for a difficult schedule, but the film was completed for the now unbelievable sum of £162,000 and proved to be the most profitable and popular one I ever made. Would that we could still make films for that sort of money, indigenous to our own country, for only by returning to our origins will we ever revitalise the British industry.

When I was head of production at Elstree studios, of which more later, I had the pleasure of casting writers and directors as well as actors. Just prior to taking up that appointment an old chum of mine, that very fine comedy actor Lionel Jeffries, sent me a script he had written based on E. Nesbit's classic tale of *The Railway Children*. I thought it was superb and when I got to Elstree I included it in my first programme. Then came the question of choosing a director.

'I know it's a crazy idea and not on, but I've always secretly harboured a longing to direct it myself,' Lionel said hesitantly.

I stared at him. 'Why didn't I think of that? It's the obvious answer. You wrote it, you know it better than anybody, you must do it.'

He did go on to direct it with great style and warmth and it became an enormous popular success. What Lionel has always had is a great feeling for period detail and this was brought out in the film. Quite remarkable for somebody making a début, he was also able to bring true emotion to the screen and there are sequences in the film that make me cry whenever I rerun it. He went on to make two other excellent and unusual films, stamped with his own personality and then, inexplicably, shamefully, his talents as a director were ignored. I find this neglect hard to understand when one thinks of the opportunities that occur every week on television.

Another of my lucky finds while I was at Elstree came out of the blue. John Brabourne and his partner, Richard Goodwin, asked to see me one day to enquire whether I would be interested in making a film based on the stories of Beatrix Potter.

'My God,' I said, 'have you got the rights?' I knew that Disney had been after them for years.

29

'Yes,' they said.

'How do you intend to do it?'

'We want to make it as a ballet film, using the Royal Ballet with choreography by Freddie Ashton and music by John Lanchbury.'

They produced some startling pictures of the masks and costumes the dancers would wear. The masks, in particular, were quite brilliant and indeed the whole conception of the film was highly original. I did not hesitate.

'You're on,' I said. 'Get to work. I'll see you at the studio. Let me know what you want and the money will be there.'

The entire conversation had taken ten minutes at the most. It was one of the most rewarding moments of my entire time in office. They later confided that they stood outside on the pavement in a state of shock.

'Did he say what I think he said?' John asked.

'I think so,' Richard replied.

'He said yes, didn't he?'

'Yes.'

'Is that it, then?'

'Must be.'

The story has a postscript. Under the terms of my contract I had total artistic control up to a figure of one million pounds. All I had to do was report new acquisitions at the monthly Board meeting. My fellow directors were mostly of the old guard and from the outset many of them regarded me with unconcealed suspicion. I was once asked by the chief executive why I came to Board meetings dressed like a cowboy, a remark prompted by the fact that I was wearing a perfectly ordinary safari suit. It was not a good omen. I was the only one who had practical knowledge of the workings of a film studio and from day one I was resolved to remove the arcane factory atmosphere which permeated the entire complex. I inherited an office from my predecessor which resembled a stage set for a provincial tour of a Ben Travers farce, complete with a fake fireplace plus an adjoining shower room where one could have contracted athlete's foot without removing one's shoes. One of my first acts was to get rid of the clocking-in procedure, which horrified head office, and I suspect marked my card as a dangerous radical. In the beginning I believe I enjoyed the confidence of Bernard Delfont, who had first offered me the position as head of production, though I subsequently felt that he never completely had the courage of my convictions, and as time went on I was proved right. We shall come to that.

Following my meeting with Brabourne and Goodwin I duly reported my decision to make *The Tales* at the next Board meeting. The faces around the Board table began to resemble a Bateman cartoon.

'Who's Beatrix Potter?' asked Nat Cohen, one of the fixtures of Wardour Street at that time.

'Ah!' I replied, choosing my words with care, 'well if you don't know, it's difficult to explain. I would say she is one of the most successful children's authors that ever lived. She has sold and continues to sell millions of copies every year and is a household name. To anybody who reads that is.'

'What's the film about?' another director chipped in.

'It's a ballet film.'

'Ballet films are shit,' he observed with that candour for which the film industry is noted.

'Don't minute that,' the chairman said hurriedly.

Delfont played the peacemaker. 'I'll discuss it further with Bryan. I'm sure he hasn't made a definite decision yet.'

'Yes, I have,' I said. 'I've given my word. We're going to make it.'

And make it we did, again with success. For the American version it was retitled *The Tales of Peter Rabbit*, for reasons I failed to comprehend. But there is nothing film distributors like more than to change titles. When I made *The Raging Moon*, the American distributor junked my music and commissioned a new title song which came out as *Long Ago Tomorrow*, whatever that means, and the film appeared under that title. I myself fought against the title of *International Velvet*, which I considered puerile, but I lost the battle. Likewise *Ménage à Trois* appeared as *Better Late than Never*, and when I adapted Kingsley Amis' novel, *That Uncertain Feeling*, originally purchased one would imagine on the strength of the author's fame, it was changed to *Only Two Can Play*.

The London opening of *The Tales* was a gala première attended by the majority of the young royal princesses and princes. When the lights went up at the conclusion the chairman's wife turned to me and in all too loud a voice remarked that her husband hadn't fallen asleep. 'So that's a good sign,' she added.

The film went on to garner a number of international prizes. And who went to New York to collect one of the awards? None other than Nat Cohen.

FOUR

Between my first published book, *Truth Lies Sleeping*, and *The Distant Laughter*, there was a gap of some twenty years. I had begun *The Distant Laughter* in a grim little rented house on West Knoll Drive in Los Angeles in the dying days of my unhappy first marriage. I had no money and eked out an existence by answering Stewart Granger's fan mail for him, a kind suggestion he made to save my face. To be unknown and out of work in Hollywood was then, and doubtless is now, a fate I would not wish on anybody. The unsuccessful in tinseltown are somewhat lower than a Hindu road sweeper on the social register. I remember I existed on salted peanuts, orange juice and the occasional hamburger in a pre-McDonald's eatery called Biffs on Sunset Boulevard. In an effort to remain sane I slaved at the novel on a borrowed typewriter, but it refused to take flight and it wasn't until I resigned from Elstree that I found those first few aborted pages and began again.

I might never have survived my early Hollywood days had it not been for the kindness of a veteran director, Raoul Walsh. Even today when anything goes it would take a brave screenwriter to commit the plot of Raoul's life onto film. The son of an Irish emigrant, reared in a New York brownstone, as a child Raoul met Mark Twain on his deathbed, once sat on Sitting Bull's lap, went to sea, became the reckless lover of General Gomez's mistress at age seventeen, served as an unqualified and occasionally lethal anaesthetist to a French doctor in Butte, Montana, became an actor by accident when movies first caught the popular imagination, went West to Hollywood with D.W. Griffith who cast him as John Wilkes Booth, the assassin of Lincoln, in *Birth of a Nation*, had his right eye taken out by a jack rabbit which jumped through his windscreen while he was driving to a desert location for the first outdoor talking western, *In Old Arizona*, went on to become a director, shooting well over a hundred films in fifty years, bought his suits in Newmarket, his hand-made boots in Jermyn Street, and in his eighties survived major surgery on a diet of jelly beans and Jack Daniels sour-mash whiskey.

Raoul was a self-made, literate, cultured roughneck who fast learned in the hardest film school of all that if you cast your bread upon the waters the chances were it would come back to you sopping wet. For most of his working life he made defiantly commercial films on a production line that turned them out as fast as Ford's Model Ts; then woke up fifty years later to find he had been guilty of producing Art. Finally recognised and elevated to a cult figure, he was given retrospectives all over the world (the 1974 Walsh festival at the Museum of Modern Art lasted three months and spanned sixty-seven of his films). He was sardonically amused by the late arrival of such flattery. 'I was a thief making films for bigger thieves, that's all, and now instead of sending me to jail they've given me the freedom of the city.'

It would be a gross injustice if I gave the impression that Raoul was some swaggering loudmouth from the dark ages of Hollywood. Nothing could be further from the truth. He was an engaging mixture of swashbuckler and would-be English squire, always impeccably dressed, quiet spoken, unfailingly courteous, and with his eye black patch he cut a dashing figure.

I once accompanied him on a shopping spree in Burlington Arcade where, to my amazement, he purchased a dozen Eton ties, telling the assistant that they were intended for me. Once we were outside the shop I tackled him as to why he would make such a strange purchase.

'Let me tell you something,' Raoul said, 'I make a lot of westerns on the Indian reservations and whenever I need a dangerous stunt, I hand out the ties. They'll do anything for an

Eton tie. There's a whole tribe of Apache back there who wear nothing else.'

I'm sure many of his anecdotes were apocryphal but he told them with such conviction and obvious enjoyment that I give him the benefit of the doubt. There was another occasion during the making of a film when we flew into France. Raoul travelled with a large travelling trunk crammed with bottles of his favourite tipple. As we approached the customs hall I asked him if he was going to declare his hoard.

'Watch me,' he said.

When asked by a weasel-faced customs officer whether he had anything to declare, Raoul did not bat his eyelid, but slapped a 10,000-franc note on the counter. 'That's all I've got to declare, Captain,' he said, looking straight at the man with his one good eye.

With the skill of a card-sharper, the note disappeared from view, the chalk came out with a flourish, the trunk was marked and we passed on.

'Always try the straight bribe,' Raoul advised. 'But never put it into their hand. That's dicey. If they don't pick it up you're none the worse off. But I don't have too many failures.'

I never had the nerve to emulate him.

Early on in his career Griffith sent him to Mexico to film Pancho Villa. There, at considerable risk to his own life, he shot some amazing footage, and was befriended by the notorious bandit to the extent that before he left Villa made him a Mexican millionaire. Sadly, before the train home steamed into Los Angeles Villa had been killed, and the bundle of banknotes Raoul carried was now worthless. That was his version, but one always had to take Raoul's stories with a pinch of salt.

Later he directed everybody from Theda Bara to Gloria Swanson, Jimmy Cagney and Errol Flynn, Gregory Peck and Anthony Quinn. Cagney remained his favourite and they shared the white heat of the roaring Thirties. Then, much of Sunset Boulevard was little more than a horse-track leading to the smog-free beaches of Santa Monica and Malibu. There were orange groves stretching all the way to Palm Springs and an all-British

35

cricket team that took to the field on Sundays. Off-screen morals were loose but carefully shielded from the public gaze; on screen the Hays Office saw to it that even married couples slept with one foot firmly on the bedroom floor. It was the age when the moguls kept *their* spare foot firmly on the jugular vein of those they employed.

It was at Santa Monica that William Randolph Hearst built Marion Davies, his longtime mistress, a mere 'cottage' with 110 rooms and 37 fireplaces: Versailles by the sea, with a deer-park atmosphere. Even this was a minor folly compared to the Shangri-La Hearst constructed for himself further along the coast, assembling it like some antique Lego set – the fabled San Simeon, where the favoured ate in a baronial hall with ketchup bottles at each place setting. Of the many splendours to be seen at San Simeon Dorothy Parker wrote:

> I've just had the honour
> To see a Madonna
> In a most peculiar niche,
> It was outside the door
> Of the favourite whore,
> Of the world's greatest
> Son-of-a-bitch.

Miss Parker shared Orson Welles' jaundiced view of Mr Hearst and the power he wielded, but Raoul remembered him less critically. He became a member of the San Simeon inner circle almost by accident, having been chosen by Hearst to direct Marion Davies in a film called, appropriately, *Going Hollywood*. He told me many stories of Hearst's lavish hospitality and the subterfuges Marion's friends employed to smuggle her in a drink, for Marion had a 'problem' that had to be concealed from her lover and mentor, but from all accounts she was a loyal and generous friend, accepting the uneasy role of courtesan, though was never the whore of Dorothy Parker's savage limerick. The fear Hearst newspapers inspired protected her and, although their long affair was common knowledge, the public were kept in ignorance until after Hearst's death. The parties she and Hearst threw (and he indulged her every whim) were legendary. Once on Hearst's birthday, she brought in an army of gardeners who worked throughout the night. When Hearst woke the day of the party the entire garden had been transformed – it was a sea of his favourite flowers, white lilies. Raoul told me that if one of her friends was down on her luck, they would be invited for the weekend and find that an entire wardrobe of clothes had been provided. He said that when he was a guest he slept in a bed once used by Napoleon, on one occasion sharing it with an accommodating English countess whom, with typical discretion, he declined to name for he was always unfailingly courteous towards women. Under Hearst's roof he got to know the younger Winston Churchill who like many ambitious men was irresistibly attracted to power, especially if that power was concentrated in a press baron (witness his later friendship with Beaverbrook).

In later years Churchill numbered Raoul's *Captain Horatio Hornblower* amongst his favourite films. Emulating the Hearst style of entertaining, Raoul took Churchill to the races and when they returned to his own home instructed his butler not to pour *a* drink for his distinguished guest, but to offer him the bottle. Churchill was also present when Raoul swiftly dispatched a lecherous minor Balkan prince who attempted to cut in on Hearst and Marion while they were dancing. 'When you're in England,' Churchill said, 'be sure to look me up. I'll point out a couple of Members of Parliament I'd like you to work on.'

'But politics were never my line,' Raoul confided. 'Especially studio politics. In those days it was a rough, tough game if you wanted to survive and I stayed out of range.'

If the life he and his bosom companions once led now seems larger than the fictions they fashioned for mass audiences, it is because it *was* larger, an extension of the dream factories they slaved in six days a week. They had every reason to take their pleasures seriously; the routine of the studio system was a merciless merry-go-round, designed for the survival of the fittest. The major studios were each turning out some forty films a year, the actors were cosseted like battery hens but seldom forgiven if they laid too many dud eggs in a row. An in-demand director like Raoul would make at least three, maybe five, films in a year, and the director was not high in the pecking order. 'I took what was offered to me. You didn't think too much about the script in those days. I can remember times when I would get a script late on a Friday night and start shooting the following Monday morning. You just turned up, had a cup of coffee, and said action. The actors knew what they were doing, the crews knew each other, the cameramen knew how the stars liked to be lit, and we got on with it. We just told stories. It was fun. That's the word. In those days it was fun. There were quite a few bottle men around. We worked hard, we played hard and when we relaxed some of us drank hard.'

Nowadays it is fashionable to deride the studio system, but Art has a habit of intruding into the most blatant commercial enterprises, and if we now acknowledge that many of the films churned out can be regarded as classic examples of the cinema, we must also allow that those who controlled the studios were not just ugly faces. 'They were monsters, many of them, dictators in a sense,' Raoul said, 'but they had something which this latest mob don't have: they loved films, films were their whole life.'

The same could be said of Raoul himself. He loved film. Like John Ford, Michael Curtiz, Howard Hawks, William Wellman and other contemporaries, he hacked away at the coal face. Less protected than the stars they helped to immortalise, the directors' main assets were speed and versatility. Raoul directed westerns, gangster movies, comedies, second features when the going was hard, war films, adventure stories, melodramas. 'When in doubt,' he used to say, 'I always start a fight.' His bar-room brawls were something to watch.

Of the many quixotic episodes in his life, few approach his encounter with Hitler. It came about when he was visiting London as a member of Hearst's holiday party and received an invitation to have lunch with von Ribbentrop, then the German ambassador. Raoul had previously known him as a wine salesman in Hollywood and was intrigued rather than impressed. During the lunch, a fellow guest, Baron Eugene von Renslaw, enquired whether Raoul would be prepared to consider making a film in

Germany. Never one to refuse a challenge, Raoul agreed to explore the matter and was flown from Hendon to Berlin in the baron's private plane the same day. In Berlin he was given the bridal suite at the Adlon and provided with two nubile Rhine maidens to help stave off any night starvation. They showed him the town, including a visit to a night-club where, in true *Cabaret* style, the famed German sense of humour was displayed: Raoul was introduced to and persuaded to dance with 'Marlene' – a drag act. These sexual formalities dispensed with, he was given a guided tour of the UFA studios, taken to the Sports Palace to hear the Führer speak, and later attended a performance of *Die Walküre* at which he met Hitler face to face. Raoul described him as 'frozen with discontent'. During all of this there had been no further mention of his making a film. It was only now that the real purpose of his visit was revealed by Goering.

'Goering laid his false teeth on the table and offered me any picture in his own art gallery if I could get him a portrait of a General von Steuben owned by Hearst. He wanted to give it to Hitler as a present. Naturally I stalled. I had a pretty good idea that Goering was a horse thief and that most of his paintings had been stolen. I also had the feeling that the hospitality would run dry the moment the deal went cold. So I played for time by telling him that Hearst had never recovered from the loss of four Grecian columns, intended for San Simeon, that had gone to the bottom of the Atlantic as a result of a U-boat attack during World War I. I did a bit of heel clicking to impress them and said, "Herr Marshal, I firmly believe Mr Hearst would only part with the painting if you returned the columns." That brought the proceedings to an abrupt end. The next day I was escorted to the airport by one of the two hookers. She made a last pitch. The Minister of Finance would cough up over two million Reich-marks if I delivered the goods. They say it takes a thief to know one, but I wasn't in Goering's league. I think the bastard really wanted me to steal the portrait.'

On the flight back to Hendon he pondered how life often encroaches on Art. There he was, the man who portrayed the assassin of Lincoln, who had been within shooting distance of

Hitler. 'That night at the opera I could have played the role again and got better billing. Certainly better reviews, world-wide!'

During that first stay in Hollywood he gave me the only job I had, casting me in a potboiler he was making on the old Universal backlot called *The World in His Arms*. I have no idea why he chose me, for the role called for an American and I suspect my assumed accent left much to be desired. During and after the film he went out of his way to befriend and advise me and when my marriage failed in very ugly circumstances it was Raoul who tracked me down and rescued me – perhaps even saved my life, for I had reached rock-bottom and might well have taken desperate measures. A battle-scarred veteran of several marriages himself he prised my sorry tale from me and swung into action.

'I'll tell you what you're going to do. You don't go back to the house, you don't ever see her again, you get the hell out of this town before you become a bum or put a bullet through her.'

'Where will I go?'

'I'll show you.'

We got into his car and he drove to the TWA offices in Beverly Hills where he bought me a one-way ticket back to London. Then he drove me to the airport and waited with me until the plane boarded.

'How will I ever pay you back?' I said.

'Oh, we'll meet up, maybe sooner than you expect. Don't worry about it, you'll pay me back one day.'

I returned home and licked my wounds for six months. Then out of the blue I got a call from Raoul. He was in London preparing to shoot a new film. 'It's a crock of shit,' he said, 'but I might be able to make something of it. Now listen, you'll get a call from the casting director in a couple of days to come and meet me. Don't shave, speak with an American accent and you never saw me before.'

True to his word, I duly got the call to present myself at the Dorchester Hotel for an interview. When I arrived a queue of hopeful actors stretched halfway down the corridor. Eventually I worked my way to the head of the list and was shown into his suite. Raoul had his back to me as I entered and I was greeted by

40

the producer, David E. Rose, a kindly but ineffectual soul. He was flanked by the casting director.

Raoul swung round and fixed me with his one good eye. 'Who's this young guy?' he asked.

'Bryan Forbes, Mr Walsh.'

'What've you done, kid?'

'Well, I've played in quite a few films, both here and in Hollywood.' My accent was thick and unconvincing.

'The kid looks good to me. Virile. Look at that beard. Certainly a change from some of the fruit-cakes you've been showing me all the afternoon.' He took out his small bag of Bull Durham tobacco and began to roll a cigarette, cowboy style, as thin as a toothpick. When lit they were apt to spray red-hot ash, like a weak firework. Those in the know kept their distance.

'Bryan's a good young actor,' the casting director said. 'I'd got him spotted for the young sailor in the first sequence.'

'You trying to insult him? What about the part of Willy?'

David Rose spoke for the first time. 'You don't mean Willy, surely, Raoul? That's earmarked for Barry Fitzgerald.'

'Yeah, well I've had second thoughts. We got to get some young blood in this epic. We're starring Rock Hudson, so we don't want to pitch him against a lot of old Irish ham cut straight from the bone. Let's cast the kid here instead.'

David Rose and the casting director looked as though they had both been struck by the same bolt of lightning. In the first place nobody ever told an actor he'd got a role until the price had been negotiated, and secondly you certainly didn't switch Barry Fitzgerald for Bryan Forbes, virility and five o'clock shadow notwithstanding.

'Let's you and I talk about it and ask Bryan to come back later,' David Rose said when he found his voice. He was visibly ageing.

'What's to talk about? He's the pick of the bunch and I'm bushed. I've interviewed every out-of-work actor in England today and the kid here is the only one who impresses me. Settle it now otherwise you'll lose him. You in demand, kid?'

I took my cue. 'As a matter of fact I am considering a couple of other offers.' Before his call I had been considering slitting my wrists in a warm bath.

'But the part's written for an old man.'

'Then let's rewrite it.'

I walked out of the hotel with a firm contract.

The basis for the film, Victor Hugo's *Toilers of the Sea*, had already felt the dead hand of a hack scriptwriter; any resemblance to the original was insanely coincidental. Now it was called *Sea Devils*, plotted around pirates and swooning heroines with unspeakable dialogue. Even without Raoul's chicanery on my behalf I doubt whether the estimable Barry Fitzgerald would have entertained it unless anxious to commit professional hara-kiri. The leading roles were to be played by Yvonne de Carlo and the then virtually unknown Rock Hudson. The finished film now reappears on television with unfailing regularity and reminds me both of happy times and, less agreeably, my ludicrous performance in a fairly ludicrous film.

The inexperienced Rock Hudson was not yet the major heart-throb and few, if any, had an inkling of his true nature. He confessed his homosexuality to me while we were on location in Concarneau, Brittany, in 1952, so his secret which was to have such tragic consequences was never a secret to me. He was a funny, totally engaging character, devoid of any pretensions, absurdly good looking and a great companion. I always admired the way in which, starting from scratch, with no training as such, he slowly fashioned a spectacular career. I grieved for his hideous end, but perhaps his death served one last and much needed purpose, for as he died in the full glare of publicity he brought about the turning point in the public's awareness of the dread disease. Suddenly they could put a face to death.

During our stay in Brittany there was another aspect of Raoul's character that has always stuck in my memory. We were taking lunch in a small restaurant when the proprietor came up to our table and said that Raoul was wanted on the telephone. He took the call and returned with a broad grin.

'You a betting man, Willy?' he asked me. (It was one of his idiosyncrasies to call you by the name of the character you happened to be playing.) 'That was a jockey I know in Ireland. One of Nature's noblemen. He just gave me the name of the winner for the four-thirty at Newmarket this afternoon.'

'The *winner*? How does he know the winner in advance?'

'Oh, he always knows the winners in advance,' Raoul replied. 'Give me what you've got and I'll place the bets.'

I gave him my money. The horse duly won by two lengths at incredible odds. I have steered clear of horse-racing ever since.

Raoul never referred to my Hollywood episode, nor did he ever ask me to repay the air fare he had provided. Many years later I went to Hollywood on my own terms to direct *King Rat* – and one of the first things I did on arrival was to take Raoul to dinner. After we had killed a bottle of Jack Daniels I handed him an envelope.

'What's this?' he said.

'It's the price of an old air fare,' I said, 'with twelve years' interest.'

'What air fare?'

I reminded him. He looked at me in genuine astonishment. He had forgotten all about it.

We remained in touch until he died at a ripe old age. By then his other eye had failed and he was totally blind. The last time I visited him at his home in the valley he sat, back upright, wearing his cowboy hat, his impeccable cavalry twill breeches and polished boots, chewing on jelly babies and drinking milk and soda water instead of his beloved Jack Daniels. His devoted wife of thirty years, Mary, attended to his simple needs. We sat and reminisced in the thin sunlight that penetrated the afternoon smog. Behind us a hen was sitting on some eggs in an ancient armchair, worried by a randy cockerel that in turn was chased by the cat. Numerous dogs basked beneath the orange trees that, sadly, sported no fruit.

'Didn't we have fun?' Raoul said.

It was an epitaph for the days the locusts had eaten, said without bitterness by a blind buccaneer who, to the end, was a man for all seasons, a true friend I shall never forget.

FIVE

As well as having a wife and two daughters with an infectious sense of humour, I have also been blessed with friends who make me laugh. Michael Caine, Roger Moore, Leslie Bricusse, Arthur Marshall, Elton John, Keith Barron, Richard Briers, George Segal, Nigel Havers and, not forgetting the ladies, Penelope Wilton, dear departed Avis Bunnage, Angela Douglas, Jennie Linden and Kate Hepburn share a pronounced awareness of the ridiculous. It is something the majority of actors have in common. Perhaps because the profession is so precarious the humour is often cruel, often self-denigrating, for whereas it is considered bad form to boast of the occasional triumph, all are adept at turning failure inside out.

Like the friends listed above, I am no stranger to hard times – hard in the sense that in order to practise our art we have often been compelled to work in circumstances that many would find intolerable. I am thinking of early days when the weekly repertory system flourished throughout the land which, together with numerous touring companies, provided much needed employment for those starting out. The average wage was just above starvation level – three pounds ten shillings in my first engagement – but I can't pretend that I felt exploited. On the contrary I considered myself privileged, only too happy to be able to realise a cherished ambition. One stayed in 'digs', or 'diggings', originally an American slang term anglicised in the nineteenth century which thereafter seems to have been used exclusively in theatrical parlance. Every actor has a landlady anecdote. Most of the landladies were angels, devoted to their ever-changing clientele, some were rapacious harridans. My first taste of this aspect of theatrical life was in Rugby during the early part of the war. Three of us slept in one bed, I remember, slotted together like sardines. One of the conditions was you could either have a hot-water bottle and shave in the lukewarm water the following morning, or else forgo that comfort and be given a jug of hot shaving water. There is a typical story concerning a landlady who asked an actor whether he had a good memory for faces. 'Yes, I think so,' he replied. 'Oh, that's good,' she said, 'because there's no mirror in the bathroom.'

A famous story was told of the old comedian, Sandy Powell. Apparently he was in digs up North and found himself pursued by a very amorous landlady throughout his week's stay. When he left for the train-call on the Sunday, he got to the station and then discovered that he had left his tickets behind in his room. He rushed back to the digs to find the landlady stark naked and being serviced by the incoming comedian on the kitchen table. Unable to disengage, she looked up and said: 'Oh, Mr Powell, you must think me a terrible flirt.'

I had my share of good and bad, including a wonderful character in Leeds where I stayed during the post-London tour of *September Tide*. Gertie Lawrence had insisted that the entire company move in to this particular address, which was odd because Gertie usually stayed at a luxury hotel. When pressed for an explanation she merely said wait and see. We arrived one foggy Sunday afternoon to be greeted by a character dressed as a World War I Tommy, complete with cropped hair and swagger stick, who immediately launched into a spirited rendering of *Take Me Back to Dear Old Blighty*. Fortified by the gin Gertie provided, she entertained us the entire hilarious week. Students of the cinema might be interested to note that when I came to write and direct *The L-Shaped Room*, I used the lady as a model for the character played by Cicely Courtneidge who gave a memorable rendering of the same wartime song.

There is also a certain bitter-sweet quality to many theatrical anecdotes. I recall a time when I was a so-called 'guest star' with the Armitage Owen Players on the end of the pier in Rhyl, acting in *Damaged Goods*, a play about venereal disease, which can hardly be described as a bundle of laughs at the best of times. Playing it in mid-winter to an audience of ribald soldiery during wartime required courage. As the 'star' guest artist I received the top salary, all of eight pounds. When the ghost walked on the Friday a regular member of the company told me to observe the old character man who had been a permanent fixture for some years. He came out of the Manager's office counting his salary aloud: '. . . nine, ten, eleven, twelve, thirteen, fourteen.' Apparently it was his regular habit to bolster his burnt-out ego by inserting Monopoly money between the real notes. Everybody was in on the secret, but he performed the same sad charade every week.

The major theatrical happening of my career occurred when I directed Peter O'Toole in the now infamous production of *Macbeth* at the Old Vic, or the Scottish play as Peter preferred to call it. Originally Jack Gold had been chosen as director, but he dropped out, possibly after consulting his astrologer, and Peter turned to me to step into the breach, dear friend. 'I'm doing the Harry Lauder show at the Vic,' was how he put it to me. The challenge of Shakespeare's most difficult play and O'Toole's return to the stage after seventeen years was irresistible, for without risk we all stagnate. I accepted, little knowing that in the next three months I would make my own contribution to theatrical folklore. Since there have been many grossly inaccurate accounts published, I thought I would put the record straight here.

Of course I was well aware of the curse of *Macbeth*; the superstition is burnt into every actor's soul from an early age, and the two leading roles have proved a graveyard for countless actors through the ages, though quite why this should be so is difficult to explain. The play, unusually brief, is full of sublime poetry and individual scenes but many scholars have surmised there is some hidden flaw in it though none can agree as to exactly where the fault lies. Mrs Siddons and Dame Edith Evans both pronounced Lady Macbeth as 'not female', Edith going further and telling me that the lady was 'incomplete' and that is why she never wanted to play the role. I have often pondered whether part of the reason for this is that, in Shakespeare's lifetime, the role was always played by a boy and that possibly Burbage and Shakespeare came to the conclusion in rehearsal that the role had to be truncated because the boy actor was not up to it. Scholarship often overlooks the obvious.

The witches are always difficult to make acceptable to modern audiences, though every variation in the world has been tried. Equally, the bones of the plot are laid bare very early in the piece: the introduction of Lady Macbeth being almost crude, for Shakespeare telescopes time, allows her to receive Macbeth's letter seconds before his arrival, whereupon without further ado she immediately decides their future course of action and blurts out the plan to murder Duncan as soon as her husband is through the door, thereby removing any element of surprise. Conventionally, murder stories are seeped in mystery, but in Macbeth we are given only inevitability.

All these factors contribute to the problems an actor faces when attempting the central role. In addition the role requires great physical stamina, and a few years previously Peter had undergone major surgery. Describing his career as 'tepid' he was out to prove himself in more ways than one and, whatever else, nobody could ever accuse him of lacking courage.

He had joined the reconstituted Old Vic company, under the Prospect Theatre banner, as joint artistic director with Timothy West. As an employee engaged for the first production, I quickly discovered I was serving two separate and opposing masters; Peter had total artistic control over *Macbeth*, while Timothy controlled the purse strings. The two central protagonists were poles apart in temperament and in their approach to the theatre, so they cohabited in isolation, like a warring husband and wife living under the same roof ripe for divorce. It was neither a practical nor a happy working arrangement and by the time I understood it I was committed.

My first encounter was not propitious. When I came home Nanette naturally asked me how the day had gone.

'It was very curious,' I said. 'I may have stepped into a nest of vipers. Time will tell.'

'What happened?'

'Well, to start with, Peter addresses Timothy as Eddie Waring.'

'How odd,' Nanette said innocently.

'More than odd. Very alarming.'

'Why would Peter do that?'

'I have the feeling that it isn't exactly a meeting of like minds.'

Perhaps I should have studied my own crystal ball. A year or so before, I had written a history of the British acting tradition which traced the progress of our performers from Burbage to Sir Ian McKellen. Of Peter, I had written:

> At his best, which is very good indeed, he is an actor of great presence and power, constantly swimming against the tide. A romantic by nature, he finds much to criticise in the contemporary theatrical scene and can unleash laser beams of invective against the citadels of mediocrity. There is passion and violence beneath the handsome mask . . . Flamboyant, a *jeune premier* in the classical mould, a tough matinée idol, a compelling and elegant actorish actor . . . who needs firm handling. His destiny lies not in the mundane but in the heroic – and heroism is thought reactionary these days, more's the pity.

With one or two minor exceptions, I inherited the cast of Peter's choice, including his Lady Macbeth, Frances Tomelty, whom Peter had preferred to a previous choice of Timothy West's. The seeds of discontent had been sown very early in the game, as I was quickly to realise. There was also an emotional involvement with another member of the cast that I could have done without. Many of the players in *Macbeth* were also set to appear in *The Merchant*, the second play in the proposed repertory, with Timothy playing Shylock.

Rehearsals began and I found Peter's knowledge of the play and general scholarship of the period impressive. He came to the first rehearsal word perfect and asked me not to give him any direction until the third week. Although unexpected, this request was understandable: he had been preparing the play months before I came on the scene and to a great extent had already set his performance. I therefore concentrated on the other players, many of whom were young and not over-familiar with the speaking of Shakespeare's verse. One, in particular, had been heavily influenced by Joan Littlewood and told me his acting had to 'come from within'. I swiftly discovered that it came so far from within that it was scarcely discernible. In his biography of Peter, the usually reliable Nicholas Wapshott places too much trust in supposition and insists that the first day of rehearsal was 'as expected, pretty awful and Forbes started as he meant to go on by tearing everyone off a strip'. In the first place this is not my style, I have never joined the Otto Preminger school of directing, and secondly all that ever happens on first days is that the cast sits in a circle and gently reads through the play. I have been in and around theatres since the age of sixteen and it was ever thus. Mr Wapshott is not alone in getting things wrong: most outsiders, when writing about the theatre, have little or no conception of what actually goes on. Since most of the young players were strangers to me it would have been the height of foolishness for me immediately to antagonise them.

Rehearsals in fact went reasonably smoothly with a refreshing absence of temperament or tantrums and perhaps I allowed myself to be lulled into a false sense of security. Many days I came home to tell Nanette I had found aspects of Peter's performance electrifying and as the rehearsals progressed I had every reason to suppose he would confound his critics. What soon became perfectly obvious to me was that there was an imbalance between Peter and some of the less experienced actors, some of whom were understandably in awe of him. A further complication was that Brian Blessed, playing the vital role of Banquo, was in Manchester finishing a television film, and only arrived for the last few days of rehearsal.

There were other hiccups. Peter rejected the first production designer's set (describing it as 'a Bonsak bathroom') and I was forced to begin a frantic search for his replacement at short notice. We encountered the same problems with a costume designer and increasingly I found myself in the uneasy position of keeping the peace between the management and my star artist. Most of the acrimony centred around rising costs rather than artistic interpretation. My total salary for two months' work was £1000, less ten per cent commission to my agent and it was not the policy of the management to give directors a percentage of the box-office take. So I cannot be held to have made vast inroads into the budget.

We finally solved the question of the sets, bringing in a young designer named Keith Wilson who had made a name for himself in films. He had to devise a multi-purpose set, acceptable to Peter, for the severely restricted Old Vic stage (on the prompt side the wing space was only four feet). One critic later described the set as 'a Hollywood castle', a rather cheap crack at Peter's and my film backgrounds. It is so easy to be wise after the event, but we were committed to a fixed opening date in London, there was no provincial tour when many of the crinkles could have been ironed out – we were destined to open cold with the minimum of previews.

By now the media hype was reaching alarming proportions. Peter was interviewed and photographed for practically every newspaper and magazine, and, since he invariably provided good quotable copy, his face and comments made the headlines. He is in the old-fashioned slang sense a major 'lardy', a barnstorming character possessed of unlimited charm which disarms the unwary, and fearless when offering his opinions. This proved to be a double-edged sword. I grew enormously fond of him during the rehearsal period, and remain so to this day, for I admire nothing more than true talent, and I regard the eventual outcome which produced such a bizarre, hysterical reaction from the critics as a tragi-comedy of good intentions.

Again with hindsight I realise there were several warning signs that I chose to ignore. Peter often remarked that the play was seeped in blood. 'Do you know how many times the word "blood" appears in the text, old darling?' he would say. I didn't, but he told me. Then later he volunteered the information that 'if you stab a living man, blood spurts seventeen feet.' I was prepared to believe him, but urged caution. He then gleefully informed me that he was having a double-handed sword made of the finest Toledo steel. When this fearsome weapon finally appeared the actor playing Macduff visibly paled. However, I did manage to talk Peter out of using a follow spot – what used to be termed a 'lime' – meaning a spotlight which tracks the leading man wherever he moves.

Towards the end of rehearsals HRH Princess Margaret paid us a visit. The association with Glamis Castle, the birthplace of Her Majesty, her mother, afforded Peter great pleasure. During a break the subject of blood came up again in conversation. 'What you need is some Kensington Gore,' the Princess said knowledgeably. 'We use it all the time in St John Ambulance demonstrations. It's very realistic.'

I saw Peter's eyes gleam, but little suspected that he would act on the advice as he subsequently did.

Although my star and cast seemed on an even keel, the relationship between Peter and the management had reached the critical-mass stage. All dialogue between the two parties was now conducted through intermediaries. Peter objected to the posters and tore them down; the management constantly informed me that due to his demands the production was going way over budget. I was in the middle, reluctant to take sides because, if nothing else, I had to keep up the morale of the cast. Actors are nervous enough as first nights approach and the added element of internal conflict was the last thing I needed.

Expectations were high, too high for anybody's good: Peter's performance had in many ways been prejudged as a result of his many pronouncements in the press. In one interview he had unwisely predicted, 'I will either be brilliant or plain bad but I won't be mediocre. You have to live or die by the box office and it's going to be brilliant.'

Whatever else, the box office was exceedingly healthy. Tickets for the first night were already changing hands at a premium and before we opened there was an advance of some £182,000, a quite extraordinary figure for a Shakespearean production outside of Stratford. Stars, they say, are those who put bums on seats and by that reckoning Peter had to be in the top bracket.

There was another strike against Peter and me. Both in advance of the first night and certainly post-production we were constantly referred to as rude intruders from the sordid world of films. I have noted that whereas when a Peter Hall or a Trevor Nunn turn their hand to the cinema they are granted generous approbation, those of us who undertake the reverse journey are treated as impertinent poachers by the theatrical pundits. In our case Peter was judged a mere *film* star rather than a leading man capable of handling the classics, and I was treated as somebody who had wandered into the theatre by mistake, this despite my having made my living in the theatre for twenty years.

We staggered through the first technical rehearsal which, by tradition, is always a nightmare. Ours was no exception. Little worked as planned and I had to steel myself not to scream throughout a long night. The penultimate day we had the first complete run-through with costumes and scene changes. Somewhat to my surprise I found that although Peter had barred Timothy from the auditorium he had agreed to an American television crew being in attendance. I found them an unwelcome distraction in the midst of all my other problems and the thought that all our mistakes were being recorded added to my worries.

Although this last full rehearsal had many rough edges, I thought Peter gave a thrilling reading – the first time he had truly pulled out all the stops – and that he would justify all the advance claims he had made. After it was over, chain-smoking his French cigarettes and consuming endless cups of black coffee, he was calm and relaxed. I felt far from relaxed, but I went home to snatch a few hours' sleep feeling that we were in there with a chance. I woke to what proved to be a false dawn.

The moment I got to the theatre I was handed a long letter from Timothy in which he listed what he felt were necessary and urgent changes if a full-scale disaster was to be avoided. I learned that he had defied Peter and secretly witnessed the last dress rehearsal from a seat in the gods. To be fair to Timothy, in a happier atmosphere I would have been prepared to discuss and act upon some of the pertinent comments he made in his letter, but I knew that to broach them to Peter at the eleventh hour would provoke an explosion that could destroy us all. When a jockey is mounted and already in the trap waiting for the off, the trainer does not ask him to change horses.

There were other secrets stalking the theatre that fateful day – *Macbeth* was living up to its reputation. Peter had sent one of the young assistant stage managers on a shopping errand to purchase several gallons of Kensington Gore which he then concealed in his quick-change room together with a zinc bath. The bloodbath he had mentioned so many times was now literally waiting backstage.

Equally, as the glamorous first-night audience filed in, I was totally unaware that Timothy had already composed a statement he intended to make public, disassociating himself from the production. Although this move was unknown to me, a few members of the press, scenting a good story, were apparently aware of it.

Even in the most mundane farce, few actors approach a first night with equanimity, and the challenge of Shakespeare's most difficult play scares the living daylights out of anybody honest enough to admit it. I have known some famous players who are physically sick before their first entrance, for as you stand in the wings waiting for your cue you are totally vulnerable and there is no one who can come to your aid: the arena awaits, the lions are hungry for human flesh. Historically some of our most illustrious actors have failed in the role or at best found themselves victims of the *Macbeth* curse. Olivier's 1937 production, also at the Vic, was spectacularly disaster prone. At a public preview Olivier's blade broke during the sword fight; a fragment flew off into the audience, striking a spectator who promptly died of a heart attack. On the actual opening night Olivier lost his voice and the death occurred of Lilian Bayliss. Alec Guinness did not fare any better: when he did it the entire set caught fire.

So it was with these dire examples in mind that just before the half was called, I paid the customary visits to all the dressing rooms to wish my cast good luck. There were twenty minutes before curtain rise by the time I reached Peter's room. I was stunned to find him stark naked except for a Gauloise.

'Peter, old son,' I said, as calmly as I could, 'aren't you leaving it a bit late to get into costume? They've called the quarter.'

'Can't wear them, darling,' he replied, with a smile and a faraway look as though he had just given me the obvious explanation. 'They're hopeless.'

'Ah!' I exclaimed as panic, like bile, constricted my throat. 'We don't have much alternative, do we? But let me see what I can do.'

I left the dressing room hurriedly to go in search of Brian Blessed. A close friend of Peter's and somebody Peter listened to, he was my only hope. After hearing my graphic description Brian said: 'Do you think his bottle's gone?'

'God help us if it has.'

'Leave him to me,' Brian said. 'Can't promise what he'll look like, but I'll get him on.'

Quite how he achieved the miracle I will never know, for I was partially anaesthetised with shock but I hazily recall that Peter made his first entrance dressed in a motley collection of garments which included jogging trousers and gym shoes. There was madness in the theatre that night on both sides of the curtain. Later several journalists tried to get me to admit that he was drunk. Nothing could have been further from the truth: since surgery Peter has not touched a drop. Several times during the final rehearsals I had drawn his attention to the idiosyncratic walk and stance he sometimes adopted, warning him that people might put the wrong interpretation on it, believing it to be the consequence of too much mead. But, unlike a film director, a stage director has no control over events once the curtain rises. He cannot halt the proceedings and ask for a second take, he cannot correct false moves, physically hasten the set changes or give a prompt if an actor 'dries'. He is left to pace at the back of the auditorium, powerless. That, alas, was my unhappy role that first night.

What followed was extraordinary by any standards. Perhaps

the critics caught a prior whiff of Kensington Gore; certainly Peter gave it to them in spades. I later learned that instead of the traditional blooding of hands, Peter had immersed himself in the zinc bath. The effect, when he reappeared after the deed, was as though Macbeth had killed the king in an abattoir rather than his bedroom. This produced a mixture of horror and hysteria throughout the audience and from that moment onwards the play was doomed, though to the end of my days I will never agree that his performance was devoid of any merit as the critics later contended. Not that I am trying to whitewash my own role in the proceedings. Peter wanted an old-fashioned, straightforward production, devoid of trimmings, and I deferred to him.

The first intimation I had of the scale of the disaster was when our housekeeper woke me to say that there was a reporter waiting in the kitchen and a television crew outside, both wanting my reaction to the news that Timothy had disowned the production. Since I had not seen his statement I declined to make any immediate comment. I remained besieged the entire day.

For the first time anybody could remember, a play performance took over the front pages. Placards in London actually carried emotive banner headlines more as though war had broken out than that half a dozen critics had panned a play. Nobody could recall anything like it happening before. It was massive overkill. Predictably, Peter and I came in for a torrent of scorn, not to say abuse, for much of the criticism was highly personal. One reviewer in particular, who behaves like a bitch on heat whenever he sights an easy target, went well beyond all normal standards of criticism.

For months afterwards friends would commiserate and ask me how much the episode had devastated me. I could honestly reply that I found the whole thing too bizarre to be upset and wouldn't have missed it for the world. Peter likewise took it in his stride and refused to be cowed. I remember him coming into the theatre on the second night when we all had to fight our way through a crowd besieging the box office for non-existent tickets. He greeted his bewildered cast with an extravagant gesture and proclaimed, 'It's all wonderful! This is what the theatre is all

55

about.' Kate Hepburn agreed. She phoned to tell me, 'If you're going to have a disaster, have a big one.'

The curse of the Scottish play struck again on the second night: we were the victim of a bomb hoax; the performance had to be interrupted while the audience filed out into the street and the theatre was searched. Because the cast were in such disarray, stunned by the vituperate notices, I felt compelled to speak up for them. I went on stage, unannounced, at the end of the second performance and made a short speech, saying that, far from disowning my cast, I took full responsibility for their performances. I had gone into it with my eyes open, I had enjoyed the experience and one has to take the consequences, good or bad.

Within days of the opening I had to be on location in Devon to direct *Jessie*, a film I had written for the BBC in which Nanette played the title role. Before leaving I wrote Peter a long letter* listing a number of suggestions for killing unwanted laughs and giving many detailed notes to individual members of the cast in the hope that Peter would act upon them in my absence. His reaction was to ring me in the middle of the night and urge me to helicopter back to London and take a rehearsal. Since I was then in the middle of shooting a film, the suggestion was totally impractical, and Peter should have known it. I did not see another performance until I returned to London weeks later and what I saw was disenchanting. It was still playing to packed houses, but none of the more obvious faults had been eradicated.

In one sense Peter was right: the theatre needs controversy, it needs big personalities who can ignite a little gunpowder; it needs to provoke passionate argument, drama within the drama. Unfortunately, our production also provoked bitterness and acrimony. Timothy's statement that he disowned the production was to backfire on him. It is an unwritten law in the theatre that you do not side with the enemy in the face of attack; you close ranks. I received letters of commiseration from Peter Hall, Sir Ralph Richardson and many others in the profession. The rest of the season did not flourish, Peter resigned, the Arts

*See Appendix Three.

Council discontinued their grant, the Prospect Theatre Company went into liquidation and what had started out with such high hopes ended with renewed acrimony.

But despite all the backstage sound and fury, tickets changed hands at scalpers' prices, television crews lay in wait outside, reporters arrived from America to keep the story alive, and a good time was had by all at our expense. The play was sold out during its entire London run and went on to break records during the subsequent provincial tour. So in a sense we had the last laugh. Not a belly laugh, perhaps, but a laugh nevertheless.

SIX

Early in 1991 I switched on the evening television news and was saddened to see a part of my life crumble before my eyes in a cloud of dust and rubble. The breakers were smashing up Elstree film studios to clear the site for another supermarket. Even as I watched the massive chained ball pendulated into the corner office I had occupied for over two years, the last act of violence and cynical disregard that had characterised the studio's plight for the previous decade. Few voices were raised in protest, for the needs of the high street are paramount, and concern for what remains of our once flourishing film industry is a minor consideration. Doubtless many would say I lament from prejudice, that the demise of yet another studio is of little consequence and judging by the long loud silence, they are right – as an industry we have never had any political muscle, and our voices would not influence a single by-election. Soon grocery trolleys will occupy the tracks camera dollies once travelled. The ghost of Hitchcock will make portly progress past the racks of pet food and fishfingers. There will be no special offers for the past, for battery chickens, frozen pizzas and diet meals will be the new power and the glory. Or who knows? Since writing the above, there has been a palace revolution in the company involved, so all previous bets are off and the future of what remains of Elstree is once again up for grabs. It is an all-too-familiar story. Shepperton studios went the same way, the victim of a Sixties' asset-stripper, the millionaire whizz-kid, John

Bentley, once a key figure in the operations of Slater Walker (remember them?). Nobody ever includes Art when talking of the environment, Art is something which exists in limbo if it exists at all in the minds of politicians. Asset-strippers on the other hand are still considered part of our cultural heritage, good old boys who know a quick profit when they see one.

The saga of my term of trial as Head of Production and Managing Director of Elstree was first documented with over-much acclaim, then questioned, probed and finally inaccurately dissected in my obituaries. Predictably, I was frequently accused of having too much power, whereas in truth I had too little to carry through the reforms that were necessary.

It all began early in 1970 in the old White Elephant restaurant in Curzon Street which had a predominantly show-business clientele. As Nanette and I were being shown to our table we paused to exchange greetings with Carole and Bernard Delfont. Bernie, acting with EMI, had recently acquired Associated British Pictures after a protracted and at times acrimonious take-over bid. Primarily a man of the theatre, that night he confessed to me that he was not over-familiar with the intricacies of the film world and asked if I could spare him an hour or so in order to pick my brains. We arranged to meet the following morning at his office in the Prince of Wales theatre. It was as casual as that. I cannot speak for Bernie, but certainly I had no premonition of what was to be the outcome.

We duly met the next morning and I talked very frankly, perhaps too frankly, for what I told him seemed to cause him alarm. As I left he asked whether I would write him a paper setting down my opinions and ideas in more detail. I still did not connect this request to my own situation, since it was my firm impression that he had already made a choice as to who would run the studio for him. At that time I was enjoying going from film to film. I had just finished *The Madwoman of Chaillot* and had three other projects on offer. For the first time in my life I now commanded a very large salary and the barometer of my career seemed set fair.

I gave him my views in a strongly worded document and his

reaction to it was swift and dramatic. He asked if we could meet again immediately and this time we settled down to a session lasting several hours. It was during this second meeting that he first broached the idea of offering me the job. Again I did not seriously entertain the suggestion, for it seemed to me we were both playing a game of consequences. Nor did I covet the job. From age sixteen I had been self-employed (and frequently self-unemployed) and the prospect of a nine-to-five desk job held little attraction. Of course it was flattering to be asked, and of course I treated Bernie's tentative offer with the seriousness it merited.

He called me to his office for a third time and on this occasion he put a definite proposal to me. What until then had been a fascinating, if academic, debate now assumed different proportions. I asked for time to consider my answer. I went home, told Nanette the news and booked for the entire family to fly to Dublin, returning in a mood of nostalgic fatalism to that same penthouse suite in the Gresham Hotel where Jimmy Woolf and I had spent several months during filming the remake of *Of Human Bondage* with Laurence Harvey and Kim Novak. I remembered the comfort of peat fires and monster breakfasts of sausages and eggs. The weather in Dublin ensured that I had little to divert me from the problem since it poured with rain for our entire stay.

From the very beginning Nanette had grave misgivings. We both recognised that if I accepted the job it would irrevocably change our whole mode of living. Throughout our marriage our lives together had been casual – periods of inactivity punctuated by frenzied episodes when I went off to make a film. We had two young daughters and always in the past I had ensured that the family was not separated. Whenever my film commitments required that I spend long periods abroad, the children went with us and as a result were educated in a variety of countries. Sarah, our elder daughter, stayed on to graduate from Staples High School in Westport, Connecticut where we lived during the shooting of *The Stepford Wives*. I had no illusions about the hours the Elstree job would require, it would be a full-time-seven-days-a-week job and therefore the family would see a great deal less of me. I faced a long journey every day, since there was no direct route between our home and Boreham Wood. (In the first year Reg Howell, my chauffeur, and I clocked up 40,000 miles and I trained myself to take catnaps while travelling.) Again, common sense dictated that I could hardly expect the same salary I commanded as a writer/director.

I had been genuinely thrown off guard by Bernie's offer and was now disturbed by my inability to come to a decision one way or the other. I tried to anticipate the reaction of the industry in general to somebody like myself being placed in a position of administrative authority. There would be some, I knew, who would be only too anxious to resent my elevation, just as many years later David Puttnam was pilloried for taking a similar post. Nanette read my thoughts.

'You realise, don't you,' she said 'that a lot of people will want you to fail and will enjoy watching you fail? You have to expect that.'

We argued backwards and forwards the entire week, and, in the end, often cursing the fact that the offer had ever been put to me, sometimes maddened by my own perception of the dangers ahead, I took the plunge, finally convincing myself that it would be an act of supreme hypocrisy to continue as a passionate critic of our native industry in the knowledge that I had passed up an opportunity to do something positive about its obvious ailments. Of course there was a degree of arrogance in my decision (beware the humble leader) but I had not sought the job, it had come to me by chance.

And why did Bernie choose me of all people? I was not one of his intimates. I had known him socially and had watched his climb to power, but I had never worked for him in any capacity, nor had any previous connection with the Grade Organisation which he shared with his two dynamic brothers, Leslie and Lew. I admired his chutzpah and I took him at his word when he said it was his intention to revitalise the British film industry.

Once I had given my decision I cleared the decks of other

projects on offer and briefed my lawyer to forge a contract I could live with, impressing upon him that the actual salary was of secondary importance. I knew enough to realise that responsibility without power is a poisoned chalice in such situations and therefore asked him to concentrate on establishing my authority in the area of artistic control. I was resolved that from the very beginning whatever else I accomplished I would ensure that I was able to give to others the basic artistic freedoms I had struggled for throughout my own career. I also insisted that there would be no reduction of the existing studio workforce save through voluntary redundancies.

My compensation was finally agreed at £40,000 plus a small percentage of every film made under my banner. I later learned that this sum was high compared to some executives in the parent company, and possibly cause for discontent. On the other hand for three years previously I had earned four times that amount and it meant that I had to cut back on my own living standards. For the first time in my life I became a paid employee on a fixed monthly salary. The contract was to run for three years.

At no point did I meet any other member of the EMI Board during these negotiations, though Bernie arranged for Nat Cohen and me to exchange views. Nat was then the Chairman of Anglo-Amalgamated, primarily a distribution company which had also been taken in under the EMI banner. He was an old and wily campaigner who knew where most bodies were buried and had made a considerable fortune distributing the *Carry On* series, as well as partly financing films such as *Darling* and *A Kind of Loving*. Instinct, borne out by subsequent events, warned me that until I came on the scene, Nat had every expectation of occupying the post himself. He received the news of my appointment with guarded enthusiasm, as did those retained executives of the old ABPC company, and from their immediate reaction it was obvious they were unprepared for my inclusion in their midst. Most of them were elderly men opposed to any change in their comfortable routine. One in particular, a reactionary dinosaur, was openly critical of Bernie's choice from the outset and I marked him down as somebody to be wary of.

Hammering out the critical clauses in my contract took several weeks. It was finally agreed that I would be given a revolving production fund of £4,000,000, a minuscule sum by today's standards, and not too generous even then, with which to produce a programme of films to be made in-house, employing the permanent studio staff, distributed by EMI and shown in their chain of cinemas.

At that time there was a duopoly between the Rank Odeon cinema chain and the slightly smaller ABPC chain, soon to be revamped and renamed. What it amounted to was two separate monopolies. For any independent film-maker to get his films shown on either of the two circuits, he had to submit them for scrutiny by one of two men – the Rank booker and the EMI booker. The fate of films rested on a cursory examination and I use the word 'cursory' quite deliberately, since I soon gained practical experience of the way the system operated. I was present on various occasions when potential films were screened cold in a deserted viewing theatre, with not even a token audience present and the booker taking phone calls throughout. Very often the screening was halted after a couple of reels and the film condemned. Obviously if the Rank booker gave his veto, the chances of his counterpart at ABPC selecting the reject were heavily reduced, with the result that the film was only shown, if at all, in the scattered independent houses where the box-office take was considerably lower.

It can be readily seen that this system operated to the disadvantage of the film-makers right down the line. After the cinemas had taken their cut, the distributor was next in line, charging not only a hefty commission but also recouping one hundred per cent of all expenses before the actual negative cost of the film was reduced by one penny. In glaring contrast to American accounting (the famed double-bookkeeping system) I have always found the British method to be reasonably honest, but even so the dice are always heavily loaded against the film producers.

At the press conference announcing my appointment I used an

off-the-cuff phrase in answer to a question from the floor which was widely misinterpreted and was to haunt me for years. I said I felt the industry had gone too far with 'the pornography of violence', a verdict I still hold to. Predictably this was immediately misquoted in subsequent stories and I was usually portrayed as a quasi-Mary Whitehouse figure opposed to any form of sex. What I had referred to were films of the *Texas Chainsaw* ilk, saturated with violence of the most hideous kind, that I felt were driving whole sections of our audience away from the cinema. One must remember that at the time of my appointment audiences were declining every year and it was my contention that family entertainment had all but disappeared. Violence in the cinema is cynically marketed and it has always been my belief that constant exposure to brutality, sadism and violent death must inevitably produce a dulling of normal civilised outrage. Addicts of death will always demand new and more perverted variations. The trend continues and the ever-increasing crop of video shops devote a good proportion of their shelf space to fifth-rate horror movies. All have a degree of foulness at their heart.

At the outset Bernie shared my views and recognised the need for my programme of films to try and reverse the trend. He encouraged me to include a number of films which might attract the vanished family audience back into the cinemas.

When I entered the studio for the first time I had no idea what I would find. For several years previously, Elstree had not enjoyed the cachet of Pinewood. Situated in a high street, it lacked the huge backlot facilities of Pinewood, and in addition was surrounded by suburban housing, making any exterior shooting difficult. I had worked there as an actor many years before and remembered it as a rather dismal place, smacking of an industrial site and lacking any real atmosphere. I had been allowed to take three people with me as my own team: John Hargreaves, who for many years had been the production controller on all of my own films and was generally regarded in the industry as brilliant with budgets; Austin Frazer, who in addition to being a fine writer had a parallel career as a designer; and finally my estimable secretary, Margaret Reeves, without whom I could not function.

I gave Austin an immediate brief to carry out a detailed examination of the entire studio complex and report what needed to be done. His eventual analysis of the situation made depressing reading and I had the evidence of my own eyes to confirm his findings. Nearly every building on the lot was in dire need of renovation. Dressing rooms were a disgrace, filthy dirty and lacking any comfort; in one we found excreta running down the walls from a broken toilet on the floor above. Some of the stage roofs were falling in, the backlot resembled a bomb-site, littered with scrap wood, discarded sets and squalid debris of every conceivable nature. I have mentioned the state of my own office, but the entire main administration building had an air of decay about it, like a home for transients. There was one modern block, housing two of the smaller stages and a decent cafeteria, but the rest depressed me unutterably. The workforce seemed to me a lost tribe, never consulted, unsure as to their future, badly paid, a microcosm of the whole of British industry during that sorry period. I could not blame them for the state of the studio, since it was patently obvious there had been little or no capital expenditure over a period of years.

That first day I had invited the heads of department to have lunch with me and I found myself staring at a lot of anxious faces around the table. Understandably they were all concerned about their fates, since nobody had informed them in advance of the changes or my appointment. I assured them that there was going to be no night of the long knives. I asked the middle management to get together with Austin and draw up a list of priorities. Apart from one television series there was no current production in the studio, so it was a good time to start some housekeeping.

I then arranged to meet all the shop stewards alone in my office. What followed bore a passing resemblance to *I'm All Right, Jack*. A dozen members of the joint Works Committee duly trooped in and before there had been a chance for any introductions I was handed a piece of paper. It informed me that as of five p.m. that day there would be a work-to-rule and overtime ban.

I tore it up and threw it in the waste-paper basket.

'It's a bit early for threats,' I said. 'I invited you here because I wanted to meet you all and have a cup of tea.'

Their spokesman said: 'I must ask you to take our resolution seriously.'

'Look,' I said, 'I haven't even found my way to the toilet yet. But if you want to go on strike, don't wait until five o'clock, go through the gates now. You'd be doing me a favour.'

Total silence greeted this.

'I happen to be on your side,' I continued. 'I've done my homework and I think you've got a good case. Some of the minimum wages are a disgrace and I intend to do something about it. But I can't do anything immediately.'

All this took place during the Wilson government, and, in order to give a wage increase under the existing law, employers had to negotiate a productivity deal.

'If you screw me now,' I added, and I must admit I used a more colloquial Anglo-Saxon expletive, 'you'll screw the only friend you've got.'

This finally provoked a reaction. 'I must ask you to withdraw that obscene language,' the spokesman said.

I wanted to laugh. The whole scene took on an air of unreality. 'Right, I apologise, but at the same time I hope you get my meaning. Give me one month. I promise that by the end of that month I'll come back to you with an improved wage structure. If I don't, if I break my word, you need never trust me again and you can throw the book at me.'

Their spokesman looked around at his colleagues. 'The brothers and I will withdraw and consider that.' I later discovered that they met in more or less permanent session and were always withdrawing from the shop floors to explore wrongs, both real and imagined.

'No need to withdraw,' I said. 'Tell me now to my face. There are no hidden tape recorders, nor have I got a team of lawyers behind me. I'm your new boss, just look me in the eye and give me a straight yes or no.'

There was a pause, and then somebody said, 'I think that's fair dos. I vote we accept what the governor says.'

And after a cup of tea, they trooped out. Perhaps the very nature of my blunt, unrehearsed dialogue helped dilute their inherent mistrust of management. I was not seeking instant popularity, nor did I get it. At the beginning I was just another face under the same hat to them; a younger face than they were used to, recognised as being somebody with their own background, but nevertheless somebody who had 'moved over', joined 'them' and therefore to be treated with even more caution. How many times had I heard the expression 'traitor to his class'? I really did understand their plight; the average take-home wage was pitiful and for all they knew I had come in with the intention of making wholesale firings. There was a chasm I had somehow to cross in the weeks and months ahead. I knew I had to find a way of breaking down the remoteness between management and the workforce.

The day did not end there. A short time afterwards an ashen studio manager asked to see me and reported that there had been a punch-up: one of the shop stewards had left my office and promptly knocked the personnel manager unconscious. I was told that it could well be a police matter. Discovering there were five eye-witnesses to the fight I ordered that all five put in written statements. In due course I received five complete works of fiction, each account describing totally different facts. Feeling that this was the moment of truth, and that I had to show I meant business, I fired the two antagonists on the spot. Curiously, neither man argued against this rough justice.

Retiring to my office and its fake antique furniture, I stared at the bare walls and wondered what the hell I had let myself in for. I picked up the phone. It was answered immediately by a scared voice and once more I realised I had inherited a demoralised workforce.

'Would you get my home, please,' I said.

'How is it?' Nanette said when the connection was made.

'Bloody lonely,' I said.

SEVEN

Arthur Marshall, who was as funny in real life as he was in print, once cautioned me about autobiographies. 'Don't put in a lot about granny and grandpa and your dotty old aunt who took to pig sticking in the Vale of Kashmir. Family skeletons should remain firmly in the closet, dear.'

I met Arthur and other distinguished literary figures through my long friendship with Roger Machell. For a time when I was licking the wounds of a failed marriage and totally penniless Roger gave me room and board in his elegant Albany chambers. There, over many a hilarious lunch, I met and enjoyed the company of Raymond Chandler, Arthur Koestler, Eric Ambler, Sam Behrman, John Gunther and Alan 'Jock' Dent, for Hamish Hamilton boasted a wonderful list of authors. Roger was a great editor who took infinite pains with his authors, never forcing his opinions on them but in the gentlest manner possible suggesting how they might reconsider certain passages. Since his day I detect a dramatic shift; certain editors now tend to regard their authors as a tiresome appendage to their own careers.

One of the two books I wrote for Hamish Hamilton, and which Roger edited, was a history of the British acting tradition which I entitled *That Despicable Race*, a description of the strolling tribe first penned by Charles Churchill. Following publication here, Scribners of New York bought the American rights, albeit for a somewhat meagre sum. 'High on prestige, low on advances,' I perhaps unwisely murmured when I met the son of the founder.

Shortly before the American edition went to print I received a mysterious telegram stating that Scribners were unable to pub-lish under my title. I rang them to enquire why.

'Our people here consider it racist,' I was told.

Baffled by this, I pointed out that the handsome jacket had a portrait of Sarah Siddons on it and that the only black actor mentioned in the text, glowingly at that, was Paul Robeson.

'Surely,' I said, 'nobody in their right mind could possibly find anything remotely racist in the book.'

'Our people have done market research and come up with a bad reaction.'

'What do you want to call it?'

'*Players*.'

'Isn't that somewhat dull?' I said. 'It also happens to be the brand name of one of the most popular cigarettes as well as the title of a film starring Ali McGraw currently going the rounds.'

Scribners were unmoved. It had to be *Players* or nothing. Irritated beyond measure I returned their advance and the book was never published 'over there'. A clear case of cutting off my nose to spite my face, I suppose, but one I did not regret. Graham Greene once suffered the same treatment, but in his case he handled it with more aplomb. Being told by his American publisher that *Travels With My Aunt* was an uncommercial title and would have to be changed, he promptly cabled back, 'Easier to change publisher than change title' and did!

In company with all screenwriters I have had to accept that my work will be changed by those who employ me. In my entire career I can only think of one script that I wrote at a sitting and which reached the screen without a word being altered. This was *The Whisperers*, adapted from a fine novel by Robert Nicolson. It was brought to me by two young American producers, Ronald Shedlo and Michael Laughlin, and I turned it into a vehicle for Dame Edith Evans. It was the one and only occasion when I had total artistic control, made for United Artists when that erstwhile great company was in the hands of Bud Ornstein and David Picker. Those were the days.

For the rest, nothing has ever changed over the years. I cannot calculate the numbing hours I have spent in script conferences arguing the merits or unsuitability of the banal. Not so long ago I was sent for by one of the American networks and offered a large sum of money to adapt and then direct a current bestseller. Between leaving London and arriving in downtown Burbank they had had second thoughts about the material. Greeted by the Vice President in Charge of Creative Affairs, a daunting lady with enough bangles on her arm to stock a stall in Petticoat Lane, I was immediately informed that the front office had decided the novel was politically suspect.

'So we want you to come up with a new story line,' she said, 'we'll use the same title and characters, of course, but we'll give it a new slant.'

'Might that confuse people who know the novel?' I said innocently. 'Wouldn't it be better if I wrote something completely original?'

She shook her bangles at me. 'We've paid a fortune for a bestseller, for Christ's sake!'

Being jet-lagged I did not argue further, but took myself off to my hotel room and there for the next two weeks I hammered out some forty pages of a new outline, complete with dialogue scenes, and sent it to the fount of all knowledge. In due course I was summoned for my second meeting.

'What did you think of it?' I asked.

'I haven't read it. I wouldn't read it if you'd sent me a complete screenplay. What I wanted was a two-page synopsis.'

I had forgotten that few Vice Presidents in Charge of Creative Affairs can stay the course through a complete script. They are weaned on *Readers' Digest* paragraphs.

'I'm sorry, my mistake,' I said, with heavy and unperceived sarcasm, as warning bells started to ring in my head. 'I was stupidly under the impression that you had hired me as a writer, when obviously you were looking for a stand-up comic.'

'Never mind that,' she continued. 'Give me the arc of your main character.'

'Do you mean "Arc" as in lamp or "Ark" as in Noah?'

'Is that a joke?'

'Yes, it's the only one I can muster.'

I had a sudden blinding vision of spending the next six months being driven slowly mad by this gaudy shrew and took an instant decision.

'Somehow,' I said, 'I don't think we're going to see eye to eye on this project. Tell you what, you keep the forty pages, they're free for you to do as you please with. Just pay my hotel bill and air fare and we'll call it a day.' And with that I walked out of her office.

She followed me into the corridor, jangling her bangles like a tambourine. 'You'll never work for the network again,' she screamed.

'Curiously enough,' I shouted back, 'I've been in the business over forty years and I've never worked for the network before, so it's no great loss.'

I have written two novels with films as their background, *The Distant Laughter* and *The Rewrite Man*, in which I tried to give unexaggerated accounts of what really takes place. With the notable exception of Budd Schulberg's classic of the genre, *What Makes Sammy Run?* the majority of novels about the industry, especially those set in Hollywood, never hit the mark in my opinion. Even *The Last Tycoon*, critically acclaimed as the definitive opus, is seriously flawed. Fitzgerald was always an outsider, never admitted to the inner cabals of Hollywood, and had little or no practical experience of what went on when the cameras rolled and egos sparked. His vision was essentially romantic, born, I suspect, of his wish to be accepted by those who rejected him. But Thalberg, on whom his main character, Starr, is based, was not a romantic, he was a tough little operator out for his own ends. He took on Louis B. Mayer, perhaps the most successful and the most odious of the tycoons, and you had to be tough to take on Mayer. Thalberg, like Monroe, died prematurely and therefore was a prime candidate for canonisation. It was Thalberg after all who kept Fitzgerald in the waiting room. For that matter there is still little that is romantic about the inner circle of the current bunch running what remains of the major studios. They are all cast in the same mould; they just speak better, as they say. It's difficult to imagine any of them having the wit to descend to Sam Goldwyn's brand of humour. The only major difference is that they jog and work out, rather than smoke cigars, and some are no strangers to coke and crack. From the moment when the glove merchants and carpet-baggers travelled west the prime driving force has been money; everyone seeking the elusive crock of gold that can be mined from a rich vein of sex and violence. The current bunch lose more money, make bigger mistakes than the old gang, but the spoils when they hit the occasional jackpot are beyond even Mayer's dreams of avarice. For all that, Hollywood lives and dies by the way in which it creates, manipulates, exploits (and often destroys) its various sex symbols. That is how the studio system with its façade of paternalism operated. The roster of stars under contract, with few exceptions, were cosseted slaves, groomed and perfumed, protected from their worst excesses, their public utterances written for them, told when to have an abortion, whom to marry, when to divorce, how to walk and speak – for gods and goddesses had to be perfect. Not for them any comparison with the girl or boy next door. Eventually, the gods and goddesses got wise and turned into monsters, demanding astronomical salaries to the extent that, currently, a single film can cost more than the entire yearly output of MGM in its heyday.

Inexplicably, films about films are seldom accurate. Perhaps it would be asking too much of the general public to believe some of the idiocies we have to take for granted. In a short foreword to *The Distant Laughter* I wrote this disclaimer: 'The fiction of the film industry has always been stronger than its fact, and my inventions and characters bear no resemblance to living people. Only the insanities are real.' That is not to say I have not enjoyed the insanities, for I have never been happier than when directing. Getting a film to the starting post may be hell in the current economic climate, the aftermath may be wrist-slitting time, but the period when one is actually shooting and editing has great compensations. To marshal and nurture the talents of fine actors, and see your words come to life on the screen the following day with the aid of superlative technicians, is a pleasure beyond measure. Much of filming is organised chaos punctuated by periods of intense boredom, especially when you are shooting on location and at the mercy of the weather. But to compensate there is an intense camaraderie in a film unit, for in many ways it is a city within a city, inhabited by a dedicated band of enthusiasts who, for a period of weeks, live in intimate proximity.

I have been fortunate in often working with the same technicians – great cameramen like Bernard Guffey, the old Hollywood veteran who started life as John Ford's operator on *The Informer* and who was still working when seventy; Claude Renoir, that urbane, distinguished French artist who painted with light and then, tragically, became blind – surely one of God's bitter jokes; our own Arthur Ibbetson, who guided me through my first film as a director; Gerry Turpin, Gerry Fisher and Tony Imi. Also from my very first film I was lucky enough to find a second right hand in my continuity girl, Penny Daniels. Penny had an amazing facility for her difficult and publicly unrecognised job. I cannot count the number of times she saved me from committing basic errors. Her husband, Bill, was my sound mixer until he died, and I have always felt it was a major injustice that although we make *sound* pictures, the sound men are never accorded proper credit. Whereas casting directors and a host of executive producers (a convenient misnomer for rubbernecks in many cases) are given prominent credit at the start of a film, the poor sound men are relegated to the roller at the conclusion and lumped in with the driver of the electrical generator, the assistant to the production accountant and the caterers – all worthy people, no doubt, but scarcely on a par with the team that records the words and effects with great skill. Bill Daniels' boom operator – that is the man who physically manoeuvres the microphone – is a genial character named Gus Lloyd, and on Bill's death I promoted him to chief mixer, a position he has filled for me ever since.

I have also worked with some extraordinarily gifted designers and composers. Ray Simm designed the majority of my films and I never had cause to fault him. When I went to Hollywood to make *King Rat* I chanced by sheer luck upon a modest but remarkably talented man called Bob Smith who, starting with a dry riverbed in the semi-desert, fashioned a fifty-acre set of great complexity within the space of eight weeks. Likewise for *The Stepford Wives*, I secured the services of a gentleman from Baton Rouge in the Deep South, by name Gene Callahan, who not only had exquisite taste in all things, but was also a superb cook and a den mother to the cast and crew. I mention them all for the very good reason that their vital contributions seldom get proper recognition.

As for composers, I started at the top with Malcolm Arnold and then can claim to have discovered John Barry, for I believe I gave him his first chance on a full-length feature film – *Seance on Wet Afternoon*. He went on to write the scores for *King Rat*, *The Whisperers*, *The Wrong Box* and, most notably, *Deadfall*. For *Deadfall* I asked him to give me a guitar concerto of concert-platform standard, for it had to be performed in its entirety by Renata Tarrago and at the same time underline the drama of a robbery – the film being cross-cut between the concert performance and the working out of the crime. John is a composer who has an instinctive feel for the mood of a film and whose music always complements, rather than swamps, what is being shown on the screen. This is the true gift and not always present – how many times have we sat in the cinema and thought, 'I wish to God the bloody music would let up so that we can hear the dialogue?'

John was not available to write the score for *The Madwoman of Chaillot*, but I remembered a brilliant young Welsh composer, Michael Lewis, who first came to my attention when he wrote the music for a stage musical called *The Barnardo Boys*. Although I never succeeded in raising the money for the play, I remained convinced that Michael had enormous talent. A wild extrovert character, with unlimited Celtic charm, he just needed a fillip to put him into the top rank. I was able to give him that fillip. At my suggestion he was flown to the Studios de la Victorine in Nice, given a room and a piano, and told to come up with some themes, since my American producers were not prepared to accept my word for his talents and needed tangible evidence. He staggered out of purdah a week later clutching some memorable music which clinched the matter. The finished score won the coveted Ivor Novello award the following year.

The wrong music can irrevocably change the entire feel of a film, and yet this vital ingredient is often left to chance. In the majority of cases the composer has no prior knowledge of what he is eventually going to put music to, for often he is not shown anything until the director and editor arrive at what is known as 'the fine cut', that is to say, the version everybody believes (with fingers crossed) is the definitive version of the film. At that point decisions are taken as to what scenes and sequences require an underscore. Exact measurements are taken and given to the composer who then goes away and starts working. At that point only he knows what the music will sound like and it isn't until a few weeks later when everybody comes together on the scoring stage for the recording sessions that the effect can be judged. By then it is too late and too expensive to make any major changes.

I feel this procedure is grossly unfair to a composer. A screenwriter can do several drafts of the script, a director can order any number of takes to obtain his desired result, and when the shooting period is over the trial and error of the editing process may be spread over three months. Everybody but the composer gets more than one bite of the apple. My working method is to involve the composer as soon as possible, show him work in progress during the shooting period, and ask him to come up with some simple themes, played on a single instrument if need be, which can then be laid into the cutting copy. In this way all those involved can judge whether the final orchestrated version will complement the images. If the first themes don't work, then there is ample time for the composer to have second thoughts. It seems to me this is the only fair and practical way of dealing with such an important ingredient.

I always go to the recording sessions in a joyous mood of expectation. This was especially true when I shot *The Slipper and The Rose*, my first and only musical. I had a great cast and the score by the Sherman brothers, so superbly arranged and orchestrated by Angela Morley, contained a number of delightful songs. My own favourite was the waltz and curiously this was the first number I actually shot, on location in Anif, Austria. I should perhaps explain to the uninitiated that when one is making a musical film all the songs are pre-recorded. Then when one shoots them the artists synchronise their lip movements to a playback. It goes without saying that this is a very demanding process and has to be achieved without the slightest error. Gemma Craven, who was a total newcomer to filming at that time, had to dance across a field, I remember, and at the same time sing a portion of the lyric. Unlike a stage performance, the song is broken up into segments, and every time the director changes the camera angle there has to be an overlap so that when the shots are cut together, there is a smooth transition from one shot to another. It sounds complicated and it is complicated, and the art is to conceal the complication.

I think the great difference between shooting a musical and a straight feature film is that the set no longer resembles a morgue. To arrive in the morning and conduct rehearsals to music is a joy. Unlike the French film industry we start work at an unearthly hour; the actresses, for instance, will invariably have to be in make-up and hairdressing by six a.m. ready to go on the set by eight-thirty. The French have a much more civilised approach. Their day begins at noon. One has a splendid French lunch, then work continues without the distraction of tea breaks until evening. I have several times worked French hours and they make all the difference to one's mental and physical well-being, especially on a long and punishing schedule. As an experiment I tried to introduce the French system while running Elstree, pointing out that everybody would benefit by missing the morning and evening rush-hour traffic and be able to arrive the following day refreshed after a decent sleep. Sadly I could not sell the idea to all of the unions concerned, not even on a temporary basis.

Night shooting is a bane, since everything seems to go into slow motion for some reason and one's brain does not react with its customary speed. Or so I have found. If one is compelled to have a long stretch of night shooting, the law of diminishing returns begins to operate since, like jet lag, the body's metabolism is thrown out of kilter. Filming at night presents particular difficulties for the lighting cameraman, for he has to justify his light sources. It is always a compromise, and sometimes the results are farcical. We have all seen a murder committed in the bushes where the moonlight has the intensity of a searchlight. Likewise there is the old chestnut of the hero striking a match in a darkened room and being suddenly illuminated by an intense beam. I have a particular affection for what used to be called the Joan Crawford-poking-the-fire-shot. Our heroine bends to stir the embers and the camera is then positioned where the fire should be and miraculously we are given a close up of the actress seen *through the flames*. A good one that, as is the shot featuring the bottle of poison in the bathroom cabinet. The cabinet appears to be free standing for, when the door is opened and a hand comes in to take the bottle, the camera is inside waiting for it. I have always tried to resist such chestnuts because I believe that they destroy the illusion we should be at some pains to preserve.

There is a further artifice known as Day for Night. (Truffaut, you remember, made a film with this as the title, using, as it happens, my old setting from *The Madwoman*.) By the use of filters, sunlight is converted into brilliant moonlight. It is never a happy compromise, but often forced on us by the demands of the budget. No matter how skilful the cameraman, the finished effect is usually slightly fuzzy and unreal. Personally, I regret that nowadays we are not allowed to make black and white films, the reason given is that you can't make a sale to television. This is strange in view of the number of old black and white films endlessly shown on television. Certainly thrillers look better in black and white, for colour has a sanitising effect. It would be difficult to imagine *The Third Man* being more effective in colour, though recently a new menace has crept in – the system of colourisation applied to old black and white films – which has been strongly resisted, without success, by film-makers. I regard it as an abomination, but because we have been denied moral rights, until international law is changed, we are powerless. Typically our own government fudged the issue when moral

77

rights were finally included in the 1988 Copyright Bill. We are now entitled to moral rights, but have to *assert* them where screenplays and films are concerned. The Catch 22 is that those who employ us still enjoy the contractual right to refuse to let us assert them, so we are back to square one.

EIGHT

For many years now I have kept a journal. It is not a day-to-day account, more a commonplace book, a serendipity memory aid where I record things and events that have touched my life, snatches of overheard dialogue, vague ideas for future novels or scripts, and odd items culled from newspapers. Treasuries of quotations have always fascinated me, and I confess to a passion for diaries, especially the diaries of writers.

Since commencing this book I have been rereading my own efforts and I have chanced across a number of unrelated entries that will perhaps give some indication of their diversity and flavour.

I have often wondered whether the acknowledged wits of the past first rehearsed their bon-bons then waited for a suitable opportunity to parade them. Noel Coward had genuine wit and I was present on one occasion when it seemed to me he made a spontaneous response to a social gaffe that could not have been predetermined. It was a very smart dinner party, and amongst the guests was Randolph Churchill. Before the first course was over he was involved in a violent row with our host. He suddenly flung down his napkin, pushed his chair back and strode from the room. An embarrassed silence followed. In the silence Noel said: 'Ah, there goes Randolph! Completely unspoilt by failure.'

Again at one of the Albany luncheons when the late Alan Dent was asked why so-and-so was not around any more, he remarked, 'Oh, he left the country under a cloud no bigger than a choir boy's hand.' What could be more elegant?

During one of our many visits to Beverly Hills Nanette overheard a snatch of dialogue in her hairdresser's. The very swish stylist was putting the finishing touches to a blue-rinsed octogenarian. 'Did I ever tell you,' he said, 'that I did Frank Sinatra's mother's hair? She was such a doll.'

'Was that before she died?' the elderly matron enquired.

That same trip Nanette came back from a shopping expedition with other social snippets from Beverly Hills. In the changing rooms she heard a woman tell her companion she was treating herself to a $10,000 mink coat after her four-year-old son had fallen through an open manhole into a sewer. 'I need something to steady my nerves and it's cheaper than a shrink,' she explained.

Later while wandering through the bridal department Nanette encountered another woman advising a young prospective bride on whether to buy an expensive wedding gown. 'Do yourself a favour, take it. After all, you only do it two or three times in your life.'

The journal for the year when I was making *The Stepford Wives* contains a jumble of entries. It was during this trip that we first met and became firm friends with Bette Davis. Our relationship began in Connecticut, for her house was close by our own in Westport. She lived alone and took great pride in preparing delicious meals for us. Her speciality was her own recipe for Boston baked bean stew, the succulent secret of which died with her. One night with just Nanette and me present the conversation came around to one of her past successes, *Old Acquaintance*. It so happened that I had just been approached to direct a remake. I recalled that during the making of the original there had been a legendary feud between Bette and her co-star, Miriam Hopkins. Nanette not being so familiar with the story asked innocently, 'Whatever happened to Miriam Hopkins, Bette?'

Bette was standing in front of the log fire, legs apart, a slug of whisky in her hand and the inevitable cigarette in her mouth, 'Well, Nanette,' she drawled in the voice that everybody used to imitate, 'God was very good to the world, he took her from us.' I thought it magnificent that after forty years the rancour was still there.

Many years later I got a call one night from the local police. 'I've got a lady on the phone who says she's Bette Davis,' a dubious station sergeant told me. 'She claims to have lost your number and wants me to give it to her. What should I do?'

'Don't risk your life,' I said. 'Give it to her.'

We had not seen her for several years and in the interim she had been dreadfully ill, somehow surviving a double mastectomy, a broken hip and a stroke, had a face-lift on her seventy-first birthday and didn't give a Yankee damn for most things. She did not shy away from misfortune, she met it head-on. There was no self-pity in her hand luggage as she journeyed through her last years; she knew what she had been and she knew what she was – an actresss no longer in great demand, but still a great lady with something to offer. I don't know why she sought me out as a friend in whom she could confide, but I am ever grateful that she did, and only sorry that I never had the privilege of working with her. To the very end she was always urging me to write a film for her.

That night we took her to dinner in a local restaurant. At first she could talk of nothing else but the recently published hatchet-job biography her daughter had written. She vowed she would pen her own version and in due course she did. Chain-smoking as always, she later regained her old sense of humour and regaled us with stories about the men in her life. Despite the jokes I could sense undertones of regret that none of her marriages had been wholly successful. I recall one story about an ex-beau, Fred Perry the tennis ace, who apparently ate nothing that was set before him when Betty took him home to meet her mother. Finally, exasperated, her mother asked him: 'Mr Perry, do you think you could suck an egg?'

At the end of dinner she walked unsteadily with the aid of a cane to the door of the restaurant, paused, turned to the gaping diners and delivered her parting shot. 'You all think I'm drunk, don't you? Well, you're wrong!' They applauded.

Bette was capable of terrifying many people and she certainly did not suffer fools and had unlimited scorn for many of the current crop of young actresses who gave themselves airs. During the making of *The Stepford Wives* my editor, Timothy Gee, confessed that he would go to his grave a happy man if he could once meet Bette. So Nanette and I organised a small dinner party. Throughout the meal Bette challenged and demolished everything Timothy said to the point of embarrassment. Afterwards Nanette and I felt that his long-awaited treat must have been an unmitigated disaster for him. I rang early the next morning to commiserate, but my concern was unnecessary.

'I loved every minute,' Timothy said. 'I mean, to be shouted down by Bette Davis is something I shall always cherish for the rest of my life.'

Bette's generation of actors and actresses were survivors. Dame Edith Evans also survived a heart attack followed by a stroke. A Christian Scientist, she at first refused all medical attention until she lapsed into a coma and her local GP risked her wrath and had her taken to hospital. I was rung by the hospital in the middle of the night to be told she was dying and had asked for me. I drove to Kent, arriving in the early hours only to be told I could not see her until the consultant had given permission. I did not take kindly to this but went away to grab a coffee in a roadside café. It was a cottage hospital with all the rooms on ground level. When I returned half an hour later I parked by chance right outside Edith's room and was amazed to hear her unmistakable voice. She sounded very much alive. Since nobody was about I slipped in unnoticed and found my way to her room. I found her sitting up in bed, admittedly, but a pale shadow of her normal self. She burst into tears when she saw me and asked me to find her a mirror. I took one off the wall in the bathroom and gave it to her. She regarded herself for a long time, then said: 'They all think I'm going to go, you know. *But I'm not going to go looking like this!* And I'm hungry. I fancy lamb chops and peas.'

I went in search of the Staff Nurse and told her of Edith's request.

'Impossible,' the nurse said, visibly shocked. 'She's on a drip feed. Solid foods would kill her. There's no way she can have anything like that.'

'Look,' I said. 'The lady in there is Dame Edith Evans, generally thought of as the greatest English actress of this century. You tell me she's dying, so what does it matter? If she wants lamb chops, she's going to have lamb chops, even if it means I have to kill a sheep with my bare hands.' I persisted and my bludgeoning tactics finally produced results: Edith got her lamb chops, ate them with relish and lived another four years.

Edith's remarkable fortitude was also true of Laurence Olivier. He, too, came back from the dead having survived a number of grave illnesses which would have put paid to most people and continued his distinguished career for many more years. They were both following a long tradition that stretched back to Mrs Siddons and Kean. There is a truism about the show must go on, which, although parodied by Noel Coward in one of his songs, is borne out time and time again through succeeding generations of actors. It isn't just a question of fearing the understudy's abilities, there does seem to be a unique spirit peculiar to actors which surmounts physical handicaps. I know I have sometimes dragged myself to the theatre with a raging temperature, feeling like death, only to return to the dressing room after the first act minus all symptoms. We don't, as a profession, have much time for malingerers. An actor needs physical strength as much as he needs talent, the two are indivisible.

I suppose Edith summed it all up during a radio broadcast she did in the days when the BBC broadcast a full-length play every Saturday night. Just before the red light went on for transmission she was approached by a young actor in the cast who ventured to say, 'Good luck, Dame Edith.'

Edith regarded him then, in Bracknell tones, replied: 'With some of us it isn't *luck*.'

Edith, Bette, Kate Hepburn, Enid Bagnold: all remarkable women and I often ponder my good fortune in having known them. Like the other three, Enid was a one-off, a true original. I first met her when I was researching my biography of Edith. I had written to ask if she would see me and talk about her relationship with Edith. I got one of her famous postcards in return on which she had written, 'Come at eleven o'clock on Tuesday. You can stay for fifteen minutes. Don't be late or I won't let you in.'

I duly presented myself at her house in Hamilton Terrace on the dot of eleven. She opened the door herself and took me off guard by immediately saying, 'Why do you use such a posh typewriter?'

'Do I?' I stuttered. 'It's just an IBM electric, nothing very extraordinary.'

'It's posh compared with mine. I can't write anything at the moment.'

She was smaller than I had expected, a slightly stooped figure with bright, intelligent eyes that regarded me with suspicion. I had seen pictures of her as a young World War I nurse – the sort of face one would want to wake up and see if a wounded soldier. Now age had taken its toll, but the beauty was still there. I was finally admitted and made polite conversation, convinced that the meeting would be a complete waste of time. Then to my utter amazement Enid suddenly said, 'Excuse me, I have to give myself an injection.' Whereupon she lifted her skirt, exposing heron-thin legs, and plunged a hypodermic into her thigh. I did not have time to do the polite thing and look away. 'I'm a morphine addict,' she explained. 'Costs me thirty pounds a day to get it on prescription, and I have the devil's own job when I travel to America. They need a lot of convincing I'm not a junkie.'

I later discovered that she had suffered a serious injury some years previously and the doctor had prescribed large doses of morphine to ease her pain. Consequently she became addicted.

Immediately after this startling episode, she further surprised me by saying: 'I like you. Didn't think I was going to, but I do. You can stay for lunch.' Lunch, cooked by her son, proved uneatable but that did not deter me. I sensed that any effort would be worth it to get closer to this remarkable woman. And so it proved for that was the beginning of a rewarding friendship that lasted until her death. She had been emancipated from an early age and on my second visit confided that, 'I lost my virginity to Frank Harris upstairs at the Café Royal.' She later had a happy marriage to Sir Roderick Jones, the Chairman of Reuters, which lasted until his death.

Her frequent one-liners always stopped me in my tracks. I remember once admiring a piece of Meissen china in her Rottingdean house where Burne Jones murals still decorated the damp nursery walls and her bookshelves were draped with sheets of plastic to protect them from a leaky roof. 'Oh, yes,' she said casually, 'it was given to me by Prince Antoine Bibesco.' Then almost as an afterthought added: 'He kept me in a basement under Proust.'

It was the sort of off-the-wall dialogue that peppered her plays. I think that given a new audience she enjoyed being a character and, like Edith, she was a bit of a flirt, still capable of working feminine charm and often faking helplessness in the company of a male. For much of the time she was obviously in pain, physical and mental. Amongst other ailments she suffered from chilblains, something that seemed strangely alien to somebody in her social strata; I thought of it as a condition that only attacked the under-privileged and remembered how my mother had been afflicted by the same painful blisters every winter in our unheated home.

Enid constantly confessed that she could no longer write, that her creative juices had dried up. Two or three times a week I would receive anguished postcards scrawled with her angular handwriting, asking me to help break the block. In a copy of her autobiography she wrote: 'For Bryan – who is going to save me from "Writer's Death" – Enid Bagnold (aged 87).' It was a cry from the heart all the more poignant for coming from an old woman who said to me, 'The boredom of my life is horrible. It is boredom like a pain. I know not one soul in this village although I've been here fifty years.' I did not save her, alas, but at least I think I rekindled some hope. At one point I urged her to collaborate with me on a film script and she thought this might be 'rewarding'. The idea was still-born, but I made frequent visits to

Rottingdean because, like Edith, she was a lonely woman at the end, her contemporaries all dead, *The Girl's Journey* she had described with such verve now but a fading memory. Katherine Mansfield had described her as 'almost without fear' and Humbert Wolfe thought she was 'one of the illuminate, who are born stricken with knowledge', – such a lovely phrase. Though Enid professed herself ignorant of most current trends, I would listen, open-mouthed, to her accounts of Sickert, Gaudier-Brzeska and H.G. Wells, for she had known everybody it seemed and to me it was like being shown stereographic slides of an era that would never come again. I literally sat at her feet while she reclined, bare-footed on a couch wrapped in shawls, giving herself the injections of morphine, bringing into sharp focus an age of giants.

Once, having written me a long letter, she scrawled across the top, 'This is a letter all about nothing. Don't waste your time reading it. Throw it away unread. I shan't know.' Often she signed her letters 'with real love', as though needing to impress upon me that our friendship was important to her. Perhaps it was, I hope it was. Again towards the end of her life, like Edith, she was convinced that she was penniless. I have no idea what her financial position was, but when I made *International Velvet* I persuaded MGM to make an *ex gratia* payment to her. This sparked off a shoal of postcards and letters with the recurring theme, 'Is it a dream, will the money really arrive?' As her ailments gradually took a heavier toll she had to face selling her home – 'Not easy when you're ninety,' she said. Sometimes in my eyes she resembled a character in one of her plays that Edith might have portrayed. Both ladies lived in isolation in large, empty houses crammed with the memorabilia of their crowded lives, unable to escape their pasts.

Enid had a magnificent library, hidden and unread beneath the plastic sheets: with my love of books I found it heartbreaking and I once volunteered to catalogue them for her, but by then she seemed too tired to care. Eventually her letters to me were spaced further and further apart, typed with one hand, the other being nerveless and needing an operation. 'It might help. Or not. So I chose the not.' After her death I learned, all too late, that the library had been auctioned off.

I often think of her as I think of Edith and Bette, for I was thrilled to know all of them, albeit only in the twilight of their years. When my biography of Edith was published and I sent Enid a copy she turned first to her own letters which I had included at length. She confessed: 'I am dazzled by *what was* [the emphasis was hers], I see now what my gift is. It's imagery. Imagery so quick it's like the snap of photography. But I am praising myself (in your book) and I mean to.' Later she confided that my biography had convinced her she had been too hard on Edith – 'but then she had her own golden burden to carry, as I had mine. Like two knapsacks they dangled and collided.' Yes, she did have the gift of imagery, imparting to what she wrote a wisdom which was almost the act of giving life made articulate.

NINE

I once cut out a paragraph from a newspaper and sent it to my son-in-law, John Standing, who shares my sense of humour. He has kept it in his wallet ever since. I don't think I have ever read anything that made me laugh more. It encapsulates everything that is completely dotty about show business, and at the same time points up the intrinsic sadness of some performers prepared, or perhaps condemned, to go to any lengths to maintain a toe-hold in our profession. I will quote it in full.

Bizarre hotel sex wrecked a sunshine holiday for John and Liz Shultz and their three children. They stormed out of a floor show at the exclusive Paraiso Mas Palomas on the Spanish island of Gran Canaria when a naked blonde simulated sex. They left again when a children's show was followed by transvestite dancers. 'The third evening was a comedy evening, so we thought we would be all right,' said John. But the comedian told blue jokes wearing only a mask and rubber leggings and with a dead chicken dangling from his penis.

I wish Peter Sellers had lived long enough to have enjoyed it, because I know he would have referred back to it for years and taken the situation further – acting out the backstage drama when the comedian discovered that his vital prop was missing. I can imagine Peter ad-libbing dialogue in one of his many voices: 'Nip out to the supermarket, will you, and get me a new chicken. Free range, of course, them battery birds don't get the laughs.'
Once Peter latched on to a comic idea, he loved nothing more

Me, aged 16, as Question Master of the BBC's Junior Brains Trust, my first professional engagement, for which I was paid 2 guineas.

Somewhat romanticised photo of a young soldier. Taken in Hamburg 1946.

The first photograph I ever took of Nanette during a visit to the Sussex Downs.

Top opposite: John Mills and me in *The Baby and The Battleship*, directed by the late Jay Lewis.

Centre opposite: Rock Hudson, Raoul Walsh and me as an improbable pirate. Taken on location in Brittany during the shooting of *Sea Devils*.

Bottom opposite: Richard Attenborough, Sheila, his wife and Nanette. This was taken on our arrival in West Berlin for the film festival. Our first solo production, *The Angry Silence*, was the official British entry.

A rare shot from *Of Human Bondage*, taken at Ardmore Studios in Dublin. Kim Novak, Laurence Harvey, Siobhan McKenna, me, Ossie Morris, the cinematographer and the intransigent director, Henry Hathaway.

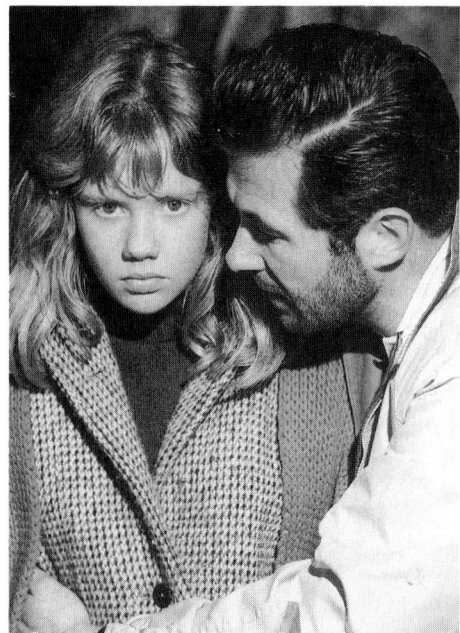

Directing the young Hayley Mills in *Whistle Down The Wind* on location in Lancashire. She was then the top box office star in the world, but entirely unspoilt and seemingly unaware of her fame.

The amazing little boy, Alan Barnes, who almost stole the film from Hayley. I discovered him in a local school. He had no previous acting experience but was a natural.

A rare photograph of Jimmy Woolf talking to Richard Attenborough and me in Notting Hill Gate for *The L-Shaped Room*.

Directing Kim Stanley in *Seance on a Wet Afternoon*. Kim went on to win the British Academy Award, The New York Critics Award and an Oscar Nomination for her remarkable performance.

Discussing the script of *Seance* on Ray Simm's set with Richard Attenborough. His nose, needless to say, was false.

The American crew on *King Rat* considered cricket a sissy game. So I sent to England for the gear and the British cast challenged them to a match. They quickly changed their minds when they found we didn't wear any protective gear.

On the set of *King Rat*, built in a dry river bed near Malibu in California, which is now a housing estate and golf course. L to R: George Segal, Tom Courtney, unknown actor, me, unknown actor, Patrick O'Neal and James ('Willie') Fox.

Left: The distinguished American cameraman, Bernard Guffey. He started his career as John Ford's operator on *The Informer* and well into his sixties photographed *Bonnie and Clyde*, as well as my own *King Rat*. I was determined to work with him after seeing his work on *From Here To Eternity*.

Below: Shooting *Deadfall* in Majorca. My beloved continuity girl, Penny Daniels.

Discussing the score for *Deadfall* with solo guitarist, Renata Tarrago, and composer John Barry.

Robert Graves and Nanette during the shooting of *Deadfall* in Majorca. Robert, I surmise, was a frustrated actor and couldn't wait to be given a role in the film.

Taken in Dame Edith Evans' garden in Kent while I was making the documentary of her life. She had only recently recovered from a stroke.

Dictating to my secretary Margaret Reeves in a graveyard during a snatched lunch break. Margaret kept me sane during the EMI period and I could not have existed without her.

than to carry it to extremes. There was an occasion when he, Nanette and I decided to go to Paris for a long weekend. We were spotted at London airport by a young and naive reporter from the then *Daily Sketch*. What was the purpose of our trip? Peter immediately began to invent. 'Mr Forbes and I are going to Paris to sign up a new pop star we've discovered.'

The reporter grabbed his notebook. 'Is this exclusive?'

'Absolutely. You're the first person we've told.'

'Can I have the name?'

Peter was inspired. 'Turk Thrust,' he said.

'Turk Thrust?' The stub of pencil scribbled furiously. 'Is that his real name?'

'It is now. He had it changed by Deed Poll.'

'And are you going to manage him?'

'We hope to. He's going to be big, really big. Bigger than Freda Clench.'

I felt Peter had now gone too far, but the reporter swallowed it whole.

'I can't tell you how grateful I am, Mr Sellers, Mr Forbes. This is a big break for me. Don't give it to anybody else, will you?'

'It's all yours.'

We flew off well pleased with ourselves, had a hilarious weekend and returned home to find that the *Sketch* had given the story a lot of space.

'We must keep Turk Thrust alive,' Peter said. 'He's too good to kill off quickly.'

We organised a fake LP complete with lurid sleeve cover and titled TURK THRUST'S GREATEST HITS. Much to our amazement nobody saw through the deception. We continued to build on the legend. I made an appearance in Peter's *Shot in The Dark*, as a nude guitarist, suitably disguised with a beard and billed on the screen as Turk. Nanette appeared on television's *Juke-Box Jury* and when asked for her opinion of a new single said, 'I like it, but I think I prefer the Turk Thrust version.' The presenter nodded in agreement. 'Yes,' he agreed, 'a lot of other people have said that.'

At one time we considered finding an unknown singer and

grooming him for the role. Given the name, and the idiocy of much of the pop scene, he might have actually made a career.

I told Elton John the story and he obviously filed it away because years later, when we joined him in Malibu for a holiday, he met us outside Los Angeles airport with a hired Greyhound bus carrying a banner proclaiming 'WELCOMING TURK THRUST – ENGLAND'S LATEST SINGING STAR'. Never the one for half measures, Elton had also hired some drum majorettes who as we appeared burst into a routine, shouting, 'Hip, hip, hip hooray, Turk Thrust is in L.A.' A crowd gathered and 'Turk' signed autographs. I love people who will go to any lengths to sustain a practical joke.

Elton has caught me on several occasions. On that same Malibu holiday, being told that my star sign was Leo (it isn't quite, I am on the cusp of Cancer and Leo), he had a fully grown lion in the courtyard to greet me when I woke up. On my fiftieth birthday, when he was touring in America, he organised a superb gag from afar, bussing the Cory Brass Band from the Welsh valleys to my home, where they played on my lawn for three hours, consumed enough beer to float a small ship and allowed me to conduct them in 'Land of Hope and Glory'. That's what I call a birthday present. One Christmas he gave me a Steinway grand piano, forgetting to check whether I can play (I can't), and on my sixtieth birthday he produced a medical wheel-chair and a comprehensive array of medications suitable for geriatrics. His generosity, like his talent, is boundless. The same was equally true of Peter.

I felt the loss of Peter as keenly as anybody and scarcely a week goes by without some fond memory of him surfacing. He was an emotional, perennial nomad, both on and off screen, often, I thought, consumed with doubts about his ability to sustain success, either soaring high on the peaks or else plunged in the valleys, there was no in between. A confirmed, hopeless romantic he could never resist falling in love and would immediately shower the object of his affections with the most lavish gifts. Such interludes often took bizarre turns as Nanette and I once experienced. Nanette was his leading lady in a comedy called *The*

Wrong Arm of the Law and halfway through the shooting Peter said he needed to talk to me on a highly personal matter. He came to the house and took up a pose in front of our sitting room fireplace.

'You know you're one of my oldest and closest friends, don't you?' he began.

'Of course, Pete.'

'And you know I'd never go behind your back or willingly do anything to hurt you?'

'Of course.'

Having established that, he went straight to the heart of the matter. 'I want to marry Nanette.'

It was a difficult bombshell to duck, but once I had recovered from the shock I tried to reply with the gravity the situation demanded.

'Well, obviously I can't fault your taste, Pete,' I said. 'How does Nanette feel about it?'

'I haven't told her yet. I thought it right to tell you first.'

'I appreciate that.'

The scene had taken on the characteristics of a Pinter play but I knew it would be a mistake to appear outraged or to mock him: that was not the way to handle Peter. The situation called for delicacy.

'I know it comes as a great surprise to you, but I've fallen in love and I have to be honest about it.'

'Well, I understand,' I said. 'I happen to love her myself. What d'you think we should do about it?'

'We'll still remain friends, nothing will change that.' It dawned on me that Peter was not entertaining failure. He had convinced himself that once he had made the confession to me and I had accepted the inevitable, all would revert to the status quo. To him it was a new role to play, a new mask to wear, and he saw nothing odd in it.

'I think it'd be best if I told Nanette, don't you?' I said, hoping that Nanette would not come into the room at that moment.

'Yes, I think that's probably a good idea. Break it to her gently. How d'you think she'll take it?'

'She'll obviously be flattered, and I know she's very fond of you.' I managed to keep mounting hysteria out of my voice. To have laughed at Peter at that point would have invited disaster. He was so patently sincere and desperate to do the right thing according to his unique code of ethics. 'I guess we'll just have to wait and see. Of course, there's the children to take into account.'

'You'd always be able to see them,' Peter said, relaxed and reasonable now, as though the conversation we were having was everyday stuff. 'Will you stay on here?'

'Difficult to say. I love it here, so does Nanette,' I ended lamely, by now infected with his madness and at a loss to make any further sense of the comedy we were embarked upon.

'You're not angry, are you?'

'Angry? No, I appreciate you being so open about it.'

Nanette joined us at that point and for the rest of the evening the subject was never mentioned. We all had a perfectly normal dinner together with Peter on top form.

Thus began two very strange years. I doubt if they come any stranger.

Peter had made up his mind that his destiny lay with Nanette and the role he had selected had to be played out with a straight face.

When we were alone later that same evening I told Nanette Peter's confession and intentions. We both agreed that we had to tread very carefully if an old friendship we both valued was not to go up in flames. One couldn't mock Peter, that would have been too cruel, for despite his fame he was always vulnerable to criticism. At that point we both felt it was just another of his infatuations which would die a natural death. We had lived through his first divorce, brought about by his conviction that he was in love with Sophia Loren, and we had held his hand while he suffered numerous other emotional setbacks. I had been honest when I said I wasn't angry with him. He was what he was, often confused, given to wild enthusiasms that usually disappeared overnight.

But we were both wrong on this occasion. His obsession with Nanette did not follow the familiar pattern. He was deadly serious and my first reaction to his bombshell had been a mistake. It fell to Nanette to handle the situation alone as best she could and she handled it brilliantly, never hurting his feelings, but gently pointing out the impossibility of the situation. Peter was nothing if not persistent and could not admit defeat, but there were moments when he was forced to see the farcical side of it all. Even at this far remove I am conscious that as I set down the sequence of events the entire episode must appear unbelievable to outsiders. Yet we remained the best of friends, for Nanette adored Peter as a companion and throughout all the twists and turns of this innocent *ménage à trois* she handled his many ploys with gentle tact that sprang from a real affection for him and an understanding of his troubled, mercurial nature. How she did it and remained sane was quite remarkable for Peter's moods could veer this way and that at a moment's notice. On two occasions he bought a gun and threatened suicide and both times Nanette somehow calmed him and talked him out of it. Then there would be periods when Peter was rational and would acknowledge the hopelessness of the situation, followed by periods when he would use every artifice in his considerable repertoire to gain his ends. We lived through seasons of unreality never quite knowing which ploy Peter would try next. One day he would attempt to buy Nanette the most expensive gifts, furs and jewellery, but always tell me beforehand and ask if I objected. When Nanette refused them, he could not understand her refusal. He pleaded to accompany us on holidays, and more than once I felt we were players in a triangle written by Coward. For two whole years we were held captive by his relentless obsession.

I have no reason to suppose that his affection for Nanette was anything other than genuine and, although the situation often became nightmarish, I could never take lasting offence because he was so open about his intentions. Nothing Peter ever did was conventional. To be his friend one had to accept that life would be full of surprises, some good, some difficult to take, but always possible to forgive. His emotions were always on the surface, nothing was ever hidden. Eventually, of course, his ardour, denied consummation, gradually lost potency like wine diluted with water. He went on to remarry three more times, seeking the perfect bluebird of happiness that sadly always eluded him.

He could be so brilliantly funny when he was on top form and relaxed, yet one always sensed the laughter was but a thin veneer masking sadness. Our friendship endured until his untimely death, though we saw less and less of him. There would be months of silence and then he would suddenly surface again and arrange a reunion. He offered us his luxurious yacht for a holiday while I was at Elstree and we accepted expecting him to be there to greet us. When we arrived at the berth in Monte Carlo, Peter had flown, leaving flowers, gifts and a note which said: 'Have gone to Vienna with the Great Bert to learn the zither. All you need to remember is the brown bits are the land and the blue bits are the sea.' The 'Great Bert' was his long-serving chauffeur, a Jeeves with infinite understanding of his master's foibles.

Whatever his marital and emotional failures, Peter's artistry, so closely encircled within his volatile temperament, went far beyond some ill-founded criticism of his worth as an actor. Because his rise to world fame started with *The Goon Show* he was often written off as a gifted mimic. I totally disagree. He was a great film artist and the characters he invented seemed to rise effortlessly from a deep well of invention. But the effort was in fact enormous, the artistry concealed the struggle he always underwent before starting a new role. But once the character was firmly in his grasp (as with his immortal Clouseau) he became possessed, delighted with the discovery in the way small boys are delighted when they find out how a toy works. He was at his best when he could efface his own personality beneath a disguise; on such occasions he was without equal. He made mistakes, he made bad films, and he was not always the best judge of material. But he gave to the screen a gallery of original portraits – the shop steward in *I'm Alright Jack*, all his roles in *Doctor Strangelove*, the old General in *The Waltz of the Toreadors*, the gardener in *Being There* and a superb vignette for me as the venal Doctor Pratt overwhelmed by cats and death certificates in *The Wrong Box*: in only two short scenes he served up the quintessence of what made him a unique performer. There was a fat man always struggling to get out of Peter and his constant longing to be a romantic leading man contributed, in my opinion, to the sadness behind the clown's mask he presented to the world at large, and hastened his death.

Now, when the memories of those years of madness have faded, we constantly remember the hilarious escapades we shared for when the good times rolled there was. no more generous or enchanting companion.

TEN

I went into Elstree studios with the hope that I might be able
to bring about a minor and much needed renaissance in our
ailing film industry. It was a modest hope, and one that I did
not realise.

For years, mirroring Britain's recurrent economic illnesses,
our native film industry had lurched from crisis to crisis, always
hampered by the fact that internal warring factions constantly
thwarted any cohesive remedy. The main exhibitors (i.e. the
cinemas) saw nothing wrong in operating the negative and unfair
practice known as 'barring'. This was a system whereby the two
largest circuits, Rank and ABC, blocked independent cinemas
from showing the latest releases until the market had been
milked dry. Television, which was cheap even for those who
actually *paid* the licence fee, had made vast inroads into cinema
attendances and was, in many cases, providing superior fare.
Governments of either hue were reluctant to admit that the
industry, if supported with incentives for investment, could
become a considerable invisible export and help the balance of
payments. Unlike many other countries, film-making on the
streets was actively discouraged. (I was once arrested in central
London for putting a camera tripod on the sidewalk, charged
under some obscure by-law. This in glaring contrast to my
experiences in France and Chicago. In the latter city, for
instance, the police department runs an autonomous film unit
and welcomes visiting crews. They will cheerfully block off main

streets, and I once shot in a working police station, moving my cameras around real-life suspects as they were brought in.) Although certainly not the prime villains of the piece, the unions played their part in refusing to read the writing on the wall. There was a great deal of petty industrial anarchy, some understandable, some deliberately engineered. I have always felt that it is a mistake to impose industrial laws on a creative process, but perhaps given the way our society remains so resolutely divided, it is unavoidable.

My appointment had coincided with the withdrawal of the major portion of American finance which, during the Sixties, had poured into our studios. At this time we still enjoyed the Eady levy, whereby a proportion of the cinema take was given back to the producers of a film without being subject to any distribution commission and was applied towards the recoupment of the film's cost. It was a welcome bonus to all independent producers, and was intended to help provide ongoing funds for future British films. But like so many laws, it could be abused. The loophole was exploited by some Hollywood studios, who operated through British companies to comply with the regulations but did not necessarily apply this bonus in the way intended.

The American invasion had come about because of our substantially lower labour costs (our unions did not enjoy pension and welfare benefits over and above the national health and pension schemes) which made film production in this country an attractive proposition. The leading Hollywood studios were more than happy to provide one hundred per cent finance to independent British producers and did so on a considerable scale. The result was a boom in home production from which I and others benefited, and in fairness it must be said that, for the most part, we enjoyed minimum interference with our projects. I can confirm that often I set up a film by a mere phone call, something unheard of today. Suddenly a number of British films found an audience in the largest American cities, and earned respectable returns, although the studios' accounting methods left a great deal to be desired. The inevitable result of this largesse was that production budgets in Britain inexorably crept closer and closer to Hollywood's own costs. In addition the Hollywood craft unions exerted strong political pressure to halt foreign runaway productions. Hollywood was not only scared of losing its virtual monopoly of the production scene, it was also undergoing a fundamental retreat from the old studio system. As their own recession started to bite, the back-lots were reduced and sold off for real estate. (Century City, an enormous sky-scraper complex, now stands on what used to be the huge 20th Century Fox lot.) A new breed took control, mostly recruited from the talent agencies, bringing a purely accountancy mentality to the scene. Instead of talking film, their language was all of deals and packages: they did not want a permanent roster of stars, producers, directors and writers on the payroll, they wanted short-term arrangements of their own choosing. Television was changing the audience patterns, box-office revenues were falling, and they were thrashing around for a panacea for their ills.

Unfortunately for the industry as a whole, the new deal-makers were often a third-rate bunch, hip with smart talk and big ideas, but short on ability and experience. Whatever else could be levelled at the old guard, the Mayers, the Harry Cohns, the Zanucks, the Warners et al., street fighters all, they at least understood film. They talked and lived film night and day and had a shrewd knowledge of their audience. Zanuck, for example, was a good editor and showed courage with films like *The Grapes of Wrath*. There was a grossness about Mayer, Cohn was a bully, but when I worked at Columbia I found that if you stood up to him and gave a good argument for what you believed in, he went along. While they reigned the moguls were also in a position to take their own decisions and the percentage of quality films they turned out on the conveyor-belt system stands the test of time – witness the number of classic black and white films from that era that nightly hit our television screens. Despite the idiocies perpetrated by the Hays Office, there was still a sophistication about the comedies they turned out. Urbane and witty, they are seldom matched by today's product, for the top writers of the day tailored their screenplays to accommodate the talents of skilled performers. When one revisits the Cary Grant vehicles, for example, we can see what we are currently missing.

Gradually, one by one, the old gang were out-manœuvred and overtaken by the television revolution. What replaced them were decisions by committees – Vice Presidents proliferated, each with their own legal pads and sharpened pencils, but grotesquely unversed in film knowhow. For all that, they seemed to lead charmed lives, fired from Fox this morning, back in position at Warners the following afternoon, an incestuous procession of the inadequate. With few exceptions they had never paid to see a film let alone made one and they were largely responsible for running what remained of the studios into near bankruptcy and further wholesale sell-offs.

This, then, was the climate when I stepped into Elstree with my meagre £4,000,000 'revolving' fund, which in the event never revolved. I did not have to be a Senior Wrangler to realise that I could never challenge Hollywood on its own terms. From the beginning I had little cloth to cut. I inherited an understandably disgruntled workforce, a run-down studio complex and a Board that displayed little or no understanding of what I wanted to accomplish. It was my first experience of the power play in a large public company and I stupidly imagined that we were all on the same side. I placed most of my trust in the Chairman, Sir Joseph Lockwood, who had steered EMI to enormous success during the Beatles era. A cultured man, poles apart from the average executive I encountered, I felt he would have an affinity with my aims, but in the event he seemed content to stay on the sidelines, observing the battle but reluctant to exert his undoubted influence.

It would be the height of arrogance for me to claim that I had all the answers or now to postulate my superior knowledge at the expense of everybody else. Such was not and is not the case. With hindsight, I can see the initial and subsequent mistakes I made. I am not by nature a ruthless person and I tend to expose my hand early on in any encounter with the result that the trust I so readily distribute is often betrayed. My brief was to provide a pro-gramme of modest films, a base camp from which to build for the future. I believed all the promises made to me when I signed, but which in certain cases were never honoured. I had been given to believe that if I held the studio together and broke even with my initial programme I would then be given some serious money to make more ambitious films.

From day one scripts and propositions flooded in from all quarters, four hundred in the initial weeks, so many in fact that I had to employ a team of seventeen readers, headed by Alan Dent, to sift through them. If three reports were favourable, I read them myself. Alas, ninety per cent of the submissions were dog-eared and hopeless, having gone the rounds many times before. Some came with dubious credentials, for I had been in the business long enough to know most of the copper-bottomed charlatans. If a project came to me from a known source, I considered it personally and immediately. Amongst the first scripts that landed on my desk was *The Go-Between*, adapted from L.P. Hartley's beguiling novel by Harold Pinter. The subject had a long history and came with a heavy price tag of £75,000, for it had passed through many hands, beginning with Sir Alexander Korda who had originally considered it as a vehicle for Alec Guinness. Now it arrived under the auspices of a producer named John Heyman. Pinter's script was, without doubt, one of the finest I had ever read and I had no hesitation in placing it at the head of my list. I met with Heyman who informed me that the project came with Joe Losey, the American director, a victim of the McCarthy era who had exiled himself in England. Losey had the reputation of being difficult and certainly I did not warm to him as a person, but he was a first rate professional at his job. The projected budget proved an obstacle – some £680,000 as I recall – and much too rich for me to tackle alone. Losey had cast Alan Bates and Julie Christie, not a bad start, and armed with this I negotiated a co-financing deal with MGM. The head of MGM at that time was a certain Jim 'Everybody has a fear level' Aubrey, also known in the trade as the 'smiling cobra'. In 1969 he became the president of MGM under its new owner Kirk Kerkorian and together with his sidekick, an ex-film-salesman named Doug Nettor, he set about reducing MGM's mammoth bank debt, beginning as he meant to go on, firing 3500 employees, turning off the heating in the Thalberg building, and cancelling twelve projected films including Fred Zinnemann's *Man's Fate* just days before shooting was to commence. He then came to England with the express purpose of closing the MGM studios at Boreham Wood, at that time one of the best equipped complexes in Europe. For reasons I could neither comprehend nor acquiesce in, the Board of EMI entered into discussions with Aubrey with a view to a quasi-merger. Sir Joseph Lockwood and Bernard Delfont seemed to be in awe of Aubrey, and I several times warned that he would take them to the cleaners. I put up a counter-argument that if there had to be a merger it made more sense to close our Elstree studios and move the combined operation over the road to MGM. The MGM studio had an enormous back-lot and superb modern facilities, whereas we were in a constricted location on a high street and badly in need of a major face-lift. I contended that, provided the profits from the sale of Elstree were ploughed back into film production, the unions would accept the situation. Above all it was a practical solution to a human problem, since the alternative would mean immediate unemployment for the existing MGM employees, many of whom had been there twenty years. But Aubrey wanted a quick resolution and there was no time to organise a campaign against his plan. I argued as forcibly as I could, but my pleas were ignored and the sell-out went ahead, signed and sealed behind closed doors. A public relations exercise was cobbled together whereby, in return for an injection by MGM of a paltry £150,000 a year and some office space at Elstree for some of their middle management, the impression could be given that this heralded a new dawn. It was nothing of the kind, of course, merely a smokescreen to obscure the true facts. A new company called EMI/MGM was formed with me as Managing Director and, with Aubrey's departure, I was left with the unhappy task of conveying the news to the MGM workforce. It was one of the saddest jobs I ever had to perform. I knew then that my own days were numbered and that nobody really gave a toss for films or the people who made them.

But even the most cynical plans of mice and men don't always achieve their original purpose. Although MGM Boreham Wood was immediately gutted (the vast, irreplaceable property department sold for a mere £5000, the central heating plant dismantled) there was a snag. The exercise had been carried out in the expectation that the site could be sold off for housing development at a huge profit. However it had been overlooked that the site fell within the Green Belt and I derived much private satisfaction when planning permission was not granted. The empty stages became a warehouse for Xerox machines. And so an era ended.

Side by side with this unhappy chapter I was putting together my first programme with *The Go-Between* as the cornerstone. MGM were unenthusiastic about Losey's involvement, but my own contract protected him and there was nothing they could do about it. Their first venture under the new banner was to try and foist Ken Russell's *The Boy Friend* into the overall plan. I was and am an admirer of Russell, one of our truly original film-makers, but I felt that his conception of this fragile, ingenuous stage musical, which had achieved its success in the theatre from the very fact that it was a nostalgic pastiche, could easily destroy its original charm. The finished product rather bore this out and it was one mistake they could not lay at my door, though I derived no pleasure from its failure.

I wish Ken had come to me with a subject that more closely fitted his considerable talents, since he was exactly the sort of director I hoped to include in my programme. I approached the cream of our native industry and asked them to join the crusade, but many of them preferred the larger spoils they could obtain in Hollywood. Others, such as Tony Richardson, came with ideas such as *Ned Kelly*, starring Mick Jagger, that I found too expensive and unpalatable. I fought to include a film of Graham Greene's *The Living Room*, which my ex-mentor Michael Powell wished to make, but sadly the negotiations floundered. I urged people I admired, such as John Schlesinger, Jack Clayton, Richard Attenborough and Lindsay Anderson, to bring projects to me but in the end I could not afford them with the limited funds at my disposal. I was particularly sorry that my partner Richard Attenborough was never able to mount Simon Raven's fine novel *The Feathers of Death* which was included and announced in my first programme.

I quickly discovered that I was caught in a trap. The EMI Board wanted me to keep the studios fully occupied, but I did not have sufficient funds to fight on both fronts. I was not only responsible for the production programme, I was also Managing Director of the studio. The studio was staffed with first-class craftsmen inadequately paid for their labours and in many instances lacking the proper facilities. I had the back-lot cleared, authorised some much needed new equipment for the stills department and put in hand general renovations in all departments until the master plan for the entire complex was approved. Even the corridor leading to my office depressed me, for it smacked of an isolation hospital; I half expected nurses to appear carrying bed pans or the odd corpse. I also made a point of eating in the staff canteen once a week to judge the quality of food being served and solicit complaints. It was a long haul to overcome years of indifference and a built-in suspicion of management, but gradually I made small inroads. The thing I am most proud of is that during my term not a single day was lost through industrial disputes and with one exception every film was completed on schedule and within budget.

On the question of wages, after prolonged negotiations, I was able to honour my promise and within the stipulated month put an enhanced pay structure to the unions. In order to comply with the government's insistence that every wage increase had to be tied to a productivity agreement, I bargained with the sacred tea break and the old factory-orientated procedure known as 'washing-up' time, a long-standing practice whereby the workforce downed tools fifteen minutes before the official end of the day and in theory took advantage of this concession to clean up. In practice they swarmed through the studio gates immediately the whistle blew. In return for the unions' acceptance of my terms I installed automatic machines, which would dispense sandwiches, snacks, tea and coffee, on all the stages and workshops. The machines serving beverages had been doctored to operate without coins – tea and coffee were to be provided free of charge. This innovation provoked profound suspicion.

A deputation from the Works Committee closely questioned me as to the number of cups of free tea each man would be entitled to.

'Unlimited,' I said.

Did 'unlimited' mean ten, twenty, thirty?

'Unlimited,' I repeated, 'means what it says. No limit.'

After my answers had been duly deliberated, two of the three craft unions accepted, but a third insisted that they must still have waitress service. I pointed out that the old method of brewing great vats of tea and then trundling them to the stages and shops in all weathers had ensured that everybody was served something the consistency of porridge – tea, in my mother's Lincolnshire expression, 'you could skate mice across'.

They were not impressed and threatened industrial action. The all-important differential had to be preserved. We were back to the class wars again, the determination, even on the shop floor, to have two classes of citizens. The dialogue continued for weeks until the sheer dreariness of the argument exhausted me. I agreed to reinstate waitress service for those employees who felt they could not live without it, but added that they would have to pay an economical price. The union official and my catering department duly met in solemn conclave to determine the true cost of a cup of tea. They arrived at a figure tuppence cheaper than that charged by British Rail. This was put to the membership who rejected it as too expensive. I patiently explained that, since they had refused free tea, they could hardly object to the price of the alternative. It was one of those mind-bending inter-union arguments that had nothing to do with the specific but was entirely motivated by the sterile philosophy of demarcation at all costs. It dragged on for weeks before being resolved. Once it had been settled I added the rider that any member of the rogue union caught helping himself to free tea risked dismissal. This provoked the cry of 'victimisation' and further dark threats of industrial action. It was a sorry, depressing glimpse into shuttered minds.

While trying to survive the climate of industrial lunacy I was being urged by Delfont to make an early announcement of our first programme of films. It was a chicken-and-egg situation. To compete with Pinewood and Shepperton, I knew that I had to improve vastly the Elstree lot and facilities if I was ever to attract the big films. Austin Frazer produced a detailed plan and models of a concept we both hoped would put Elstree back on the map as a modern studio. Careful costings were done and I went to the Board with a request for capital investment of some £800,000. After much procrastination, I was given £80,000, just enough to paint and tart up what existed. The Board were quite happy to embark on a major face-lift of the cinemas, but disinclined to spend more than fourpence on the Elstree complex. I can only recall one occasion when any member of the Board set foot inside the studios while I was there.

One of my priorities was to encourage new directors who had previously been unable to get a break into feature films. This was a calculated risk, but one worth taking. I have already mentioned Lionel Jeffries' notable début, but in addition I was also able to provide first chances for Robert Fuest who directed a stylish thriller for me called *And Soon the Darkness*, shot entirely on location in France, and a newcomer named John Hough. Dressed in what used to be called a zoot suit the young Mr Hough arrived unheralded and sat in my waiting room for the best part of two days before my secretary took pity on him. He was ushered into my office clutching a can of film and forthwith asked me to view it. It was a film about Robin Hood he had made on a shoestring with a cast of unknowns. I viewed it and thought it quite outstanding. As a result I persuaded Irving Allen, the producer, to let him direct *Eyewitness*, another thriller set in Malta, and he proved worthy of my confidence and went on to a career in Hollywood. (At Irving's instigation I somehow found time to do a necessary rewrite on the *Eyewitness* script, using a pseudonym.)

The Canadian-born director Alvin Rakoff was set to direct

Peter Sellers in *Hoffman*, a claustrophobic story that had affinities with John Fowles' *The Collector*, written by Ernest Gebler from his novel *Shall I Eat You Now?*. Unfortunately Peter entered into one of his manic depressive periods during the making of the film and immediately it was completed demanded to buy back the negative and remake it. This being hardly feasible, he then gave an interview prior to the film's release in which he stated that the film was a disaster, thus doing everybody, including himself, a disservice. Not surprisingly, the film did not prosper. There was never any rational explanation why Peter acted in the way he did. His performance and that of his co-star, Sinead Cusack, were fine and Alvin's direction polished. It was an outcome I could not have anticipated, but for which I had to take the blame.

Perhaps my greatest disappointment was my failure to solicit the necessary finance and enthusiasm for a subject called *The Long Loud Silence*, brought to me by Richard Condon and his associate, the distinguished American photographer, John Bryson. The story had a terrifying premise: a train carrying lethal nerve gases is derailed near a small American town and most of the inhabitants are wiped out. The few survivors are then deliberately and callously isolated from the rest of the world and left to their fate. It was a topical and chilling piece and very cinematic. One of the most dramatic episodes was when a busload of children is sent across the only bridge out of the town in a desperate attempt to break the siege. They are fired on and the bridge is then blown up. I managed to get the ear of the State Governor of Georgia, as I recall, who said they had a bridge they were willing to sacrifice (talk about co-operation), but the budget went beyond my existing funds and the Board was not prepared to meet it. I remain convinced the subject matter would have made an outstanding film, but, like many of the projects I tried my damnedest to further, I ran up against a brick wall. The main criterion was a quick profit with little or no risk. As one Board member put it to me: 'We wouldn't be unhappy if you gave us a *Sound of Music* every week.'

I did have an original musical set for the programme, for I

resurrected Michael Lewis' score for *The Barnardo Boys*, potentially, in its appeal, another *Oliver*, and capable, I felt, of finding a world-wide audience since the subject matter was universal rather than insular. Musicals are always expensive to make, and I had another battle on my hands which, ultimately, I did not win.

I did take one calculated risk, and that was with *Forbush and the Penguins* brought to me by an (to me) unknown American director and his partner. It had an intriguing script by Anthony Shaffer from the novel by Grahame Billing. Apart from a few scenes set in London, the bulk of the action took place in Antarctica and this presented some formidable logistical problems. John Hurt was cast in the leading role of a young naturalist who elects to leave the city flesh pots for Antarctica to study the penguin colony life cycle. Once there, isolated and alone in Shackleton's hut, he forgets his original mission and gradually becomes maniacally obsessed to save the helpless penguin chicks from the predatory skua gulls. His one-man war fails, as fail it must. Admittedly a far cry from *The Sound of Music*, but positively different and worth attempting.

Once the unit were safely there communication between them and the studio was out of the question. Equally the exposed footage could not be seen until they returned, for as I remember the supply ship only called once every three months. Despite these obstacles, I felt the subject matter justified the risk and I was full of admiration for John Hurt's courage in accepting the role. In addition to the main unit, I also engaged the noted cinematographer Arne Suksdorff to shoot the all-important wildlife sequences – there could be no faking, they had to be shot for real. I crossed my fingers, gave the unit my blessing, and they set sail. It was in many ways the most exciting of all the projects and I will later describe the sad and muddled denouement.

Looking back I have tried to determine why, having given me the job, the Board did not lend more support. Perhaps my comparative youth worked against me. I was forty-three when I took the post, while most of the other members of the Board were fifteen years my seniors, set in their ways and resented any attempt to change the old status quo. I did not share their interests, aims or humour. I was in effect isolated at Elstree and ill placed to counter the criticisms that went on behind my back. I do not offer this as the main reason for my inability to bring about the required changes, but it was a factor I neglected to counter. I later heard that it was felt I received too much publicity, but that struck me as strange since the film industry as a whole lives and dies by publicity. I did not actively court self-publicity, indeed the press attention was often an unwelcome intrusion into more urgent matters on my desk, but I was the spokesman they sought and I did my best to keep a balance. I had the sole responsibility for the studio and production, but lacked any real muscle in the other two vital areas of distribution and exhibition where a finished film is made or broken. That is where the real power always lies.

But no regrets. I would do it all again and I do not number my years at Elstree as wasted. They were years of high hopes, of excitement, often of fulfilment and, contrary to what various pundits said after the event, the programme proved a commercial success, returning according to the latest figures a profit in excess of £16,000,000 on a capital outlay of £4,000,000. Admittedly small beer indeed against the likes of *Rambo* and *E.T.* but nobody goes broke making a profit.

My successors were handed some £30,000,000 and managed to get through this within a very short time on only three films. They were of course applauded for their efforts and went on to greater glories. There is a moral hidden there, but my inherent good nature inhibits me from stating it.

ELEVEN

Every time I hear a political speech or read those of our leaders, I am horrified at having, for years, heard nothing human. It is always the same words telling the same lies. And the fact that men accept this, that the people's anger has not destroyed these hollow clowns, strikes me as proof that men attribute no importance to the way they are governed. – Albert Camus, Notebooks, 1937.

I copied the above passage into my own journal many years ago when my own disenchantment with our endless political polarisation had reached its zenith. Now as I write this, the Gulf war recently finished, it seems particularly apposite to think of Camus' words in relation to the regime in Iraq where, in the teeth of the appalling carnage wreaked on the Iraqi army, Baghdad radio is still proclaiming victory. Truly we are hearing nothing human.

Do we ever hear anything truly human or is every piece of information affecting our daily lives only couched in party-political jargon, often incomprehensible, saturated with meaningless and juggled statistics, invariably an abuse of straightforward English and economical with the truth? There is a depressing sameness about one evil being replaced by a greater evil and an even more depressing realisation that one half of the world feeds on hatred while the other half starves. Another French novelist and philosopher, Henry de Montherlant, put it succinctly when he wrote:

We are born under a layer of superstition and false ideas; we
grow up under it, go on living under it, and say to ourselves we
shall die under it, without ever for one single day of our lives
having lived otherwise than in subjection to the ideas of idiots
and the custom of savages which we cannot infringe or even
denounce without danger to ourselves.

I am not a political animal, and have never been a member of any
political party, but as a writer the behaviour of politicians holds a
fascination for me. The pursuit of power in whatever guise it
takes is always worthy of closer examination. Over the years
socially and professionally I have come into close contact with
many of our own politicians, including five Prime Ministers and
three Chancellors. While I admire their fortitude in enduring the
archaic, naughty schoolboy rituals enshrined in the day-to-day
business of the House, I am still at a loss to understand what,
apart from a naked desire for power, makes politicans take that
first step towards the hustings. I imagine there must be some who
enter the arena in order to devote themselves to the betterment of
mankind, but if so they swiftly conceal their concern for others
and concentrate on themselves.

Throughout my lifetime England has always been politically
polarised, each succeeding government hell bent on reversing
whatever legislation its predecessor has put on the statute books
regardless of its merits. We are seldom confronted with ideas,
only dogma. Consequently we have been shunted backwards and
forwards on the same length of track and real progress towards a
unified, classless society has been exceedingly slow. Denied a
proper revolution since Cromwell, the British content themselves with an endless wrestling match, the trainers and managers
snarling catchphrases at their opponents from opposite corners.
All the participants are at pains to tell the spectators that this is
the highest form of democratic debate. Nobody ever throws in
the towel and admits defeat and consequently the dreary spectacle is perpetuated, avidly reported by a whole army of corre-
spondents who know that the bout is fixed, but go along anyway.
Truth is the only real casualty.

My first contact with the body politic in a non-political sense was when I had a short, private meeting with Sir Winston Churchill. This came about when I was researching a commissioned screenplay based on his early life, a marathon undertaking which ultimately never saw the light of day for various murky reasons. Towards the end of my labours permission was granted for me to visit the great man one afternoon at his London home in Hyde Park Gate. He received me in a downstairs room seated in front of a fire and wearing a dark blue siren suit. Greeting me with the gravity he had usually accorded to more auspicious occasions, he wasted no time in offering me a drink.

'Pour me one while you're about it,' he commanded, gesturing towards a decanter. I poured a large tot for him and a smaller one for myself. We drank. He stared at me for a long time while I hesitated to open the conversation. During the months of research I had uncovered a number of hitherto unknown facts about his life and longed to discuss these with him but, face to face with the legend, no words came, I could recall none of my carefully prepared questions. I was stupefied with nerves and as a result drained my glass too quickly. Sir Winston motioned me to refill it.

'Mine too,' he said.

As I handed back his replenished glass he suddenly said, 'You must lead a very interesting life, Mr Forbes.' Conscious of the incongruity, the comparison between the vast canvas of his own life and my paltry experiences, I stumbled to find a suitably gracious reply. Looking back at the notes I made at the time, I am aware that apart from the thrill of meeting him I made little use of the time I spent in his presence. I remember that I attempted to draw him out on the subject of his father, for if ever a son strove to overcome the tragic failure of a father, this was a textbook example. His own son, Randolph, made the same effort but history did not repeat itself. 'I didn't know my father,' Sir Winston answered finally. 'Not at the time.' Afterwards repeating, 'Not at the time.'

I later wrote in my notebook, 'It was as if his mind was like a lighthouse: sometimes the beam came round and illuminated the past, then revolved again and all was blackness.' He seemed very tired, his eyes watery, and it took him a long time to raise the glass to his lips, though once it was there he dispatched its contents without hesitation. Fixing me with a stare he returned to his original and devastating opening remark, 'You have a very interesting life, Mr Forbes.' For the second time I could find no adequate rejoinder to it. I did manage to frame some questions about his early life, and he seemed more at home there; probes about more recent events drew no response. We sat and looked in the fire and the combination of the heat and whisky made me torpid.

Sitting there, I recalled a strange weekend I had spent with his son, Randolph, in his Essex home. Our first and only meeting began with insults and ended with drunken meanderings. He first expressed his resentment that I should be embarked on a film of his father, treating me like a poacher. Repeatedly he informed me that he had prior right to all biographical material and if I infringed his copyright he would not hesitate to take legal action. I had first been appalled and then fascinated by his invective. His voice, thickened by incessant smoking, often lapsed into a parody of his father's delivery and he reminded me of a ravaged Roman emperor. After a rich dinner his manner softened and at the conclusion of another more drunken, one-sided discourse he suddenly pulled himself out of his armchair, opened the French windows, pissed into the night, then led me outside and unlocked the specially built brick storage building resembling a street air raid shelter. This guarded Aladdin's cave proved to house his father's private papers. At that time he was embarked upon the definitive biography of his father, a mammoth task he never lived to complete and which was taken over and brilliantly completed by Martin Gilbert.

Much to my amazement, given his earlier behaviour, Randolph proceeded to show me a variety of documents never intended for public scrutiny. I was more than conscious that in the sober light of day he might well regret his impulsiveness. Suddenly he began to shake as though seized with a sudden ague. These violent contractions ceased as abruptly as they had begun and his manner changed once more; he became distant, as if I did not exist. He stared at me and then handed me the keys and asked me to lock up securely when I had finished and stepped out into the night to vanish from my life.

For a few solitary hours I had the place all to myself. I sensed that I had no right to be prying into the intimate treasure trove. Now as I walked between the rows of filing cabinets I felt the chill, not only of the January night, but of history itself. Perhaps wisely, or some might say foolishly, I did not abuse the opportunity. I opened a few of the cabinets, studied a variety of letters and official documents, many marked confidential, but made no attempt to record what I read.

I thought back to that strange encounter as I sat opposite Sir Winston that afternoon. I thought of what he had meant to me as a schoolboy, of how his broadcasts in the darkest days of the war had imbued me with the courage and resolve to join the Home Guard and patrol the Cornish cliffs absurdly armed with a useless rifle. To the schoolboy in the ill-fitting uniform he had been something akin to a god, somebody who inhabited another planet, for never in my wildest dreams could I have imagined that our lives would ever touch in later years.

He urged me to have a third glass together before an acolyte entered the room and silently indicated the audience was at an end. He signed the two-volume biography of his father and I took my farewell. Shortly afterwards he was dead. On the day of his State funeral I stood with Sarah, our eldest daughter, on the embankment at Virginia Water station as the train carrying his coffin passed on its way to Bladon, and I shall never forget the sight of all the cranes being lowered along the Thames as his body began its last journey.

That late February afternoon I walked unsteadily out of his room convinced that I would be arrested by the policeman on duty outside if I attempted to drive home. In desperation I asked a secretary if I could have a cup of tea and something to eat. She made me some slices of toast and I remained in her office until confident enough to face the world.

There was a curious aftermath. Since I had not been sworn to secrecy about my visit, I gave an interview, duly published, in which I recounted my drinking bout with the great man. I immediately received an irate letter written on Lady Churchill's behalf stating she took exception to my version of events and insisted that I retract them. It seemed odd to me that at the end of her husband's life she would seek to deny what he had never concealed, namely that he enjoyed a drink or two, but doubtless it was the same protective urge that made her have the Sutherland portrait destroyed. I apologised for unwittingly causing offence, but I did not retract; it was the truth and I was proud to have been drunk in such distinguished company.

Apart from being called to appear before various Commons Select Committees and give evidence on the state of the British film industry, I had little or no contact with our political masters until Edward Heath took over the leadership of the Tory Party in opposition. Watching him deliver a desultory political broadcast on television I was appalled at its ineptitude and with a certain temerity sat down and wrote to him. In my letter I said I had been a communicator for most of my professional life, that I felt he had many good ideas but that they were not coming across because of the antiquated technique he was subjected to. I never expected anything other than a polite thank you, but to my amazement he rang me early the next day and suggested we should meet and discuss what I felt was needed. At that time he was trailing far behind Harold Wilson in the opinion polls and most commentators predicted he would lose the next General Election.

I met him for the first time in his Albany chambers, elegantly furnished and with a grand piano as a centrepiece. I had been told that he was a difficult person to get close to, cold and withdrawn, but I cannot say I ever found him so. Over drinks followed by an excellent dinner he asked me to advise him where I thought the television presentations failed. Up until then both main parties invariably stuck their spokesman behind a desk and had them speak, glassy-eyed, straight into camera, reading off a prepared and usually cliché-saturated speech from the teleprompter. They were invariably lifeless and unconvincing.

'How could we change it?' Ted Heath asked.

'Why have a set formula at all? Why do the same old thing every time? Why not have a film crew follow you around the country talking off the cuff to people and then edit it down to length. Shoot in the streets, not in some mock-up of an office which adds to the unreality. And no prepared speeches, just say what you really feel.'

'Would that work?'

'Well, it couldn't be worse than the present system,' I said.

A week or so later he sent for me again and announced that he was prepared to try out my idea. He had to make a tour of the North of England shortly and felt this would be a good opportunity to test my theory. I said I would accept on condition that he and he alone decided on the edited material and that I be allowed a free hand to shoot as I felt fit. Beyond that, he would control the content and the final result. 'You lead, I'll record,' I said. 'It will be *cinéma vérité*.'

'What does that mean exactly?'

'The truth as you see it, as it happens, nothing prepared in advance. You say what you like and we photograph it.'

Although remaining dubious, he agreed to give my suggestion a trial. I selected a small unit of friendly technicians, including my senior cameraman, Tony Imi, who is brilliant at shooting over open sights with a hand-held camera, and we set off for Newcastle. It so happened that the day we arrived Newcastle were playing Benfica in that year's European Cup Final and I suggested that for the opening of the film we should have Ted seated amongst the fans. 'If it looks like *Match of the Day*, we might fool them into not switching off in the first few seconds,' was how I bluntly put it to him. Ted went along and after the match went to the dressing room to congratulate the winning Newcastle players with my camera close behind.

The next morning I stationed him outside the local Inland Revenue Office and as disgruntled taxpayers exited he tackled them as to how they felt about the punitive taxes they were paying under the Wilson administration. He got some very pungent replies. At lunchtime we followed him into a pub and recorded his conversations with the locals over a pint of beer.

Although he began rather stiffly, by the end of the first day he was more relaxed with us and able to forget there was a camera photographing his every move.

On the second day we accompanied him on a tour of the shipyards, though here we encountered some resistance from the management and at one point I was manhandled by a bowler-hatted official and told to bugger off. Later that same afternoon we were rained out and I accompanied Ted on a tour of the depressed areas of the city, many of which resembled a Gustave Doré etching. In those days the Leader of the Opposition did not rate a police escort. Seated together in the rear of a Ford Granada we looked out on the grim and rain-sodden scene. Ted was silent for a long time, then he said, 'If I lived here, I wouldn't vote for me, I wouldn't vote for Harold. There's only one person I'd vote for.'

'Who's that?' I asked.

'Robespierre.'

That evening there was a stag dinner in our hotel attended by luminaries of the local business community. Just as the coffee was being served, one of the captains of industry, heavily in his cups, leaned across the table and addressed Ted. 'You'll never make bloody Prime Minister,' he said.

The conversation around the table died away.

'You don't think so?' Ted answered affably enough.

'I bloody know so! I tell you what you ought to be thinking about, you ought to be thinking what old Enoch's saying if you want to get anywhere.'

This was shortly after Enoch Powell made his notorious 'rivers of blood' speech.

'Curiously enough,' Ted said, still speaking calmly, 'I've thought about it a great deal. But, I'll tell you something, it won't be black power that takes over your shipyards, it'll be the Japanese. So perhaps you should turn your mind in that direction if you want to stay in business.'

This silenced his boorish critic, but when the party broke up and we left to go to our rooms the same man, no doubt advised to make his peace, came up to Ted by the hotel elevator.

He stuck out a hand. 'Put it there, Heath, and let's bury the hatchet.' Ted shook his hand without much enthusiasm.

'Shall we share this lift?' the man said.

'I don't think so,' Ted replied. 'You see, we're going up and you're going down.'

It was a masterly squelch. I have often wished that he had shown this side of his personality more forcibly and more often and I remember many instances of his radical, mordant wit. For some reason, and increasingly so during his years in the political wilderness, he has publicly stifled his sense of humour in favour of an implacable dourness. I often saw his other face which presented an entirely different picture from the public image of a disgruntled, bitter man.

When shooting finished I took the train back to London with him. Again he was not given any VIP treatment and we occupied two seats in a crowded compartment. There had been an accident further down the main line and our train was halted for the best part of two hours. During the long wait we cracked a bottle of British Rail claret together and he relaxed, speaking tenderly of his mother and father and his upbringing as well as voicing his love of music and sailing. He also startled me by suddenly volunteering that if he lost the next election he would leave politics for good and choose a new career.

The finished film produced a favourable response from viewers when transmitted and I was asked to do others. There was nothing very special about my innovations, but they did have the effect of humanising what had previously been a sterile exercise in public relations. I suspect a few eyebrows were raised in the Tory Central Office especially when I went on to direct Tony Barber, then Chancellor of the Exchequer. He was not a natural performer in front of the cameras and the Treasury script he had been handed required him to mouth a mass of unintelligible statistics. From behind the camera I listened appalled and then, forgetting that I was not on one of my own film sets, heard myself say, 'Cut? It's no good, darling. Let's have a cup of tea and rethink it.' Everybody froze like a Bateman cartoon – The Man who called the Chancellor 'darling'. Tony Barber took it all in good part and to this day whenever we meet still chuckles about it. We had the cup of tea and once again I persuaded him to put what he wanted to say into colloquial language.

Right up until Ted Heath's unexpected victory I was entrusted with all of his television appearances, and in fact made a suggestion he included in his acceptance speech, although in the event he paraphrased the quotation I had given him. My quote had been 'There is only one way to govern men, and that is by serving them. The rule is without exception.' Ted's version was cut down to 'To govern is to serve' which to my ear lacked a certain ring.

The morning after election he included me in a small celebration gathering at Smith Square. There was a television in the room and while celebrating we watched the late returns coming in. I remember Ted looking soberly at the screen as the Revd Ian Paisley made a fiery acceptance speech.

'Northern Ireland will be my cross,' Ted said. 'If I can come anywhere near solving that it'll make everything else worthwhile.'

Immediately after he had moved into Number 10 he threw a party for everybody who had helped in the campaign and insisted that all my film crew members and their wives be included. It was a gesture typical of him, just as was the letter he found time to write to me on his first day as Prime Minister.

For the want of a nail, the shoe was lost, as the old adage begins, and in Ted's case misfortune struck his administration very swiftly. The untimely death of Iain Macleod who, with Angus Maude, had been primarily responsible for 'One Nation – A Tory Approach to Social Problems', one of the most sensitive and humane papers ever issued by the Conservative Party, was a severe blow, depriving Heath of a key member of his Cabinet and a formidable debater in the House, one that Wilson feared. Tony Barber later confided to me that at the very moment he learned of Macleod's death he was himself contemplating giving up. At the time he was in Brussels conducting the intricate negotiations for Britain's entry into the EEC and suffering from an attack of kidney stones. The pain was so excruciating that he felt unable to continue. It was at this moment that he was informed that Macleod had died and that he must return to London at once and take over the office of Chancellor of the Exchequer. The shock was such that he passed the stones. Thus, in the space of a few hours, Ted Heath might have been deprived of two invaluable colleagues. As it was he lost one of the prime architects of Tory policy and Tony Barber found himself forced to switch horses and take over one of the great offices of State for which, by his own admission, he was ill prepared.

After Ted became Prime Minister I did my best to keep the television experiment going. I still believe that, in their small way, the films my team produced during that period were the first to try and present a political philosophy in layman's terms instead of the usual heavy-handed, we-know-what's-best-for-you approach. I was not alone in observing that shortly afterwards the Labour Party began copying the technique.

In politics timing is everything, and John Donne's much quoted sermon that includes the famous 'no man is an island' passage had particular pertinence to England when the Middle East war and the oil crisis struck. Ted Heath's government was overtaken by events beyond its control. I believe history will show that the biggest mistake made by his administration during the fateful three-day week was to reinstate the normal hours for television when the hasty General Election was called in the teeth of the miners' ultimatum. Life by candlelight was readily accepted; it had a war-time feeling and brought out the best in people, I found – we British seem to thrive and come together in adversity. In spite of dire predictions, production did not fall, indeed in certain cases it increased. The curtailment of television seemed to be the main talking point and the biggest single factor that convinced the electorate something was sorely amiss. The dead screens in the living rooms meant that a basic dependence had been removed; once television reverted to normal scheduling the threatening siege atmosphere evaporated. Since the election was a close-run thing, I have always felt this might well have been the deciding factor. Even so, Ted gained the largest percentage of the popular vote, though he was unable to cobble together a coalition with the Liberals and the Queen sent for Wilson by default.

Although the majority of politicians cannot wait to be on the box, few of them have taken the trouble to understand the medium by which, in election times, many of them are made or broken. David Owen is an exception as is, in a quite different way, Tony Benn, who brings a maniacal intensity to his close-ups which serves to mask the poverty of his arguments. Ken Livingstone is a natural, but the majority would do themselves and mankind a favour if they kept the cameras at a distance. Harold Wilson fondly believed he put himself across as an honest, homespun character, but to my mind there was always something too calculated – he always seemed to me the actor playing the role of Prime Minister in a play by J.B. Priestley. Out of office and relieved from any responsibility, Harold Macmillan on the other hand ran rings around everybody else, conducting a love-affair with the camera with all the confidence and aplomb of a matinée idol.

I enjoyed the hours I spent in Ted Heath's company all those years ago and found him a fascinating companion. It is to be regretted that he chose to isolate himself from the mainstream of British politics, though I have often wondered whether a verdict Violet Cazelet-Keir once delivered to me contained the germ of truth. She said, 'Ted is a natural musician and an unnatural politician.' There have been many rumours but we shall have to wait for some future historian or a Freedom of Information Act to discover what post Margaret Thatcher offered him after her victorious bid for the leadership. Whatever it was, he obviously took it as an insult, and smouldered for her entire reign, finally to erupt on the subject of a united Europe. A loner by choice, a courageous man in so many areas, in the final analysis an enigma, Ted Heath nevertheless played a major role in revitalising the image of the Tory Party in the latter half of the twentieth century for he consistently saw the need for Britain to become part of a unified Europe which would finally lay to rest the curse of nationalism – the cause of two horrendous world wars.

When Margaret Thatcher grasped her nettle and succeeded to

the leadership I was once again asked to supervise her Party Political broadcasts. I had known her from the time when she was Minister of Education and asked me to serve as her representative on the BBC's Schools Broadcasting Council, an unwieldy body that pontificated at length and achieved very little to my mind. As with Ted Heath, in those early days she was not completely at ease in front of the cameras and I persuaded her to adopt the same technique we had used to good effect with her predecessor. She was quick to grasp the advantages of using the medium in this way and I made a point of pitting her against young people. By now we had slightly bigger budgets and were able to shoot the Party Politicals in colour, though everything was still done on a shoestring. Mrs Thatcher readily and enthusiastically co-operated and appeared more relaxed once she trusted me. However I soon became aware that the pundits at Tory Central Office resented the fact that she was prepared to act on my suggestions. There were some stunning small minds around at that time, and for all I know still are; they wanted to manipulate her and shape her image in a different, and to my mind, false way. I was just an outsider, I had no axe to grind, nor did I put words into her mouth. As with Ted Heath, I merely tried to portray her personality on film in a straightforward manner and nothing I shot for either of them was ever scripted. I survived for two or three films with her before falling foul of the advertising agency brought in to mastermind a Greening of Maggie campaign. The crunch came when, handed a pathetically inept script full of clichés and double-speak, I persuaded her to withdraw on the grounds that it would be a grave mistake for her to mouth such banalities as a substitute for her own sincerely held views. She listened and she agreed with me. My actions provoked consternation and outrage and sealed my fate. The dodgy baton was passed to Michael Heseltine who dutifully went before the cameras and spoke the puerile word, directed by somebody else. I was never forgiven, nor was I invited to play any further part. The agency and their political cohorts went in an entirely different direction, one which owed more to the marketing of pet food than the propagation of a political philosophy. The new concept was quickly aped by Labour, so that by the time the next General Election came around both parties were vying with each other to produce something that was a cross between *The Sound of Music* and a school lesson for the under-fives. They began to talk down to their audiences, to my mind insulting everybody's intelligence, for the electorate is not that stupid and can see through the artificiality of obvious propaganda. It is an exercise that both main parties have still to correct.

My own efforts were just an attempt to humanise one aspect of politics and for two brief periods I played a small part in helping to show Ted Heath, Margaret Thatcher and others talking not in the usual platitudes but in straight, unrehearsed, unscripted dialogue with average citizens. As a writer the episode provided me with valuable insights into the political mind. Politicians of all hues crave television exposure while at the same time harbouring a deep distrust of the medium and commentators. I find it curious that whenever our Prime Ministers and senior members of the Cabinet have to make an important statement they are compelled to step outside Number Ten and make their pitch on the pavement. This in stark contrast to the well-organised weekly press conferences with open question-and-answer sessions staged by the White House. Likewise we can manage to support a Royal yacht but not the equivalent of Air Force One. Curious, as Alice said.

I can't say that my brief skirmishes with Whitehall changed my basically cynical attitude towards politics or, to put it another way, altered my view of those amongst us who feel compelled to thrust their beliefs onto others. It was my one and only stroll through the corridors of power. I enjoyed it while it lasted, but I did not miss it once it ended.

I must add that, at the outset, I found Margaret Thatcher extremely feminine; she seemed totally different from the majority of Tory MPs in attitude and streets ahead in intelligence; the steel was always there, but not obviously so at the beginning. Whatever verdict history eventually delivers on her time in office, I don't think even her most vitriolic critics can deny that she changed the face of British politics, arriving in office at a time when the country seemed to be drifting towards a banana republic status. But like most revolutions, the one Margaret Thatcher brought about over-stretched itself, becoming increasingly divorced from reality. Perhaps it is inevitable that, under a system which allows the chief executive almost dictatorial powers until finally challenged, anybody who occupies the supreme office inevitably loses all contact with life as it is led by the majority of citizens. The work-load is horrendous, the glamour of dominating the international scene demands time that would be better spent solving the equally urgent problems that persist at home, and the inner cabinet of intimates, often not answerable to Parliament and ever-mindful of their livelihoods, perpetuate a dangerous sycophancy. It was ever thus and to my mind the isolation inherent in the job contributed in no small measure to Margaret Thatcher's predictable dismissal. Ordinary people do not live in the rarefied air of the Commons where everything is reduced to a Treasury statistic; ordinary people long for stability and have no wish to be made to stagger from crisis to crisis brought about by two warring factions who insist, despite the evidence, that their answers are consistently the right ones.

Even so, I found much of the vitriol Margaret Thatcher inspired, especially from our more trendy feminists, difficult to understand even on their own terms. I once had a violent altercation at a dinner party when the hostess described her as 'an evil woman'. I felt compelled to point out the misuse of the word, reminding my hostess that Hitler, Stalin and Idi Amin could justly have the word 'evil' applied to them, but whatever her opinion of Mrs Thatcher this was a bigoted misuse of the word. The fact is that Margaret Thatcher brought a reinvigorating strength and common sense to much of our national life during the early years of her reign, which for decades had been lacking in governments of both parties. All her achievements were eventually obscured by her latter-day mistakes, some of which had fearful consequences. Led by the increasingly bereft and unfunny *Spitting Image* she was invariably depicted as some crazed harridan. Now I am all for politicians being reminded that they only govern us by sufferance, and I am all for genuine satire and cartoons that remind our masters of their frailties, but in

Margaret Thatcher's case the venom was on an unprecedented scale that allowed of no mercy whatsoever, purporting to demonstrate that she had no redeeming qualities, which was patently untrue. She brought to politics a moment of promise, rare enough to be commended and all too easily forgotten.

The manner of her dismissal, shocking to many, greeted with glee by others, and completely incomprehensible to several of our allies, was a salutary example, just as the impeachment of Nixon was a salutary example, of Anglo-American democracy at work. For most of her term in office she was a giant amongst pygmies, and it is fascinating to reflect that both she and Ted Heath surfaced from working-class backgrounds and each in their own fashion put their stamp on the traditional Tory image. Whatever their personal animosity, they were personalities the country needed.

In due course we can confidently expect a spate of political memoirs to provide us with a blow-by-blow account of how the Great Age ended. In Regency days politicians often committed actual suicide rather than resort to the more cumbrous method of writing their memoirs.

Bringing it back to my own mundane level, I once experienced another, brief, personal insight into the world of minor politics. A number of my fellow technicians once asked me to stand for election as president of the film technicians' union, the ACTT. I did not engage in any electioneering and in fact I was in Hollywood when the voting took place. I remember I was woken up early one morning and told that I had won by a sizeable majority. Before I had time to celebrate I received a second phone call. This time a member of the Standing Orders Committee said that the election was to be rerun as the result of a complaint, upheld, that I had broken the rules. I asked what rules I had broken *in absentia*. Apparently my election statement had exceeded the statutory number of words. I enquired why there hadn't been a word count *before* the voting took place, thus giving me an opportunity to correct the heinous fault, but this was received by deaf ears. I did not stand for the second ballot.

I guess that is another reason why I am not a political animal and never will be.

TWELVE

The germ of a novel, rather like a summer cold, often appears out of nowhere. I doubt if any of us who earn our living by the pen really understand the creative process. I know I don't. I have long barren periods when my addled brain refuses to disgorge a single idea and then something clicks when I least expect it. Journalism and screenwriting have their disadvantages, but they teach one to write to a deadline, because the Muse, a difficult bitch at the best of times, does not descend to order; she has to be wooed, coerced, stroked.

The genesis of one of my novels, *The Rewrite Man*, is a case in point. I was in the South of France directing David Niven, Maggie Smith and Art Carney in a slight comedy originally called *Ménage à Trois*, and all my energies were concentrated on the film, thoughts of a new novel were not uppermost.

For many years, dating from the period when I lived in Albany, I enjoyed a friendship with Graham Greene. Until his death he made his home in a small and modest apartment in Antibes. After the film had been shooting a couple of weeks, I dropped a note into his letterbox on my way to the location, telling him that I would be at the Hyatt, Nice, for the next three months and would love to take him to dinner. That night when I returned to the hotel I had a message to ring him. I suppose it was around ten o'clock at night when I made the call. Graham answered and without further ado plunged into a bizarre and complicated account of what he was currently experiencing. He told me that he felt his life was in danger because of the stand he had taken about corruption on the Côte d'Azur. Much of what he related that night eventually appeared in his published pamphlet *J'accuse* but at the time I was in ignorance of the background. He told me that a girl had disappeared and had probably been murdered. I listened and made sympathetic noises from time to time, and was finally able to break into his disturbing account.

'Look,' I said, 'you're obviously having a rough time, why don't we have dinner and talk about it? How is Friday for you?'

Friday was okay.

'Well, if I'm on location I'll call for you at seven-thirty and if I'm at the studio, we can make it eight-thirty.'

Graham said: 'Are you anything to do with the Bryan Forbes film?'

Not unnaturally this took me by surprise. 'Graham,' I said, 'this is me, this is Bryan you're talking to.'

There was a long pause, then he said: 'Oh God, what have I told you?'

'Nothing that I can't forget. I don't know the people concerned, so don't worry about it.'

To this day I have no real clue as to who he thought he was talking to. Perhaps I woke him out of a deep sleep or perhaps he was expecting somebody else to call at that time. Graham's life was never far from mystery of one sort or another.

We did meet for dinner that Friday, and he turned up at Chez Felix, his usual watering hole in the old port of Antibes, carrying a plastic supermarket bag which he said contained a gun and a bottle of Mace. It was all vintage stuff from Greeneland. 'If they do succeed in killing me,' Graham said and, I am sure, enjoying the effect it had on me, 'you'll be the only one to know who did it.' It was not a confidence I wished to harbour. Since we ate in the open, every time a black Citroën cruised by I instinctively shifted my position. I thought, if they're out to kill him and their aim isn't too hot, I'm the one who'll get the bullet between the eyes. He elaborated on the drama while we had our meal, betraying no fear, merely stating the situation in a way that echoed the revolver in the corner cupboard of his childhood. Perhaps throughout his life he had always invited a violent death for himself, going to Mexico, Vietnam, the land of Papa Doc and other far-flung outposts in search of burnt-out cases, putting himself in the firing line.

At the end of the meal I walked with him to his apartment block in the Avenue Pasteur and said goodnight on the pavement, the plastic shopping bag swinging between us.

That night I wrote a brief account in my journal, but it wasn't until a week or so later that a way of using the incident as the basis for a novel occurred to me. I twisted it of course. My plot revolved around an unsuccessful screenwriter living in New England who returns home one night to find a message on his answering machine. It is from a film director in the South of France asking him to call back. He does so and, as with Graham's startling conversation with me, the director launches into a story of love unrequited – he is in the middle of a film and has fallen hopelessly in love with a young actress. A married man, he is desperate to keep his infatuation secret. The screenwriter listens politely and at the end says, 'Well, I'd like to be able to help, but it's a bit difficult when I'm four thousand miles away.'

This is the cue for the director to echo Graham's shocked cry. 'Who am I talking to?' he says. The outcome, to cut it short, is that to protect himself he offers the screenwriter a rewrite job on the script. When the screenwriter arrives in Nice he becomes the beard for the director. Or at least that is the idea. The twist in the novel is that the screenwriter falls for the young actress and has an affair with her that ends tragically.

These were the bare ingredients that came to me and I eventually wrote the novel.

The idea for *Familiar Strangers*, on the other hand, came about in quite a different way. Curiously it also began in the South of France. Leslie Bricusse had lent us his house in St Paul de Vence over the Easter period, but sadly the weather was hideous: gales, trees blown down – it was Scunthorpe in January rather than the famed Côte d'Azur. I mooched around the house for days, then discovered a portable typewriter. I sat down and suddenly thought of a cousin of mine who had died recently. He was the odd man out in the family, although I believe that only my sister,

Betty, and I knew his true character. He had been extremely good looking in his youth, had a brilliant career at Cambridge and went on to become the headmaster of a minor public school. My mother could never understand why he never married. 'He couldn't find a girl good enough for him,' she would say in all innocence. Betty and I would exchange knowing glances since we were well aware that, even if he couldn't find a girl, he found a lot of young men. I was always amazed, pre-Wolfenden, that he did not end up in jail. He made me the executor of his Will and when he died I realised that my first priority would be to get rid of incriminating evidence since I saw no point in destroying my dear mother's illusions.

What I found in his disordered house proved to be sadder than I had imagined for, even in his old age, he still subscribed to those gay magazines that specialise in soliciting partners interested in 'corrective treatment' and other spanking delights. My instincts were correct. I found collections of photographs, even eight-millimetre films, inexpertly shot, depicting my cousin in lederhosen being beaten by other elderly gentlemen dressed in SS uniforms. They made sad viewing. There was also a large amount of Fascist literature; apparently at one stage in his life he had joined Mosley's Blackshirts. I burnt all of it and apart from Betty nobody in the family was any the wiser. A total eccentric, he had never thrown away a newspaper or magazine for thirty years and had even saved train and bus tickets, together with boxes of used postage stamps, cigarette cards, old coins and the like, all piled around his bed in such profusion that the mind balked. He lived frugally with his cats, but died a rich man and left a small fortune. Unfortunately his eccentricity extended to never signing his Will, and consequently, although he left it all to my mother, she died before receiving a penny, and the spoils were eventually divided amongst a legion of relatives as the law demands. This caused acrimonious rifts, for in the process of proving their entitlement I stumbled across two bigamous marriages.

My first idea when I sat down at the typewriter in Leslie's house that Easter was to use my cousin's life as the basis for a novel about a brilliant man who never fulfilled his early promise.

At that point I had no inkling that by the end of the first chapter my story would veer off in a totally different direction and that I would end up writing an interior thriller that encompassed Burgess, Maclean and Philby and my conception of the still-concealed Fourth Man, using a fictional version of my cousin as the catalyst.

Once that idea entered my mind the rest of the novel fell into place. I should add that I am not one of those writers who maps out everything in advance; that is not my method. I think most writers will agree that, beyond a certain point, our characters start to dictate what should happen and, once I surmount the first hurdles, I have relied on a continuous and often subconscious process that pushes the novel on.

I always had the feeling that the Fourth Man would prove to be artistic, don't ask me why, it was merely a gut instinct. I made my Fourth Man a novelist and, before anybody jumps to conclusions, he was not modelled on Graham Greene. The novel was published in advance of Anthony Blunt's exposure and when that gentleman was eventually unmasked there was a great deal of conjecture as to where I obtained my privileged information. Several commentators suggested that I must have had an inside track, but it simply wasn't true. I had never heard of Blunt until he was named, but my instincts were sound. Even if I had known of Blunt's duplicity in advance, it would have taken a braver novelist than me to portray a spy working inside Windsor Castle, knighted, in a position of influence and enjoying the patronage of the Monarch. That would have been laughed out of court – literally.

When *Familiar Strangers* came to be published by Doubleday in America, they too decided to change the title. They called it *Stranger* and gave me a dust jacket which would have served as a poster for a Humphrey Bogart film during the Thirties. Once informed of their decision I cabled, 'Stranger than what?' and back came the reply, 'One word titles are in this year.' They weren't and sales on that side of the Atlantic were disappointing.

But if my moments of inspiration only occur at lengthy intervals, Nanette has a new idea roughly every twenty-four hours. Starting much later than me, she has so far produced thirty-seven books, many of them translated into other languages, and all of them successful, an achievement she constantly shrugs off. Her career as an author began casually with a collection of children's sayings entitled *God Bless Love* which went on to sell a million copies and the entire royalties from which she donated to her favourite children's charity. Eventually she published another five similar collections before writing some highly original stories for children and five cookbooks. Very often when she accompanies me on a film location I will say goodbye to her in the morning only to be greeted when I return at the end of the day with, 'I had an idea today, see what you think.' Whereupon she reads me a complete book and when I express suitable amazement, her inevitable rejoinder is, 'Oh, well it's not like your proper writing, it's not a very long book.'

Our elder daughter, Sarah, wrote poetry from an early age. We had always encouraged her, and when she was seventeen an enterprising publisher (not my own I hasten to add before another accusation of nepotism is hurled at me) brought out a small collection under the title *I Thought We Were Friends*. Written during the transition years, there is a distant echo of innocence about them, coupled with a mounting awareness of the world she had grown up into. I have always been affected with this one.

> What does she think
> as she lays down her head?
> (*She* placed the bomb
> and twenty are dead.)
>
> What does she say
> as she watches TV?
> Does she pray to her God
> saying 'Be proud of me?'
>
> What does she do
> when she sees crying eyes?
> Does she wear her dark glasses
> to cover her lies?

What does she think
when she lays down her head?
(*She* placed the bomb
and twenty are dead.)

When bad news is good
and like Christ you feel
Do your facts and your motives
become now unreal?

Where does she turn
when she's just killed a child?
Does she sing, does she dance,
are the parties quite wild?

How does she sleep
and live with her fame?
Is her happiness deep
or is she insane?

What does she think
when she lays down her head?
(*She* placed the bomb
and twenty are dead.)

I thought it was a stunning debut and it remains a source of pride to me. Later she turned to journalism before becoming the mother of three and hanging up her pen. It is still my hope that one of these days she will resurrect the sleeping talent I know she possesses.

Not to be outdone, Emma, her younger sister, was determined to get into the family act and when my *Notes for a Life* appeared Emma suddenly produced her own variation, with the inspired title *Spiders for a Life*, complete with illustrations, the price pencilled on the cover and a dedication. Having made her point she has rested on her laurels ever since, though when an accident put paid to a promising career in the ballet, she stifled her disappointment and, again with no assistance from me, forged a career of her own, at one time editing a small trade magazine before finding her niche in television. Neither she nor Sarah has ever thought the world or their parents owed them a living and, although they have always known that Nanette and I are here to pick up the pieces when things go wrong, they have never traded on our careers. Totally different in character, they have always been able to twist me round their fingers and to me they are quite stunning. Their beauty stems from Nanette, but perhaps I contributed their outrageous sense of humour.

It might seem unfeeling of me to confess that the jumping off point for my thriller *The Endless Game* was the death of my mother, but such is the truth. Like her mother before her and my father's mother, she lived beyond ninety and for most of her days enjoyed rude health. (I frequently observed that women of my mother's generation and background often said, 'I don't have time to be ill.') Alas, towards the end, Alzheimer's disease struck her down with all its distressing consequences. In the final months of her life she recognised nobody and was virtually a vegetable. The last images of her in the nursing home where she died are burnt into my mind. When I visited her she would raise her eyes to meet mine and a slow flicker of recognition, like a delayed shutter on a camera, passed across her face. All I could see was a great weariness as though she wanted to be done with it all – the tiredness, the unfamiliarity, even the kindness, perhaps most of all the kindness which then had no face, for between our visits she was administered to by dedicated strangers. I used to wonder if she had ever known real happiness. Perhaps she had always worked too hard, this Lincolnshire farmer's daughter, the last survivor of a family of seventeen. She was never young to me, for she bore me in her forty-first year, the year of the General Strike, but always on the go, first up in the morning, laying the fires, working, washing, cleaning for dear life – so house proud, blacking the grate, my father's shirts ironed to perfection, as though if these tasks were not done every day her world would come to an end. She brought up my sister and me on three pounds a week household money, with none over for herself. I remember that when I was a small boy and expressed a longing for a clockwork Hornby train, she went out charring to earn enough to buy it for me. It did not seem unnatural then, but now the memory of my mother scrubbing floors on my account haunts me. Even after my own fortunes increased and I was able to buy my parents a bungalow in the country, she still could not relinquish the habits of a lifetime. Her squirrel energy was unabated, the house had to be kept spotless, for dirt was a crime. I employed a daily help for her, but that made no difference. 'They don't clean properly.' she said, and gave everything a second going over.

Now as I watched her life slip away, I felt endless regret for things unsaid. She shared the room with two other women, both in the advanced stages of senility and never, as far as I could judge, even visited by friends or family. 'They're dumped here,' the Matron told me, 'out of sight, out of mind, most of them. Don't talk to me about relatives.' One old woman sat in the window, smiling, dusty sunlight haloing her wispy hair, and occasionally she would ask me whether she was going on holiday. The other lady lay curled up in the foetal position, her stomach bloated as though in the ninth month of a pregnancy; she always mistook me for the doctor which was most disturbing. There was no contact between the three of them, they each existed in their own twilight worlds, my mother restrained by straps in her armchair, for towards the end she would try and remove all her clothes. She was in no physical pain, but God knows what went through her mind as she waited for a merciful death to creep up on her. I don't think she recognised me, though occasionally there would be a spark of memory, a mumbled reference to faraway, halcyon days in Lincolnshire.

She died in her ninety-third year and seemed to go with a sigh as I pressed my lips against her cheek. My father was unable to make any coherent comment except to tell the Nursing Sister that during the course of his ambulance duties he had seen many others die. Later, at her funeral, he asked me the saddest question: what ought he to write on the card accompanying his wreath. Put 'with all my love', I said.

I came home to Seven Pines and wrote a poem, though I am not a poet, but the thoughts I held demanded to be set down.

Rodent-like she sleeps
With open eyes
And gaping mouth
Hearing nothing
Not even the echo of our
Whispered love

Too late
And yet not late enough
For Life clings tight.
Life
That thief
That comes and goes by stealth
Stealing
From we who stay and watch
Waiting
To be relieved
Of her last pain.

Those last images surfaced again when I sat down to write *The Endless Game*. I used the memory of my mother's final days as the jumping-off point for the story, for she became in my imagination a British agent who had been returned from Russia. Tortured by the KGB she was now little more than a vegetable, abandoned and secreted away in a private nursing home because she is an embarrassment to the authorities. There she is visited by a hired killer and murdered. When eventually I made a film of the novel I recreated that room and the other two inhabitants. Why did I do it? Was it to try and expurgate a certain agony of remembrance, or is it that writers use all the material of their lives in some form or another?

I used other echoes of my parents in my film *The Whisperers*. There I tried to paint a portrait of two people, played by Dame Edith Evans and Eric Portman, who could not communicate with each other. I believe that was the tragedy of my parents' lives during the last two decades of their sixty-year-old marriage when they seemed to withdraw into separate shells. 'People have to talk, have a conversation,' I made Eric Portman say, for there is a special poignancy about two people sharing the same house and bed, yet having no common interests. I witnessed such a slow deterioration between my parents and was powerless to do anything about it.

Do any of us ever know our parents? And do they know us? From the moment that I announced, aged sixteen, that I was not going to pursue a career in accountancy, as they had fondly imagined, but instead intended to become an actor, a decision that, bless them, they never argued against, I doubt whether either of them ever comprehended my world. Although over the years I believe I gave them cause for pride, my experiences were beyond their ken. When I was writing a book, for instance, my father would take Nanette aside and ask: 'When's Bryan going to get a proper job?' It was a question asked with genuine concern. The idea of somebody being self-employed all his working life, dependent upon the chance offer of an acting or directing job was a frightening, unknown country to him. I don't believe my father ever read one of my books, or if he did he made no comment about them to me. In fact I cannot recall ever seeing him read a single book although I took him many. He would study the newspaper with intense concentration, and held passionate, often violent and always distorted, views on the twists and turns of the country's political fortunes. On certain topics he was apt to make Alf Garnett sound like a liberal, though at heart he was a kindly, generous man, always willing to put himself out for others. For the best part of his active life he devoted himself to the St John Ambulance Brigade, rising to become Superintendent of the 88th West Ham Division. He was twice commended for bravery during the London Blitz when he commanded a flying squad of ambulances. I remember him coming home begrimed and weary when the All Clear sounded, eating his breakfast in silence and then, once shaved, going off to do his normal daily slog. He never boasted about this aspect of his life and I only heard of his bravery by chance and long after the event. Even when he had retired he still put on his uniform and took groups of disabled children on outings. During the Heath government I tried to obtain an MBE for him, in recognition of his devotion to that worthy, voluntary organisation. I knew that if I succeeded it would have put the seal on his whole life, but sadly my request was dismissed out of hand.

Once, when he was a widower, I paid him a visit to find him crying. He had read a report about a worker who, claiming wrongful dismissal although found asleep on the job, had gone to the Industrial Tribunal and been awarded £7000 compensation. 'I had to work ten years for that amount of money,' he said. In many ways the world had passed him by. He cared passionately for the old values he had once known, but at heart he was a frustrated and lonely man. He left school at age eleven, sent out to work first as an assistant in a drapery store in the East End of London, then as a tram conductor before finding reserved occupation in World War I. 'If I had had a proper education,' he would say, 'I could have made something of myself. It's held me back, you see.' I think, against all the odds, he did make something of himself, but what held him back was an inability to articulate his innermost thoughts and hopes. He had a quick and agile mind which had never been stretched; his approach to life remained somewhere in the Thirties – the Depression and the need to survive scarred him forever. To be in debt was a crime and he portioned out his meagre salary every week into a black cash box: a half a crown for the Insurance, five shillings for the annual holiday, so much for his cigarettes and baccy, so much for the housekeeping. As the result of a small legacy which came his way late in life, he left a few thousand divided amongst all the grandchildren. I many times urged him to spend it on himself, but he felt compelled to leave something he would be remembered by and this stemmed from what I know was his longing to feel important. Important people did not die penniless. That same urge drove him to buttonhole any new audience and regale them with lurid tales of his past exploits. The family had heard them many times, and with each retelling they became more and more embellished.

There was another side to him which caused us all endless secret amusement. He would come out with the most extraordinary statements. I remember he once had a goldfish and when I paid my weekly Sunday visit I found it floating, dead as a doornail.

'What's happened to your fish, Pop?,' I said.

'She's not too frisky this morning,' he observed (all animals were female to him). He stared at the floating corpse for a long time before pronouncing: 'Though I did read somewhere you can revive them if you put cotton wool in their ears.' David Attenborough could build a whole series from that single remark.

When I went to Hollywood for the best part of a year to make *King Rat*, I returned home to find that he had chopped down all the trees at the bottom of his garden, thus revealing a particularly ugly view of his neighbour's house.

'Why did you get rid of the trees?' I asked.

My father sucked in his breath. 'I had to get the air to my rhubarb,' he said, for another of his mistakes was to believe he was an inspired gardener, a cause of much annoyance to my mother who did have a country girl's green fingers.

'It's a pity,' I said, 'because now you haven't any privacy. You can see everything next door are doing.'

'Yes, yes,' with another prolonged intake of breath. He looked towards the mock Tudor edifice. 'I haven't quite got their measure yet. They're either Canadians or Turks.' I never did work out that one, since it conjured up a mental picture of a lumberjack in a fez.

On another occasion when they were both in their seventies I arranged a holiday for them in a quiet, luxury hotel in Cornwall, recommended by Lionel and Eileen Jeffries. I became aware they were strangely unenthusiastic about the prospect, so I enquired if they were looking forward to the trip.

'Seems a bit dull from the brochure,' my father said.

'Not much going on, dear,' my mother chimed in. 'We like a bit of excitement.'

'Well, would you like to go somewhere else? No problem, you choose.'

'We rather thought Butlin's would be nice.'

'Fine. Butlin's it is, I'll cancel the other.'

It so happened that they went during one of the hottest two weeks in recorded memory, yet returned home white as sheets.

137

'Didn't you get good weather?' I asked.

'Oh, yes, very good, but we didn't have time to get outside much,' my father said.

'I did lie down on the bed two or three times with the window open,' my mother volunteered, 'but of course Pop was too busy most of the time.'

'Busy?'

My father assumed a Stanley Baldwin pose. 'Matter of fact,' he said with unconcealed pride, 'they made me Chairman of the Complaints Committee. They gave me a badge which I had to wear at all times. We had to meet every morning at eleven. Course, we were given free coffee and biscuits, that went with the post.'

'What sort of complaints did you have to deal with?'

'Give you an example: The Talented Children Under Eleven Contest.' I stared in total incomprehension. 'The girl who won it turned out to be *thirteen*!' he explained with vehemence. 'She cheated. We had to hold an enquiry and send a report to head office.'

Then he embarked on a lengthy story which epitomised why there will always be a class war in England. When in order to divert him from the saga of bogus eleven-year-old talented children I asked if the food had been satisfactory, he gritted his teeth. 'Very fair, very fair. Except' – there was a long pause for effect – 'we had a duff waitress. I canvassed all the other tables, and we were the only one who had to *ask* for seconds. And I'll tell you something else, Bryan' – and now, my mother having left the room to make a pot of tea, he assumed a conspiratorial whisper – 'I don't want to say this in front of Kit, but I saw this same waitress *having a drink in the bar with some of the male guests*.' He chopped one hand into the other for extra emphasis. 'Bryan, *the two classes don't mix!*'

My mother, I later discovered, had taken cleaning materials with her and had religiously tidied their room and made the bed every day. 'I didn't want the maid to come in and find the place a mess. She thought the world of me.' I was reminded of this years later when David Hockney told me that when he first brought his mother to California she made the observation: 'All this sunshine and no washing out.' I guess there will always be an England.

Another year I gave my father a first-class ticket for a cruise on the *Queen Elizabeth*. My mother wouldn't accompany him because she was terrified of making a journey abroad. He returned blissfully unaware of the countries he had visited, but having enjoyed a seaboard romance with an American widow who subsequently wrote and invited him to New York. I doubt whether it was a consummated romance, though one never knows. He laid siege to my mother during World War I. From snapshots taken at that time I can see that he was an extremely handsome man with an engaging smile and a touch of Jack the Lad about him, cocky and self assured. My mother had a delicate, period beauty and no shortage of suitors from all accounts. Although his prospects were virtually non-existent when first they met, my father apparently pursued her with quiet confidence. My mother was a chief welder at Sopwith's and earning good money, whereas my father had some menial job that paid little. In later years, with I hope unconscious cruelty, she would often remark, 'I didn't want him, but you see my real sweetheart was killed in the war.' If the barb ever went home, my father never betrayed the fact.

Towards the end of his life I took him for a holiday in the South of France. It was the first time he had flown since World War I when he had made several flights in the legendary Sopwith Camel as a passenger. The drama started as soon as we arrived at Heathrow. The moment my father stepped through the electronic security arch, alarm bells sounded. He was searched and two pairs of scissors and a Swiss Army knife were discovered on his person. 'These are offensive weapons,' the security guard told him. My father cheerfully agreed: 'Of course. You could stab somebody with those.' He then explained he always carried them in case he was called upon to perform an emergency. This stemmed from his long association with the St John Ambulance, but the rationale failed to impress the authorities and the offending articles were confiscated.

As a small child I regarded him as somebody akin to a brain surgeon and I well remember an amazing incident which took place at Upton Park, the home of West Ham Football Club. My father regularly attended the matches there together with other members of his ambulance brigade to render first aid. In those happier times there was little violence and the spectators were not hemmed in with wire fences. If anybody fainted they were passed over the heads of the crowd and laid on the grass touchline where my father's team revived them. On this particular occasion a truly enormous woman collapsed and by the time my father arrived on the scene she had turned an alarming shade of purple. My father was equal to the occasion and immediately issued his first instruction: 'Search for foreign bodies in the throat!' I had no idea what this meant – 'foreign body' had a sinister, cannibalistic connotation: did it mean his assistant would extract a fragment of a German soldier? To my disappointment all that came to light was a full set of dentures. Whereupon my father acted decisively. 'Scissors!' he commanded, and was handed a pair. Vastly impressed, I imagined he was about to perform emergency surgery. With great aplomb he proceeded to slit open the lady's dress and pink corset. She came apart like a sack of potatoes, revealing large expanses of flaccid white flesh. This was dramatic enough, and in fact medically correct, for the sudden release of pressure brought the lady back to life. But far from thanking him, when she had taken in what had happened, she turned on my father, shouting abuse. Clutching her shredded garments she then proceeded to chase him around the perimeter of the pitch much to the delight of the crowd. In after years my father often recounted this story with sorrow. 'The public are never grateful,' he would say, 'I saved that woman's life.'

Thus, on our journey to Nice, I was not surprised he had been relieved of his surgical instruments. During the flight I made the mistake of telling the friendly Air France steward that my father had not flown since 1918. The steward mistakenly took this to mean that Pop had been a World War I ace and he was invited into the cockpit and remained there until we landed. He emerged well pleased with himself. 'I haven't lost my knack of flying,' he said.

During the week I took him to a small restaurant which Maggie Smith and I had frequented during the making of *Ménage à Trois*. It was run by a family and served the most delicious fresh fish. The wife of the owner, a buxom lady, waited on the dozen or so tables. My father regarded her with a discerning eye. 'Translate for me,' he said suddenly.

'What d'you want to say, Pop?'

'Tell her she reminds me of the postmistress in Sunninghill, and that she's got wonderful tits.'

Why not, I thought? I duly passed on these two pieces of information and the lady took it as a compliment, flung her arms around my father and gave him what can only be accurately described as a real French kiss. For the remainder of the holiday we ate there every night and the service was superb. The episode confirmed my suspicion that in his dandelion days my father had been a smooth operator.

Both sides of the family were long-lived. My father's mother lived to be ninety-eight, and my maternal grandmother also passed the ninety mark. Pop's mother, a wispy little woman who to a child's eyes seemed to exist on small pieces of bread dipped into weak tea – 'sops' as they were called – was bombed out during the Blitz and spent her remaining years with us. I remember that I bought my parents their first black and white television set. At Christmas my father religiously observed all the rituals and placed particular importance on the Queen's speech. He would bring out the Wincarnis and pour everybody a glass in preparation for the loyal toast at the conclusion of the speech.

On this particular Christmas, Granny Clarke was carried into the living room and seated a few inches from the television set. By then she was virtually stone deaf and had cataracts on both eyes. I doubt whether she even comprehended the miracle of steam radio let alone television, but Christmas was Christmas and my father was adamant that she be included. We solemnly watched the Queen make her speech and then raised our glasses as the anthem was played.

I turned to my grandmother.

'Could you hear it all right, Granny?' I shouted.

She nodded.

'Did you enjoy it?'

'Always like Gracie Fields,' she said.

When, as a child, my father took me up to London we invariably had tea and a sticky bun in one of Messrs Lyons' famed Corner Houses where we would be served by Nippies, as the waitresses were called – erotic creatures to my young mind, with shiny black blouses that accentuated their breasts. My father, I remember, seemed to be on intimate terms with all of them and there would be innuendo exchanges that I could not decipher at that time. He once impressed me by taking his umbrella and smashing a chipped teacup. 'The public are fully entitled to take the law into their own hands,' he told me. 'You can catch dangerous diseases from a cracked cup, diseases which would prevent you ever getting married to a decent woman.' I imagined he would be immediately arrested, but much to my amazement nobody turned a hair. He was promptly served a fresh cup of tea and rose in my estimation. I was grateful he had saved my future married life.

THIRTEEN

It was a perfect summer's day in July, the eve of my forty-ninth birthday, when the specialist delivered the verdict that I had Multiple Sclerosis.

The first disturbing symptoms had occurred a month or so previously while I was shooting the snow sequences for *The Slipper and the Rose* high in the Austrian Alps near Anif. I became aware that something was odd when, returning to the hotel after work, I stepped into a hot bath which mysteriously felt ice cold. Conversely when my bare flesh touched the rim of the porcelain washbasin I felt a searing burn. It was as if wires had been crossed and I was receiving contra-reactions. A day or so later I developed agonising sensations in my right leg as though a fire was raging within. My eyes were also affected and I began to lose my balance.

Every film director is compelled to take a rigorous medical examination before shooting commences, and it is a contractual requirement that the insurance company must be immediately notified of any subsequent conditions that might jeopardise the progress of the film. I forced myself to believe it was just a temporary aberration brought on by an intensive work schedule in bitter weather and bent the rules by first consulting my own doctor on my return home. He sent me to a neurologist who proved to be a somewhat dingy individual with a marked lack of any bedside manner. After he had prodded and stuck needles into me he said gloomily, 'Well, one can't rule out cancer of the spine, or even the possibility of a brain tumour. You'll have to have some extensive tests and go on the scanner.'

After this horrifying prognosis, my condition deteriorated. I began actually to fall down, my eyesight weakened and I was compelled to notify the film insurance company, although I did not stop working. They demanded I had further tests so every day before going to the studio I was seen by at least six specialists at various hospitals, none of whom came up with any conclusive diagnosis. Finally they pooled all their findings and one of them was delegated to come to my home and pronounce sentence. There had been no further change in my condition; apart from pains in my right leg I felt reasonably well and convinced myself I had picked up some rare bug which the medicos would eventually isolate and treat with modern drugs.

It was a Sunday evening in July when the light has special qualities that the spokesman came to Seven Pines. Nanette was out when he arrived and he made a special point of saying he would wait for her return before telling me the decision reached. I took this to mean good news. When Nanette eventually came back he asked us both to sit together and then began to read a typed statement, rather like the governor of a prison telling a condemned man that all appeals had been exhausted and the execution would now go forward. My first reaction was anger, not so much at the verdict but the manner in which it had been broken to me in front of Nanette.

'So what is the treatment?' I managed to say. At that point I was totally ignorant about the disease.

'The first thing is you must give up work, it's important that you don't have any stress.'

'If I give up work you won't be paid,' I heard myself saying, 'so I wouldn't suggest that. What else can be done?'

'The standard treatment is cortisone,' he replied.

Again I heard myself saying, 'I'm not taking that, I'm told it has disastrous side-effects. What's the alternative?'

'At the moment, very little, although research is going on all the time.'

The rest of the conversation remains hazy, but I know that I dismissed him shortly afterwards and never consulted him again. Apparently when showing him out Nanette asked how long I had to live and he gave a bleak answer. Throughout the next two years Nanette's anguish was far worse than mine because from the moment I was told I became bloody minded and refused to believe the worst.

The following morning I was scheduled to shoot one of the large musical numbers in the presence of Her Majesty Queen Elizabeth The Queen Mother, Princess Margaret and her two children, all of whom were paying a rare visit to the studio. I got through that day somehow and the curious thing is that while I was on the set and concentrating on the direction of the film, all the symptoms disappeared. It was only at the end of the day that they returned. This further strengthened my resolve to rely on mind over matter, a potent force for good.

The only person I told was my producer, Stuart Lyons, and he agreed to keep the confidence. I promised him, with God knows what justification, that I would finish the film come what may and he agreed to share the risk. I had no idea what came next or how long I could continue to function but trusted to luck and will power.

Nanette refused to trust to luck and although greatly distressed she set to work to find the answer. Everything that followed I owe entirely to her. I have to be careful how I set down the rest of the story because I am told that there could still be an element of risk to the main character involved. Equally it would be dangerous for me to pretend a medical knowledge I do not possess and which might give false hope to others. I can only report my own case and the treatment I administered to myself and which has given me some fifteen years' remission (if that is the correct term) for which I am profoundly grateful. I will resist describing a miracle panacea and merely record the facts as they were presented to me and which I acted upon. There are many cures being hawked around for every imaginable condition since alternative medicine captured the public's attention and we are all entitled to a personal choice where our own health is concerned.

It happened like this: Nanette remembered what I had forgotten, namely that an old friend of ours, Roger McDougal, a successful playwright (*To Dorothy a Son*) and at one time a Professor of Logic at, I believe, UCLA had also been struck down by MS. His situation had been far worse than mine and eventually he went blind and was confined to a wheelchair. His friends used to go and read to him. Although blind and immobilised, his brain was still as active as ever and he applied logic to his plight, approaching it methodically step by step.

First he took the mystery out of the name of the disease. Multiple = many. Sclerosis = hardening. As he understood it the disease caused the sheaf protecting the nerves to be destroyed, leaving them bare like electric wires. Next he argued that if he cut his finger the body's restorative powers grew new tissue over the wound. Therefore, why wasn't the body able to repair the damaged nerves? What attacked them in the first place? He continued researching and discovered that MS was virtually unknown in countries where the staple diet was rice and maize. He then caused further research to be undertaken and found that there was an absence of gluten in rice and maize, whereas it was present in wheat, barley, oats and rye. He put himself on a gluten-free diet for a period of several years and slowly his eyesight and general condition began to improve, but the progress was too slow for his liking. Although he had satisfied himself that the gluten element in wheat, barley, oats and rye was a contributory factor, by cutting them out entirely he had also deprived himself of valuable trace minerals. So he formed a company and began to produce a highly potent vitamin supplement which he took with concentrated B12. Again, this produced positive results in his case. Anxious to share his good fortune he wrote several papers for scientific journals and immediately ran into conflict with the medical establishments on both sides of the Atlantic. His findings were derided and dismissed; he was threatened with prosecution if he continued with his claims. Nevertheless he persisted, going underground as it were, and distributing a pamphlet which described his own experience to anybody who asked for it. Staying within the law, he was careful never to solicit fellow sufferers, but equally never refused to share his experience with anybody who found their way to him for advice. What had started out as a personal mission became an obsession and he was determined not to be silenced. From that moment onwards he devoted his entire life in an effort to convince the sceptical that what had happened to him through his own unaided efforts was at the very least worthy of closer examination.

This, then, is the background to my own story.

Nanette tracked down Roger the day after the fateful pronouncement. At first she pretended she was ringing on behalf of a friend. Roger quickly saw through her subterfuge. 'Are you really talking about Bryan?' he asked. She broke down and confessed the truth. Roger immediately calmed her by saying, 'Well, dry your tears because your troubles are over. He's going to get better, no question about it. Throw all the medicines down the toilet and stop distressing yourself, otherwise we'll have you ill. Bryan's ill, but he's not going to die.'

The very next day he came to have lunch with us at Pinewood. I met a man nearing seventy, bent but still sprightly, no longer blind and able to drive his car and, as he put it, 'run up the stairs'. He inspired immediate confidence and stated his case with measured emphasis, never exaggerating his claim, never promising an overnight miracle cure, but telling us how he had fought and overcome his own troubles and the troubles that came after. I am not somebody who scorns the enormous advances made in surgery and orthodox medicine, but even before meeting Roger I had always felt that there had to be other routes worth considering. If people want to go to faith healers, or take herbal cures, visit holy shrines, then good luck to them and they should not be mocked. I am not religious, nor did I turn to religion at this crossroads in my life. I listened to a man who spoke from bitter experience and decided that in the absence of any real aid from conventional sources, I could lose nothing by giving his regime a trial. He was not telling me to take any drugs, he was not selling me any magic potion and he wanted nothing in return. All that concerned and sustained him was a burning belief in his own life

147

story. He was so quietly reassuring that I did not hesitate to test the diet he outlined. He provided Nanette with a book he had written and a diet sheet. I went back on the set after lunch with renewed hope.

For the next three years I stuck to his gluten-free diet supplemented by vitamins together with daily doses of oil of evening primrose which I continue to this day. I was also compelled to forgo my favourite tipple, whisky, but was allowed a modest amount of wine, indeed any spirit that came from the grape. Nanette proved brilliant at finding palatable alternatives to my favourite foods and closely scrutinising every tin and packet for the forbidden ingredient before buying them. I can't say that my taste buds suffered one iota thanks to her dedication. It was as a result of her endless experiments that she came to write her first cookbook – *The Fun Food Factory* – designed primarily for children, which showed them that there is life beyond junk food. It proved an enormous success and led to her having her own programme of the same name on London Weekend Television and was followed up by a second book, *Fun Food Feasts*. So there was a pleasant aftermath to our initial troubles, and no more than she deserved. Throughout the first months of trial I continued to direct *The Slipper and the Rose*, often working a fourteen-hour day and travelling long distances to the various locations. The film went on to be chosen as the Royal Command Film the following year. I found I had much more energy on the diet and can honestly report that I suffered no extra ill-effect. Gradually my symptoms became less severe; I regained my balance and the aberration in my eyesight corrected itself.

I often think back to that traumatic period and shall never forget that first meeting with Roger McDougal when he tore aside my layers of fear and ignorance and replaced them with hope. There was a stark contrast between the romance I was attempting to record on film and the backstage anguish that Nanette, much more than I, endured. Without her love and unwavering support, I doubt whether I would have lasted the course. I know that I could never have sustained my own resolve without her as we journeyed through unknown seas with only one map to guide us. I have met some remarkable women in my life as this account has noted, but nobody comes anywhere near my wife. She is not just a beautiful face: let anybody or anything threaten her family and she becomes a tiger not to be tangled with. Between us we somehow managed to keep the secret from our two daughters and with the exception of a handful of our closest friends, nobody suspected anything untoward.

Subsequently I have undergone several insurance medical examinations when beginning other films, and naturally I have to disclose any past illnesses. When I reveal the MS diagnosis I am always told, 'Well, yes, there's no actual proof that a gluten-free regime helps. On the other hand doesn't do any harm, I suppose. You have to realise the disease often goes into remission.' To which I say, I'll settle for a remission that has lasted fifteen years. I took no drugs, not even an aspirin, and have been able to keep up my usual punishing work schedule. I still get occasional pain when overtired and I have long since gone back to a careful, but normal, diet, semi but not rabidly vegetarian. Apart from the minor ills that all flesh is heir to I seem to be holding together.

FOURTEEN

It was during the holiday Nanette and I spent in Malibu with Elton John that I first met Groucho Marx. He came into the room like the last of the great French Resistance fighters, a hero who had just fooled the Gestapo, his doctors, various wives and current agent, and come to terms with his own legend. He was accompanied by a very presentable young lady whom he introduced as his secretary. 'Our relationship is purely physical,' he said.

The black beret he sported seemed to have replaced his Havana trademark of old and in any case the small cigar he flourished had never known Cuban thighs. The smudged moustache was also thinner, hardly perceptible in the evening light, but the eyes at eighty-one missed nothing that moved, especially if it was wearing a mini-skirt.

He had come to dinner at Elton's invitation and arrived promptly wearing a black Vicuna overcoat even though the temperature was in the seventies. 'What a dull party,' he said as he came through the door, 'where's the piano player?'

As Elton greeted him we caught a sacred and profane glimpse of the Groucho who used to insult Margaret Dumont with such Pisa-leaning ease. 'They tell me you're Number One, but I'd never heard of you until I went into my office this morning and said I was having dinner with Elton John. They all fainted.' He looked straight into an imaginary camera. 'After that I lost what remaining respect I had for you.'

He told us he wanted to use the evening as a warm-up for his coming concert in San Francisco in six weeks' time. 'At my age you need a long warm-up,' he sneered, flourishing the cigar. After a leisurely and hilarious dinner his own pianist arrived and we sat around him on the floor prepared to do homage. Just as he was about to begin his secretary reminded him that he ought to use the bathroom. Groucho did what used to be described as a 'slow burn', finally allowing his sad eyes to come to rest on Nanette. 'She always makes me go to the bathroom before I sing,' he said. Then, with perfect timing, the tag line was dropped into the silence: 'That's because *after* I sing, *everybody* wants to go to the bathroom.' He was led away, still gently protesting.

His pianist, a young man obviously devoted to his employer, played the introduction to *Hurrah for Captain Spaulding*, a vintage favourite of mine. Groucho stood by the piano, twirled the dead cigar between his fingers, leered at Emma and started to sing in a voice filtered through a lifetime of simulated lechery. He sang some fifteen numbers for us, enjoying himself, opening up as old pros do when the house is with them.

It was an evening of total nostalgia for some of us, and for others a first glimpse of what the good old days were all about. He did three encores and then sat down while Elton took over the piano and gave him a preview of his latest and as yet unreleased LP. Groucho listened gravely, signed as many mementoes as were put in front of him, then departed into the Californian night, back to his vast and empty house on Hillcrest.

We saw him on several occasions after that and took him to see *Jesus Christ, Superstar* which was being performed in the open-air theatre on the Universal back-lot. On the way there, driving over Coldwater Canyon, he told us he was hungry, so we stopped at a drive-in for a hamburger. Between the journey from the cash desk to our table he somehow managed to date an attractive young blonde and invited her to join us. She went home to change. Groucho ate a stack of pancakes saturated with maple syrup and, when the waitress enquired whether he had everything he wanted, he said, 'Everything's perfect except the food.' The waitress took this as a compliment, the young blonde returned, breathless and in her Sunday best, and we continued our journey.

The Universal auditorium is vast and it took us fifteen minutes at Groucho's leisurely pace to reach our seats, by which time the overture was being played. He was recognised every inch of the way and four usherettes vied to light his path with their torches. We sat in the third row, stunned with the volume of amplified noise. Groucho watched the opening scenes without expression, then turned to me and, in a voice that made Pontius Pilate falter, said: 'D'you think this'll offend the Jews?'

In the interval he took another slow promenade and was soon surrounded by admirers of all ages. He accepted the compliments without false modesty, but half the time I sensed he did not enjoy being reminded of the golden days when Chico and Harpo were alive. During the second half when the actor playing Christ was climbing to the massive tubular cross and the high-flying 747s winked soundlessly in the clear night sky above the stage, he made his only other comment on the proceedings. 'Tell me,' he enquired, 'does this have a happy ending?'

On the way out he somehow managed to lose the first blonde and acquire a second, linking arms with her while her boyfriend walked alongside resigned to such unbeatable competition.

We took a beer with him that night in the empty house on Hillcrest, sitting in the cinema that was filled with photographs and memorabilia of all the brothers Marx. He told us that deer came down from the hills to eat his flowers and then, switching abruptly, asked whether people in England still remembered him. All he remembered of England was a past failure during an early stage appearance. Our efforts to convince him of his immortality were in vain. He autographed a copy of his collected letters for me, then walked us to the front door and said goodnight.

The last time we saw him we went to a private suburban house in the valley where there was to be a showing of *Animal Crackers* which he had not seen for fifteen years. 'I always thought I was pretty good in that one,' he said, 'but I could be wrong.' When we arrived at our destination, which Groucho said was close to where W.C. Fields drank his last, it appeared to be a fairly nondescript bungalow as Californian houses go, but outward appearances proved false for the interior had undergone major architectural surgery. We were conducted through a room housing an enormous organ, the pipes disappearing through holes in the ceiling. En route to the underground cinema, reached by a spiral staircase, we glimpsed a man putting the finishing touches to a monster jigsaw. In the basement we were led through another chamber where two or three ladies were using aerosol cans of what passes for cream in America, spraying a collection of unappetising cakes laid out on a long table and presumably for our benefit. By now we were all caught between unease and hysteria. Finally entering the cinema we were faced by another mighty Wurlitzer organ standing beside a concert grand piano obviously once used by Sparky for, as we took our seats, the piano was electrically activated and started to play *Sonny Boy*. 'God, don't tell me Jolson's gonna show up!' Groucho remarked. 'Though I could believe it in this joint.'

As it turned out that was the best laugh of the evening since Groucho watched himself in silence and afterwards pronounced the revival disappointing.

After he died the young lady he had facetiously introduced as his secretary, but who in fact was a devoted companion, came in for a great deal of flak when his Will was published and she was named as a beneficiary. In my opinion the abuse she suffered was unfair. Groucho obviously adored her and depended on her in his last years; certainly she did everything for him with obvious dedication while we were around.

I shall always picture him sitting there in that empty house, being told when to go to the bathroom but still out-foxing everybody, not resting on his laurels but adjusting them, a superstar watching the deer eat his flowers and getting ready to sing for the last time in San Francisco.

FIFTEEN

During a period when film criticism seemed to be going through a particularly arid patch, as typified by the gibberish then being published in the official organ of the BFI, *Sight and Sound*, I was asked by *The Times* to concoct a fictitious epic and review it. The idea appealed to me and I laid the satire on with a trowel just to make my point. Much to my amazement a great number of people took it to be the genuine article, so much so that, prior to running it in the paper, *The Times* lawyers wanted an assurance from me that they could not be attacked for libel. It is perhaps worth quoting the entire text.

Sade with Flowers
Last night I was privileged to attend the first screening of *Merde*, Hentes-Modra's eagerly awaited new film, which has its British première next month in aid of the Metropolitan Police Widows Fund.
I can report that Hentes-Modra has lost none of his daring and flair and consolidates his position as a superhip master of cinema. Not since *A Clockwork Orange* has rape been so tastefully handled on the wide screen. This simple and for the most part plotless story of a blind Jewish homosexual is loosely based on an unpublished fragment of Kafka's, but Hentes-Modra, working from his own screenplay, has brilliantly transformed this obscure vignette of Europe in the mid-Twenties into a parable for today. He is quoted as saying: 'I see my hero, eyeless on the Gaza Strip, doomed by his own impotence and rejected by society, yet somehow funny with it.

Death and violence have to be seen as fun things, otherwise we're in danger of taking ourselves too seriously.'

Throughout the film he guides his leading actors to tread the thin line between comedy and repulsion, agreeing with Honorat de Bueil, 'Rien au monde ne dure Qu'un éternal changement.'

From the savage opening frames which immediately follow the director's amusing solo credit, we feel we are *there*, taking part in the full frontal rape of the Negro servant girl. The programme notes state that Hentes-Modra shot this sequence in his own bathroom over a period of three weeks, and in lesser hands the deliberately out-of-focus images would seem amateur. I doubt if anybody will ever forget the blind hero groping helplessly on the blood-slippery tiles as, in a fit of remorse, he attempts to give mouth-to-mouth resuscitation to his victim. This shattering sequence, with its imaginative use of Schubert's Fourth Concerto, takes up nearly a third of the film's length and leaves five of the main characters dead. I have no hesitation in saying that it will serve as a textbook study of how to photograph acts of ultraviolence without giving offence to any except the most prudishly squeamish.

I won't spoil anybody's anticipated pleasure by revealing the rest of the plot, but suffice it to say that the rape is only incidental to the main theme. Hentes-Modra is stating, in effect, this is the universal sickness of mankind as typified by his blind protagonist. There is no homosexual camp in the film, and indeed the homosexuality is only touched upon by one glimpse of a drag party being brutally suppressed by a score of lesbian fashion models. Here again what places Hentes-Modra in a class apart from his many imitators is his ability to inject flashes of real humour into the most likely situations. This was all the more apparent when *Merde* was compared with the unofficial British entry at the Venice Festival, *The Charabanc Kids*, which was received in silence.

We hear so much ill-informed criticism of the way in which violence is depicted on the screen today that I think it is worth restating a truism – namely that if the cinema is to survive as an Art form it must remain commercially viable. Hentes-Modra knows this instinctively and yet makes no extravagant claims for his own work. In a long interview he granted to *Cahiers du Cinéma* last year following disturbances at the Cannes Festival, he spelt out his own position with his customary and engaging frankness. 'I have a social conscience which I reconcile to a percentage of the gross. My films are message films and the message is that you can fool most of the people most of the time.' The honesty of the man is apparent in every frame he exposes.

I shall see *Merde* again and review it at greater length. Not for the important things it says about the pathology of violence, but because I believe passionately in freedom of expression at all levels, and I think the time is fast approaching when those of us who view with alarm the creeping cancer of censorship in our society should stand up and be counted. All credit, therefore, to the censor for refusing to be influenced by majority pressure groups and granting Hentes-Modra's masterpiece – yes, one must use that word – a General audience rating. Had I children of my own I would not hesitate to expose them to this film.

Lord Chesterfield held the view that ridicule is the best test of truth, while Swift noted that 'satire is a sort of glass wherein beholders do generally discover everybody's face but their own.' I should perhaps have ignored Chesterfield and Swift and heeded Benjamin Franklin who said, 'Strange that a man who had wit enough to write a satire should have folly enough to publish it.'

As it happens dear old Hentes-Modra, may his tribe increase, was all too real for a lot of people. (I chose his name from one of Nanette's cookbooks; he is of Hungarian origin and a concoction of pork chops, ham and pickles.) Within hours of the article appearing in *The Times* my phone had to be taken off the hook. This was followed by an avalanche of mail, most expressing horrified astonishment that I, of all people, could praise such a revolting film. A few were openly abusive and some unquestionably threatening. Some of my colleagues in the industry rang to enquire after my mental health and one anonymous caller breathed the title (in English translation) into my midnight ear. One of the Sunday papers drew attention to the film and my justification of it and suggested that my head should be examined.

What did alarm me was that few of my critics *questioned* that there could be a film called *Merde* having a London première in aid of the Metropolitan Police Widows Fund. I could only sadly assume that they accepted the perverted story as being nothing out of the ordinary. I agree with Paulene Kael, film critic of the *New Yorker*, who once wrote: 'How can people go on talking about the dazzling brilliance of movies and not notice that certain directors are sucking up to the thugs in their audience?'

The Times article was not my only excursion into satire because I was bold enough to have another go for the pages of *Punch*. On this occasion I parodied the style of various critics, this time inventing another film *Kaernemaelkskoldskaal* (English title *I am Inexplicably Orange*, Cert. X) with a splendid director named Kottbullar.

I still have a certain affection for this piece, especially the one written in the style of *Sight and Sound*.

I Am Inexplicably Orange is at once too remote and yet not remote enough, and clearly demands our respect if not our complete understanding. Kottbullar has regurgitated Peckinpah in the same way that his ex-circus hero rejects the rats, and yet here, in his fifth film, he explores the religious syncretism inherent in the subject matter in a way that brilliantly illuminates Eric Pollen's thesis on 'The Life and Death of the Non-film Film'. Pollen argued that 'to understand Kottbullar's post-Brechtian techniques, you have to accept that the director is primarily talking to himself.'

Or how about my stab at *Time*?

I Am Inexplicably Orange is a rat-infested comedy that pulls out the laughs the way a catheter drains urine. The latest offering from true Danish blue director Mansson (*Douche-Moi*) Kottbullar throws more than a few Schlagobers in the spectator's kisser. With all the delicacy of a Chicago slaughterer, he sets out to prove there are more ways than one to sever the jugular, and labors in vain. His leading actor, Jan Tunberger, should give celluloid a rest and ply his talents on Fifth Avenue where mugging is a fine art. The rest of the cast consists of reformatory teeny-boppers selling-out love for lustiness. If you liked *The Singing Nun*, *Orange* will peel you off.

The readers of *Punch* proved more sophisticated than the readers of *The Times* and I received no hate mail, only compliments. I do think there is a great deal of esoteric rubbish written about films in the more highbrow publications. In recent years, of course, the television critic has subordinated his film colleagues, and television criticism, with few exceptions, is often little more than a gossip column which leans more heavily on the private lives of the performers than on their talents. In any event television criticism is a dead-end, for like yesterday's newspapers it is here today and gone tomorrow. The audience is captive, has a choice of flipping through the channels and for the most part is indifferent to the opinions of others. The best of British television is without equal anywhere in the world in my opinion, but there is much that is puerile – inescapably attractive, I suppose, to the commercial channels aiming for the advertisers' mass markets, but short-sighted where the BBC is concerned.

It is a lie to pretend that artists are not hurt by bad reviews or that they never read them (there is always a friend who will draw our attention to the worst!). The most poverty-stricken criticism is when it takes the form of character assassination rather than constructive analysis of our faults. Even Kenneth Tynan, fine and erudite critic though he was, often lowered his standards in this respect. One has to take the rough with the smooth and I have had my fair share of brickbats. I seldom reply in kind unless it is to correct a question of fact, but I never hesitate to defend others if I feel they have been grossly maligned.

John Simon, the feared critic of *New York* magazine, once described Nanette as the 'unattractive wife of Bryan Forbes'. It so happened that the launch of *The Raging Moon* in New York coincided with the film festival there and I was invited to conduct a seminar. Nanette was in the audience accompanied by an assigned publicity man who introduced her to John Simon, seated next to her, with the words: 'I don't think you know Miss Newman, John.'

Afterwards Nanette told me, 'the opportunity was too good to miss. I said, "Oh, yes, Mr Simon does know me. I'm the unattractive wife of Bryan Forbes as he once wrote." '

The publicity man went into shock, fearing an explosion and the possible loss of his job. To his credit John Simon reacted with suitable grace, sent Nanette a large bunch of red roses the following morning, took her out to lunch and in a eulogistic review of our film described Nanette's and Malcolm McDowell's performances as 'unimprovable upon'. As a final act of contrition he sent her a copy of one of his books inscribed: 'To Nanette Newman, with gratitude for having taught me a lesson – useful to men and invaluable to critics – that I can be just plain wrong.' Game, Set and Match for once!

We don't seem to have fared well with American publicity men over the years, engaging though they often are in what is often a thankless task. I recall that when *Whistle Down the Wind* went to America the distribution company handling it decided, for reasons that still seem obscure, to open it in Dallas, Texas. It was an odd choice for a small black and white British film that demanded to be quietly launched in New York and left to find its own level. However, the decision was out of my hands and we were told that on arrival in Dallas there would be a lunch in our honour.

We were duly flown across the Atlantic and changed planes in New York. There we were met by a publicity man who had been instructed to take care of our every need on the second leg of the journey. He proved to be four feet tall, wore an enormous Stetson, and greeted us rather the worse for wear. The plane was late taking off and he continued a non-stop sampling of hospitality liquor, taking care of his own needs rather than ours during the flight to Dallas. The inevitable result was that after throwing up he passed out and had to be given oxygen.

Because of our late arrival we were rushed to the luncheon venue which was held in what I took to be a night-club. Lunch was already over and the gathering of media people assembled to welcome us were likewise fairly soused. I managed to make a short speech, but it fell on ears that had long been tuned out to all coherent conversation. The only question I can remember being put to me was when a Texan giant rose unsteadily to his feet and asked: 'Mr Forbes, why didn't you shoot your film in sunlight?' I explained that the film had been made in the North of England during the winter months when sunlight was a sparse commodity. 'That's the point I'm trying to make,' he said gravely. 'You should have shot it in sunlight.'

The next treat in store for us was a gift of charge cards for Neiman Marcus, then as now the most exclusive shop in America. We were given a VIP tour, but since we only had a hundred or so dollars between us, it was difficult to decide between the his-and-hers helicopters on display, or buy ourselves a mink-covered toilet seat that played a tune when lifted. Promising to come back when we had rested, we made our escape and were then deposited in the Dallas Hilton. We found ourselves in a suite the size of a hockey pitch complete with a circular bed of heroic proportions. Before we had come to terms with this there was a knock at the door. I opened it to be confronted by a total stranger.

'Mr Forbes,' the stranger said, 'I've come to apologise to your gracious bride and your gracious Queen of England for the insult done to you today. We're gonna rub out the Greek tonight.'

'The Greek?' I said. 'What Greek?'

'The chef. That was a disgusting lunch.'

'Well, I must admit I've tasted better, and it's very kind of you to take the trouble to apologise, but please don't rub out anybody on our account.' By now I was convinced I was dealing with a madman.

'No, the insult to your gracious bride needs to be taken care of, and we're gonna take care of it.'

He prattled on with this lunatic dialogue for several minutes until I finally managed to get rid of him. I turned to Nanette. 'Don't unpack,' I said, 'we're getting out of here.' We used the service elevator and took a taxi back to the airport where we caught a plane to New Orleans and thence home. Fade to black screen as we say.

Some years later during the week that President Kennedy was

assassinated our long-time friend Alexander Walker came to dinner with us. Like most people we were glued to the television news and it had just been announced that Lee Oswald was to be moved from jail to another location and that there would be live coverage of the event. We watched and together with the rest of the world saw the figure of Jack Ruby move in from the right-hand side of the screen and shoot Oswald at point-blank range.

I immediately recognised Ruby as the man who had come to our hotel room that strange afternoon with the Greek chef's demise in mind. I later discovered that it had been his night-club where our bizarre luncheon had been held and that he must have been as crazy as a fox even then. The long arm of coincidence had really stretched out to touch our lives on that occasion. It still seems unreal that by chance we came in contact with a man who changed the course of history, and to this day I remain obsessed with the mystery that still surrounds the death of the President.

SIXTEEN

On our frequent journeys into London from darkest stockbroker Surrey we inevitably pass a sad, demented man who stands motionless in all weathers, bare head bowed, his arms splayed outwards in the crucifixion pose on a street corner close to the Hammersmith flyover. He appears to be unaware of the constant stream of traffic thundering by and has become such a familiar sight that passing pedestrians pay no heed. I often wonder about his life and what brought him to such a pass for sometimes he wears campaign medals denoting that he was in the armed forces. Occasionally he leaves his favourite pitch and sits on a thin strip of grass by the roadside, grass so stunted by highway pollution that it resembles little more than a green stain stippled with empty beer cans and discarded plastic. There he is often joined by a gaggle of like unfortunates, winos, meth drinkers and other inner-city human flotsam, bonded together by a common despair. The loneliness of this group is almost tangible, reflecting as it does the gaping divisions that still persist in our so-called affluent society. There is something shaming to glide past in a comfortable car.

Does anything ever change? Was it always like this or is nostalgia for a Britain we thought we once knew a falsely coloured memory, a sort of Camelot that as one grows older seems infinitely preferable? Edith Evans always maintained that counting the years is a sign of deterioration, and perhaps for a variety of reasons this held true for her. Because of her lifelong dedication to the theatre she had removed herself from life as it is lived by the majority, and that is no criticism of her, for without such dedication we would have been the losers. But she had no children, and children signpost the passing of the years to most of us, constantly reminding us of our mortality. Edith knew great loneliness; denied a lasting marriage, she had one short affair and then withdrew behind the mask of a great actress.

Every time I see that man standing on the street corner, my thoughts hark back to my own childhood in Forest Gate. I had a poor but happy childhood in an area where the inhabitants struggled to maintain a genteel façade of respectability – the doorsteps always pumiced, the dark privet hedges, shorn like conscripts, clinging to life in a few inches of soot-barren soil. The food placed before me was simple, but wholesome: crusty cottage loaves spread with Golden Syrup, dumplings the size of tennis balls floating in stews made from the scrag end of lamb, fourpence worth of fish and chips on a Friday, sometimes winkles for tea, chicken a rare luxury, steak and scampi unheard of. Real poverty was absent for the simple reason that we lived in a community where everybody knew each other and when the hard times came whatever was available was shared, the pain of keeping afloat hidden from the children. There was little crime, you didn't steal from your neighbours, you borrowed from them – the odd cup of sugar, half a packet of tea, always repaid when the pendulum swung the other way. The only violence I was conscious of was when Mosley, looking like Mighty Mouse, came with his black garland of close-cropped bodyguards to Wanstead Flats and screeched his upper-class impersonation of Julius Streicher until bottles were flung on the wire cage protecting him and the Jewish community gave battle. I can remember seeing mounted police swinging out from behind the small bandstand and laying about the fighting mob with their long batons. But no mugging, old age pensioners were not clubbed down for the few shillings they carried. Nobody saved for their old age, they saved for the annual fortnight's holiday and for their funerals, paying a shilling a week to the man from the Pru who called to collect it and was given a cup of tea.

So it isn't violence and mayhem that remain fixed in the

memory, but a glimpse of madness. We had a thin strip of garden where my mother toiled to bring forth a few blooms of London Pride and lupins which backed onto the garden of an identical house in the next street. It was there one summer's morning that I saw a woman move all her furniture and belongings into her back yard. I watched from my upstairs bedroom window which for the first thirteen years of my life I shared with my parents. She did it very methodically and to a child there appeared little that was odd about her behaviour: she might have been embarking upon a spot of spring cleaning just as my own mother was fond of doing. It wasn't until she began to hang pictures on the garden fence that I dimly perceived that her behaviour held other portents, some secret adult game I could not immediately recognise. When everything was arranged to her apparent satisfaction the woman stripped naked – Ophelia with a crêped belly above the dark triangle of hair – and began to dance very slowly. While she danced she held her breasts in her hands and sang verse after verse of 'Ain't it Grand to be Blooming Well Dead'.

Shortly afterwards two uniformed men appeared and after a struggle she was overpowered and put into a strait-jacket. By dint of eavesdropping I later learned that she had smothered her Down's syndrome child.

That is the connection I make whenever I drive past the crucified man on the street corner, for he takes me back many years when the human factor was an unknown quantity to a child and I had a sort of innocence that fifty years of living has corrupted.

SEVENTEEN

One of the penalties for anybody in the public eye is that journalists cannot resist pinning labels to us or placing us in (for them) convenient pigeon-holes from whence we are never allowed to escape. For example the noted columnist Mr Nigel Dempster never fails to refer to me as 'the Queen's favourite film-maker'. Now I number quite a few queens amongst my most fervent admirers, but I have no evidence to suggest that Her Majesty is amongst them.

The Press in general prefer personalities who throw up in restaurants, pick fights with bartenders or constantly reveal the intimate details of their marital squabbles and deliver such deeply philosophical revelations as 'I've finally found who I am and where I'm at' when asked why they are walking disaster areas. For a budding young actress to appear topless guarantees a four-page spread in one of the colour supplements and sets her on her way to instant stardom in a sitcom series.

I think one of the most obnoxious examples of this attitude occurred when I cast Tatum O'Neal in *International Velvet*. Long before she arrived in England to commence filming she had been dubbed 'Tantrum Tatum' and was universally depicted as an unpleasant, spoiled little brat who earned too much money. Journalists who had never met her in the flesh rushed to describe her as a pubescent horror. She was thirteen at the time and had deservedly achieved fame with a captivating performance in *Paper Moon*. Her father, Ryan O'Neal, had long been cast as

Peck's Bad Boy and it was a case of like father like daughter to most of the scribes of Grub Street.

The idea for a sequel to *National Velvet* had come from Richard Shepherd, the then head of MGM, who had been my Hollywood agent at the time of *King Rat*. He was much too nice for the job, and had a vision of returning to the old days of MGM when they produced a string of family-orientated films. I was dubious about the project at first, but he invited me to Culver City, installed me in the Thalberg Building and asked me to try and come up with an original story that would complement Enid Bagnold's classic. The atmosphere at MGM during that period was refreshingly different from the other major studios. A very personable young lady named Sherry Lansing was in charge of the story department; she later went on to become the first woman production head of 20th Century Fox before launching out as an independent producer with such films as *Fatal Attraction* and *The Accused* to her credit. I enjoyed my time there and eventually thought of a story outline that encouraged Dick Shepherd to okay the project.

The main role had to be played by a teenage girl who could not only act but also ride superbly. I knew next to nothing about horses except that I never wanted to get on one, a conviction that was confirmed over the following twelve months. I think it takes an act of courage to feed a horse, let alone ride it, so I wisely left all the equestrian decisions to the experts – notably Bill Steinkraus, a three-time gold medallist in the American Olympic team, and our own Commander John Oram.

The action of the film centred around the demanding Olympic three-day event and it was left to Bill Steinkraus to pronounce whether Tatum had the will and the spunk to tackle such a challenge. Tatum had some rudimentary riding experience but had only ridden cowboy-style before on well-trained film horses. Riding the much larger and high-spirited beasts was another proposition altogether. After some professional tuition Bill Steinkraus gave her a trial and she proved to be a natural and fearless. Our biggest problem on the film was to convince her that some of the scripted action was too dangerous for a novice to tackle. Although we used the brilliant Virginia Holgate to double for the dressage, Tatum did seventy per cent of the cross country and arena riding. Many times I had my heart in my mouth but my two advisers insisted that she was up to it.

As I have said, she was only thirteen when she arrived in England to start filming, still a child, seven thousand miles from home, isolated from all her friends in an alien environment and carrying the burden of being the principal star of the film. I'm sure it would give pleasure to some of her detractors for me to report that she lived up to their expectations as a spoiled brat, but such was not the case. Throughout a long and arduous schedule she was always on time, knew her lines, couldn't wait to get on her horse and did everything asked of her. I was not only her director but also her surrogate father and I grew very fond of her. Logistically, the film was a nightmare and, had Tatum been the character sections of the press had predetermined, the film could not have been finished on time and within budget.

We shot on many different locations, hundreds and once thousands of miles apart and this meant we not only had to transport, house and feed a large cast and crew, but also some forty horses and their handlers. Horses, I swiftly found, have to be treated with kid gloves and are more temperamental than divas. There was one sequence in the film, based on fact, where a horse goes mad and has to be destroyed during a trans-Atlantic flight. We built a full-scale replica of a cargo jet at Pinewood. This was constructed on top of an elaborate platform that, hydraulically, could be rocked and twisted to simulate an aircraft encountering turbulence. Five horses as well as my cast were involved in the sequence. Four of the horses were placed in rigid stalls, but the fifth horse, a stallion, the one required to go beserk, was placed in a stall constructed of much flimsier wood with all the securing bolts partially sawn through, since the object of the exercise was to ensure that the animal did not suffer any injury.

We then had to decide how best to trigger the horse. John Oram came up with the idea of using cold air. He volunteered to conceal himself in the stall and, when I gave the word, aim a quick jet of compressed air on the stallion's testicles.

'Will that make him kick?'

'I don't know about you,' John said, 'but it would make me kick!' He assured me that this would do the trick without harm to the animal. Even so I approached the moment of truth with some trepidation, although John seemed supremely confident. In retrospect we were too careful. The flimsy stall was easily demolished and once the horse found he could kick his way out the sudden freedom went to his head. He started to demolish the entire set. Understandably my cast jumped to safety, Tony Hopkins leaving for the day and vowing never to come back. It was certainly a very hairy episode, though my principal camera-man, Tony Imi, never deserted his post but kept shooting and secured some vital footage until he and I finally left the bridge and took to the lifeboats. Certainly we were never going to have the luxury of a second take. John Oram spent fifteen long minutes quietening the beast, an act of courage above and beyond the call of duty. Apart from the wrecked mock aircraft and our nerves, there was no lasting damage and the horse was taken out to graze, none the worse for wear and presumably well pleased with himself.

I was going over my script later that night when my phone rang. It was the newsdesk of the *Daily Mirror*. They understood from 'a reliable source' that I had grossly mistreated an animal during the course of shooting.

'In what way mistreated?' I asked. The same 'reliable source' had informed them that I had inserted an electrode into the horse's anus and caused it untold suffering. They intended to print the story and wanted my comments.

I denied it categorically and demanded to know who had fabricated such a gross slander, but naturally the 'reliable informant' was given a protection denied to me, a curious practice whereby the victim's rights are ignored in the name of freedom of the press. 'If you refuse to accept my rebuttal and print such a filthy lie, I shall have to sue, as will Commander John Oram,' I told them. They remained unimpressed.

Greatly disturbed I made several phone calls of my own, trying to track down the possible instigator. I drew blanks until I had a sudden hunch as to who it might have been. One of the stunt riders had several times crossed swords with John and had finally been dismissed from the film for another misdemeanour. I rang the *Mirror* and said, 'I know you won't divulge your source, but can I ask you to write down this name?' I gave them the name of the man in question. 'You don't have to say anything, but if I'm right, and the name I've given you is the originator of the story, which is totally false, then you'd better let me know who your lawyers are, because, in addition to refuting the story, I can also prove malice. The man in question was fired more than a month ago and was not present on the set today. Everything he told you is a gross lie.'

There was a long pause, and then the news editor said, 'We'll think about it.'

They thought about it and the story was killed.

I quote this because there was a strange follow-up. Some months later, long after Tatum had departed, another curious story appeared, this time in the *Mail on Sunday*. With great prominence it was reported that Nanette had taken such a dislike to Tatum that during one scene she had struck her a number of times, so much so that shooting had to be halted and Tatum given medical attention. It was further reported that I left the set and never returned and this was such a preposterous fiction that I rang the editor himself to protest. Once again I was given the 'Oh, our sources are impeccable' routine. I pointed out that films are shot with a great number of people present, that because Tatum was a minor we were required to have a state registered nurse on the set at all times, and that had Nanette been stupid enough to lose her temper and strike Tatum even once in anger, it was hardly likely that eighty members of the crew would allow the prolonged attack as described. It was such a patently fabricated non-story, full of holes and so easily and conclusively disproved, that one wonders what brain of the year thought it worth running. After the lawyers were brought into the act, an apology was given equal prominence as the original bunch of lies and a large settlement was agreed out of court and donated to Nanette's favourite charity.

The true story is that while we were on location in Devon there was a dawn scene where Tatum has taken and ridden Nanette's horse without permission. She is caught and given a slap. We only had a very short time in which to get the shot and the moment Nanette slapped her Tatum stopped acting, looked to me behind the camera and asked, 'Why did Nanette do that?'

'Because it's in the script,' I said.

'Oh, I never read those bits,' Tatum said cheerfully.

By then the rising sun had burned through the dawn mist and we had to call it a day. There was no chance of rescheduling, since the entire caravan had to move on to Burleigh, and months later we faked it in the studio. So much for the reliable source syndrome.

Tatum is now married with children, providing the truffle hounds with more ammunition, since they can write about the film brat marrying the tennis brat – perfect copy for the scurrilous-minded. If you can't stand the heat get out of the kitchen, as the saying goes, but it isn't that easy. Fame is a poisoned chalice in many cases and as the rewards grow ever more astronomical so the pressures increase. Television provides instant notoriety, often to those ill equipped to deal with it, and television devours talent, especially comedic talent. Whereas in the old days of variety a comedian could use the same basic material for a year or more, travelling from city to city, now his act is exhausted in a single night on the box. The mass audience is quickly jaded, avaricious for new gimmicks, even the news bulletins have to be fashioned as entertainment.

One victim of fame who comes immediately to mind was Tony Hancock. I directed him in what I believe was his last screen appearance. I had always been an avid admirer and I place him alongside Sid Field as the two greatest native comedians of my time. Tony, I think, fell into the oldest trap of all – he was an inspired clown who wanted to play Hamlet. Self-destructively he turned his back on the character he played best, tailor-made for him by the writing team of Galton and Simpson – the truculent, aggressive know-it-all who somehow could never admit defeat and who epitomised many of our own unsuccessful battles against bureaucracy. He was Strube's Little Man with a funny face, a suburban Don Quixote tilting at officialdom, a bigot who made us recognise our own failings and laugh at them. It was a portrayal of genius and it made him a household name that eventually he longed to escape from. I remember one occasion when we shared a holiday together in the South of France and for the first time I saw behind his public face. By then he had parted company with Galton and Simpson and relied heavily on alcohol to get him through the empty days. It was painful to see him ward off the well-intentioned plaudits of British holiday-makers on the beach who weren't interested in him as a man, only as his alter ego they remembered from television. They wanted him to reply in character, to be funny, and they brought him to the edge of desperation. Invent a catchphrase and it remains with you for life like a vivid birthmark.

Nanette played a role in one of his feature films, *The Rebel*, but, as with Sid Field, his particular brand of humour did not catch fire on the big screen. She remembers a location trip to Paris with him where between the airport and the hotel he made half a dozen stops for refreshment and that during the entire two days she was there he never went to bed. He was a kindly, generous man to his friends and a marvellous raconteur, steeped in the folk lore of the variety world.

When towards the end of his life I cast him in *The Wrong Box*, the fire had gone out of him. There were occasional glimpses of the old genius, but he seemed unsure of himself. On one occasion, I remember, I took him to one side and suggested a piece of business. He responded like a drowning man who had been thrown a lifebelt. 'Nobody ever helped me before,' he said, 'I think they were all frightened of me. They thought I had all the answers, but I didn't.' He seemed ready to accept that he was no longer the star everybody wanted to employ, and, who knows, perhaps by then he had already decided to end the agony. Shortly afterwards he took his own life in Australia. It was as though, like a wounded animal, he had crawled away to die alone far from East Cheam and the madding crowd.

EIGHTEEN

My last months in the job at Elstree were fat with drama. At one point in an effort to clear my brain and rid my body of a few toxins I took us off to a health farm, as they were amusingly described. Nanette, fully brainwashed by the diet industry, thought of it as a treat, I was resigned to a few days of intensive boredom combined with the odd glass of expensive lemon juice. We drove to Buxted, I had my last salad meal before the fast commenced and plunged into the sauna. There I found an old friend, Wolf Mankowitz, already ensconced and, somewhat surprisingly, an Irish priest throwing pine-scented water on the sullen volcanic rocks. (I later made use of this encounter in *The Distant Laughter*.)

Wolf has always been a hybrid grafted onto the film industry establishment, a larger than life character possessed of considerable talents combined with a refreshing cynicism, a trait he shares with Frederick Raphael. I never meet either of them without taking away a feeling of delight, for they are two opposites of a kind: Freddie academically precise, Wolf an earthy street fighter, both veterans of many battles with the front office. Their Jewish chutzpah is very much to my taste and they are both fellow survivors in the jungle we inhabit. As we sweated together that day – the priest having heaved his solid mass of carbo-hydrates off the slab and gone for his pummelling – Wolf told me that he and his family were leaving England and settling in Ireland to take advantage of the new and friendly Irish tax laws for writers and artists. We swopped views on the current parlous state of the industry and I related some of the problems I was encountering at EMI.

Wolf spoke a lot of good sense about the basic inability of creative people to survive in the corridors of power. 'The trouble is,' he said, 'the artist becomes an easy victim of his own artistic paranoia in that environment. Kicking against the pricks is an exhausting way to spend your time and ultimately a waste of your life.'

I couldn't argue against the truth of that for in the months just passed I had felt increasingly isolated. The promised revolving fund had never materialised, so I now had no spare cash with which to commission a second programme and my efforts to elicit a decision on the future of the studios were consistently put on the back burner as the Americans say. The marketing of my films as opposed to those put out by Anglo-Amalgamated, Nat Cohen's subsidiary company, left much to be desired. Rumours about my impending resignation were rife and for all I knew might have been deliberately planted in order to flush me out. I could no longer look for much support from the other members of the Board and my relationship with Bernard Delfont, although outwardly normal, lacked the intimacy I had previously enjoyed. John Read, the chief executive, had little practical experience of the film industry having come from Ford Motors, and was therefore more at home discussing time and motion studies than creative matters. He also developed a fixation about the number of cleaners employed at the studio. These were mostly sweet old pensioners who had been there for years and were totally honest and reliable. I therefore consistently resisted Read's urgings to switch to unknown contract cleaners, arguing that the minimal savings achieved by such a switch were not worth the risk. I did not have a seat on the main Board and so Sir Joseph Lockwood, the one person who might have been expected to understand my problems, remained firmly in the background and was disappointingly no help at all. Those remnants of the old ABPC Board sat like figures from Madame Tussaud's, saying nothing, and the newcomer, Peter King, who now had sole responsibility for booking films on the EMI circuit, was an unknown quantity. The hand of friendship I extended to him on his arrival was sadly not returned in kind.

So, despite the regime, I found the few days we spent at Buxted mentally stimulating. We woke to wintry sun streaming across the misty landscape. Below our windows the deer grazed like shadows, the back light so strong as almost to pierce them. We went for walks along the dank paths where underfoot were masses of small black fungi and the first nipples of daffodils showing yellow-green and tumescent through uneven grass. It is at moments like these that I find myself drawn to the countryside as a lemming is drawn to the cliff's edge. Albeit city born and bred, whenever I wake up in a strange city I am a dead person; in the countryside I am immediately excited and fulfilled.

My batteries recharged, drained of toxins and a few pounds lighter, I was better able to take stock of my current situation and see certain events in perspective.

Matters had been brought to a head at the time I delivered my own film *The Raging Moon*. Although I was perfectly entitled under my contract to direct while remaining Managing Director, the announcement that the film was going ahead had provoked veiled criticism in the trade journals. It was conveniently overlooked that the main reason for my decision was to keep the studio open and avoid wholesale redundancies amongst the permanent workforce. I took no extra salary for directing and scaled the budget down to a modest £260,000. I believed passionately in the subject and felt that in casting Malcolm MacDowell I had a potential star. He had achieved great success in Lindsay Anderson's *If* and had immediately been snapped up by Stanley Kubrick for the leading role in *A Clockwork Orange*. The fact that I cast Nanette opposite Malcolm inevitably gave my critics something else to snipe at. Bernie asked me whether it was wise to risk adverse press comment by employing my own wife, to which I replied, 'Wait and see.' I had every confidence that Nanette would triumph in the role and so it proved, for she was to win the Variety Club award for Best Actress the following year.

I also felt that I owed it to her. She and Edward Woodward had been the innocent victims of a fiasco earlier in the programme. They had both been cast in *A Fine and Private Place*, adapted from one of A.E. Coppard's brilliant short stories. The project had been brought to me by a young director whose previous work had been confined to television documentaries. Even so, I felt his enthusiasm and approach merited the risk; the screenplay contained all the ingredients for a compelling film and I gave him the go-ahead. As an insurance policy against his inexperience in feature films I appointed a veteran producer to hold his hand and guided him towards a first-class crew, including Julie Harris the Oscar-winning costume designer who provided some ravishing period clothes. The unit duly departed to his chosen locations on the wild North coast of Cornwall. As was my policy I kept well clear, especially since Nanette was involved, and it wasn't until I rang her one evening to ask how it was all going that I had the first premonition of disaster.

'Edward and I didn't work all day,' Nanette said. 'The weather's frightful. Nobody can stand up against the wind, and it's pouring with rain. We spent the whole day sitting in our trailer.'

'What about a cover set? Didn't they go inside to shoot?'

'No. As far as I know we didn't shoot anything.'

(It is standard practice, vitally important on British locations, to schedule safeguards against the inclement elements. These are known as 'cover sets' and ensure that time is not wasted. Before the unit left the studio I had carefully ensured that the film was adequately protected against bad weather.)

The next morning I asked to see the latest weekly reports and to my horror I found that after two weeks a third of the budget had been eaten up for only ten minutes' screen time. I immediately took a train to Cornwall to find out at first hand. Although I had previously seen photographs of all the locations and enthusiastically approved them I knew only too well how the best-laid plans can go awry when subjected to the vagaries of the British climate. Nanette had not exaggerated; the winds were gale force when I arrived. I got an immediate sense of doom emanating from the crew, and asked the young director if he would allow me to screen what he had already shot. I viewed his rushes on a portable screen in the hotel and was appalled by what I saw. One sequence in particular made no sense at all and would obviously never cut together.

Despite this I did not want to panic him, but tried as tactfully as I could to point out the errors and told him that the sequence would have to be reshot for it broke all the rules and would never cut together. The cameraman and continuity girl agreed with me, but he remained adamant that we were wrong and he was right.

I stayed up most of that night trying to convince him that he was on a collision course but won few arguments and finally took to my bed very depressed. The next morning the weather had changed and I woke to brilliant sunshine. I asked the producer to take me on a tour of the various locations, in particular the place where the butterfly sequence was to be shot. This had been a favourite of mine from first reading of the script. Edward was playing a plebeian village schoolmaster who entered into an ultimately tragic affair with the lady of the manor – Nanette's role. In this particular sequence he invites her to present the awards at the school prizegiving and has prepared a surprise for her. The schoolchildren have collected butterflies and at a given moment these were to be released within the school hall. Except that the surprise goes wrong, his mistress is terrified as hundreds of butterflies flutter around her head, some becoming entangled in her veil. It had always been obvious that this would be an extremely difficult sequence to mount and shoot but, if successful, would be a stunning visual set piece. We had gone to enormous trouble to have many thousands of white butterflies bred and the timing of the sequence was critical given that the lifespan of a butterfly is very brief.

So under bright sunny skies, I set out that morning with renewed hope. I had already arranged for a second camera unit to join the first team and help retrieve some of the lost time by shooting those action sequences which did not involve the principal actors. I also felt that my pep talk had cleared the air and that all was not lost.

'Show me the school hall first,' I said. The producer looked dubious, but said nothing. We set off in a Land Rover and he took me down narrow lanes and over ploughed fields for several miles until we reached a farm. We turned into the yard which was knee-deep in straw and pig shit.

'No,' I said, 'you misunderstood me. I want to see where he's going to shoot the butterfly sequence.'

'Here,' he replied, not looking me in the eye. 'This is where he intends to shoot it.'

I stared at him. 'Here? In this filth? You are kidding me, aren't you?'

'Unfortunately, no.'

'But how could you even let him dream up such a thing? You're an old hand, you know it has to be a total cockup! The scene can't possibly work as an exterior. It has to be shot inside.'

'I agree, but I couldn't talk him out of it. We had a stand-up row about it, but he's the director and you told me he had the last word.'

With sinking heart I realised that my determination to give new talent maximum creative freedom had misfired in a major way on this occasion.

'His idea is to have all this filth cleared and build a platform in the middle.'

I was listening to a lunatic scenario. 'Madness,' I said. 'Utter madness. How can he possibly shoot it here? The moment the butterflies are released they'll disappear and never be seen again. All that effort for nothing. It's an exercise in futility!'

We got back into the Land Rover and went in search of the unit. I arrived to find Nanette sitting on an enormous, restless horse at the bottom of a grass dell. I looked at the clapper board which denoted that there had been numerous takes. Taking the continuity girl to one side I asked her what the shot was.

'Just a close-up of Nanette,' she said, 'but they can't get the horse to stand still. We've been at it all morning.'

I called the First Assistant over and suggested that if they took Nanette off the horse and stood her on a rostrum they would achieve the same effect and get it first take. Since it was a close-up and the horse was not in frame it was the obvious answer. He gave me an old-fashioned look and said, 'Perhaps you'd like to suggest that, governor. We haven't had much luck persuading him.'

It so happened that the scene was taking place a short distance from a magnificent piece of coastline: crashing waves on the rocks, spume rising like mist against an azure sky of bright perfection. Choosing my moment, I asked the director why, instead of shooting in a dell, which on the screen would look identical to a suburban lawn, he wasn't taking advantage of the magnificent scenery? 'Oh, I don't want the sea in the film,' he said airily as though this was the perfect answer.

I stayed another day, wrestling with my conscience and weighing up the few options left to me. I saw some more footage, beautifully played by Edward and Nanette, and to be fair competently directed, but the latest progress report showed that half the budget had now disappeared with very little to show for it. The final straw was when I was told that the young director intended to shoot a night love scene between the two lovers *au naturel* in the woods. I called a production meeting and asked the director to explain and convince me how he intended to sur- mount the obvious pitfalls. Quite apart from the certainty of both actors catching double-pneumonia, it was patently obvious that a simple scene, scheduled for a day in the studio, would almost certainly need a week of night shooting to complete in the open air and subject to unpredictable weather. I knew that by now the young director regarded me as some dinosaur, incapable of grasping his superior vision, but I insisted that I could not permit an uncontrollable situation such as he envisaged to go ahead. I was in despair.

I took my lunch alone and tried to think if there was still any way in which I could retrieve the situation, but came to the conclusion that the film had already passed the point of no return. Immediately after lunch, and without giving Nanette or Edward any prior warning, I called the entire cast and crew together and told them that I was reluctantly closing down the production, and that everybody would be paid off. To save the young director's face I placed the entire blame on the weather. It was the most agonising decision I ever had to take on a film. I felt sorry for everybody concerned and I knew that I would come in for heavy criticism. But everything is relative and this was my *Heaven's Gate*. I did not have the luxury of increasing the budget and, even if I had, I had lost confidence in the ability of the director to deliver. It was a tragedy of good intentions, a blight on Nanette's and Edward's careers and a sad loss of income for the crew.

When I returned to Elstree and broke the news to Bernie he was understandably appalled. I pointed out that the money already spent could never be retrieved and that to have continued would have inevitably cost more than the film was worth. To emphasise my dilemma I tried to make him see that, because of my own wife's involvement, the decision had been doubly heartbreaking. The logic convinced Bernie, for he could relate it to his own experiences in the theatre when he had been forced to close a production, but he remained gloomy about the Board's reaction.

Publicly I stuck to my story that the weather had beaten us, for there was nothing to be gained by naming the director as the main culprit. I was in the kitchen, I had to stand the heat. It was a hideous time and the trade press comments were predictably hostile and damning, one piece hinting that it was time for me to go.

During the following two weeks while the crew were still on salary I made strenuous efforts to investigate remounting the film with another director. I brought in John Hough who I felt had the necessary drive to tackle the problem. We investigated other locations closer to the studio, rewrote sections of the script, but in the end we had to admit defeat. All that remains of that venture are some stills of Julie Harris' stunning costumes.

Because of this fiasco I was determined to vindicate my lifelong belief in Nanette's abilities as an actress when *The Raging Moon* came along. In many ways my career has acted to her detriment. As a mother she always put the family before her own ambitions and when the children were young turned down many opportunities in order to keep the family together. Unlike me she comes from a theatrical background, for her father and mother were both in variety during its heyday. She was performing in her father's act at a tender age and made several films as a child. She gained a Leverhulme scholarship to the Royal Academy of Dramatic Art and had considerable experience in repertory before entering films. She has only appeared in ten of my twenty-one films, often in quite minor roles, so accusations of nepotism are exaggerated. She has worked for a great number of other film directors, had three mini-series on television, presented the TV AM breakfast show, her own talk show and cookery programme. For her part she insists that she made no sacrifices, but merely decided to do what she wanted to do. I apply the same criterion to Nanette as I do to every actor: are they talented and do they fit the role? I have never felt any need to justify working with her.

The subject matter of *The Raging Moon* was fraught with pitfalls of a creative kind. My task was to avoid any patronising of the disabled, shun sentimentalising the core love story and bring out the humour which, during my research, I quickly found was characteristic of genuine paraplegics. Nanette struck an immediate rapport with Malcolm and before principal photography commenced they both went to Stoke Mandeville hospital to learn the technique of handling a wheelchair. They also had to train themselves never to move the lower parts of their bodies. The technique of getting in and out of bed and into the wheelchairs was particularly difficult to master. I used as many real paraplegics as I could in the film, including the late Michael Flanders who was an invaluable help throughout.

The next problem was to find a large empty house within reasonable distance of the studio since I had to be in touch with base at all times. The one chosen, a mock Georgian standing in its own grounds, was big enough to pass as an institutional home for the disabled and once my art department had gone to work it was swiftly transformed for all our needs. There were enough spare rooms to provide make-up, wardrobe and canteen facilities. The fact that, apart from a few exterior locations, I could shoot the entire film in one place not only meant a considerable saving in set costs, but was also helpful to the cast. They were playing the inhabitants of an institution and therefore being in a real building, each with their own rooms to which they returned every day, added to the reality.

As the first day of shooting approached the old adrenalin started to flow. It felt good to get out from behind my desk and I knew that John Hargreaves, Austin Frazer and the management team would hold the fort in my absence. I dealt with my mail and urgent studio business during my snatched lunch breaks, then spent two hours or more at the end of the day on routine matters. It meant working sixteen hours at a stretch, but I have always found that doing what you enjoy is seldom fatiguing, it is boredom that exhausts me.

Bruce Cohn Curtis, my young American producer, was related to the infamous Harry Cohn of Columbia but had inherited none of Harry's grosser qualities. He had a wicked sense of humour, though not quite as black as Malcolm's, and the film progressed in a relaxed and happy atmosphere. Apart from my beloved Penny Daniels and her husband, I was working with more or less completely new crew. I had engaged Tony Imi as cameraman on the strength of his work on that landmark television documentary *Cathy Come Home* and my faith in him was justified from the first day. I did not want glossy photography, I wanted utter realism. It has always been my style to avoid as far as possible weird and wonderful camera movements which to my way of thinking detract from the performances of the actors. This was especially necessary in a delicate subject like *The Raging Moon*; too much artifice and it could easily have slipped over into bathos, which would have been a gross betrayal of Peter Marshall's autobiographical novel on which the film was based.

An example of Malcolm's wicked humour occurred while we were shooting one of the few exterior sequences in Canterbury. I had a scene where he and Nanette had to buy an engagement ring in a jeweller's shop. They were both wearing radio-microphones and from a first floor window on the opposite side of the road I prepared to film with a concealed camera fitted with a zoom lens. While we waited for the light, Nanette and Malcolm sat in their wheelchairs. I spotted the Archbishop of Canterbury striding towards them and cursed the fact that we weren't ready to shoot. Malcolm also had spotted him and, as the Archbishop drew level, he flung the rug covering his legs to one side and staggered out of the chair, crying, 'It's a miracle, I can walk!' The poor old Archbishop, visibly shocked, made off at speed, as well he might. It was all in extremely bad taste, but very funny.

The finished film was lovingly assembled by my editor, Timothy Gee, and I had the benefit of a haunting score for guitar and orchestra by Stanley Myers and played by John Williams. I was proud of the final result. The film had a rock-hard central performance from Malcolm, superbly complemented by Nanette's tragic heroine, and despite the grim subject matter contained the germ of hope for those afflicted with such a distressing condition. I therefore unveiled it with considerable expectations to Peter King believing it to be a worthy addition to my programme.

The screening took place in the private viewing theatre at Golden Square. In addition to Peter King there were only two others present – Jack Goodlatte, one of the old guard, and Eric Maxwell, the son of one of the founders of ABPC, a gentleman who seldom ventured an opinion. They started without me, just to establish their good manners. Goodlatte snorted and fidgeted noisily throughout, Peter King made phone calls and then left during the last reel, followed by Goodlatte, without either of them saying a word about the film to me. My anger was such that I was capable of doing physical injury. I went to Bernie's office and helped myself to a stiff whisky from his drinks cabinet. Bernie came in shortly afterwards and I related what had happened and told him in no uncertain terms how I felt. He urged me not to do anything precipitate and said that he would ask for an explanation from King. I recalled something Wolf had said to me in Buxted: 'Bernie's a killer who hates the sight of blood.'

I then went to take part in a stormy session of the BBC's *Any Questions* broadcast from Bedford College where the students staged a riot and guard dogs had to be brought in to quell them. All in all it was an extraordinary day.

The following morning Bernie informed me that King wanted to apologise for his behaviour (he sent me a wire) but that both he and Goodlatte loathed the film, holding the opinion that it was neither commercial nor art house material and would prefer not to show it at all. I told Bernie there was no way I would accept such a verdict, for it placed me in an impossible position. How could I possibly remain in charge of production if my own film, made with one hundred per cent EMI finance, was shelved and buried?

I immediately asked for a meeting with Sir Joseph Lockwood and that very evening drove down to his house to have dinner with him and his young assistant, William Cavendish. I gave him a detailed reasoning as to why I thought the film division was floundering, but as far as the Peter King episode was concerned confined myself to the bare facts. Sir Joseph listened attentively, asking the occasional question, but would not commit himself either way. The only positive thing that came out of the discussion was agreement for me to hold another screening with an invited audience, including as many friends as Sir Joseph wished to include. If at the end of that screening the majority opinion sided with Peter King, I would accept that verdict. If on the other hand my faith in the film proved justified, I would be entitled to a proper release on the EMI circuit. I left at midnight even more convinced that if I was to fight I would have to fight alone.

I started to plan, booking the private cinema in Warwick Square, and prepared my own guest list which included a lot of young people together with Alexander Walker, Roger Machell, Lionel and Eileen Jeffries, Dickie and Sheila Attenborough and Roger Cook. Bruce Curtis gathered together his own group and on the night Sir Joseph, William Cavendish, Bernie and Carole Delfont, Nat Cohen and Robert Webster (Goodlatte's son-in-law) together with a number of strangers were also present in a representative audience that totalled around fifty. Nanette was too emotionally involved to face it and stayed at home.

This screening proved to be a total success, the young people present being visibly affected, many in tears as the final credits rolled. At the conclusion Bernie stood up and made a generous speech, saying that although he could not predict the commercial success of the film, he was proud his company had made it. He also praised my integrity. Sir Joseph, whilst wishing it had had a happy ending, was also fulsome though he confided that after our dinner he had thought, 'Poor old Bryan, perhaps he's lost his touch.' I telephoned Nanette to put her out of her misery and then went with Lionel and Eileen to the White Elephant for a celebration dinner. Alas I celebrated too well and ended the evening drunk and very much the worse for wear.

In view of the initial lack of enthusiasm shown by Messrs Goodlatte, King, Maxwell and others, perhaps I can be allowed to record that the film was a triumph in America, the New York critics calling it 'an eloquent reminder of what great and lasting moviemaking is all about', 'deeply moving', 'a tender and touching revelation', 'a civilised rarity', and adding that I had 'elicited remarkable, poignant performances from Nanette Newman and Malcolm McDowell, with a depth and sincere pathos far surpassing other actors in similar roles'.

When I look back on the term I spent at Elstree, I cannot help thinking how different the outcome could have been. My programme of films, the last ever attempted in this country, returned a handsome profit for a modest outlay. If further finance had been forthcoming, and had successive governments granted us the same concessions they extend to other industries, we would still have a native industry instead of empty or derelict studios. The French do not regard culture as separate from economic, social or foreign policies, and consequently have an enlightened approach towards French cinema. (In 1990 they invested £330 million in 146 feature films; during the same period we made 39 films with domestic investment £44.8 million only.) Here the cinema has been crushed as a part of our national culture. We have had no less than twelve Films Ministers in twelve years, and what have they achieved? Sweet f-all.

A shot I took of Kate Hepburn while we were in Paris for *The Madwoman of Chaillot*.

Explaining a shot to Tatum O'Neal during *International Velvet*.

The Madwoman of Chaillot: Katharine Hepburn in the title role flanked by her co-stars: (Left to right) Oscar Homolka, Nanette Newman, Donald Pleasence, Charles Boyer, Paul Henreid, John Gavin, Yul Brynner, Giulietta Masina, Margaret Leighton, Edith Evans, Claude Dauphin and Richard Chamberlain. Danny Kaye, as the ragpicker, stretches out on the curb outside the cafe in the Chaillot section of Paris.

Eric Portman in character for the role he played in *The Whisperers*. He was such a superb actor.

Tony Hancock during *The Wrong Box*.

A shot I took of my father towards the end of his life.

Dudley Moore clowning on *The Wrong Box*. I thought he enjoyed the film, but in his biography he said it was an unhappy experience for him. Certainly I enjoyed working with him.

Michael Caine and Nanette spooning for *The Wrong Box*. Michael saved Nanette's life during filming when the team of horses drawing one of the Victorian hearses bolted.

Nanette and me arriving for work in the Royal Crescent, Bath, during the location for *The Wrong Box*.

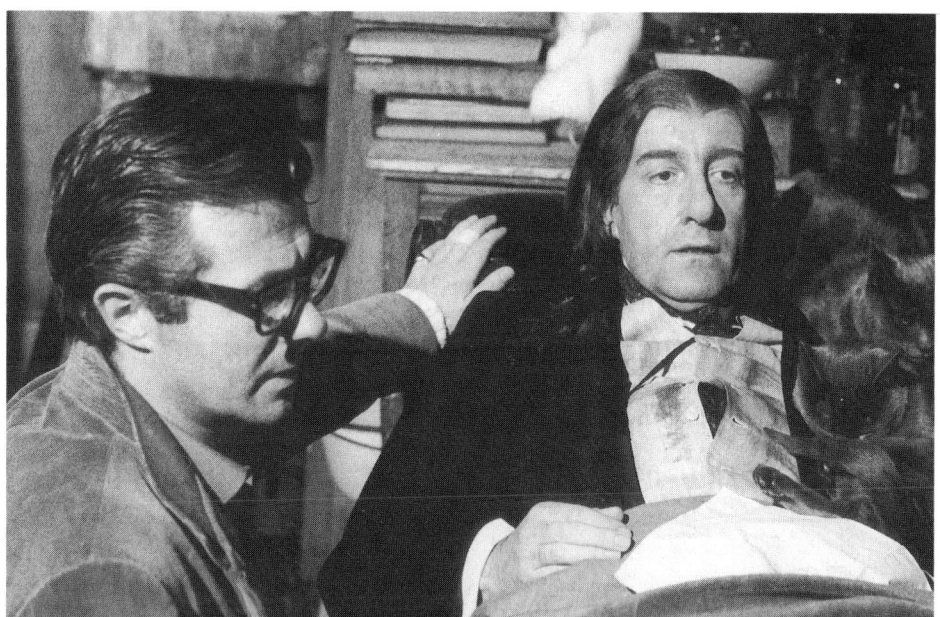

Peter as Doctor Pratt in *The Wrong Box*, a role he delighted in. To the end of his life he always signed letters to me, *Pratt, M.D.* We had over 60 cats on the set and by the end of the week's shoot the smell was indescribable.

Peter and Nanette during the making of *Wrong Arm of The Law*. It was at this time that he proposed marriage to her.

Our youngest daughter Emma and her husband Graham Clempson.

Sarah and her husband the actor John Standing.

Nanette's favourite shot of Sarah as a teenager
which she says epitomises the spirit and freedom of childhood.

Producer Bruce Cohn
Curtis, me and Nanette
during the making of
The Raging Moon.

Malcolm McDowell in
The Raging Moon.

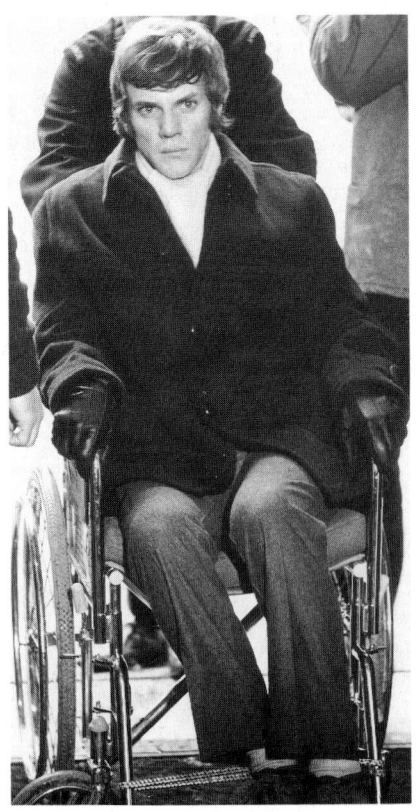

NINETEEN

Nanette once remarked that, given a free hand, I would build bookcases round the bidet. I sometimes think I should form BCA – Book Collectors Anonymous – for wherever I travel I cannot resist the lure of a bookstore, I am drawn to them like a moth to a flame. The ridiculous thing is I own a bookshop and have no need to buy elsewhere, but the compulsion never leaves me and I invariably return from one of our many trips to America with a suitcase full of titles that a few months hence would be available, much cheaper, from my own shelves.

Shortly after we moved into Seven Pines, a bookshop opened in the local parade. It was a modest affair, but I greeted it like a dying man coming across an oasis in the desert and immediately became the best customer, much to the delight of the owner. The shop had been started by an engaging woman called Peggy Pegler, the daughter of a notable publisher, A.S. Frere. She knew a great deal about books but very little about finance and the shop was pitifully under-capitalised. Much to my delight she asked if I would consider taking a half interest. I did not hesitate. Once in a position to take stock I found that the shop was virtually insolvent, but even this did not daunt me. Shortly afterwards Peggy was involved in a horrendous car crash suffering terrible injuries from which she subsequently died. Her husband had been the driver and, although he survived, the trauma caused him to have a nervous breakdown; he became a patient in the local Holloway sanatorium. On Peggy's death the executors asked if I wished to acquire her remaining half. Thus I became the sole, proud owner of a somewhat impoverished bookshop that I have continued to run ever since.

I made many mistakes at first, going through a succession of less than adequate managers until I found a remarkable young man called Patric Glasheen whose love of books equals, if not surpasses, my own. He has been with me ever since, stamping his own personality on the shop, and has become a fixture in the community, as a good bookseller should, knowing all our regular customers by name and willing to go to any lengths to locate their most obscure choices. I have many times heard him faced with enquiries which go something like this: 'Patric, there was a book published sometime last year – I don't know the title, but it had a red cover or, wait a minute, it could have been green, and I think it had a picture of a dog on it. Do you think you could get it for me?' Nine times out of ten Patric somehow dredges his memory and comes up with the right answer. Because my work takes me abroad for long periods, the day-to-day running of the shop is Patric's although when I am at home I spend part of every day behind the counter and always serve on Saturdays. I don't think I have ever lost that sense of excitement which comes from opening a parcel of new books. The smell of fresh print gives me a fix like a glue-sniffer.

I won't pretend that the shop has made my fortune, because it hasn't. The individual bookshop is locked in an endless battle against the large multiples and the only area in which we score is that we can offer a more personal service. The overheads are daunting and because books are still an occasional luxury for the majority of the population, sad to relate, the going is hard. My own shop could not have survived for twenty-two years without constant injections of cash from me, and my other activities subsidise it. The latest blow has been Community Business Charge which was introduced alongside the failed Poll Tax. Overnight our rates were doubled and I have seen many of my neighbouring small businesses go under. Very soon every small shopping area will consist of nothing but estate agents, take-away junk food emporiums and betting shops, which is tragic, environmentally ugly and sad for the communities thus impoverished. When we first moved to Virginia Water we had a variety of splendid little shops sufficient for all our needs. Bookshops in particular are amongst the hardest hit, for they cannot raise the prices of their wares to keep pace with inflation. We can't even *lower* the price of the stock that sticks on our shelves since we are legally constricted by the Net Book Agreement. Margins are minuscule and in order to survive we have to rely on a friendly atmosphere, personal service, and a little madness. Obviously Patric and I are mad with much heart.

Where did it all start, this compulsion to be a purveyor of books? It began as far as I am concerned with a shop called Better Books which used to stand in Charing Cross Road, before the whole of the St Giles area fell prey to the planners and the architectural phallus of Centre Point dominated what had been an annexe to Soho. Better Books was the realised dream of a remarkable friend called Tony Godwin. When he was demobilised from the army in 1945 he sank his entire savings into what was then a derelict second-hand bookshop in a prime position and set about transforming it into a haven for the like-minded. He had a superb eye for the layout of a bookshop and was the first bookseller to commission a well-known artist – Ronald Searle – to illustrate the advertisements he placed in the Sunday papers. I still have Searle's original illustration for my first book, *Truth Lies Sleeping*, which Tony kindly paid for. Like everything else Tony touched, the advertisements had wit and style for he was consistently ahead of his time.

While still in the army myself (I had a much lower demob number than Tony and did not revert to civilian status until late in 1947) I always made a beeline for the shop when home on leave and in the course of time became a firm friend. Tony allowed me to serve in the shop and it was there in the company of Frank Powys and Kenneth Fyfe that I graduated from being an enthusiastic amateur to a semi-professional. Ken was a bespectacled, stooped and prematurely aged young man who lived entirely for books. In personality he was identical to my Patric, possessed of a remarkable memory and steeped in knowledge. It was he who introduced me to authors I had never heard of – John O'Hara, Horace McCoy, dos Passos – guiding my immature taste without condescension.

I remember those days with enormous affection. None of us had much money, I was still a struggling actor, and Tony had to plough every penny he earned back into the shop. We shared meals in a cheap little Italian restaurant in Old Compton Street and it was there I met some of the minor literary figures of the day: Gerald Kersh, Paul Capon, the dandyish J. Maclaren Ross with his silver-topped cane and black cape who held court round our table while we drank cup after cup of bitter coffee. Minor they might have been in the public eye, and now all but forgotten, but to me they were published authors, set apart from ordinary mortals. Sometimes the Olympian figure of Sir Osbert Sitwell would appear in the shop. He had just written the first volume of his autobiography which I immediately bought and consumed at a sitting, just as I devoured Durrell's *Alexandria Quartet* and the still-banned Henry Miller, pirate copies of which were always available under the counter. Today, with so much hard-core pornography available in paperback, it is odd to recall that in those days even such a mild example as *The Well of Loneliness* was considered capable of corrupting anybody bold enough to read it. And this after the obscenity of Hiroshima!

Perhaps, in retrospect, my most notable companion from those days was the young Paul Hamlyn. I remember he used to pay Tony regular visits and cart away all the remainders. According to legend he then sold these from a barrow outside Selfridges, a humble, and I trust not apocryphal, beginning to his later meteoric career which transformed the publishing world and still continues to introduce much-needed innovations. We were a strange trio gathered together in Tony's dank cellar which served as his office and stock room, all three possessed of individual visions. Tony was also a frustrated novelist like me, returning home after a long day to churn out page after turgid page of unpublishable prose. As a friend I was required to read his efforts but never had the heart to tell him that he had no talent. Eventually he gave up the struggle, moved on from Better

Books to join first Weidenfeld and Nicolson, then progressed to Managing Director of Penguin, where he introduced illustrated jackets, eventually emigrating to New York to launch his own imprint and where, tragically, he died from an asthma attack. But the era when he ran Better Books, pointing the way that many others have since followed, remains a shining memory for me.

Better Books remains a landmark in my early life for another reason. It was there that the loss of my virginity originated. After completing my initial training I had been posted to the Intelligence Corps and was enjoying my first weekend pass after escaping from my baptism as an infantryman of No. 5 Platoon 'A' Company in Warley Barracks, Brentwood. There, I had been instructed in the noble art of war, *circa* 1914, encouraged to charge with a bayonet to cries of: 'Get behind it, you useless twot, poke it around until his guts fall out. Don't stick it in like you would a woman. You're trying to kill the bleeder, not fuck him!' Over the previous two months the copulative verb had been casually applied to every activity known to man. Indeed it acquired an almost poetic rhythm in the mouths of my fellow unfortunates. 'Pass the fucking HP sauce and get your fucking laughing gear round this fucking piece of horsemeat, or else fucking hand it to me, you dainty fucker,' was a typical mealtime exchange. Or else, during one of the lectures intended to give the British Army of that day a semblance of culture, we would be treated to such gems as: 'This morning you useless fuckers are going to be told about Keats, so sit up fucking straight and pay attention, because I don't suppose any of you know what a fucking keat is.'

Such consistent exposure to the grand all-purpose verb must have triggered a sublimated desire because my last act before leaving Warley had been to indent for a free ration of contraceptives. I viewed them with a certain amount of suspicion because according to the old lags they had been left over from the Boer War. The elderly lance-corporal in charge of the prophylactic station must have been a humorist because he handed me four dozen. At that stage in my non-existent sexual career they seemed destined to last me to my grave. I filled one with water to test their efficiency and packed the rest with hope.

Shaven of head, resplendent in my best battledress, regulation cap at the correct angle, fondly imagining that I looked like an 8th Army veteran, I set out for my first taste of freedom in many weeks. It was a Saturday afternoon, I remember, when I arrived in London and made straight for Better Books for I was parched for the sight and smell of new books. (Reading was considered a suspect and sissy occupation in Warley Barracks.) There Ken Fyfe introduced me to a friend of his, a young woman some ten years older than me. I will call her Alice, though that was not her name. She had a voluptuous figure and a mass of auburn hair and, amazingly, seemed to be immediately attracted to me. At that point in my retarded development I carried with me a Charles Morganesque view of the perfect woman, a rosy picture of love pure and undefiled that would one day be mine to claim. Apart from the fantasies inspired by the tattered copy of *No Orchids for Miss Blandish* passed around at school, my knowledge of the feminine mystique was virtually nil. So when the delicious Alice suggested I take her to tea I detected no innuendo. Indeed, at that point I was more concerned not to queer Ken's pitch, since I assumed he had prior territorial rights. As we left, I whispered to him, 'Is it okay by you?' 'Absolutely,' he replied. 'And if you want to use my flat, go ahead.' Greater love hath no bookseller, I thought, as I conducted Alice to a nearby Express Dairy. There over a cup of tea and a wartime rock cake she propositioned me without further ado. 'I'm very lonely,' she said, 'will you come to bed with me? I want you to make love to me.' The four dozen contraceptives danced before my glazed eyes like rubber Tiller Girls. I managed to maintain an iota of *sang froid*. She then told me that she was married but hadn't seen her Merchant Navy husband for over two years, so in the space of a few minutes I was not only potential lover but also that most despicable of individuals, a wartime adulterer. It was heady stuff, but as she gripped my hand across the table all scruples vanished. What she neglected to tell me was that she had recently undergone an operation for appendicitis.

I remembered Ken's offer of his flat since I did not relish the added complication of searching out a seedy hotel, and the thought of deceiving her husband in the marital bed was too appalling to contemplate. So Ken's flat it was and, suitably armed with an abundance of the necessary equipment supplied by the British Army, soldiers for the use of, I set out for the great unknown.

Which brings me to the critical aspect of dear Alice's post-operative condition. This was to have a profound effect on my future well-being. It has to be understood that until this point I had never seen a completely nude woman. I had viewed artistic photographs in which all traces of pubic hair had been meticulously airbrushed out, so when Alice first revealed herself to me in all her naked glory my first impression was that a photographer had been to work on her. Only then did it occur to me that she had been shaved for surgery and that, like the razor ads, she had been left with a five o'clock shadow. I registered her appendicitis scar which shone like a smear of lipstick on her white abdomen; it had been crudely stitched and filled me with alarm because it looked insecure. Such was my ignorance about what was to come that I wondered whether the pending exertions would burst the the stitches. I had a vision of myself lying on top of a corpse and the term *in flagrante delicto* assumed a new dimension. These and other morbid thoughts tended to dampen my ardour and I searched for a plausible, eleventh-hour get-out.

I can't remember my exact words, but it went something like this: 'Look, don't take this the wrong way, but, having thought it over very carefully, it would be a terrible betrayal of your brave husband for us to go through with this.'

But Alice was not to be thwarted. Alice was a tiger burning brightly in the night. 'If you don't do it,' she said sweetly, advancing on me, 'I shall scream the place down. I shall tear down the blackout and switch on all the lights and when the air raid wardens arrive I shall say you were trying to rape me. You know what they do to soldiers who rape innocent women?'

I didn't, but I could guess. Thus the reluctant virgin was finally initiated into the second oldest mystery. It was a long night, a night of revelations. I can't say that I found the position ludicrous or the pleasure momentary for Alice was out to take a crack at the title, and there was more than one position and repeated pleasures. Since I had nothing to compare it with, I found the experience both exhilarating and alarming – none of Charles Morgan's heroines behaved with such abandon or uttered such crude commands to their lovers. In short, I was not merely seduced, I was obliterated.

It wasn't until the following morning that I realised that the Song of Solomon had variations. Alice's belly had not been like a mound of wheat, but rather a field of stubble. During the course of the, to me, extraordinary night this had produced what I can only describe as an alarming clinical reaction to my penis. Like all soldiers I had been compelled to attend various graphic lectures on the dangers of venereal diseases. A limited knowledge was certainly a dangerous thing, for as I examined my changed and ravaged body various snippets of information resurfaced. Syphilis, I recalled, could be identified by (a) loss of hair – Alice had ripped out a few locks in her moments of ecstasy (b) a rash around what, in my case, could no longer be called my 'private' parts – Alice's pubic-grater had ensured that condition (c) headache and general malaise – both of which were present. I convinced myself I was already in the tertiary stage and all that lay ahead was general paralysis of the insane. In the space of a few tumbled hours, I thought, your mother has lost her only son, the Intelligence Corps has been deprived of a future secret agent and the British theatre denied a great actor – there was no room for modesty at the end of one's life.

Aware that failure to report such a condition was a probable court martial offence, I duly took myself off to Wellington Barracks and joined the queue outside the M.O.'s office. In the fullness of time I stood to attention on my diseased legs before an elderly, chain-smoking major in the Medical Corps.

'Name, rank and number,' he said without looking up and with an inch of ash about to fall.

I gave them.

'What's wrong with you?'

'Syphilis, sir.'

'Drop your trousers.'

After balancing his cigarette on the rim of a saucer, he picked up a wooden school ruler and used it to lift my penis then rock it from side to side.

'That painful?'

'Bearable, sir.'

'You're lucky it didn't drop off. Was she a pro?'

'Sir?'

'Tart, man, tart. Was she a tart or your girlfriend?'

'More a woman friend, sir.'

He went back behind his desk and took a nicotine fix.

'Right. Give me the details. When did you have contact?'

'Last night, sir.'

He looked at me for the first time, '*Last night?*' The ash finally dropped.

'Yes, sir.'

'What's your game, soldier?'

'Sir?'

'Fuck off.'

This did not seem to be a considered medical opinion. 'But, sir, have I got it, sir?'

'I'll tell you what you've got, soldier. You've got a bloody nerve, that's what you've got. Now get out or I'll put you on a fizzer.'

Over the next few months I swore off women and kept a careful check on my health; every day I remained alive was a bonus. By then I was in the Isle of Anglesey, training to be a member of Field Security, and being propositioned by a gay padre. Sex, it increasingly appeared, was turning out to be a very complicated matter.

TWENTY

At the midway point during the French revolution of 1968 I wrote in my journal: 'Kate Hepburn is a combination of Jekyll and Hyde, Mary Poppins, Lady Hester Stanhope with perhaps a touch of Gandhi and Falstaff thrown in.'

At that time she and I were to all intents the sole inhabitants of the Hotel Plaza Athénée, Paris. Except for the very curious or foolhardy (the CRS were no respecters of nationality when making a baton charge) most of the tourists had fled. We were numbered amongst the foolhardy, trapped as we were in the middle of making *The Madwoman of Chaillot*. There was real danger on the streets such as I remembered from wartime riots in Cairo, especially during the critical few days when de Gaulle disappeared to make the trade with his generals. The students and the unions had formed an uneasy alliance without defining their mutual ultimate aims, and this added to the chaos. Like everything else connected with that particular film, there was an element of unreality, of things happening by pure chance. There was always a film within the film.

The genesis of my involvement with *La Folle* had a strange twist to it. Early in January 1968 we entertained Cicely Courtneidge to dinner at Seven Pines. She came accompanied by Patric Walker, the well-known astrologer. Although I have never conducted my life according to the behaviour of the stars in the firmament, during the course of the evening I enquired what the future held for me. Patric was alarmingly concise. After he had ascertained my birth date he said, without hesitation, 'You will shortly be required to live abroad for a long period, and you will be making the biggest film you have ever tackled. It will start on February fourteenth.' I listened attentively but was too polite to tell him that his prediction was hopelessly wrong. I was committed to direct Iris Murdoch's *A Severed Head* in England from a fine screenplay by Freddie Raphael, plans for which were far advanced.

Later that same month, on 26 January to be precise, my guest book for that day contains the entry 'Help!' over two signatures – Ely Landau and Henry Weinstein, at that point complete strangers. They arrived unannounced at my front door, two desperate roly-poly men of enormous girth, to inform me that they were the producers of *The Madwoman of Chaillot* and were in dire straits: the original director, John Huston, had walked out following irreconcilable 'artistic differences'. Ely told me he was locked into a start date for his expensive all-star cast that could not be shifted. In addition he was constricted by contract to giving Katharine Hepburn, his principal star, director approval. I explained that, sadly, I was not available because of my prior involvement with *A Severed Head*. 'We'll buy out your contract,' was Landau's immediate response. As it happens that wasn't necessary; Elliot Kastner, the producer of *A Severed Head*, generously agreed to release me.

I stepped into the minefield for one reason only: the opportunity – possibly the only one I would ever have – to work with Katharine Hepburn. The following morning I flew to Marseilles and thence by car to Arles where Kate was finishing *The Lion in Winter* directed by my ex-editor Tony Harvey. Her long-time lover Spencer Tracy had died but a few months previously and, typically, she had thrown herself into a punishing schedule which included the taming of Peter O'Toole. 'Make her like you,' Landau said on our journey into the unknown, 'you're my only hope. But be strong. Don't let her think she can walk right over you. She's a formidable lady and right now feeling a little sore that Huston took a walk. You've got to charm her.'

Kate and I were introduced in her small hotel room. She greeted me dressed as a ravishingly attractive member of the

French Foreign Legion, or so it seemed to my dazzled eyes, for she was wearing an old shirt of Spencer's, a kepi at a jaunty angle on her tousled head, no make-up and baggy trousers complete with a tear in the seat.

Her room was at the top of a flight of stairs down which, I had been immediately told by Tony Harvey, she had recently tumbled Mr O'Toole during one of his more exuberant moods. This information did not add to my composure.

Like a skilled interrogator she steered me into talking too much about myself, extracting those salient bits of information about my career and attitudes towards work that would enable her to decide whether I was the right choice. Later I realised I had been totally seduced by a lady whose true mission in life should have been to run the United Nations. On that extraordinary winter morning it seemed I had made the long journey for one reason only: to fall in love.

After three hours and a hilarious lunch, had she suggested it, I would have jumped from her third-storey window. Apparently she liked me, for I was given her seal of approval and set out on another long car journey along the coast to Nice. There I was installed in the Negresco Hotel, occupying a suite that would have served as a *fin de siècle* brothel complete with a fur counterpane on the bed. It was a room to go mad in and indeed over the next two weeks I often teetered on the brink.

The Studios de la Victorine at Nice, one of the oldest studios in the business, can be seen from the air as the jets make their final approach and therein lies its major disadvantage. In 1968 it resembled a quaint village that had seen better days. The executive offices were housed in a wedding-cake-pink villa surrounded by a jumble of assorted buildings and stages, some modern, some on the verge of collapse. There was a café where one ate under grape vines and the permanent staff quaffed litres of rough red wine, noisy as a flock of starlings. Beyond them the set and empty swimming pool, constructed for *The Comedians* starring Taylor and Burton, still stood on the back-lot, and were being taken over by undergrowth spotted with red poppies. Lizards made tiny, darting movements, like contestants in *Come*

Dancing, across the cracked concrete of the pool and the air was filled with the sound of cicadas. I saw it all through a haze, my brain grappling with a hundred problems.

The set for *The Madwoman* was still under construction, for work had been halted until Huston's replacement had been chosen. I arrived to find a bewildered skeleton crew of Huston's choice and my immediate task was to establish whether they were prepared to accept me. There was no time for polite finesse, all indecisions had to be final. The Art Director and First Assistant felt their first loyalty was to Huston and departed. I was more than happy that Claude Renoir, the cinematographer, was content to stay on, and put in urgent calls for Ray Simm and my usual sound crew to catch the first plane and begin sorting out the mess. Huston had okayed the location for the main set during the off-peak tourist season when take-offs and landings at Nice airport were minimal, but the runway was so close that one could almost recognise the pilots and the Air France jet in common use at that time was the Caravelle, one of the noisiest flying. This was to prove our major time-waster when shooting began.

Huston had also allowed the set to be built at the wrong angle and as Claude Renoir quickly pointed out this meant he would have to use an enormous amount of artificial light to compensate against the fierce sun and achieve the necessary colour balance. The budget did not permit a turnaround; I was stuck with the existing layout and could only hope that Ray could galvanise the French construction crew into action and, with his own adjustments, finish it by the deadline. The reason for the panic was that in order to meet his budget Landau was working to very tight individual contracts with his expensive all-star cast. If any of them did not start and complete their roles on time they could evoke serious overage money. Artists such as Yul Brynner, Danny Kaye, Charles Boyer, Margaret Leighton, Giulietta Masina (Fellini's wife), Donald Pleasence, John Gavin, Oscar Homolka, Paul Henreid, Fernand Gravet et al. did not come cheaply. For the most part they were an unknown quantity to me, though naturally I knew their work and their worth.

Having left various instructions I took off again for Paris, there to audition and engage a number of French actors for the secondary roles. I also made the acquaintance of the distinguished but distressed old costume designer chosen by Huston. He showed me his sketches between bouts of crying. They seemed to be designs for a pack of playing cards, jacks, queens and kings dressed as for a production of *Alice in Wonderland*. I had all the fantasy I could cope with at that moment and he was paid off and departed, still crying, though mostly I suspect from relief. His successor, chosen without hesitation, was a sensuous French lady called Rosie de LaMarr who had a quick grasp of what was needed in the time left to us. She never gave me cause to regret my choice, and remained a delightful ally and companion throughout the long and often difficult schedule. What I do regret, with hindsight, is that the situation did not allow me time to form an overall conception of my own. Had I had this luxury I would have jettisoned all of Huston's ideas and taken an entirely different route. Certainly, had I known Kate better, I would have asked her to appear in her everyday clothes – they were certainly eccentric enough for the role she was playing.

As it was I inherited a screenplay by Edward Anhalt who had elected to update Giraudoux's wartime play, bringing in a sub-plot about an atomic bomb which sat uneasily on top of the original, slender fantasy. Later, when the strikes and riots began, Landau and Weinstein insisted I include a new sequence, showing Dame Edith and Richard Chamberlain caught up in a student demonstration. It was a further mistake for us to try and update a creaky period piece that Anhalt had already tampered with. A certain madness of the times infected us all, typified by the Belgian First Assistant who arrived every morning on a motor-cycle with his large Alsatian dog riding pillion, complete with crash helmet.

The only thing I inherited with joy from Huston was a villa on Cap Ferrat, with its own private beach and dock, which was the most luxurious house we had ever occupied. It came complete with an engaging French couple, Anne-Marie and Gabriel, plus the owner's vicious parrot. Our bedroom was high in a circular tower and overlooked the bay towards Villefranche. Although

Nanette and I subsequently discovered that we were keeping a legion of Anne-Marie's relatives, she and Gabriel could be forgiven everything for their superb cooking. Every time I came home I would be greeted at the door with a glass of freshly squeezed orange juice and the villa would be permeated with the smell of garlic and herbs as Anne-Marie prepared a succulent dish of local fish and her speciality *pommes frites* that were worth killing for. Our grocery bills were astronomical but we ate like kings. Had I been really smart I would have bought the villa, for it was offered to me at an affordable price. The last time it changed hands I am told that it fetched $4,000,000. The story of my life.

So the stage was set for a remarkable experience. I have already described how I wangled my old friend George Hillsden into the cast, now I recruited Gerald Sim, another founder member of my film repertory company, to play the role of Yul Brynner's secretary. Advance reports of Yul were not encouraging; he was said to be extremely difficult and reluctant to take direction. He was much maligned, for he proved to be one of the nicest and most stylish actors I have ever worked with. He had completed his role by the time the riots took hold and was safely back in Switzerland. By then we were virtually isolated. All commercial flights from Nice had ceased, petrol was unobtainable and basic foods had to be bought on a quickly established black market. France was in the grip of a general strike and eventually our film was the only one still shooting. Union officials travelled to coerce our own French crew and finally a deputation came to me and with the utmost politeness confessed they had no alternative than to join the strike. In the best traditions of French farce they went on to tell me that they had arrived at what they hoped would be an acceptable compromise: they said they intended to honour the union's strike call, but only striking during their lunch break. This enchanting solution might well have come from Giraudoux's pen, but it was, alas, doomed to be challenged. More union officials arrived and the film was finally brought to a standstill.

It was impossible to phone out of France although incoming calls were okay and through this period Yul rang us twice daily to check whether Nanette and the children were safe. 'You'll have to take your chances,' he said to me, 'but if it gets too dangerous I have a small private plane standing by night and day. I promise I'll get Nanette and the kids out to safety.' Now to make that offer once is commendable, but to make it twice a day every day was the act of a real friend. Others said he was arrogant, but he was never arrogant with me and we remained friends until his death.

Yul travelled first-class through life; he drank the best wines, ate the best food and wore totally individual clothes and jewellery. A more than generous host, his homes always reflected his life-style – elegance and comfort. I first saw him on stage with Gertie Lawrence in the original performance of *The King and I* way back in the Fifties. While we were together in Nice he confided, that, although that first attempt at the role had made him a star, he had never been satisfied. 'Now I'm old enough to play it properly,' he said. Play it he did, though racked with constant pain; pain that necessitated sleeping on a custom-made surgical bed; pain that needed powerful drugs before he could get on stage. He was consumed with the role as some men are consumed and destroyed by a love affair, and he died playing it to the hilt. It remains one of the most staggering theatrical performances I ever witnessed and his friendship meant a great deal to me. You have to take people as you find them and I never found him wanting.

Charles Boyer, whom I had never met before, was one of the great heroes of my early cinema-going days. He also proved to be a consummate, malleable actor, a true gentleman possessed of the most exquisite manners. His personal life had harboured tragedy. Despite his reputation as the great screen lover he was happily married, but his only son had committed suicide on his twenty-first birthday. As a consequence his wife cut herself off from everything and became a sad recluse. Three days after she died, Charles took his own life. I shall always remember him as an urbane, witty man, never in a bad mood, with infinite charm and with an accent that had given rise to a thousand impersonations, but which remained inimitably his own.

It was such an extraordinary cast to direct. Sometimes looking through the camera I could not believe my luck. Going to the set every day was pure joy. One drove through near-deserted streets in that early morning sunlight peculiar to the South of France. There would be the scent of herbs and lavender, salt water and fresh bread. Along the sea front the beaches were being raked smooth, the sea itself like mirror glass, now and then gently disturbed by small fishing boats returning to Antibes with their catch. At the studio, strong hot coffee would be waiting in the make-up rooms, the air thick with Gauloise smoke as the actors prepared. Outside on the huge set the crew and extras were assembled, the prop men watering the flowers, the electricians trundling the huge arc lamps into position through groups of gossiping extras. There was such a feeling of gaiety always, it was all so totally different from anything I had encountered before.

In the evenings the same atmosphere prevailed amongst us. We often gathered together for dinner at the Voile d'Or, shamelessly taking over the entire restaurant, a rowdy lot like children released from school after exams. Maggie Leighton, then married to Michael Wilding, would suddenly burst into an operatic aria when in her cups; Danny Kaye would invade the kitchen to cook lemon chiffon pies; Giulietta produced amazing pasta and carried on involved conversations in unintelligible English which only Mike Wilding professed to understand.

I had cast Nanette in the small role of the waitress at the café and the first time she went before the camera I went and kissed her after I had a print. There was a splendid French actor playing a waiter with her and she told me that following my embrace he had taken her to one side and whispered: 'He likes you. Play your cards right and I think you could be on to a good thing.' She didn't have the heart to tell him she was already sleeping with the director.

The first actor I worked with was Paul Henreid. He was playing a corrupt French General. We shot the opening sequence in the empty, baroque Hotel Ruhl which was shortly to be demolished. I had devised a complicated tracking shot, following

Paul from the exterior of the building into a large hall where a detachment of troops was waiting to be addressed by him. Paul then had to mount a podium and deliver a long speech. He has since given his own account of what followed in his autobiography, but I fear that the passage of time eroded his memory. What really happened was he fluffed his lines take after take. Having been an actor myself I knew how bloody lonely it is with the cold eye of the camera staring at you, especially on the first day when you are thrown in at the deep end. I thought I was patience itself. I never embarrassed him, I found technical excuses for going again and again, I changed the camera angle several times to give him a breather but it was a wearisome début for both of us and when, at the end of the afternoon, he finally managed a complete take I felt totally drained.

When I got back to Cap Ferrat the experience still troubled me. I felt convinced that he must be sitting alone in his hotel room in a state of anguish: I would have been if the roles had been reversed. So I rang him and suggested Nanette and I took him out for dinner. Over dinner, as gently as I could, I said, 'Look we all have off days. It doesn't matter, the audience never sees the numbers on the clapper board. All that matters is that you got it in the end. Don't feel upset about it.'

He looked at me in amazement. 'Why would I be upset? I'm not in the least upset. Film's cheap.'

Any sympathy I had brought to the table disappeared at that point. Fuck it, I thought, why did I bother to drive all this way at the end of an exhausting day? The conceited bastard hasn't got the grace to apologise. Mr Henreid gave an entirely different slant to the episode in his memoirs. According to him I did not know what I wanted and that after the first day he had no respect for me as a director. Alone out of that large and distinguished cast he was the only one who introduced a sour note and remained an outsider. Charm is not confined to the skill of lighting two cigarettes at once for Bette Davis.

The other actor who surprised me in a different way was Danny Kaye. Like many others of my generation I had been transfixed by his early screen appearances and worshipped at his one-man Palladium appearances when he took London by storm. I was totally unprepared for his lack of confidence. Early on in the film he came to me and asked to be released – would I somehow talk to Ely and explain that he could not go through with it. I talked him out of such a drastic course, using every flattery I could think of to make him reconsider. In the end I succeeded and he stayed, but perhaps I did not ultimately do him a favour for his performance was heavily criticised when the film came out. I thought he acquitted himself with distinction, but critics often seem peeved when their past favourites forsake the familiar mould. In *Madwoman* they were presented with a sombre Danny Kaye, denuded of all his zany gestures and quirks of speech. That was what Giraudoux's character demanded and he played the role honestly. I always regret that I was not able to give him the swan-song he longed for. After *Madwoman* he more or less retired from films and devoted the rest of his life to Unicef, piloting his own plane all over the world raising funds for deprived children.

Recent biographies have contended that he was a closet gay who conducted a long affair with Laurence Olivier. Since neither gentleman can now answer for himself, I must say that, from my close knowledge of them, I strongly doubt the veracity of such a claim. They may have jokingly 'camped it up' when together but there is slim evidence to support a love affair and I suspect that, following recent trends in the lower echelons of show-business biography, the suggestion was introduced to attract attention and increase sales. Christopher Plummer and I also 'camp it up' so doubtless when we have both fallen off the perch a similar story will surface.

Kate was Kate. 'It's tough being a living legend,' she said. She suffered a great deal from the heat, drank pints of iced water and had to get out of her costume between takes. I discovered she had a sweet tooth, and every afternoon sent her driver into Nice to buy large quantities of orange peel dipped in rich, dark chocolate. ('When I die they should have me embalmed in Bournville.') She also insisted on ordering and serving my lunch every day. 'Your husband is as quirky as Spencer,' she used to tell

Nanette. 'I know exactly how to deal with him.' Nanette happily bowed to such superior knowledge.

Kate had rented a house on Cap d'Antibes which she rapidly transformed, buying pieces of furniture and rugs to make it seem more like her New England home. She was up early every morning for her swim and her first entrance on the set always caused a flurry; Yul had given her a bicycle and she invariably did a circuit of our mock Parisian square, a white scarf tied around the inevitable kepi, tattered sneakers on her feet and the arse of her trousers hanging out. Her off-screen appearance was of supreme indifference to her, but in professional matters her eagle eye spotted anything out of keeping. She was the den mother to all the young players, a sort of Pied Piper they followed with slavish devotion. She never came to see the dailies. 'Jesus! After all these years I know how I look, why would I want to remind myself?' I took this as a sign that she trusted me. The only days we had off were Sundays and often we would picnic at Kate's villa, or else take lunch at the Colombe d'Or in St Paul de Vence, surely one of the most elegant restaurants in the world. To our two young daughters Kate was certainly Mary Poppins; anybody who bought chocolates every day and passed them around was not your average adult. On one occasion she took them both to the palace at Monaco and finding that her old friend, Princess Grace, was not at home, scaled the walls rather than disappoint them. I don't think they ever thought of her as a famous film star, she was just a gloriously unpredictable figure who broke all the rules and made everything fun.

The filming proceeded very smoothly considering the size of the cast and the logistics involved. The only thing that slowed me down was the incessant noise of aircraft, often so loud that the cast could not hear me shout 'Action' and threw Bill Daniels and Gus Lloyd, my sound crew, into despair. As the tourist season hotted up landings and take-offs occurred every ten minutes or so and we would sometimes lose two hours a day from the delays. I instigated an early-warning system, positioning one of the assistants on a high vantage point, where he could see the runway and flag us when it was clear of aircraft. The constant stops and starts were murder for the actors, for acting for films is all about keeping your energy level up – the surgical eye of the camera is quick to detect momentary lapses of concentration. Time after time I had to abort a good take. Equally, Claude Renoir's appraisal of the set had been correct. By mid-afternoon when the sun had moved round he had great difficulty obtaining a balance of light no matter how he repositioned his arcs. To overcome the problem great gauze 'scrims' had to be erected because otherwise the actors could not keep their eyes open against the glare. We just had to be patient and sweat it out, though I was ever conscious that I had an increasingly anxious producer looking over my shoulder as the clock ticked away his money.

Halfway through the shooting period the Greek actress, Irene Papas, playing one of the four madwomen, came to me and confessed that she was deeply unhappy and felt it would be better for all concerned if she was released from her role. I felt desperately sorry for her, but I knew that she found the language difficult, especially since she was up against Kate and Margaret Leighton who both had highly individual deliveries. So we exchanged sad farewells.

Giulietta on the other hand learned her lines parrot fashion, but gave them such enchanting, if unusual, emphasis that it worked. I confess that I was somewhat thrown by the arrival of her husband, the great Fellini, who sat on the set while I was directing Giulietta. He wore an enormous black hat, I remember, said nothing, but stared relentlessly.

Finding a replacement for Irene threw us all for a loop. By now the demonstrations and strikes were sweeping the country and growing ever more ominous. Taking a chance, and with Ely's blessing, I put in a call to Dame Edith. I realised that there was no point in being other than totally frank with her, since I could hardly pretend that she was my original choice for the role. I put the position to her and Edith didn't hesitate. 'Sounds fun,' she said, 'of course I'll come.' She was then in her eighty-first year. Since there were no direct flights to Nice, the only route was to come via Milan then take the long car journey into France. She arrived dressed in a pale lemon outfit by Norman Hartnell, looking for all the world as though she was about to step into the Royal Enclosure at Ascot. The production had been closed down until Edith arrived and I felt it only politic to immediately introduce her to Kate. 'I guess I'll be taking a back seat now that your steady girlfriend's arriving,' Kate had remarked, firing a warning shot over my bows. They met for the first time on the veranda of Kate's house. I was content to be an unobtrusive witness to this meeting of gladiators. Over iced tea they conversed about Ruth Gordon and other mutual friends, then Kate asked, 'Where're you staying, Edith?'

'They've put me in a hotel.'

'Hotels are a bore,' Kate said emphatically. 'Nothing worse than staring at four hotel walls when you've done a hard day's work. Why don't you treat this place as your own? If you want somewhere quiet to study your lines, Phyllis will hear them for you.' (Phyllis Woburn was Kate's unflappable long-time companion.) 'This is open house with only one house rule. I like to go to bed early because I get up early, so I'm usually in bed by half past seven. Apart from that you're welcome to come and go as you please.'

There was a long, beautifully timed pause while Edith looked out across the bay. 'That's very generous of you,' Edith said. Then another shorter pause. 'But what do people do who *don't* go to bed at half past seven?' Edith enjoyed the freedom that filming allowed, having spent the greater part of her disciplined life chained to the strict routine of the theatre. Now, in France, determined to enjoy herself, she became a night bird and liked to have dinner with the cast and even, on one occasion, sample a disco.

It was difficult to decide what these two amazing creatures really made of each other, but side by side on the screen they sparked their own electricity. To Kate life was a continuous adventure, to Edith life was 'a lark' and the unexpected bonus of spending a few months on the Riviera something she relished. Unlike Kate, much of her declining years had been spent alone in that vast Elizabethan manor house in Kent and although she kept up with friends by correspondence, few except me came to visit her. She would never admit that she was lonely, just as she would never admit that age had slowed her down.

It so happend that both Edith and Kate were up for Academy Awards that year. For Kate it was the second year in succession, and Edith had been nominated for her performance in my own film *The Whisperers*. The morning after the awards I stepped out of my car to be greeted by an excited First Assistant. 'She won,' he shouted. 'Great!' I said and was walking away when I stopped and turned back. 'Which one?' I asked.

'Kate.'

To her credit Kate's first call that morning was to Edith. 'You should have had it,' she said. 'They only gave it to me out of sentimentality.'

Because of the various delays Claude Renoir had to leave the film to honour his next commitment. Cameramen of his skill do not often grow on trees and if they do they are usually fully employed. It was a considerable blow with the film only two-thirds finished. I phoned Burney Guffey in Los Angeles on the off chance. Since our *King Rat* days his career had happily received a deserved fillip and he had just won an Academy Award for *Bonnie and Clyde*. As with Edith I was not offering him a plum job, since few cameramen could be expected to relish taking over from a distinguished colleague. I explained my dilemma and he told me that, because of his recent award, he was once again in great demand. 'But I'll catch the next plane,' he said. 'I owe you one. When you took me for *King Rat* I couldn't get myself arrested.' He was as good as his word, arrived forty-eight hours later and went straight to work. It was an act of friendship I shall never forget.

Shortly after Burney took over we completed the Nice sequences and shifted to Paris where I had several long sequences to shoot, notably in and around the Palais de Chaillot. I also needed to find the madwoman's house for the opening of the film and miraculously I struck gold. I chanced upon a derelict house sandwiched between two modern highrise buildings on the Rue Scheffer. It was partially obscured from the road by a high wall daubed with obscene graffiti directed at de Gaulle. I walked over to a garage on the opposite side and enquired as to the ownership of the house. The proprietor made an extravagant gesture of despair. 'It belongs to a madwoman,' he said. 'The old fool refuses to sell.' Then he reconsidered and pointed to the skyscrapers dwarfing the house. 'But maybe she's not so mad at that. Maybe she's holding out for more money.'

I could hardly believe my good fortune. Ray Simm made urgent enquiries and somehow tracked down the eccentric owner. Using powers of persuasion known only to film art directors, he obtained limited permission for us to shoot in the house and overgrown garden. It was perfect, a house preserved in aspic evoking shades of Miss Haversham. Kate immediately fell in love with it and more or less moved in, insisting that she get made up in one of the empty bedrooms, amidst the bird droppings and debris. As long as it made her happy I didn't argue. Burney Guffey was as thrilled as I was, for the place was seeped in atmosphere and the juxtaposition of the house with the bustle of modern Paris gave us a contrast we could not have found elsewhere.

It was unbearably humid in Paris that week and because of the riots any police co-operation was out of the question – film companies were definitely unwelcome. The logistics of moving our circus around the streets were formidable. When we did get ourselves organised and started to shoot we invariably attracted a crowd, for even in the middle of a revolution the *sans-culottes* of Paris were not to be denied the spectacle of La Hepburn who stopped traffic whenever she appeared. I resorted to diversionary tactics, using a bogus second camera unit on one location while I grabbed the action involving Kate elsewhere.

Looking back I don't know how we got away with some of the shots. We actually dropped explosive charges into the Seine on one occasion, got the take and then made a run for it before the gendarmes arrived. On another occasion I needed to see the general's car drive into Les Invalides. I used a double for Paul Henreid, put him in a black Citroën with a four-star general's insignia flying and surrounded by a posse of outriders and simply drove the convoy straight at the gates. The guard turned out and did the honours as the Citroën swept in with sirens going, did a smart U-turn and drove out again. What officialdom made of that I will never know, but again we lived to tell the tale and the shot was in the can.

On one particular day the call was at the Palais de Chaillot. As a consequence of Kate insisting on getting made up and costumed in the real madwoman's house on the other side of town we were kept waiting and by the time she arrived we had lost the light and filming had to be abandoned.

It was the only occasion when she and I had a slight spat. Dismissing the crew I went back to the Plaza Athenée and was lying in the bath feeling depressed about the episode when the phone rang. It was Kate. 'Listen,' she said with her usual directness, 'It's ridiculous for you and me to quarrel. Come to my room and have a glass of champagne. Let's bury the hatchet.'

We kissed and made up over a bottle of Dom Perignon. 'I've got a great idea,' I said, 'put on some glad rags and I'll take you to dinner.'

'I never go out to a restaurant. The last time I tried it I near fainted from claustrophobia. Besides, I've got nothing to wear.'

I wasn't going to let her off the hook that easily. 'You travel with half a ton of Louis Vuitton luggage,' I said, 'they must contain something other than torn trousers and tennis sneakers.'

'No, it's no good asking me.'

I remained masterful. 'I shall go back to my room, finish changing and then make a reservation.'

'Where?'

'That's my privilege. I'm taking you out and I'm paying. I shall return for you in half an hour. If you're not dressed to kill when I knock on your door our love affair is over.'

'Oh, shoot!' she exclaimed. 'Son of a bitch, what sort of invitation is that?' But she seemed to be weakening.

I drank my champagne and left. Half an hour later I duly presented myself at her door and was confronted by a transformation. No Foreign Legionary greeted me: Kate was dressed in a stunning black outfit with matching accessories.

'I found something,' she said.

I offered my arm and we tripped the light fantastic to L'Hotel, where I had booked a private room. I guess to dine alone in Paris with Katharine Hepburn in the hotel where Oscar Wilde died and the Dolly Sisters once cavorted must rate three stars in anybody's personal *Michelin*.

Where we dined reminded me of the setting for a Victorian seduction, and perhaps that is not so far from the truth, for Kate seduced me all over again that night. We sat in armchairs in front of a blazing fire and lived it up until the early hours in splendid isolation. She was a different Kate, a totally relaxed Kate, who beguiled me with stories of when, fresh from a stage triumph on Broadway, she had stepped off the train to conquer Hollywood. She spoke of her long and loving association with Tracy; of how he died in the kitchen of the house they had shared and how, faithful to her principles, she had stayed away from his funeral in deference to the wife he would never divorce. Relaxed, with no hint of claustrophobia, she exuded femininity, Kate the all-time charmer with the face that photographer John Bryson has said was 'made for Mount Rushmore'. People have often asked me what makes a star. There is no simple answer, but I have my own theory: it is a combination of ambition, energy, a face and a voice that cannot be duplicated, all fused to inherent talent. I sat across from her that memorable night thinking, this is a story to tell my grandchildren. How once in Paris, beneath the barricades while the world above exploded into violence, I dined with one of the most extraordinary women who ever set the screen alight, a lady of infinite variety – perverse, funny, flirty, immensely generous, indomitable, a one-off.

The film was still prey to more dramas. As the weeks slid by without the end in sight, Bernard Guffey also had to leave and Gerry Fisher photographed the last sequences until we marked the final take on the clapper board 4 July, an apt date. We had a riotous end-of-picture party at the Studios de la Victorine, dancing under festooned lime trees, exchanging gifts and letting off fireworks. There is always a sadness when a film comes to an end and the cast and crew with whom one has lived in such intimacy over the months scatter. Some one never sees again.

Perhaps Christmas cards arrive for a few years, but more often the emotional arteries are severed. I kept in touch with Yul until he died; we saw Maggie Leighton and Mike Wilding until they too were gone, and of course Edith always remained close as I have related – but they were the Europeans. Of the others only Kate and Richard Chamberlain keep in touch. Whenever we visit New York we never miss seeing her. At one point when our elder daughter, Sarah, was getting over a broken engagement, Kate had her to stay for a few months, giving her own inimitable advice – 'You can't go through life in a leaky boat, Sarah, dump him!' When Sarah asked whether she should return her engagement ring, Kate's rejoinder was, 'Keep the stone, send him the setting.' She still has a remarkable zest for life, still swims, still plays tennis despite having nearly lost a foot in a car accident, a lady who once she has decided to give you her friendship never takes it back.

I was to remember those long months spent on the *Madwoman* and that feeling years later when, alone in New York, I took myself to see Truffaut's *Day For Night*. He had used my set and it was all there – the Chez Francis Café, the cobbled square where once Kate practised for her Tour de France, the fake Metro entrance, my own office; nothing had changed except I had moved on, we had all moved on and that particular time and the many friends who had shared that time were gone and no longer part of my life. I sat in the cinema and cried.

TWENTY-ONE

I was in Arizona working on this book when Sarah phoned from London to tell me that Graham Greene had died. I cannot claim to have been an intimate friend, though he always treated me as one whenever our paths crossed in the four decades from our first meeting in the Rope Walk at Albany where at one time we were both residents.

Shortly before leaving England I had written to him in the Swiss hospital where he spent his final days and the last letter I had from him mentioned his illness but made light of the gravity of his condition. 'I am in a sort of retirement because of my health,' was how he put it. 'It's simply a matter of patience and injections and blood transfusions and pills!'

Now never again will any of his friends welcome that minuscule signature or have the joy of opening a new book from him. I had a premonition that he was clearing the decks, for in the past year with his own sense of occasion he had called the final collection of short stories *The Last Word* ('sweepings of the bottom drawer') and a few months later published *Reflections*. Both seemed to me to signal that he was getting ready to draw the curtains.

The last time I saw him we said goodbye on the Avenue Pasteur, Antibes, outside his apartment building. As always he might have given strangers the impression that he was an expatriate university don eking out an existence on a small pension, for little about him smacked of success or wealth. Tall, still handsome, slightly stooped, slightly shambly, giving no hint of his world-wide eminence, he nevertheless had an aura about him coupled with an old-world courtesy. In my experience he always had a concern for those in his company, an interest in them that was not put on for the occasion but which you felt was always present.

Nanette and I had just had lunch with him at his customary Chez Felix, where he had picked at a few whitebait but enjoyed his wine ('I always say I eat only to drink') while enchanting Nanette who was meeting him for the first time.

'He was so different from what I had imagined,' she said afterwards. 'I thought he would be intimidating and that I wouldn't have anything to say. You had told me so much about him, and you admire him so much, that I felt I was bound to be disappointed. But he was so gentle, so softly spoken, I just fell in love with him. You said I would, and I did.' Before lunch he had inscribed a limited edition of *The Third Man* to her after serving us both the wrong drinks and chattering about the security measures he now had to take for his safety since a recent break-in. There was something so incongruous about the way he lived; without the view of the old harbour, the apartment might have been in Pinner; there were none of the acquisitions usually associated with fame and wealth. It was the habitat of a writer who had few material wants, but who demanded no distractions while he worked.

During our lunch the topic of Salman Rushdie's continuing dilemma came into the conversation. 'I know what I would do,' Graham said. 'I would let it be known to the authorities that I would appear in public on a certain day, at a certain time and place, so as to invite the threatened assassination. I could not contemplate a lifetime spent in hiding, but at least this way I would ensure that when I was killed, my murderer would be caught.' He appeared deadly serious, just as he was serious when he outlined a story (which he later wrote and published) about the Channel Tunnel. 'Most of the labour is Irish,' he said. 'So what could be easier than to plant the explosive in the wet concrete and wait until the tunnel is open and operating then blow it by remote control?' It was a chilling scenario and I hope that his indisputable knack of anticipating events does not prove true in this instance.

By now completely relaxed in his company, Nanette asked him about his affection for opium and what effect it had. This launched Graham into a series of anecdotes which he obviously relished telling to a new and fascinated audience. I almost expected him to produce a pipe and give a practical demonstration, such was his continuing enthusiasm for the drug. He recounted one story of how, finding himself in a country where opium was banned, he had been taken to a safe house by the local Chief of Police; it was the sort of ironic situation that characterised so much of his writing: corruption mixed with the mundane.

More than any other writer, living or dead, Graham influenced my own efforts, for Nanette is right, I admired him extravagantly and see no reason to conceal the fact. No writer had the ability to excite me more, or cast me down so quickly when I compared my own puny efforts with his mastery. There is no shame in trying to aspire to the best and to me Graham was the best although having seen the scrawled and crossed out words on the yellow legal pads he used I know that he struggled as we all struggle despite the final result appearing effortless. I have many instances of his encouragement, for he always found the time to read what I sent him and his comments were invariably pungent and helpful. The same was true with so many other authors, for he was consistently generous in this respect.

Though he denied the coincidence to me, his wanderings invariably took him to places that were on the verge of transition. It was as if he had an in-built radar for detecting what was about to happen in the world. His novels were suffused with innocence contaminated and time after time his imagination revisited a country of lost illusions that came to be known as Greeneland. There was something of the eternal schoolboy, the suppressed practical joker, about him to the end, as though the long journey he had taken had never destroyed that urge to push himself towards the frontiers of danger – the revolver in the corner cupboard still beckoned from the lost childhood. The austere letter writer to *The Times* on divers topics believed that the writer had a genuine duty to society to be a piece of grit in the State machinery, possibly giving the impression to strangers that he was devoid of humour. Such was not the case; he enjoyed telling and hearing jokes. In certain photographs taken when he was near the end of his life I felt the lens gave him the face of a sad clown – somebody who had always entertained others while concealing inner doubts.

Towards the end of 1987 I was given the chance to direct a revival of his first play *The Living Room*. I remembered the original production which brought Dorothy Tutin to fame and in which Eric Portman gave another memorable performance. As already related I had tried to include Micky Powell's film version in my EMI programme and the opportunity of restaging it for the theatre was something I welcomed. I was fortunate enough to find another fine young actress, Katharine Schlesinger, for the central role, and the emotionally crippled wheelchair priest was played by my old friend, Paul Daneman.

In varying degrees the critics were lukewarm about the thirty-four-year-old play, some of them dismissing it as a period piece that had not stood the test of time – the mixture of sex and religion seemed to make them uneasy. Graham made the journey from France with his long-time companion Yvonne Cloetta to attend one of the performances. He had several times written to me before and during rehearsals, and was obviously delighted that the play was to be given a second hearing. He professed himself pleased with the production, signed copies of the poster for all the cast before we dined at Rules – one of his favourite haunts when he lived in London. During that meal, and again in that last lunch we had in Antibes, I probed him about Philby and the other defectors of that period. I don't believe his defiant friendship and defence of Philby was another of his calculated tilts at an Establishment he had little time for; I think his affection for Philby was genuine on a human level and that it was no coincidence that his last novel on divided loyalties was called *The Human Factor*. In an address given at the University of Hamburg as far back as 1969 he spoke of the story-teller's need 'to act as the devil's advocate, to elicit sympathy and a measure of understanding for those who lie outside the boundaries of State approval'. Graham's lifelong fascination with the theme of innocence betrayed – read one of his early, and masterly, short stories called, simply, *The Innocent* – contains many of the map references to Greeneland, but as the reader ventures deeper into the later works he finds that what occupied Graham was the continuing issue of loyalty and disloyalty. Unquestioning loyalty, he felt, confines us to accepted opinions; disloyalty, he wrote, 'encourages you to roam through any human mind' and gave the novelist an extra dimension of understanding. He made articulate to me many of the paradoxes of human existence and that, surely, is the justification of a great talent.

Curiously enough I spotted that he had used *The Innocent* again in *The Human Factor* and asked him whether he was conscious of this. He replied that the repetition was intentional – 'In the first passage Daintry is alone, in the second he has a companion. The image has grown in his mind.' So in this instance the twin themes of innocence and betrayal were married.

A year or so before he died he sent me another play, *A House of Reputation*, but despite all my efforts I could not conjure any enthusiasm from theatrical managements or, indeed, the BBC. It seemed extraordinary to me that a work by arguably our greatest living writer could not find a taker, when television and the West End happily accept a goodly proportion of the third rate.

He was not honoured until late in life for England is ever neglectful of the giants in our midst, preferring to ennoble failed politicians and indifferent businessmen rather than those who have made a more lasting contribution to the quality of life. Equally he was disgracefully passed over for the Nobel Prize in favour of writers who could hardly be mentioned in the same breath, but Graham never voiced his disappointment, if disappointment he ever felt. He refused to let any of his novels be considered for lesser literary prizes, arguing that these should be the domain of writers hoping to make their mark and more in need of financial help. Perhaps he was content to let his huge body of work stand as the monument that would survive such transient baubles of fame. Can anybody quickly name the last three recipients of the Nobel?

Likewise many of the obituaries were not over-generous. This saddened but did not surprise me: charity is mostly an absent guest amongst the literary set, and those who sought to cut him down to their size revealed more about their own inadequacies than his. Anthony Burgess allowed his antipathy towards Graham as a person to influence the judgement of his worth; another critic headed his piece 'Our Man Overblown' and talked of Graham's 'uncomfortable presence' on the basis of a single meeting. Anita Brookner, John Fowles, Anthony Powell, Malcolm Bradbury (who during a broadcast introduced the thought that Graham had been termed the leader of the second rank) also added some discreet hatchet work, while the unsigned piece in the *Daily Telegraph* stated that 'even his admirers might balk at attributing greatness to him.' Burgess could not resist mentioning that he found Graham's morals 'dubious', a curious comment for a fellow writer to make, for since when did morality have any bearing on creative genius? Using this criterion Michelangelo, Proust, Tolstoy, Wilde, Balzac, Picasso, to name but few, would have to be ruled out. I prefer Graham's own statement that he found mortal sin a difficult idea to accept 'because it must by definition be committed in defiance of God. I doubt whether a man making love to a woman ever does so with the intention of defying God.' The common thread running through many of the obituaries was that Graham was too popular, and therefore suspect. Redressing the balance, Robert Harris deplored the snobbishness that was rooted in Graham having written accessible, non-experimental books which sold in prodigious quantities and had been made into films – a vulgarity for which sections of the literary establishment had never forgiven him.

I have no means of telling whether his Catholicism sustained him at the end, for in the long interview he gave to Marie-Françoise Allain he confessed that 'with age, doubt seems to gain the upper hand. It's my own fault. I've never been much of a religious person', and he went on to confound the majority of the obituary writers who labelled him a Catholic writer. He said, 'I'm simply a Catholic who writes.' I cannot recall that he ever discussed religion or his own faith or beliefs with me, nor did he question me as to mine. That secret died with him, but the secret lives of the characters he created in his novels and entertainments were given to posterity.

Attending the High Mass given at his Memorial Service, my first encounter with Catholicism, I confess that I found it a particularly unjoyous occasion, conducted for the most part by grim-faced priests more concerned with ritual than with humanity. I have never understood why both the Church of Rome and the Church of England go out of their way to preface entry into the Kingdom of Heaven with such emphasis on gloom. Whenever, on holiday, I witnessed a funeral in Barbados the mourners wore white and followed the coffin playing uninhibited music. This seemed to me in the spirit of the occasion, since presumably, if one is a true believer, going to meet one's Maker should be cause for celebration. At the service Muriel Spark spoke eloquently of his kindness to other writers, citing her own experience and telling how, when she was struggling at the beginning of her career, he regularly sent her a stipend 'always with a bottle of wine to temper the charity, as he put it'.

I believe that Graham's particular alchemy was to transform 'the panic fear that is inherent in the human situation' into a unique vision. He exerted a greater influence on writers of my generation – whether acknowledged or not – than anybody else, but beyond that, as a friend, he was willing to share his knowledge of the world, fight for lost causes, while at the same time pursuing without compromise his chosen craft.

TWENTY-TWO

Towards the end of my time at Elstree I was invited to make the principal speech at a Variety Club luncheon honouring Ted Heath. It seemed as good an opportunity as any to slip a personal comment into my peroration, so in the course of welcoming our then Prime Minister I reminded him that 'nothing recedes like success'. It was a remark pertinent to both of us as it happens. Ted was then riding high, but the miners' strike was fermenting just over the horizon and unlike the late George V my own days were not drawing peacefully to a close. Behind the scenes all hell was breaking loose and I was fighting on half a dozen fronts at once.

The spectre of James Aubrey had reappeared in my nightmares. By now *The Go-Between* had been completed and I considered it a potential winner. Mr Aubrey had other ideas. He cabled Bernie that he intended to open it at the Bruin Theatre in Westwood, California – a nice little village cinema close to the university campus, but hardly a number one date for the première of an important film. For a British film to break free of the restricted art house circuit in the United States, any production of quality has to be unveiled in New York, hopefully there to garner some important and influential reviews which will persuade the distributors to give it a full release. In my experience any other route guarantees commercial failure.

Under the terms of my contract I retained full artistic control until such time as the finished answer print was handed over. So

219

with Losey's and John Heyman's knowledge and approval I employed delaying tactics, much to Aubrey's annoyance. I screened the dubbed cutting copy for Bernie, hoping to impress him, but he was loath to take on Aubrey and pronounced the film non-commercial. 'It's mostly about the boy,' he told me incredulously as though by some strange process hitherto unknown to man Losey had managed to distort Hartley's original plot.

'Yes,' I said, 'the go-between.'

'Well,' said Bernie, 'he runs forever, for miles and miles.'

He then made determined efforts to get me to change my mind and allow Aubrey to proceed as he demanded. I refused. Bernie's fear at that point was that Aubrey would pull out of the partnership and ask for his money back. The cables flew backwards and forwards across the Atlantic, with Aubrey's language becoming more and more intemperate. With nothing else to lose, since the writing was on the wall, I continued with my own plans. Losey, I knew, enjoyed a cult following in France, the Cannes Festival was a few months hence and I was determined that his film would be considered as the official British entry. Behind the scenes I worked to this end, sneaking a copy of the film to Dilys Powell who was on the selection committee that year and whose judgement I had always trusted. My covert efforts paid off: the film was chosen as the British entry. This further provoked Mr Aubrey who informed Bernie that the festival had no commercial clout and that, unless his territorial demands were satisfied, he would withdraw MGM's financial involvement. Panic set in at EMI's Golden Square offices. But by then I had ensured that the festival committee's choice had received national publicity, and any change of heart would have been damaging to EMI's standing. I was not scared of Aubrey's continuing anger, for I rightly judged that his own days were almost certainly numbered, and that he was merely casting around to cut his losses. I had played him at his own game and won, just as the film won, coming away with the major prize at Cannes and going on to achieve a deserved artistic and commercial success.

With petulant bad judgement and timing Aubrey took his money out a few days before the festival jury made the awards and John Heyman – no slouch in these matters – swiftly sold the film to Columbia. Dogs have no scruples about eating dog in the film industry, and Columbia garnered all the kudos and the profits from Aubrey's mistake. Losey, who was not noted for expressing gratitude, acknowledged his debt to me in a letter I treasured. It had been a long and at times bitter struggle, but it was the kind of film – intelligent, visually compelling, beautifully directed and acted – that in a small way vindicated everything I had tried to accomplish at Elstree. Had I lasted longer, had I been given the proper backing and funds, I know we could have attracted more films of the same calibre to the studio. But it came too late.

Although *The Go-Between* had been neatly disposed of, I still had other fights on my hands. Firstly I had to ensure that the remaining films in the programme were at least given the minimum chance to succeed. Every aspect of the operation needed careful policing. By now the *Forbush and the Penguins* unit had returned from the Antarctic and at long last I was able to screen the material they had brought home. Despite John Hurt's dedicated and certainly courageous efforts, which could not be faulted, the stunning location footage did not sit happily with the more conventional scenes shot in the studio. Because the budget had been beyond my own resources British Lion and the National Film Finance Corporation also had stakes in this venture. As such they were entitled to make their views known. British Lion was then controlled by two notable teams of film-makers – the Boulting Brothers and Launder and Gilliatt. All four were adamant that drastic changes had to be made. They insisted that the director be replaced together with the leading lady and that the Boultings take over the rescripting and reshooting with Hayley Mills, then Roy Boulting's wife, recast as the female lead. I felt that such drastic surgery was bound to make matters worse at such a late and critical stage but I was outvoted and landed with the unhappy task of conveying these decisions to those concerned.

Understandably John Hurt was not amused by these machinations. Having done everything asked of him and having

endured lonely and often unpleasant months away from civili-
sation, he did not relish the prospect of starting all over again and
refused point blank to co-operate. I faced up to the unpleasant
job of convincing him that, if he persisted, he was on a collision
course. 'I know how you feel, but sadly you're in a no-win
situation. They will sue you if you don't turn up for work and it
will blight your career.' We sat up one whole night, sinking an
entire bottle of brandy until, rightly reluctant, he gave in and
accepted his fate. I felt no pleasure at my Pyrrhic victory, for he
faced a loathsome few weeks of shooting new scenes with a
different leading lady and a director he had every reason to
resent. It was a sad conclusion to a brave venture and the result
was a confused, unsatisfying film. Since that fateful night my
only consolation has been that John's subsequent brilliant
achievements might never have happened had he taken another
route, but I am not proud of my enforced role in the affair.

It was while all this was happening that Bernie discovered a
lame duck he wanted to rescue. He had been asked to consider
bailing out an unfinished documentary on the life of Rudolph
Nureyev. I was asked to fly to Paris and view what existed. The
documentary had been shot on sixteen-millimetre by a young
French director and originally intended solely for French television. I took Nanette with me for the ride and we sat on fruit
crates in a ramshackle office while the film was projected onto a
bare wall. Basically all that existed were some unedited interviews with Nureyev and Ashton's ballet *La Dame aux Camélias* in
which Rudolph was partnered by Fonteyn. This in isolation was
certainly exciting and likely to prove valuable archive material,
but the whole came nowhere near making a film. I duly reported
back to Bernie and convinced him that if EMI became involved
additional ballet sequences would have to be shot and that we
would need to blow-up the sixteen-millimetre to the standard
thirty-five-millimetre format. A quick decision had to be made
because of Nureyev's restricted availability. He was managed by
the formidable Mr Gorlinsky, long noted for striking a hard
bargain. After some tricky negotiations a balance was struck and
Bernie asked me to budget, shoot and edit the additional scenes.

I had met Nureyev once at an intimate dinner party given by Lee Radziwill who was then hankering after an acting career. Rudy lounged and pouted throughout the meal, confessing to Lee that he had had a bad day and thrown what he described as 'a tiny tantrum'. I was aware of his reputation for being difficult if he did not get his own way in all matters. Our first discussion about the film was not encouraging, for he obviously viewed me with some suspicion. I finally persuaded him that my intentions were honourable and I promised that he would have the final say regarding his own performances. It was decided that he would dance one complete modern ballet, the erotic *Field Figures*, with music by Stockhausen and choreographed by the young American, Glenn Tetley. I had no prior knowledge of this work, but remembered that a critic had once described Stockhausen's music as the sound of sheep being grated to death on a corrugated iron roof. I am sure I am woefully lacking in musical appreciation where this composer is concerned, but the cacophony accompanying *Field Figures* made me feel I was having root canals done on all my teeth simultaneously. In *Field Figures* Rudy was to be partnered by Diane Bergsma. The other selection was the *pas de deux* from *Sleeping Beauty* with Lynne Seymour as prima ballerina.

In view of the fact that Rudy would only be available to me for a very short period, I decided to use multiple cameras, with Tony Imi as the cinematographer. Although I had gained much valuable experience watching the development of the *Beatrix Potter* film, and in particular the way Sir Frederick Ashton fashioned the dance sequences, it was my first venture into the closed world of the ballet with its own particular codes, language and temperaments. The amount of money at my disposal allowed of no grand sets and we shot *Field Figures* on a small studio stage and *Sleeping Beauty* on a Sunday at the London Coliseum, using an existing backcloth.

Both sequences produced their moments of high drama. At one point during *Field Figures* I had to head off a potentially ugly situation when Rudy saw fit to insult my inoffensive stills photographer, George Courtney Ward. Suddenly dissatisfied with his own performance Rudy chose to say he had been distracted by the sound of the shutter noise from George's Nikon, and vented his annoyance on the most vulnerable person present. Had he done it to one of the electricians he would probably have been laid flat on his back and that would have been the end of the film. I did obtain a grudging apology before allowing filming to proceed, but the incident left a nasty taste. I suppose if you are continually lionised and your every whim catered to by sycophants, all normal patterns of behaviour go by the board. It wasn't as though his genius had ever been questioned or that he had to fight for recognition: his path had been strewn with roses ever since his defection. Adulation, like power, corrupts, more's the pity. I admired him, but I could not like him.

For the Coliseum sequence I had five camera crews in position by eight o'clock on the Sunday morning, but waited in vain for Rudy to arrive. It wasn't until after lunch that he condescended to put in an appearance, strutting on stage tetchy and argumentative, and immediately announcing that all my cameras were in the wrong position and that furthermore Lynne was too heavy for the lifts. She immediately burst into tears and fled to her dressing room. I sent out for flowers, then returned to tackle Rudy.

'Look,' I said, 'I admire you extravagantly as a dancer, but we've been hanging around all day waiting for you to show up. Either you get changed and dip your feet in the rosin and we shoot it, or else I'm going to dismiss the crews, who are on double salary, and you'll have to pay them out of your own fee.'

This homily was delivered in front of Sir Joseph Lockwood who had come as a spectator and remained a silent observer.

The mention of money brought about a startling change in him; I had struck where it hurt most. He flounced off to his dressing room, I dried Lynne's tears and an hour later we were finally able to commence shooting. Rudy was still at the height of his powers, dazzling to watch when he executed his seemingly endless *grands jetés*, giving the impression that his feet never touched the ground. It was a heart-stopping spectacle that made all the previous difficulties fade into insignificance. A perfectionist, he demanded half a dozen takes before pronouncing himself satisfied, and I was happy to accommodate him. Where he summoned the renewed energy from time after time amazed all present and, despite our differences, I shall always consider my brief association with him a fascinating experience.

The film appeared under the title *I am a Dancer* and is memorable for the chance to renew acquaintance with Fonteyn's exquisite dancing and Rudy's *tour de force* in *Sleeping Beauty* if nothing else. It also contains some penetrating insights into the life of a great dancer in his prime which I have not seen duplicated elsewhere. I took no credit for my own contributions and the film appeared as the sole work of the French director.

By now *Dulcima* had finished shooting and *The Railway Children*, on which I pinned great hopes, was in the cinemas, doing good business as a result of the excellent notices. I liked Lionel Jeffries' story of how, after the première of his film he had rung Bernie and told him that he had gone to Mass to thank Jesus for his success; Bernie enquired: 'Who?'

Dulcima had been taken from a short story by H.E. Bates and directed by Frank Nesbit with John Mills and the ultimately tragic Carol White giving beautifully judged performances. Frank was another young director starting out on a career and again I felt he showed great promise in his handling of this melodramatic, bucolic tale, shot entirely on location. But as with *And Soon the Darkness*, the cinema and distribution arms of the company showed no great enthusiasm for either film. Purely from a commercial standpoint it seemed an irresponsible waste of the shareholders' money. Properly marketed with a little imagination and given a chance to succeed, their fate could have been quite different.

I had not given up the struggle to overcome the indifference shown towards *The Raging Moon*. After I had threatened to take ads with my own money, Bernie was persuaded to increase the sparse advertising budget. Then Malcolm, Nanette, Bruce Curtis and I embarked on a whirlwind tour of the provinces, appearing on stage after the final showing of the film and answering questions in an effort to drum up the enthusiasm lacking in other quarters. I was also in negotiation with an old friend in New York, Don Rugoff, the owner of the prestigious Cinema V, and eventually he bought the film for the USA, gave it an inspired campaign and showed how it could be done. But as far as England was concerned we were written off.

The only pleasant interlude during this entire period was when I arranged a private showing for Her Majesty Queen Elizabeth The Queen Mother at the Warwick cinema, with dinner afterwards at the Empress. Together with a group of Her Majesty's friends I invited Yul Brynner and his then wife Jacqueline, who flew over from Paris, Julie Harris and my lawyer, Michael Oliver. We had drinks at Clarence House before the showing and Bruce was anxious to get the protocol correct. He was such an ebullient character and so hyped up at the prospect of meeting royalty, that I urged him to keep his usual high spirits in check. 'Stay cool, Bruce,' I cautioned. The showing went off successfully and we progressed to the Empress where the estimable Mr Negri received us and magnums of Taittinger '64 awaited. The pianist played all the Queen Mother's favourite tunes and we ate, drank and were merry until midnight. It was only when we all stood on the pavement to say goodnight to Her Majesty before she sped off in her Rolls that Bruce's control snapped. 'It was so kind of you to do us the honour, Your Majesty,' he said.

'Oh, I enjoyed it immensely,' she replied.

Bruce gave her the lightest tap on the shoulder – it could not be termed a shove – although later the story became heavily embroidered. 'Then tell all your friends,' he said.

Her Majesty carried this off with her customary charm. 'Oh, I will, I will,' she said.

'If only we could use that in the ads,' Bruce mused, as her car disappeared. 'What a quote! Just imagine what it would look like on the posters!'

'Don't imagine it, Bruce,' I said. 'Otherwise you'll end up in the Tower of London.' He immediately rang his mother in Los Angeles and gave her a somewhat exaggerated account of his life and times with royalty.

That was the high point of those troubled weeks. In an effort to push the Board into a decision about the future of the studio and my own position I wrote a long memo to John Read, offering to take a ten per cent salary cut if this would help matters. I was seeking to smoke him out and get a positive response, to have somebody consider causes rather than the usual monthly recitation about effects. The reply I received was an inconclusive 'wait and see'. I then had a private meeting with Bernie in which I asked him either to give me his full support or else accept my resignation. I think my frontal attack took him off guard. He confessed that he had not been sleeping for weeks and wished he had never got involved with a public company. 'I never minded losing my own money,' he said.

Once I had mentioned the word 'resignation' I could almost hear Bernie's brain ticking. I had given him the opening he had been reluctant to suggest. 'When you go,' he said, immediately assuming the fact, 'we must make sure it looks as though you and I are parting good friends. I think you should have a firm contract to direct two films, two big films, and we should name them and set the dates.' He also felt that I should remain on the Board in a non-executive capacity. After elaborating on this idea, we discussed the possibility of my doing *The Barnardo Boys* at long last, and by the end of the conversation he was already ad libbing a press release, but adding that, of necessity, I should stick to 'no comment'. It was a fascinating insight into his personality. I like Bernie and he is a great theatre showman, but films were a foreign country to him where, quoting from Hartley's novel we put on the screen, 'they do things differently there'. Used to being a one-man band and in his own words 'spending his own money' I think he found corporate decisions within a public company restricting.

A few days later the mechanics for my departure were in place. Michael Oliver met with his EMI legal counterpart to finalise the resignation instrument and to prepare a draft of the statement to be issued. I had private meetings with Sir Joseph and John Read, but neither offered any comfort. Read felt that I had made too many enemies to continue and Sir Joseph sat on the fence as I had come to expect. Although I had been promised complete

227

confidentiality until the day my resignation was announced, I laid my own plans, a wise precaution as it happened, for a story was leaked to the *Daily Sketch*, purporting to come from a 'close friend', headlined SHAKE-UP OF FILM BOSS and describing me as a 'frustrated actor'. Since I had given up acting ten years previously, I must have borne my frustration with remarkable fortitude.

I began the dismal chore of clearing my personal papers at the studio, letting John Hargreaves, Austin Frazer and my secretary Margaret into the secret and assuring them that my settlement included guaranteed provisions for their futures. Whatever enemies I had or had not made outside the studio, I could still count on the loyalty of the studio staff; my publicity chief tipped me off that the story of my resignation was already in Fleet Street. This gave me time to put Alexander Walker and the editor of the *Evening Standard* into the picture, and subsequently I spent a long evening with Alex giving my side of the story. Looking back it all seems so unimportant and petty, but at the time it had a bloated importance. My appointment had been heralded in a blaze of publicity and, doubtless because it was another dull day, when the announcement of my going was released I again made the headlines. Most of the stories were conjecture, some predictably insisted that I had been fired rather than resigned, but due to my foresight the *Evening Standard* account, spread over the two centre pages, gave the only accurate report.

That day I got to the studio early and asked all the heads of department and the entire works committee to join me in the conference room. I spoke first of my dear friend Basil Dearden who had been killed that week in a particularly horrifying car accident, before turning to my own situation. I thanked them all for the part they had played in keeping the studio a living entity over the previous two and a half years and for the loyalty and support they had shown me. I left the room abruptly before anybody could reply, going straight to my office and locking the door so as to conceal the emotion that had suddenly overtaken me. Sitting at my bare desk I thought back to the first days when

I had believed I could somehow bring about a change. Well, I had won a few and lost the rest. I had given a handful of young people the chance they sought and they had repaid me to the best of their ability. I had kept the studio open and ensured the talented workforce was not shoved on the breadline. It was a small victory and a hard price to pay for it.

Recovering I went downstairs to say goodbye to the switchboard girls and walked around the studio lot for the last time. It was cleaner than when I had arrived, that much I could say, and it had the look and feel of a studio rather than a run-down factory. Old craftsmen, all of whom I knew by name, came up to me and commiserated. When I went to the canteen for the last time my regular waitress, Maureen, cried. Tony Lumkin, the brilliant head of sound, who had done so much to upgrade the facilities of his department, said: 'Well, they got you in the end. You were too honest for them. But fuck them, they never created anything in their lives. Never forget we're the ones who make the films. All they have at the end of their lives is money, nothing for the history books.'

It was a day like no other. Before I drove out of the studio I was handed a book signed by every employee. Many wrote personal messages. By coincidence Nanette and I had a prior engagement with Princess Margaret and Tony Snowdon. I rang Kensington Palace and left a message, saying that I would quite understand if, because of my situation, they would prefer to make it another day. By the time I got home Tony returned the call: 'What the hell are friends for?' he said.

We all had dinner at the Tiberio then walked across the road to the Curzon cinema to see *The Owl and the Pussycat* starring my old friend George Segal in hilarious form with Barbra Streisand. When we left the photographers were lying in wait. Princess Margaret said, 'Put on a smile.' Afterwards we went on to San Lorenzo in Beauchamp Place where Pete Sellers was throwing what he called a Goodbye or Good Riddance party. We paid our respects and then left, with the photographers still hounding us around town. I felt battered.

The next day, somewhat to my surprise, Nat Cohen asked me

to have a farewell drink with him in his apartment. 'Do you know what your mistake was?' he said to me.

'I'm sure I made a great many, Nat. Which one are you referring to?'

'You threw your lot in with Delfont, instead of with me.'

It was significant that he said 'Delfont' and not 'Bernie' since I had always imagined they were very close. 'But it was Bernie who gave me the job, not you, Nat.'

He shrugged. 'It could all have been different my way.'

Perhaps he was right. I never did understand all the politics and manoeuvring that went on behind the scenes, nor did I have much time for them. The one person who behaved scrupulously towards me throughout was Leslie, the third Grade brother, who sadly died at an early age and who had been the dominant figure in the agency that established their combined fortunes. When Nanette was a small child he had lived in the same block of flats in Streatham, and told me he had pushed her in her pram. During my term at Elstree he brought me *On the Buses*, a small budget film we made for £100,000 and which returned a million pounds in profit. And after I left he went out of his way to try and generate other projects for me.

Without waiting for the dust to settle I took off with Nanette, the children and their devoted Scottish nanny, Mary Malcolm, for our first trip to the West Indies. We had chosen, on Harry Secombe's recommendation, to book into Sandpiper hotel in Barbados. There for the next month I recharged my batteries, dived for shells and contemplated my navel. While we were there I had an offer from Hal Wallis to direct a film of Rattigan's play, *Bequest to the Nation*, about Nelson and Lady Hamilton. None of the long-distance telephone conversations I had with Wallis convinced me he had any real respect for the material and in the end I did not have the energy to fight the endless battles I suspected lay ahead. Instead I got out my notebook and took up the novel I had abandoned twenty years previously. I used the title I had always wanted to use – *The Distant Laughter*. It seemed the right one for many reasons.

TWENTY-THREE

When William Styron and I took off in an ancient Austin Seven for a tour of England way back in 1952, I doubt if either of us guessed what the future held. I was still a struggling actor and would-be novelist, Bill had just published *Lie Down in Darkness* and was in England at Hamish Hamilton's expense to give interviews and drum up some publicity. Sadly, there was little interest in a first novel about the Deep South of America by an unknown writer but Roger Machell happened to be his editor. Desperate for ideas how to entertain his young guest, Roger turned to me and asked if I would chaperone him around the countryside for a couple of weeks. I don't know how Bill took to the suggestion at first, but I was out of work and jumped at the opportunity. Bill and I were complete strangers to each other and the relationship had to start from scratch. Happily we hit it off immediately.

We set out for Lincolnshire; I thought I would combine business with pleasure and revisit some of my childhood haunts. Both my mother and father had numerous relatives in the fens, the majority of them farmers, and it was there that I had spent most of my early holidays. In particular there was one house called Simbooth Grange, the family home of the Leggatts, distant cousins of my father, that to me retained romantic connotations. It was situated just outside Woodhall Spa and within sight of a small chapel made out of corrugated iron sheets, painted rust red, which on Sunday evenings reverberated and shook as the faithful pitched into rousing Methodist hymns. There was also a Kinema in the Woods, I remember, where the patrons sat in deck chairs, and to a London child the whole area was an alien landscape under wide, Constable skies, where anything could happen.

I remembered Simbooth Grange as being vast, a place where for the first time in my life I had a bedroom to myself, and it had been the inspiration for one of my, mercifully unpublished, works. Of course it wasn't vast, just a rambling old farmhouse, but to a child sizes appear exaggerated. Rumour had it that there was a secret passage from Simbooth to nearby Crowthorne Abbey that had been used by priests during the Cromwellian period, and this added to the mystery I weaved in my imagination. The moment one entered the house had an odour all of its own – a mixture of so many things, carbolic soap and rainwater in the damp, stone-flagged kitchen where often laying hens intruded; the slate-cold larder gave off other scents – freshly separated cream stood in an earthenware pot alongside the jar of sugar-water where wasps met their end; bricks of home-made butter were laid out beneath the salted hams and sticky fly papers. There were buckets of brown eggs gathered from the hedgerows, the churn of foamy milk. Stored Bramley apples, big as melons, had slept through winter in the darkness and added their musky scent.

It was in Woodhall Spa that I spent the first year of the war – the 'phoney war' as it was termed – a reluctant evacuee compelled for a time to attend the village infant school where, because of my age, they could teach me nothing. I remember solitary bombers droning overhead on their way to drop leaflets into Germany. In those days we went to sleep in feather beds by candlelight and the house groaned during the night as rats scuttled in the eaves. Downstairs one of the rooms had been sealed against a gas attack and the window sandbagged though, from what I later experienced having returned home just in time for the London Blitz, the crude sanctuary would have afforded little protection.

Simbooth Grange and nearby Walcott Dales close to the Norman keep of Tattershall Castle were the first ports of call for

Bill and me that trip. I was greeted as a creature from outer space by all the relatives, for they had not seen me since the first year of the war. Then I had been a scrubby schoolboy, but in the intervening years I had not only served in the army, but more impressively I had become an actor, had my name in the papers and been to Hollywood, the only member of the family to achieve a degree of notoriety. Bill and I were received and treated like royalty and stuffed with food. Bill later confessed he had never seen anything like it: breakfasts of home-cured bacon, new-laid eggs, fried bread and potatoes, tea tables laden with whole hams, sausage rolls, a variety of cakes and tarts, for in those days nobody dieted if they could help it and the word cholesterol was unknown. Although farmers lived hard in 1952, they lived well. Many with small acreages still used shire horses for ploughing; sugar beet, one of the staple crops, continued to be cut by hand and only the more affluent could afford electric milking machines. Although the word organic was not yet in general use, most spread animal manure on their land and the eggs were certainly free range, taken warm from the nest and popped straight into the frying pan.

We escaped their hospitality before obesity set in and travelled south and west since Bill had a hankering to cross Dartmoor at night. He confessed that the ambition had been with him ever since reading *The Hound of the Baskervilles*. I was somewhat dubious, for our Austin Seven was a temperamental beast and the prospect of it conking out in the middle of nowhere was not inviting. We worked out a timetable that with any luck would bring us to Princetown, the site of the infamous jail, around midnight since Bill had decided that if we were going to do it, we should go the whole hog. Dartmoor lived up to its Sherlock Holmes reputation and was shrouded in fog; wild ponies assumed ghostly shapes in our weak headlamps and I confess there were many moments when I became convinced the moor would claim us as victims. Bill found the whole journey exhilarating. 'Wouldn't it be great,' he mused, 'if the alarm suddenly sounded for an escaped convict and we heard the baying of bloodhounds?' All his fantasies about England had a literary origin and while we took turns at the wheel (another madness, since he had never driven on the left-hand side before) he said how he had been affected by the graveyard scene in David Lean's version of *Great Expectations*.

For my part I close questioned him about the American Deep South. I envied him the fact that he had actually finished a long novel; his writing seemed so complex and mature compared to my own, hinting at a sexuality that was at once alien and exciting. He seemed to possess a knowledge far beyond his years, expressed in assured, sinuous prose. It is hard to write about youth when you're still young, but in his own country and on the strength of one novel, Bill was already being rightly hailed as a future giant. I think he was impressed by my familiarity with the American scene, for throughout the journey we traded favourite authors and traced our own longings to be numbered amongst them. But whereas my own writing at that time was derivative, his seemed to spring from an original source, a further cause for admiration.

We arrived outside the prison some time in the early hours and Bill could hardly contain his delight. We seemed to be the only two people on earth; the fog blanketing everything, dulling sounds but heightening the sense of disquiet we felt standing under the formidable walls. It was not somewhere to linger and, since there was nowhere to put up for the night, as soon as Bill had satisfied his curiosity, we resolved to drive on. I had already phoned ahead to the vicarage at Porthleven and asked Mrs Gotto if we could stay for a couple of days. We somehow managed to remain awake and completed the journey without a stop, arriving in time for breakfast. Mrs Gotto and the Canon treated us both like long-lost sons, and I suppose in many ways I was the son they never had. Going back to the vicarage was a very emotional moment for me. Nothing had changed, my bedroom seemed as perfect as I remembered it, the distant view of the harbour and sea beyond like a cherished painting long stored and now brought out into the light. Just as I had been many years before, Bill was enthralled with the library. The books and the Canon's favourite armchair looked dustier and older than I remembered, but the dining table still gleamed with silver and we ate by candlelight; it was a kind of time warp for me, for Bill an introduction to an England and a way of life that was soon to disappear in many small communities.

I took Bill to the church where once I had served as an altar boy and listened fitfully, cheeks bulged with boiled sweets, to the Canon's fiery sermons. Incense had seeped into the fabric of walls over the years, for this was an Anglican High Church and considered the first step on the downward path to Rome by some of the inhabitants of the Canon's parish. As he had often told me, Cornish people consider anybody who lives over the county border as foreigners; even to marry somebody from the next village provokes disquiet.

Leaving the cool interior of the simple church I walked Bill to the clifftops where wartime concrete blockhouses still stood, now the haunt of sea birds and half concealed by undergrowth. Below us fishing boats rocked gently in the small harbour and beyond the serpentine beaches flashed in the sun. It brought back searing memories of my stay there. I looked up into the sky, half expecting to see Beaufighters wave-hopping to strafe the German positions in Occupied France. As an Air Training Corps cadet, desperate to become a fighter pilot, I had once been given an illicit and highly dangerous joyride in a Beaufighter from the squadron stationed on the Lizard. I stood behind the pilot's seat, there being little spare room in the cockpit, right over the escape hatch. Quite apart from the illegality of the jaunt, the chances of being shot down must have been considerable. At the time it never entered my head, I was mad keen to fly, aped RAF slang and regarded the pilots as gods. I told Bill how armed with a useless rifle I had once been part of the Home Guard, spending nights in such a blockhouse. I remembered the Canon in his Major's uniform careering around the countryside and ensuring that all of his Dads' and Boys' Army were at readiness in their posts.

'You mean you didn't have any ammunition?' Bill said.

'Some of us didn't even have rifles.'

'So what good would you have been if the invasion had come?'

'We'll never know,' I said. 'Fortunately we were never put to the test.'

'Jesus!' Bill exclaimed. 'You sure you're not kidding me?' I assured him that in the immediate aftermath of the fall of France, even rifles were a luxury. He had served three years in the US Marines and he found it difficult to comprehend those post-Dunkirk days. Later he drew upon his own experiences in his second, short novel *The Long March*. He was also surprised to find that a degree of rationing was still operating seven years after the war had ended, not apparent on the farm we had recently left, but very much in evidence at Mrs Gotto's table where we ate well but simply.

I have often thought back to that trip we spent together, and from time to time Bill and I have touched base again. The last time I saw him was in New York, just after *Sophie's Choice*, the masterpiece he always threatened to write, was published. Last year he wrote what he called 'A memoir of madness' under the title *Darkness Visible*, an account of his climactic nights of despair which engulfed his life and left him on the brink of suicide. Told with remarkable candour, the book described the process of meltdown. In Bill's case it began with a severe attack of that malady simplistically known as 'acute depression' – which attacked him without warning when he was sixty and, to all outward appearances, at the height of his powers. In Bill's case it first manifested itself as an aversion to alcohol. He admitted he had been abusing the substance for forty years. 'Like a great many American writers, whose sometimes lethal addiction to alcohol has become so legendary as to provide in itself a stream of studies and books, I used alcohol as the magical conduit to fantasy and euphoria, and to the enhancement of the imagination ... although I never set down a line while under its influence.' Reading and being greatly moved by his descent into near madness before the slow climb to recovery, I was hard put to recognise the young writer who had once shared that ancient Austin Seven on a voyage of discovery, though I could relate to every word. It so happened that the same week I came across his book, I had been rereading Katherine Mansfield's journal and had been haunted by her last entry: 'We all fear when we are in waiting rooms. Yet we must pass beyond them.' A writer spends the greater part of his or her life in waiting rooms and only passes beyond them when the imagination soars. I am thankful that Bill emerged from his particular hell for I don't want either of us to lose the hopes and aspirations we once shared crossing the foggy wastes of Dartmoor and which far more than me he later realised. Art is the only method we have for arresting time, flash-freezing memories in a way palatable to strangers who have not shared the original experience. Bill's writing, at its best, has this quality. *Sophie's Choice* distils the horror down to one human being and through its art leads us to the core of his heroine's nightmare. It is a book I shall never forget.

The American South has spawned so many distinguished writers – Faulkner, Willa Cather, Capote, Tennessee Williams – all of whom seem to possess a terrifying knowledge of the secrets of the mind, injecting into their steamy settings the sad music of people in torment, and they are not afraid to seek out the last taboos. There is a melancholy romanticism in everything that Williams ever wrote and few of us who love the theatre will ever forget the first time we were exposed to the magic of his verbal beauty. He once said, 'I think we are all winners and losers in rotation . . . Losing is a hard habit to break.' Sadly, unjustly in his case, the rotation from winner to loser in the public eye warped the end of his life, but as Fitzgerald put it, 'There are no second acts to American lives.' To my lasting regret I never met him, though friends such as Christopher Isherwood often tried to bring us together.

I saw a lot of Isherwood during the period when I was holed up in the old Beverly Wilshire Hotel writing screenplays. A gentle, compassionate man, like Aldous Huxley he turned his back on Europe, deserting his origins and thereafter never completely recaptured the creative splendour of his early work. He once confided that *Goodbye to Berlin* had given him a pension in his old age. 'Just imagine,' he said, 'a novel became a stage play which became a film which became a hit stage musical which became a hit film musical. You can't complain at that.' He made his last home in Santa Monica with his long-time lover Don Bachardy, the extremely gifted portraitist, whose work is exhibited in a number of countries. Nanette sat for him on several occasions, the last being when I brought him to Connecticut during the making of *The Stepford Wives* and he drew all the portraits used in the film. Don also produced a book of drawings he had made of Christopher dying and these reminded me of the savage, uncompromising works that came out of Germany in the late Twenties, the period when Christopher first turned his camera eye on Sally Bowles and the last convulsions of pre-Hitler Berlin.

The reason I succeeded in meeting Capote was because he was another of Roger Machell's authors. I remember that he lay on the rug in front of Roger's fireplace in B.1, Albany, hands behind his head, talking non-stop scurrilous gossip in a high-pitched voice, half child, half garden gnome. His comet started to fall to earth when the very people who had first lionised him closed ranks against him. I happen to have the same editor, Joe Fox, at Random House, Capote's publisher, and Joe maintains that despite an exhaustive search the complete manuscript of Capote's last book, the one that cooked his social goose, has never been found. It had been 'work in progress' for many years with, from time to time, tantalising extracts leaked into circulation. Unlike Proust he never lived long enough to make good his boast that he would spill the beans on the very rich who had taken him onto the dance floor and tangoed. Both he and Williams were hosts to the virus of self-destruction, Capote corrupted by the belief that his bitchy wit would ensure the dance never ended, Williams driven into a corner by premature neglect, and both hastening the end of their immense talents by drug abuse.

Their stories again encapsulate part of the American dream – the Gatsby-like yearning to go further than anyone else. Capote and Williams came so close to their personal Xanadu and then deliberately turned away. Both were capable of startling the reader and the playgoer with a wondrous poetic vitality; they saw the world with a completely fresh eye. The best American fiction is saturated with this quality. I go back in my own life to the moment when Ken Fyfe pointed me towards the early Saroyan who took the story apart, shook it like a Jack Russell shakes a rabbit and then reassembled it. He seemed to have unlimited inspiration, always zeroing in on the familiar from a new angle. Like the daring young man on the flying trapeze who made his reputation, Saroyan took enormous risks. Most English writers don't risk enough. Is it the vastness of America, the violence that I always feel lurks just below the surface of American society, the feeling that anything is possible, that gives the best American writing such a charge? There is something in the American psyche, a dark menacing quality, reflected also in the current American cinema. The greatest American screen actors all seem to possess this same quality of brooding danger coupled with extraordinary range. What British screen actor, for example, can be set beside Gene Hackman for sheer versatility? Where are our Al Pacinos, our Robert De Niros, our Meryl Streeps? We produce fine actors in abundance, but perhaps because of our classical tradition they all seem cast in the same mould, and again, does it hark back to our national character – the fetish for stifling emotions, the stiff-upper-lip syndrome? Those who do break away and make it usually make it in Hollywood where they appear to throw off the old restraints. It is fashionable to sneer at the brashness of America, but Americans I find know how to enjoy themselves without embarrassment. And they have a pride, again often derided, that we have lost, a simplicity curiously married to glitz and high-tech, state-of-the-art machinery. I am not trying to draw an unflattering comparison between a materialistic Utopia and our own staid way of life evolved over the centuries and nihilistically cemented into a class system that defies all efforts to dislodge it, but I have to confess that without frequent visits to America I would feel I had lost out on something. We cling too much to the past, America reaches out for the future. We are grudging towards literature and the arts and have a miserable penny-pinching attitude to anything that smacks of culture or else institutionalise all enjoyment out of it. Perhaps the difference between the two attitudes to popular entertainment is best illustrated by the fact that in England *Coronation Street* tops the ratings year after year, whereas in

America *Dallas* and *Dynasty* are a way of life. The average American wants to be lifted out of himself and shown the impossible dream, his British counterpart is happier with the old familiarity.

There is the other side of the coin, of course – the manufactured American novel for the bestseller lists, pap for beach reading, with its depressing sameness of plot, a mixture of sex, greed and power designed expressly for a mindless mini-series, thus completing the circle of banality. But if one searches, the American literary scene contains gems any week of the year and this is reflected in the amount of space devoted to reviews. Despite the fact that to lift it often necessitates a visit to the chiropractor, the Sunday edition of the *New York Times* encompasses the whole spectrum of the arts and does not treat television quiz shows as the pinnacle of achievement.

Through Bill Styron I met and became friends with another Southern writer, Calder Willingham, who also made his début with a remarkable novel, *End as a Man*. Calder swears that his most vivid memory of me is an occasion when, dining with Bill, all three of us more or less penniless, I picked up the tab for the meal. It's a story I would like to think is true, although I have no recollection of the occasion. I often wish we could return to the days of the literary salon where writers met and exchanged views. I number a few writers amongst my closest friends but see too little of them there is no cross-pollination because it is the nature of the beast to work alone. I was a founder member, with Carl Foreman, Ted Willis, Galton and Simpson, Frank Muir and Dennis Norden, of the Writers' Guild, originally formed in order to elevate the status of writers in television and films. We met in a small basement room in, of all places, Harley Street – a case of the impoverished living below the affluent. I was treasurer for a time and remember that at the outset we struggled to survive on a total yearly income that rarely exceeded £2000. *In the Beginning was the Word* had little significance in the early days of television and although we have never attained the muscle and influence of the Writers' Guild of America, over the years we have raised the profile of the writer in the visual media and ensured that our vital contributions are accorded proper recognition. Even so, the writer for films and television continues to be fair game, constantly 'interfered with' as the old *News of the World* used to put it primly when reporting a sexual attack. So the struggle continues.

I occasionally cross paths with friends like Len Deighton, James Clavell, Brian Garfield, Kingsley Amis, Morris West and Frank Muir, but by choice I don't swim with the literary mafia. Graham Greene was the only mentor I ever wanted, and the only one who consistently inspired me to go a yard further than before.

TWENTY-FOUR

It might come as a surprise to many people to learn that Capital Radio, the flagship commercial station, was the brainchild of a practising Weybridge dentist with the engaging name of Barclay Barclay-White.

Following my departure from EMI I found it difficult to get a job. Whether or no I made too many enemies, as Sir John Read contended (he was knighted shortly after my departure), nobody was too keen to offer me a film to direct. Unbeknown to Nanette I applied for a variety of jobs outside the film industry though without success. Usually when I walked in for an interview I was greeted with amazement.

The Boultings commissioned me to write and direct a screenplay based on the stage hit *Conduct Unbecoming* but the rights were subsequently sold on without further reference to me and whereas my version was a *screenplay* the eventual film was merely a photographed stage play. I began to feel I was a pariah.

It was at this moment that a letter arrived from Mr Barclay Barclay-White, a complete stranger. In it he said that he intended to apply for and win the franchise for the London general radio station. He invited me to become the first chairman (I refuse to write chairperson and view the entire gender lobby as an affront to common sense). Like most people in the public eye I get my fair share of lunatic mail, sometimes my morning post consists of little else, and at first I thought that Mr Barclay Barclay-White was merely another eccentric. But there was such a disarming sincerity about his letter that I showed it to Nanette and asked her opinion. Women are much more intuitive than men and many times during our marriage she has saved me from making a fool of myself. 'Meet him,' she said, 'what have you got to lose?'

'But a *dentist*!' I said.

'So? Perhaps he's tired of pulling teeth. See him. You'll soon make up your mind whether he's a phoney.'

I remained sceptical but took her advice.

A Bill had recently passed through Parliament authorising the IBA to launch the first commercial radio network in direct competition with the BBC's hitherto unchallenged monopoly. The initial applications were for two London-based stations – an all-news station (which eventually became LBC) and the larger, general entertainment station which was the one our unknown dentist was going after.

As with the advent of commercial television many years before, the preliminary announcement provoked emotional and mixed feelings. There was a voluble and influential lobby which felt that any diminution of the BBC's position was a retrograde step and would lead to a swift debasement of the air waves. But times had changed from the days when Lord Reith had insisted on the unseen news readers wearing evening clothes and black tie while informing the nation. Pirate radio stations, operating outside territorial waters, were proliferating, proving very popular with young listeners and defying efforts to put them off the air. The champions of commercial radio argued that by legitimising the use of advertisements the pirates would be put out of business. Both Labour and the Conservatives suffered periodic bouts of paranoia about the BBC, Harold Wilson being convinced that there was an ongoing subversive plot against him (witness the famous Dimbleby interview), and the Tories equally convinced that Broadcasting House and the TV Centre were staffed with covert fellow-travellers plotting to undermine the Establishment. In the general run of things it can be assumed that the majority of journalists, wary of anything that encroaches upon their freedom of expression, lean towards a liberal, rather than a reactionary, philosophy. There were several cases during this period when journalists and broadcasters refused to reveal

243

their sources and were taken to court, one editor actually serving a term in jail for refusing to comply with the court's ruling. Heath was in power and, like Wilson before him and Callaghan after him, was heading for a confrontation with the unions. The wind of change was blowing in all directions and change is what the established bastions fear most.

I duly took my meeting with Mr Barclay Barclay-White and found him very engaging. He was totally convinced, and fired me with his conviction, that he would be successful. Still a practising dentist, he was, as Nanette had surmised, bored with staring into people's mouths and wanted to launch out in another direction. He felt that if he persuaded me to join him I would attract the necessary consortium to mount a serious application.

It so happens that I began my career as a broadcaster. Before I left school I had written to a number of radio personalities, picking their names from the *Radio Times* at random – Sir Malcolm Sargent, Alvar Liddell, Ben Lyon, Tommy Handley and the entire cast of *Happidrome*, a North country comedy team – asking for help and advice to enable me to pursue an acting career. My ignorance at the time went beyond bliss. Few bothered to reply, but I did get a kindly response from Tommy Handley and struck the jackpot with Lionel Gamlin who was then the voice of Movietone News and a distinguished broadcaster of the old school. I had sent him my ludicrous rave review for Shylock in the school play, and he told me later he felt anybody with that amount of nerve deserved a hearing. The moment I finished school I was on his doorstep. He solemnly interviewed me at the BBC's Bush House studios where throughout the war he had played a major role in their European service. I was given a microphone test in an underground studio where I read, strangely enough, Lincoln's Gettysburg speech.

After the interview he took me for tea in the Aldwych Brasserie. To the strains of gipsy music much favoured in tea rooms those days, surrounded by genteel matrons up for the day from their suburban haunts, I munched a wartime meringue that looked and tasted like something you push between the bars of a birdcage, while Lionel outlined a possible future for me.

'If you are hell bent on a theatrical career,' he began, 'I think I should warn you of all the pitfalls ahead.'

He proceeded to outline the dangers that lay in wait for a would-be young actor.

'You'll probably starve. All actors starve at some point, making do on nothing more than a currant bun and a glass of milk at the Express Dairy.' At that moment a currant bun held more nutritious attraction for me than the meringue I was still trying to swallow.

'I don't mind starving,' I said manfully.

'The other thing you should be aware of . . .' Lionel fixed me with a penetrating look . . . 'You'll almost certainly be chased around a great number of desks.' My eyes widened. What the hell was he talking about? He elaborated. The perils of Pauline, it appeared, were chicken-feed compared to the dangers that lay in wait for juveniles in the West End theatre.

'Queers,' he said and waited. Of course in those days we had not progressed to the word 'gay'. In fact there was a musical currently playing in London called *Gay's the Word*. I stared blankly at him.

'Do you know what I mean by that?'

'Not really, sir.'

'The theatre is largely controlled by queers. You can't avoid them. Most of them escaped being called up by shaving their armpits and you're going to have to make up your mind very early on which way you're going to go.'

I was too bewildered to confess to further ignorance on the subject, although it crossed my mind that shaving one's armpits seemed a small price to pay for fame.

'I take it you're not queer?' Lionel continued.

'I'm not sure, sir.'

'Do you prefer girls to boys?'

'What for, sir?'

'Sex.'

'Oh, that,' I said. 'I thought you meant something else. No, I prefer girls for that.' The sum total of my sexual experience at that point was confined to a fumbled game of doctors and nurses played with a nubile and, I suspect, extremely naïve cousin.

'Well, good. The important thing in life is never to be a tease. Don't tread both sides of the line, in other words. As long as you remember what you are and stick to it, you'll never lose friends. And when you are propositioned, as you undoubtedly will be, always say no gracefully.'

'Oh, I will, sir.' I had a quick mental picture of a queue of people waiting to pop the question. For the rest he might have been talking in Hindu.

'You don't think you'll change your mind?'

'What about, sir?'

'Going on the stage.'

'Oh, no.'

'Well, don't say I didn't warn you. Now then, there's one other thing. Your name.'

I had been christened John Clarke and this, Lionel said, would not do. There was already a young actor of the same name who had recently made a success playing the leading role in the *Just William* series, and it was explained to me that Equity, the actors' union, did not allow identical names. So, as the rock-hard meringue crumpled another school filling, Lionel began to write alternatives on the back of the menu.

'How does that look?' he asked, pushing the menu across the table.

I stared at the word 'Forbes'.

'Forbes-Robertson, you know,' Lionel added. I didn't, but I nodded. 'Old theatrical family, has a good ring to it. Now then, if you're happy with that, we must put a first name to it.' He jotted down several before pronouncing 'Bryan' as his favourite choice. 'Bryan with a 'y', I think, it'll look better on the bills. See what you think.' He blocked out the entire *nom de plume* in capital letters. I studied my new self between the Brown Windsor stains on the menu. Already I could visualise my name in lights.

'I'm sure you're right, Mr Gamlin,' I said. I was so impressed with the whole encounter that had he suggested I call myself Nigel Hitler I would have agreed without a murmur.

246

'Fine, that's it then. From now onwards you're Bryan Forbes.'

Can it be that easy, I thought, wondering how my parents would react.

Lionel later guided me towards the Royal Academy of Dramatic Art where, like Nanette in later years, I gained a Leverhulme scholarship. My Cockney accent was flattened and I learned in no uncertain way that I did prefer girls. He also provided me with my first professional job, making me Question Master of the BBC's Junior Brains Trust, a programme he produced. I was paid the princely sum of two guineas (a BBC financial quirk), and had my first taste of publicity when I was photographed for *Illustrated* magazine. From that I progressed to having my own programme called *Hello India* which was beamed every week to that continent. It was now that Lionel's warning came true. *Hello India* was produced by a shock-haired Indian who from the first day had designs on me. Although I was not chased around his desk, I was grabbed under the table just as the red light went on to signify we were on the air. My voice jumped three octaves, producing something like 'Hell-looooooo India!' I suppose in its own way it was a broadcasting first.

In later years when I knew Lionel better and could talk openly about his homosexuality, we laughed over our first encounter. He admitted that the advice he gave to the young player to the accompaniment of a gipsy band had an ulterior motive. He was a lonely, underrated man, a superb natural broadcaster whom I shall always remember with gratitude and affection. As my own fortunes improved, so his declined, for he fell foul of the BBC hierarchy for some reason and was cast out in the cold. When I became a director I was able to repay his kindness to me by employing him as an actor, but he died penniless and alone. I learned of his death when the police rang me late one night to say that his body had been found in a one-room flat in the unfashionable part of Hampstead. They had traced me from a photograph found amongst his meagre belongings. I paid for his burial since I could not wish him a pauper's grave. It was the least I could do for the man who had invented me.

I have digressed from the genesis of Capital Radio to emphasise that from an early age I had a great interest in broadcasting. I was one of those who felt it would be beneficial for the BBC to experience some competition. While remaining the best broadcasting system in the world, it had become top heavy with administrators, many of whom gave the impression that they were above criticism. A shake-up and some competition, I felt, would do no harm.

I therefore agreed to throw in my lot with Barclay-White and we set about recruiting our team. I approached Richard Attenborough, David Jacobs and George Martin because I felt it vital to have working professionals in the forefront. Dickie Attenborough solicited the theatrical impresario Sir Peter Saunders, we recruited John Whitney as our first chief executive and Barclay set about the task of finding the necessary financial support. The successful applicant would be required to equip and go on air in a very short period after the franchise was granted. This was a formidable challenge since it had never been done before and everybody was sailing in unchartered waters. We took temporary premises in Piccadilly and engaged a skeleton staff. Our priority was to produce a highly detailed document outlining our technical plans and programming intentions which had to follow closely the IBA's requirements. The document also had to show exactly where the money to pay for the station was coming from, and to give binding undertakings from those concerned. I was instrumental in drawing up the basic programming guidelines and together the team we had assembled worked to a tight deadline. There were half a dozen other consortia in the race and secrecy was of the essence. The fact that our team was headed by a dentist led us to be considered as the underdog without much of a chance, for on paper several of the other hopefuls looked formidable. It was a chicken-and-egg situation in more ways than one. Large sums of money had to be spent in advance without any guarantee that they would ever be recouped. Possible permanent premises had to be found and earmarked; schedules for the vast amount of necessary technical equipment had to be drawn up and budgeted. The calculations revealed that we would need some £750,000 to be viable. In addition to the written evidence of our intentions, we were required to appear before a selection committee and be questioned. It was decided that Dickie, David and myself would be the spokesmen and shortly before the actual day I was asked to stand down as chairman in favour of Dickie since it was felt that his name would carry more weight. By now the bookies were quoting us as the dark horse in the race and the odds shortened. We duly appeared before the assembled worthies, many of whom patently had little knowledge of broadcasting, and were closely questioned. We had done all we could and now had to await the jury's verdict.

Barclay's conviction that we would emerge the winner never faltered, and amazingly he was proved right. The franchise was awarded to us and then began a scramble to get the station on air by the predetermined date. We had chosen Euston Tower as our headquarters and immediately after the victory celebrations the work of putting the station into operation began. It was a frantic but exciting period and we made the deadline. Nobody knew how the advertisers would react and for the most part they played a wait-and-see game. Our colleagues at LBC faced the same problems and in many ways had a far harder task, since the BBC's news service was a hard competitor to beat. Both stations had to provide a twenty-four-hour service and the most obvious innovation we introduced was the talkback concept. Of course we made many errors, for in certain areas we had been over-ambitious, but our initial signal went out on time as planned. We thought we were on our way, but we had not allowed for the miners' strike and Heath's three-day week. The advertising, meagre to begin with, dwindled to nothing and we woke up to the fact that we were trading insolvently. A crisis Board meeting was called, a new bank loan was hastily arranged, but every director had to give a joint and several guarantee for £25,000. All this happened within two months of going on air. For the next five years, unlike the commercial television companies when they were first launched, we did not have a 'licence to print money' in the infamous phrase of Lord Thomson and were fortunate to survive. But survive we did and eventually went public. The anonymous dentist from Weybridge proved to be an unsung hero.

My subsequent flirtations with the BBC, that strange, sometimes brilliant, always top-heavy, bureaucratic, autocratic, pompous, wasteful, often wonderful and certainly indispensable organisation, provided many episodes of drama and farce.

I took part in the last television play broadcast from Alexandra Palace, R.C. Sherriff's *Journey's End*, directed by the brilliant Michael Barry, for which I was paid the princely sum of seventeen guineas and a pittance of rehearsal money over a month – for some reason the BBC still calculated all fees in the arcane guineas, an anomaly aped by the intelligence services who paid officers in sovereigns! In those pioneering days everything was live, there were no recordings and one performed the same play twice – first on the Sunday evening, and a repeat the following Thursday – and if an actor dried or missed an entrance it was a disaster. The audience was a small, unknown quantity and of course there was no opposition. The actors and presenters wore bright orange make-up inches thick and faced crude and unwieldy cameras that had a red electric light bulb fixed on top – mobile brothels we called them. If the light was on it denoted that the camera was working. The viewfinder gave the cameraman an inverted image, which must have presented considerable problems since, if an actor moved to the left, they had to pan right to follow him. I often wondered if, after a heavy day, the cameramen went home, wound the cat up and put out the alarm clock. The cables for the equipment were the size of boa constrictors and presented a hazard on the studio floor. I well recall that the cameras frequently broke down during transmission and on several occasions I turned to face what I fondly imagined was the right camera only to find it being dismantled by demented engineers and a frantic floor manager waving me to find the nearest red light district in order for the play to continue. It was pioneering stuff and kept the adrenalin flowing.

Many years later I recalled these early days when I was suddenly summoned at short notice by Bill Cotton Jnr to a mysterious dinner date one evening. I drove to a restaurant in Kensington High Street to find other members of the top brass of the day awaiting me: Brian Wenham, Aubrey Singer, as well as Bill Cotton. The mystery was quickly explained: they wanted to know if I would be interested in heading up a new film division with a budget, as I remember, of some £80,000,000, responsible for producing a given number of filmed dramas every year. They asked if I could give them a quick answer and pressed me to meet with the chief negotiator the following morning. I duly went home and thought, why not?

So the following morning I drove to Television Centre and was shown up to the executive floor where coffee was provided in china cups. There I met the negotiator who began brightly. 'Let me tell you what the job commands,' he said from behind his desk. 'Firstly, you get a car, a Ford Granada.'

'Wonderful,' I murmured. 'Actually, I have a car already.'

If he heard this he ignored it. 'Then you also get a free television set and a VHS recorder.' Warming to this litany he continued: 'Plus all your telephone calls, and you can sign for your entertaining expenses.'

'A generous package,' I observed, with just a smidgen of sarcasm. 'What is the actual salary?'

'Ah! Well now. How old are you?'

I was fifty-eight at the time and told him so.

'Oh, dear. Retirement is mandatory at sixty, so that doesn't leave much room for a pension.' He looked down at his papers.

'Well, let's not worry about a pension,' I said, wondering whether the onslaught of senility was evident in my face. 'Let's discuss the salary.'

'There is of course a scale set down for salaries at your level.' He mentioned a figure only slightly above what I was currently paying my secretary. I got up and started to walk to the door.

'Where are you going?' the negotiator said, visibly startled.

'You've just made me bankrupt,' I said.

I came back and sat down again. 'Now, let's go through it again. I don't want the Ford Granada, I don't want the television or the VHS recorder, I'll take my chances with personal telephone calls and expense lunches, so let's agree what that little lot is worth, add it to the sum you've just mentioned, then double it and I might be your man.'

His face registered real pain. 'But that's not possible,' he said. 'It's right off the scale.' I had a mental picture of a computer somewhere in the building suddenly sending out an earthquake warning as my proposed salary came up on the screen.

'I'll have to take advice from a higher authority,' he said. He left his desk and went to Mount Olympus, returning with a senior executive who took me to one side and, with a conspiratorial wink, tapped me on the shoulder. 'Salary isn't everything,' he confided. 'Do it for the glory.'

I interpreted this to mean that at the end of my two years I would be put up for something in the honours game.

'I've had my share of glory,' I said. 'The most pressing consideration at the moment is how to pay the gas bills.'

He frowned. This was not the answer of a keen applicant. And that was goodbye to all that. I heard nothing more, except that a few months later I went through the same routine again, this time being offered a senior appointment with the Pebble Mill division. Again I was wined and dined and encouraged to think that the job was mine if I toed the official line, but that, too, came to nothing. I guess I didn't have the acceptable Establishment face. Or something.

TWENTY-FIVE

Lionel Gamlin may have given me a highly coloured account of theatrical life, but it was not entirely exaggerated way back in 1942. At the time when I embarked on my stage career the theatrical scene in England was vastly different from today. In the first place there was a thriving repertory system spanning the entire country; few large towns were without their own theatre and resident company; variety had not yet been killed off by television and, in addition, once they had finished their London run most plays went out on long tours. Wages were just above the poverty level for the average actor, especially in the provinces. I received three pounds ten shillings for my first engagement in Rugby Rep once I had left RADA, and could just about survive on this with Woodbines at sixpence a packet! Aged sixteen, I either played juveniles during my baptismal season or else, grotesquely made up, totally unconvincing old men. London salaries, except for the stars, were equally parsimonious.

I was lucky in that I gained a measure of professional experience before being called up into the army. I had played in a number of repertories up and down the country before being spotted on tour in a play called *Fighters Calling* by Terence Rattigan and offered a role in his long-running wartime success *Flare Path*. Immensely cultured, and with an urbane wit, Terry became my mentor and a very close friend, though possibly not as close as he would have wished. Still somewhat naïve in the ways of the world I had entered I told him of Lionel's advice about saying no gracefully. Terry listened gravely. 'Yes,' he said, 'a very useful piece of advice. Of course, on the other hand, you could always say yes gracefully.'

As a callow young man I could not fail to be impressed by Terry's lifestyle. He lived in Albany, an oasis far removed from anything I had ever known – period furnishings, silver on the table, the rich food he managed to serve even in wartime, wine, a butler – to my eyes it all seemed something out of a film (and in fact the Albany setting was faithfully reproduced for Terry's next success *While the Sun Shines*). I had never been close to such wealth before, nor the influence that comes from wealth.

In appearance he was not unlike the young Scott Fitzgerald and, certainly when I first knew him, he could have passed for the sort of handsome leading man who graced so many plays of the period. He wore Savile Row suits, chain-smoked with a Dunhill crystal-filter holder and loved nothing better than to hold court and indulge in theatrical gossip and high camp. (It was the first time I had ever heard men referred to as '*Mrs* So-and-so'.) His conversation was sprinkled with anecdotes about the theatrical greats; it was Larry and Viv, Emlyn and Johnnie G., Katie and Rex, heady stuff for someone at the start of a career for, unlike today, junior members of a company risked being frozen out if they immediately addressed the stars by their Christian or nicknames on the first day of rehearsal.

Terry not only encouraged me as an actor but was immensely helpful in guiding my attempts to become a writer. He patiently read and passed constructive criticism on the turgid novels I was writing at the time, though I am sure this was a chore he could well have done without. Later he persuaded A.D. Peters, the doyen of literary agents, to take me under his wing and this eventually led to my first published work.

It is a matter of record that Terry's craftsmanship as a dramatist was often derided and it followed him to his grave, for many of the obituaries gave depreciating emphasis to this. It was left to Harold Hobson to pen the most perceptive summing up when he wrote that 'Rattigan had the greatest natural talent for the stage of any man this century'. Yet throughout his life the implication had been that he had not fully realised that natural talent. He several times confessed to me a longing to break out of the light comedy mould and tackle more serious themes, and throughout his long career strove to prove his critics wrong, but even so their praise was often grudging. This was especially true when dramatists such as Osborne, Pinter and Beckett came to the fore. Terry was labelled old fashioned, dismissed as part of a *passé* theatrical establishment which churned out plays with no social content. Terry went on the attack in his own defence, inventing a fictitious character, 'a nice, respectable, middle-class, middle-aged, maiden lady . . . a hopeless lowbrow', typifying the average theatregoer, whom he named Aunt Edna. He contended that playwrights ignore the Aunt Ednas of this world at their peril: those who were 'unfortunate or unwise enough to incur her displeasure' would soon pay the price, expanding his theme with humorous but serious intent, for it was obvious that his detractors' barbs had gone home. Alas, his invention and his well-reasoned argument lived to haunt him until the last years of his life when his reputation and talents were finally reappraised in more generous terms.

He used many aspects of his own complicated emotional life within his serious plays and he saw no crime in his efforts to popularise serious themes, nor did he believe that it was necessarily worthier to make an audience weep than to make it laugh. The pose which, in his own words, he had 'often assiduously tried to assume' – that of the urbane, even-tempered, world-hardened cynic utterly indifferent alike to praise or blame – was a false picture. He had a true sense of theatre and consistently struggled to widen his horizons. *Separate Tables*, *The Winslow Boy*, *The Browning Version* and *Ross*, indeed the whole body of his serious work, proves this point should it still need proving, but in two instances I was witness to a curious weakness in his make-up which illustrates that he sometimes lacked the courage of his fiercely held convictions.

Shortly before I was called up for my war service he arrived unannounced in Swindon where I was appearing with the local repertory company. He gave me the manuscript of a new play, at that time titled *A Little Less Than Kind*, which he said he had written for Gertrude Lawrence. The second largest role was that of her character's son which he wanted me to play. There was a third starring role and this he had earmarked for Ronald Squire. It was a very flattering situation, but a few weeks later, staying in a Berkshire pub he often escaped to when writing, he found that the Lunts were fellow guests. At that time Alfred Lunt and his wife Lynn Fontanne were indisputably American theatrical royalty with a large following on both sides of the Atlantic and accustomed to dictating their own terms. Terry gave them his play to read – not, as I understood, for them to consider, but merely to get their opinion of its worth. They came down the next morning and announced that if he was prepared to do certain revisions, they would be willing to appear in it. Terry found himself unable to confess he had intended the play for Gertie Lawrence. The 'certain revisions' the Lunts demanded were quite major: they wanted the man's role built up and the boy's role reduced. And that is what Terry did. The promised role of the son, now greatly truncated, never came my way. Instead I went into the army and the Lunts eventually returned to the West End in what was now retitled *Love in Idleness*.

That was merely my loss, but in the second incident I always felt that Terry cheated himself, although I could understand why he acted in the way he did. Once again he showed me the first draft of a new play, *The Deep Blue Sea*. It was vastly different from the version that eventually proved such a great success with Peggy Ashcroft and Kenneth More in the leading roles. In the early manuscript I read, Peggy Ashcroft's role was that of a young man, for the play was Terry's anguished effort to purge the memory of a tragic love affair he had had with an actor named Kenneth Morgan. Morgan committed suicide by gassing himself and theatregoers will recall that *The Deep Blue Sea* opens with the heroine lying in front of a hissing gas fire. The earlier draft had no heroine, instead it was a brave attempt to put across a homosexual love affair without sensationalising it. Once again it was Terry's intention to ask me to audition for the role based on Kenneth Morgan. Had he been successful in getting the first draft of the play produced there is little doubt in my mind that it would have been a watershed in British drama. Sadly, he was talked out of it.

In his defence it has to be remembered that these were the pre-Wolfenden days; homosexual acts, even between consenting adults in private, remained criminal offences incurring severe prison sentences. Although Terry's sexual preferences were common knowledge within the closed theatrical circle he inhabited, his natural shyness allied to a very real fear of being blackmailed made him conduct himself discreetly. Prior to his tragic and one-sided affair with Kenneth Morgan, he had earlier been the lover of the MP, 'Chips' Channon, irreverently known as 'the iron butterfly'. Terry was well aware that if any whiff of scandal about his private life escaped, the whole pack of cards would come tumbling down. Just as we were warned during the war that careless talk cost lives, careless talk cost careers, and if I appear to place undue emphasis on the homosexual aspect of theatrical life during this period, it is not an indulgence out of prejudice, for I have none, preferring to judge people by their talents rather than their private lives, colour or religion. But nobody who grew up in the theatrical scene during the war and post-war periods could be unaware of the homosexual dominance exercised by, amongst others, Coward, Novello, Rattigan and, of course, the ubiquitous Hugh 'Binkie' Beaumont who controlled the largest and most influential theatre empire, H.M. Tennent Ltd.

Binkie had flair, taste and a morbid eye for detail. His productions were always lavishly mounted, even in wartime. He was nothing if not an astute business man and found a legal loophole of avoiding the despised Entertainment Tax, which not only enabled him to enlarge his activities but greatly reduced the financial risk. Something of a snob, he liked all-star casts. Very loyal to a small band of intimates, he recruited the best technical staff, employed the top directors and designers and ran the empire he had inherited at an early age with ruthless efficiency. No career was advanced by crossing him.

When Terry showed him the first version of *The Deep Blue Sea*

Binkie's first reaction was panic. I had Terry's word for it that he ran scared, and not only scared, but outraged. How could Terry possibly contemplate such a dangerous, foolhardy venture? It would ruin everybody connected with it. From conversations I had with him at the time, I think Terry was of a mind to take the risk, Binkie or no Binkie, for there was a masochistic streak in his make-up, sometimes revealed in his public acceptance of humiliation from his lovers who all seemed cast from the same mould. He reasoned that there were other managements, braver than Binkie in this one respect, and he recalled that Binkie had once before declined to mount another of his plays – *The Browning Version* – in a double bill with *Harlequinade*. But in the end, pressurised on all sides, he bowed to Binkie's judgement and rewrote it as a star vehicle for a woman. Had he stuck to his guns he might have changed the face of British drama and drawn nearer to his dream of being regarded as the supreme exponent of a natural talent. It was not until many years later that a company I was associated with treated the forbidden subject with the gravity it deserved. This was a film called *Victim*, directed by Basil Dearden, which was widely acclaimed and put its star, Dirk Bogarde, into a different category overnight.

It is curious how many times in life previous memories overlap. While writing this chapter Nanette and I went to look at Terry's old house in Sunningdale where I enjoyed many hilarious weekend parties. Semi-derelict, having fallen into the hands of a speculator who later defaulted, it had the air of Daphne du Maurier's Manderley as we wandered through the unkempt walled garden. Staring through the dusty windows into the indoor swimming pool I remembered that when it became obvious that Terry was dying I was asked to fly to Bermuda and film an obituary television documentary. I did not have the heart to accept, for it seemed too ghoulish a journey to undertake where an old friend was concerned.

My stage career went into hiatus for nearly four years while I served first in the Intelligence Corps and then, six months after the war ended, I was seconded to a unit which might well have been devised by the Monty Python team. This was first called

Stars in Battledress, and later Combined Services Entertainment Unit. There, together with Sergeant Harry Secombe, Lieutenant Roger Moore, LAC Peter Sellers, Sergeant Terry Thomas and other luminaries of a motley army, we sweated out our last months before being demobilised. As can be imagined, the marriage of army and show business was destined not to be made in heaven. Officers were not allowed to act in the plays we produced, acting being considered infra dig by the War Office brass, the squalid stuff was confined to other ranks. We journeyed all over occupied Germany and Austria visiting various camps and presenting one-night stands.

I appeared in five plays, as I remember – *Charlie's Aunt*, *The Case of the Frightened Lady*, a grim little number called *The Day is Gone*, *The Hasty Heart* and Bridie's *It Depends What You Mean*, in which I played the role of a padre originally created by Alastair Sim. It required a considerable stretch of the imagination to accept a twenty-one-year-old as a Church of England padre, but our audiences were not over-critical and I did my best to appear holy. It was another army ruling that only officers were allowed hard liquor and the company I was in charge of found this irksome since all we could obtain on the black market was a fearsome local potion we suspected was three parts wood alcohol with many of the characteristics of U-boat fuel. Purely by chance one evening I discovered that I was taken for the real thing. We were setting up for the performance and I was already in costume supervising the stage management when I was approached by a private soldier who asked my advice, as a man of the cloth, about a desperate marital problem. Although taken aback, I remained in character and did my best to console him as a diabolical idea began to form in my mind. If this man accepted me, maybe others would too.

Emboldened by the encounter I decided to test the water and I arrived at the next camp already wearing my padre's uniform and made straight for the Officers' Mess. I was admitted without challenge and buttonholed the Quartermaster Sergeant in charge of the bar. Assuming a slight Irish brogue which I thought gave a little verisimilitude to my impersonation, I spun him a tale of having just visited some wounded in hospital who were thirsting for a drop of the hard stuff. Could he possibly help out? Of course, Father, anything for your lads.

I blessed him and came away with a crate of whisky and gin, repeating the deception many times until the tour finished. Looking back I am amazed at my nerve, for impersonating an officer was a court martial offence, and impersonating a padre probably carried a life sentence!

Immediately after my demobilisation from the army, I was lucky enough to go straight into a new play called *Gathering Storm*. I had created the role during my days in Rugby Rep and the author, Gordon Glennon, asked for me again when Sam Goldwyn Jnr remounted it for the West End. I played a simpleton falsely accused of murdering his grandmother. Nancy Price, in the role of the grandmother, was the star. She was variously and irreverently known as 'Nancy Half-Price' or 'Nancy-not-at-any-Price' and as far as I was concerned lived up to her reputation. It was a cold January when we started rehearsals and she pleaded hypothermia and said she could only rehearse her scenes with me in the warmth of her own depressing flat. Required to present myself there promptly every morning I would greet her with, 'Good morning, Miss Price, I hope you're feeling better,' and get the snarled response, 'Don't want your sympathy, just get on with the dialogue.'

The other hazard was that she rehearsed with a particularly vicious parrot on her shoulder. Her greatest success had been in *Whiteoaks* in which she shared the honours with this parrot, named Boney. It took an instant dislike to me and whenever, as the action required me to, I got close to its mistress it went on the attack. More than once while we were in the middle of the scene, the bird would relieve itself, depositing a trail of green slime on the shawl covering Nancy's shoulders. This did not faze her.

'Cloth!' she would shout before continuing her dialogue and an ancient crone would appear and remove the offending slime. All in all rehearsals were extremely unnerving.

I should also add that my role demanded that I had a dog on stage with me most of the time, and that it was to the dog that my character confided all his secrets. The question was, where could we find a docile, compliant hound? Several were auditioned, but in every case the owners withdrew their pets when they discovered that the play would tour before coming into the St Martin's theatre. It was then that the management dispatched me to the Battersea Dogs' Home to select a potential star performer. Not a wise decision as it turned out. Appalled by the pounds full of abandoned pets, most of whom were destined to be put down, I chose one at random. Naturally the poor animal regarded me as its saviour and for a time behaved impeccably, doing everything required of it on stage and captivating audiences.

That is until we got to the Theatre Royal, Brighton. I was staying in some lodgings called Ross Mansions, mostly populated with skaters from the ice show at the Hippodrome. Ross Mansions consisted of a series of small cubby holes where the transient occupants were expected to survive with self-catering: the establishment did not boast a restaurant and room-service was unknown. They provided a small electric ring concealed in a cupboard and a few pots and pans that looked as though ferrets had slept in them. At the time it was all I could afford, for I came out of the army virtually penniless. During my week's stay I had a visit from a midnight cowboy. One of the male skaters entered my room while I was asleep and lisped in my ear, 'The moon could shine for you tonight,' perhaps not the most memorable suggestion I have ever received and it was an occasion when I did not say no gracefully. I hit him with a shoe.

Not only wasn't I very good at fending for myself, I also had the responsibility of caring for the stray dog. Since I had never had a dog of my own before, I made the mistake of buying and trying to cook dogfish. (Readers might well wonder whether I was totally retarded despite four years in the army.) It looked big enough to last him the entire week. This was before frozen food so there were no instructions on the packet; without degutting it I cooked it whole in one of the ancient saucepans, with the result that it swelled up like a balloon and then exploded, covering the walls and ceiling. I spent the entire night trying to remove the stinking debris before the management got wind of it.

There was a further disaster on the Wednesday matinée. Perhaps the poor dog was crazed when I rescued him from Battersea, or else he had read his notices, but during a love scene played by Emrys Jones and Mary Mackenzie, he cocked his leg against the sofa they were sitting on and peed endlessly. The rake on the Theatre Royal stage was acute and the pee ran down into the footlights which immediately fused and went off like a series of firecrackers. My faithful hound, doubtless exhilarated by the hysteria and applause from the audience, then jumped through the phoney fireplace, bit the fireman standing in the wings, ran out of the stage door and was never seen again. Between the matinée and the evening show the author did some quick rewriting and thereafter my character talked to an *imaginary* dog.

Nancy Price was killed off at the end of the second act, and this did not sit well with her. Every night whether the applause justified it or not, she stepped forward at the curtain and made a speech which began, 'When we dead awaken'. To our cringing embarrassment she then went on to solicit gifts of food from the audience (rationing was still in force) and exhort them to buy copies of her latest book.

The play opened at the St Martin's during a February blizzard and only survived three weeks. I was relieved to get away from grandma and my ghostly dog and was lucky enough to be spotted by Dennis Van Thal, then the talent scout for the Rank Organisation, which resulted in a film contract at Pinewood Studios. After my first featured role in a guileless and parochial British comedy called *All Over the Town*, I resumed my stage career.

One of Binkie's innovations was to employ a full-time casting director who scoured the country looking for new talent who would then be brought to London, first as understudies and then, if they behaved themselves, given minor roles. The casting director's name was Daphne Rye, a remarkable lady by any standards who stood at one remove from the Tennent inner circle, part of it but not engulfed by it. She gathered around her a small circle of young actors often giving them bed and board, and they were known as Daphne's Lodgers. I was one of them, so was Richard Burton, and for a period Richard and I shared Daphne's superb cooking and indeed a girlfriend.

It was to Daphne that I owed my rise through the ranks, for she was entirely responsible for my major West End engagements, casting me as Gertrude Lawrence's son in *September Tide*, Daphne du Maurier's romantic play, which marked Gertie's return to London after seventeen years. It ran to packed houses at the Aldwych for nine months and then we subsequently toured it around the major cities. After that I was put into Wynyard Browne's haunting Chekhovian drama *The Holly and the Ivy* which this time ran for eighteen months after a shaky start in Cardiff.

The opening week in Cardiff gave me an illustration of the way in which Binkie operated. The play is set in a Norfolk vicarage at Christmas and centres around the moral dilemma posed by the return of a journalist daughter who has had and lost a child out of wedlock. The result of her tragedy, unknown to her widowed father, the vicar, is that she has become disillusioned and a drunk. Daphne Arthur, a superb young actress, played this role and I played her brother, a serving private in the army, who also returns to the family hearth for Christmas. There is another sub-plot involving the elder sister, played by the delectable Jane Baxter, who has sacrificed her life in order to look after her father. The role of the vicar was played by one of the finest actors I ever worked with, Herbert Lomas, inevitably nicknamed 'Tiny' because of his height. There were various secondary roles one of which was filled by a distinguished actor, the husband of one of our revered actresses, who had, but was alleged to have conquered, a drink problem. All went well during rehearsals and he appeared to have got everything under control. The auspices for success were good.

Towards the middle of the first act Daphne and I, unable to take the atmosphere in the house, go out to a pub and return much later the worse for wear. Coming in from the snow to the sudden warmth, Daphne passes out in front of her father and the others. At which moment the character played by the alleged reformed alcoholic steps forward and says: 'Leave this to me, Martin. I've been dealing with drunks all my life.'

The stage directions then require him to lift the unconscious Daphne and carry her upstairs.

It was unfortunate dialogue as it turned out. On the first night the poor man stepped forward, delivered his line, bent to pick up Daphne and pitched forward on top of her, never to rise again. He had obviously fallen off the wagon, doubtless to try and stifle his first-night nerves. There was nothing Tiny Lomas and I could do to save the situation; we stood transfixed as the curtain fell for the end of the act.

Now since it was the very first time the play had ever been performed, some members of the Cardiff audience might well have thought that this was all part of the plot. Not so Binkie Beaumont, who was out front. He came backstage and fired the actor on the spot, then instructed Frith Banbury, the director, to go on and read the role for the remaining two acts. The dismissed actor made a botched attempt at suicide and to the best of my knowledge never worked again in any major production. His wife supported him until he died. It was a revealing example of the ruthless side of Binkie's nature.

During the subsequent run of the play I was to be given a further insight into his personality. His office was at the top of the Globe theatre in Shaftesbury Avenue and could only be reached by a small elevator that held two people in tight proximity. The inner sanctum was guarded by his secretary, the formidable Miss Byers. Binkie was further protected by his publicity lady, known throughout the business as 'No news is good news', since she was under orders to keep Binkie's name out of the papers. He shunned personal publicity and was rarely photographed, though it is interesting to note that, having granted a rare session to Angus McBean, he allowed himself to be shown as a manipulator of puppets.

While *The Holly and the Ivy* was enjoying its long run at the Duchess theatre I was summoned to the Globe and the presence. I made the ascent in the confined lift, feeling distinctly uneasy: had my performance slipped, was I about to be fired, had I made some unguarded remark about my employer that had been reported back to him? It was in this mood that I was shown into Binkie's holy of holies where I found him with his long-time lover, John Perry. Much to my relief I was greeted warmly. The chain-smoking Binkie always spoke slowly, stretching and giving equal value to every word.

'We're very p-l-e-a-s-e-d with you, very pleased indeed,' he said, in that soft, silky way he had, and I breathed again. 'I slipped in to see the last act the other night and I thought your performance was still very good.'

Then he went straight to the point. 'But we've got a little problem.' Pause. Again the smile that implied anticipated complicity, 'We're very b-o-r-e-d with Claire Bloom's virginity and we thought you could do something about it.' 'Bored' was given a special emphasis.

Why he ever made such a preposterous statement remains a mystery. Daphne Rye later told me that there had been some conflict between Binkie and Claire's mother, but I was never able to corroborate this. Equally astonishing was the suggestion, delivered with a hint of menace, that I could and should help matters. Shamefully, but firmly believing that my career depended on it, I nodded and heard myself say: 'Yes, of course, Mr Beaumont.'

After a few more pleasantries I was sent on my way to solve the problem. At that time the ravishing young Claire was appearing in *Ring Around the Moon* and was the toast of the town. I knew her to say hello to since we all ate in a small sandwich bar called Taylor's in nearby Wardour Street, a sort of New York deli where actors, who made up most of the clientele, were given favoured treatment and often allowed credit when out of work. The next time I saw her there I asked if she would like to see a film with me one afternoon and have tea afterwards and she accepted. Without Binkie's prompting I would have been more than willing to squire Miss Bloom and counted myself a fortunate man, for she fulfilled all my ideals – having recovered from my initial, traumatic encounter with the opposite sex I had been transformed into a fervent romantic. During my time in the army

I had had several affairs, including one in occupied Austria which had left an emotional scar, and I tended to fall in love with alarming regularity, my heart heavily influenced by literary parallels.

Claire and I had two or three totally innocent dates but I made no progress in complying with Binkie's suggestion for the simple reason that she was not ready for any deeper relationship with me or anybody else. Looking back, the fact that I even made the attempt to go along with Binkie's dictum I find craven and pathetic, but incredible though it may seem in this day and age, I felt convinced that my future would be blighted. In the end I found the necessary resolve to ignore his wishes and felt the better for it. Curiously I never again worked for Tennent's – whether this was coincidence or connected in any way with my failure as a Casanova hitman I will never know.

I should add that years later I revealed my hideous secret to Claire and we had a good laugh about it. As for Binkie, he had no affinity with the New Wave plays pioneered by George Devine at the Royal Court which climaxed with the success of Osborne's *Look Back in Anger*. To Binkie both the plays and the actors who performed them lacked glamour; kitchen sinks and coarse language on stage were not his scene. He would not or could not move with the times, and the times gradually passed him by. Even when Olivier went over to the opposition in *The Entertainer*, Binkie still did not get the message. He was trapped by his own legend and incapable of breaking loose. Close friends became increasingly distressed at the way in which he allowed his appearance to go to pieces. He had always been immaculate, now he drank more and more, neglected the way he dressed, his hitherto smooth hair-style left unkempt. Often he had to be put to bed, ugly drunk, at the end of an evening. He was no longer somebody to be feared, but an object of pity. I remember that during this period Nanette and I attended a large charity dinner. We were seated at separate tables and at the end of the evening Nanette said to me: 'Who was that drunk on my right? He hardly uttered and was covered in cigarette ash.'

'That,' I said, 'was the famous Binkie Beaumont.'

He smiled at me, a wan token of recognition, but said nothing as he left the table and wandered into the night. I thought back to the days of *Flare Path*, *September Tide* and *The Holly and the Ivy* when merely to have been acknowledged by him had made an actor's day, and of the power he had once wielded now wrested from him.

For all that, I retain more happy mementoes than sad ones from my days as an actor. Acting was always a joy for me; I have always had a photographic memory, so learning lines never presented any difficulty, and, because of the acute shortage of young actors during the war, I was fortunate to get some early breaks. There is no justice in the profession; the theatre squanders, abuses and, worst of all, ignores talent as often as it extols it and the actor is never, for a single moment of his existence, other than at the mercy of the entrepreneur. I know so many fine actors who have never been given that one role that takes them to the top. They make a living, they would not be anything other than an actor, yet the necessary extra ounce of luck never comes their way, and somehow they keep going, spurred on by the belief that this week, next month, maybe next year, the main chance will fall into their laps. Television has widened the scope of employment for the actor but at the same time made him less mysterious. Beamed into every living room he is sold like a detergent, discarded like a beer can, when the poverty of his material falls below the tolerance level of the lowest common denominator. Television destroyed the repertory system, closed innumerable cinemas and in the main substituted the quiz game, the formula series, the glorification of the amateur. That is why I have to admire the average actor and ignore his conceits, for they are his defence against failure and the life he leads is almost beyond the comprehension of outsiders.

Actors have a singleness of purpose which, like a condemned man, concentrates the mind. There is a story told of the late Ernest Milton, an actor of the old school, which I have always thought highlights this determining characteristic. Apparently he once appeared in a blank verse play of surpassing mediocrity in a small theatre on the outskirts of London. It was the first night and he was in his dressing room applying, as was his habit, far too much make-up. There was a knock at the door and the distraught stage manager stammered that the curtain could not go up because the juvenile had been arrested.

Ernest made no comment, merely applied more eyebrow liner.

'Mr Milton, I beg you to listen. We cannot take the curtain up. He's been arrested, Mr Milton, he's in jail.'

Again no response from Ernest as he outlined his mouth.

'We can't put the understudy on, he doesn't know a word. Mr Milton, sir, do please take in what I'm saying. There is no possibility of the play opening tonight.'

Ernest finally turned round. He smiled and then said, as though it was the only obvious response, 'Demand his captors to release him,' in a voice made for parody.

Back-stage existence for a long run assumes a pattern all of its own. Dressing rooms become second homes, cluttered with familiar odds and ends brought in to remind us that there is life beyond six evening performances and two matinees. The first night telegrams stuck around the mirror grow yellow with age, becoming like the messages of condolence on graves. There will be a small drinks bar prepared against the chance that somebody will come round after the show, but the fact is that visitors tend to fall away after the initial month and if one is in the same play over a long period friends enquire, 'What are you doing now?' and when you remind them, they say, 'Oh, that's still on is it?' You are to all intents dead and buried. If the play runs through summer, while others get a tan you endure matinees sparsely attended by old ladies who have perfected the art of dropping their tea trays during your best scene. As the winter months approach and you are still there, the tea-tray-droppers are augmented by those dying of consumption. Then the actors' nightmare rears its head: you go on stage one night and find that your mind is an entire blank. The lines you have said several hundred times have vanished into thin air. This attacks the great as well as the small part player; nobody, no matter how exalted, is immune. Or else you fall prey to the hysteria syndrome. Towards the end of *The Holly and the Ivy*'s run, dear Jane Baxter could never play the scene we had together at the beginning of the third act without succumbing to a fit of the giggles. Every night she tried to overcome it, and every night it happened. There is never any rational explanation for it and every actor I know has experienced it at some stage. Olivier, no mean giggler himself, once told me of an experience he had in a Shakespearean production. I'm sure he embroidered the account for extra effect, but why not?

A third of the way in, an actor playing a messenger mistook his cue and rushed on stage, flung himself at Olivier's feet and said something to the effect, 'My Liege, the Duke of Buckingham is slain this hour.'

Now the Duke of Buckingham had yet to come on and was certainly not slain because he had a lot of plot to impart. Taken by surprise but nevertheless equal to the occasion, Olivier replied, 'Nay, I think you mistaken, sirrah.'

The actor now assumed that Olivier had dried and persisted. 'I have seen the dreadful sight with mine own eyes, my Lord. By yonder thicket he lies, cold as the grave.'

Olivier lifted the actor to his feet and gripped him by the neck. 'Ist positive, villain?' he hissed.

'Yeah, my Lord,' the actor stuttered, greatly alarmed at Olivier's expression.

'Ist *absolutely* positive?'

'I swear it be so!'

Olivier gripped him tightly around the throat, turned him upstage and snarled, 'Then, by my troth, thou hast fucketh the entire play.'

I think the beauty of this story, true or false – and I am inclined to believe it for there are many similar stories told about Olivier – is that both participants stayed in character and invented Shakespearean ad libs. I so hope it really happened.

Missed entrances, wrong costume changes, agonising 'dries' – they all play their part in an actor's life. Laurence Naismith was once running a weekly rep theatre in a south coast seaside resort. Funds were low and he was forced to take on a variety of chores – direct the plays, supervise the box office, design some of the sets, as well as acting a number of roles. On this particular day he was in the wings worrying where he would get the money to pay everybody when one of the actors on stage looked through a fake window and hissed: 'George is off!'

Galvanised, Larry rushed to the ground floor dressing rooms and shouted: 'George, you missed your cue. Get on stage.'

Nobody answered. He ran up the stairs to the next floor and repeated the cry. Again, no response. There were two remaining dressing rooms at the top of the building and close to a heart attack he made the ascent at a run. 'George!' he screamed, 'For God's sake get down on the stage. You've been off for two minutes.'

A member of the cast appeared from one of the rooms wiping his face with a towel stiff with old removal cream. 'What's up, Larry?'

'What's up? Bloody George missed his cue. God knows what's happening on stage.'

'But *you're* George,' the actor said. 'You're playing George this week.' Collapse of Larry.

Not only actors but theatre dressers also provide amusing moments. Male or female, they are a unique breed and seem to have been pressed out of the same mould. When we appeared on stage together Nanette and I shared a gentle soul called Lou, who lived with his one-legged ex-boxer lover. He was in the habit of bringing us revolting good luck tokens, such as a moth-eaten rabbit's paw, on first nights. When we were not working he wrote every week, enclosing faded photographs of himself as a panto-mime dame in some long-forgotten production. He was hopeless as a dresser, but we never had the heart to fire him; he only lived through us and was loyal to the point of madness.

For the run of *September Tide* Michael Gough and I shared another such dear soul called Herbert. He was a chattering old worldly figure who appeared every night in a variety of bizarre clothes which I suspect were remnants of his own distant days on the boards. My role and my salary really did not warrant a dresser, but he meant so well that I tolerated him. Michael, on the other hand, had several costume changes and Herbert's main responsibility was to stand ready to assist Michael during a crucial moment in the second act. The plot was that, during a violent storm when he is alone in an isolated Cornish house with his mother-in-law (played by Gertie Lawrence), Michael dives into the estuary below to secure a drifting boat. He dived, of course, into a pile of mattresses strategically placed out of sight of the audience. Then he had to immerse himself in a bath of lukewarm water (prepared by Herbert) and reappear later suitably drenched. Meanwhile, on stage, Gertie went to a cupboard and took out some towels, ready for Michael's return. She towelled his semi-naked body – a very daring scene for 1948 – then they sat in front of the fire and cooked and ate an omelette (made with dried eggs) before falling into each other's arms. The vital point, heavily established in dialogue, was that they were cut off from the rest of the world and could thus sin in safety.

On this particular matinee just prior to Michael's dramatic dive one of the rope cleats securing the substantial set gave way. In a panic the stage manager told Herbert to hold onto a support rope while he went in search of a stage hand. Michael did his leap and then groped his way in the darkness to the lukewarm bath, minus Herbert.

It so happened that Herbert at this point was positioned directly behind the cupboard containing the towels. Gertie opened the cupboard door and revealed Herbert curiously attired in pin-stripe trousers, a collarless shirt and white tennis shoes. I should add that he also sported spectacles and a moustache, which made him look like Himmler. She was too dumbfounded to do anything, and for a few seconds she and Herbert stood transfixed. Being of the old school and knowing his manners when faced with a star, Herbert couldn't help himself. He gave a stiff little bow and said, 'Good afternoon, Miss Lawrence.' He then handed her the towels.

Until his good manners betrayed him, the matinee audience may have been surprised but not necessarily thrown by this unexpected plot twist. They had not seen the play before and possibly imagined that Daphne du Maurier had intended her heroine to be suddenly confronted by Himmler concealed in a cupboard and wearing tennis shoes. But of course when Herbert paid his respects to Gertie by name, the game was up. Unable to suppress her mounting hysteria, Gertie slammed the cupboard shut, turned away up stage and stumbled into a sodden Michael who had been greeted with a howl of laughter and now found himself playing the scene with a leading lady who appeared to be inexplicably drunk. How they got through the rest of the act including cooking and eating the dreaded omelette was further proof that necessity is the mother of invention. To her credit, when she was told the facts, Gertie refused to be angry with poor Herbert, as many other stars might well have been.

Eating meals on stage is invariably a hazard, and the egg scene in *September Tide* was particularly irksome and accident prone. After we finished the run at the Aldwych and Gertie went home, the play was then toured with an entirely new cast. Gertie's and Michael's original roles were played by a couple of somewhat advanced years. The gentleman in particular needed some help from Max Factor and also wore a toupee to aid credibility. The moment came when the infamous omelette had to be cooked. The actress went off stage to bring the wine leaving her cohort to cook the concoction over a primus stove. As he bent over his task the toupee came loose and dropped into the omelette pan. Traumatised, he stirred it into the mass of eggs. The lady returned, gay and expectant with the Nuits St Georges, prepared to play a tender scene with her young lover, and found herself confronted with a demented, bald-headed old man cooking a pan of hairy eggs which eventually they both had to eat and pretend to enjoy. It was achingly funny to watch, for at the end of the long scene they had to embrace, sharing not only passion, but strands of toupee.

TWENTY-SIX

It has always been fashionable amongst novelists writing of Hollywood to depict producers as boorish illiterates and certainly many accounts have been written from the heart, the authors having experienced a crash course in humiliation from their own Sammy Glicks. Towards the end of his life Fitzgerald wrote a number of short stories, featuring a hack screenwriter named Pat Hobby as his central character, which were thinly disguised pieces of autobiography. Raymond Chandler, Irwin Shaw, Odets, Faulkner, Benchley, Dorothy Parker, Harry Kurnitz all carried away scars from the ironically named Garden of Allah where many of them drowned their sorrows. (The Garden was still there on Sunset Boulevard when I first went to Hollywood in 1951, but by then it had become a sad trysting place for transient lovers, peopled with ghosts.)

Every studio used to have a writers' isolation ward where the inmates were kept apart from the rest of the team. Before the Writers' Guild of America obtained sufficient muscle to challenge the system it was common practice for the studios to farm out a script to three or four different writers at the same time with none of them being aware that they were not the sole author. They were the low men on the totem pole until they got organised, so it is not surprising that if and when they escaped the treadmill they sought to hit back in their fictions. I have been guilty myself because in common with the majority of my colleagues my screenwriting career is littered with horror stories.

But like everything else there are exceptions to the rule and I have enjoyed working with several fine producers who have made invaluable contributions to the collective effort. The first was, of course, Richard Attenborough. We formed a production company together called Beaver Films at a crucial point in our joint careers when we felt we were floundering and too dependent on the whims of others. I think the reason we complemented each other so well, starting with *The Angry Silence*, is that we were opposites. Dickie is a perennial optimist (witness his eighteen-year struggle to get *Gandhi* made) whereas I am inclined to be one of Nature's pessimists. Our partnership went on to make several other films, notably *Whistle Down the Wind* and *Seance on a Wet Afternoon*, before our paths went off at a tangent.

It was around this time that I was fortunate enough to join forces with a remarkable producer named James Woolf. He and his brother John ran Romulus Films and had a string of distinguished films to their credit, including the landmark *Room at the Top*. I remember I first met Jimmy when I was staying at the Beverly Hills Hotel. Passing through the dimly lit Polo Lounge a hand came out of the gloom and thrust a book at me. 'Read that,' a disembodied voice said, 'and if you like it write a screenplay for me.' When my eyes had become accustomed to the murk I discerned Jimmy sitting at his favourite table. His suits were always rumpled and he made no concessions to the Los Angeles climate – heavy tweed, whatever the temperature.

I looked at the title of the book. It was Lynn Reid Banks' *The L-Shaped Room*.

'Take it away and let me know,' Jimmy continued. That was how he always did deals, on a hunch, on a handshake, and his handshake was good. He had great taste in material and an infallible eye for talent. Jack Clayton, Laurence Harvey, Michael Caine, Terry Stamp, Sarah Miles, as well as myself, have Jimmy to thank for giving a fillip to our careers when it was most needed. In many ways I always felt he was a sad and unfulfilled man who lived his life through others. Once when we shared a suite in the Gresham Hotel in Dublin over a period of months, he confided that he thought of himself as Quasimodo. This was because he had a harelip, but I can't say that I was ever really conscious of it.

Jimmy loved to throw parties, big parties, where he mixed the famous and unknowns with himself as a retiring host. He was a generous man, and it was difficult if not impossible to return his hospitality.

The L-Shaped Room had originally been earmarked for Jack Clayton to direct, but Jack was ever slow to come to a decision and after six months or so Jimmy got tired of waiting and gave the direction to me. He had inspired ideas where casting was concerned – Simone Signoret for *Room at the Top*, Cicely Courtneidge and Pat Phoenix for *L-Shaped*. The deal, the casting and pre-production were what Jimmy liked best, once shooting began he took a back seat, content to view the rushes, have lunch at the studio, listen to the latest gossip and then go home to play gin rummy. He was a true producer in that he never chiselled on the money if he felt the film needed it. 'It's always cheaper to live at the Ritz,' was one of his maxims, though he himself kept a permanent apartment at Grosvenor House.

When *L-Shaped* was finished we ran into difficulties with the censor who sent us four closely typed pages of items that were unacceptable.* He was not happy with any references to contraceptives, breast and thigh rubbing and copulatory dancing were totally ruled out, as were all erotic visuals. I wonder what he would have made of a 'comedy' I saw recently in which the leading actress was required to remove a condom from a dead man who had expired during a frenzied sexual bout. We, on the other hand, were required to substitute 'tart' for 'whore' and even a mild joke about 'getting a bun in the oven' was questioned. Nowadays such edicts seem like messages from another planet, and by current standards the film is totally inoffensive. I saw it again recently when I was given a retrospective season at the Cherbourg festival; it sounded much better in French but I could detect nothing in the visuals that could have caused the slightest discomfort to Mary Whitehouse. I remember that Leslie Caron had to have her nipples covered with Elastoplast for the love scene, and the sequence where she visited the Harley Street

*See Appendix 2.

abortionist, played with sinister charm by Emlyn Williams, was tortuously oblique. Would it have been any better by being explicit? I doubt it. Suggestion is nearly always preferable and more erotic than a voyeur's birds'-eye view of the human sexual act. Nearly every film one sees today contains the statutory hump, or what Nanette calls 'a bit of leg-over acting'. I am not advocating that we return to the ludicrous days of the Hays Office, but it would show more creative skill and imagination if occasionally there was a variation on the boring theme of simulated fucking.

Once Jimmy and I had satisfied the censor we had another problem on our hands. *L-Shaped* had been funded by British Lion/Columbia, a joint company employing both British and American finance. Mike Frankovitch who was then in charge of the British arm of Columbia screened the final cut and asked for it to be shortened. After argument and discussion we agreed to remove seven minutes. It was then the turn of the British Lion Board to put in their two cents with Roy Boulting acting as spokesman. He sent Jimmy a long letter making the case for further and more extensive cuts and certain scenes to be deleted in their entirety and quoted the opinion of Peter King, then an exhibitor, who had urged that the film be cut by at least twenty minutes and given a happy ending.

Roy Boulting had picked out many of Jimmy's favourite moments in the film and I had never seen him so incensed. Within minutes of receiving the letter he dictated a reply, defending our version of the film with pith and passion. 'Regarding Peter King, possibly pig-headedly and arrogantly, his opinion is of no interest to me. His prime concern, like most exhibitors, is probably how fast and how many times he can get his customers in and out of the theatres for which he books.' He concluded in masterly fashion, well aware that both Boulting Brothers were in the habit of bristling and rushing into print if their own creative views were ever questioned, 'I know you believe all independent producers should have complete freedom and should stand or fall by their own judgement . . . I therefore wish the film to take its chances as it stands.'

His reply was not well received, but Jimmy stuck to his guns and carried the day. The film was shown as we wanted it and proved an enormous critical and commercial success and continues to bring in respectable sums of money thirty years later.

After the London opening we both flew to Los Angeles for a gala screening at the Directors' Guild theatre. Leslie Caron deservedly won the coveted New York Critics Award for best actress and went on to receive an Oscar nomination, a pattern duplicated by two of my other leading ladies – Kim Stanley and Dame Edith.

Planes were falling out of the sky with alarming regularity that year and Nanette persuaded me to come home by boat. I took the train from Los Angeles to New York, thinking it would be an adventure, but it turned out to be four and a half days of non-stop boredom, although the food and accommodation were superb and one's every need catered for by attendants who seemed to have stepped straight out of a Norman Rockwell cover. Jimmy refused to endure the train journey with me, but instead arranged to meet me in New York a few days before Christmas and had booked passages on the SS *France*. I travelled with a mass of Christmas presents including bicycles for the children and a mink coat for Nanette which Jimmy had cajoled me into buying from a friend of his; he loved doing deals.

Half an hour before the *France* was due to sail Jimmy wandered into my stateroom and announced, 'Don't unpack, Byron, because we're getting off.' (It was one of his quirks to call me Byron.)

'Getting off? Why?'

'Because the accommodation isn't suitable.'

'My cabin's fine,' I said, aghast, since I was anxious to get home for Christmas. 'But I'm quite happy if you want to swop.'

'Don't argue, Byron,' he said. 'You're a very unsophisticated traveller. There's no way I'm going to spend five days shut up in a French hovel. Come along.'

'Well, perhaps they can give us different cabins,' I said, desperate to change his mind. 'Why don't we go and ask?'

Reluctantly persuaded, Jimmy marched me into the first-class dining room where the Head Purser was taking table reservations. Jimmy strode resolutely to the head of the queue and immediately blamed the whole thing on me by implication. 'My friend, who is a very distinguished film director, cannot possibly stay in the accommodation you have given us. Either you change our cabins or we must get off the boat. What else have you got?'

'But we sail any moment, Monsieur,' the Purser said. 'And the only thing vacant is the Provence suite.'

'That sounds much more suitable,' Jimmy replied. 'Show it to us.'

We were escorted to the sun deck and ushered into a magnificent suite the size of a hockey pitch consisting of an enormous living area, two vast double bedrooms, two bathrooms, a bar and hallway which had obviously been designed to accommodate Heads of State.

Jimmy didn't hesitate, 'We'll take it. How much?'

The Purser did some rapid mental calculations. 'It will be another six hundred and thirty dollars per person extra, Monsieur,' he announced.

I'll give you two hundred dollars cash,' was Jimmy's swift reply.

With the boat about to cast off the Purser was not the man to forgo a handout. 'I accept,' he said.

When he had left Jimmy turned to me with a grin. 'Those grabby French are no match for a Jewish boy,' he said. We spent the voyage in splendour, though I must say that the pride of France had none of the atmosphere of the old *Queen Mary*.

The end of the journey also furnished drama of a different kind. Packed and ready to disembark, Jimmy and I were playing a last game of gin rummy when I became conscious that everywhere was very silent.

'Shouldn't we be getting off?' I enquired.

'They'll tell us,' Jimmy said. 'We haven't even docked yet. I know about these things and you don't, Byron.'

I stared out of the porthole. 'Then why am I looking at a warehouse with a large sign on it saying RANK HOVIS SOUTHAMPTON?'

In fact we had not only arrived some hours before, we were the only two passengers for England still left on board and the ship was about to cast off again. A very alarmed Nanette had been waiting on the dockside and it was entirely due to her frantic enquiries that a steward came to the suite and hurried us off. Otherwise we would have spent Christmas in Cherbourg. Characteristically, Jimmy blamed the whole thing on the French. 'They just don't know how to run a boat.'

There was another story which Jimmy loved to tell concerning a flight he had once taken to New York. He found himself sitting next to a friend, Al Burnett, the well-known London club owner who was taking the trip in order to attend a very important auction. Apparently Burnett was an extremely nervous flier and constantly asked Jimmy whether the engines were secure on the wings (the engine pods on the 707s were designed to be flexible in flight). 'Look,' Jimmy said, 'I can't sit here for seven hours listening to your fears. Take one of these relaxing pills and enjoy it.' He offered Al one of his sleeping pills.

Burnett eyed the pill suspiciously. 'What is it?'

'Nothing. Just a mild tranquilliser.'

Because he was constantly in pain from an old back complaint and in the habit of taking numerous painkillers the pills had little effect on Jimmy – he took them to snatch an hour's respite after lunch – but to anybody else they were fairly lethal. Al Burnett was persuaded to swallow one and according to Jimmy's version slept for fifteen hours, had to be put to bed on arrival in New York and missed the auction. It was a story Jimmy often repeated with great glee.

Although a bachelor Jimmy had a winning way with children and took a particular fancy to our daughter Sarah. When she was five or six he gave her lunch at the old Caprice where the great Mario Gallati presided. 'I know exactly what children like to eat,' Jimmy told Nanette as he and Sarah set out. 'Beetroot and ice cream.' He ordered an Ivor Novello Bomb as a first course; this was a gigantic ice cream concoction, a speciality of the house. Thereafter Sarah regarded him as an inspired surrogate uncle.

It was Sarah who was responsible for saving his life on one

occasion. We were all in Dublin for the ill-fated remake of *Of Human Bondage*. It was a dreary Sunday afternoon and we took Sarah to the zoo while Jimmy said he would have a nap. When we returned from the zoo Sarah wandered along to Jimmy's room to take him a present. She came back and said, 'Uncle Jimmy's asleep,' then added in all innocence, 'he's asleep on the floor.' Nanette and I rushed to his room to find him unconscious. We called an ambulance and he was taken to hospital, a Catholic hospital, naturally, staffed by nuns. There he was given a stomach pump and kept in overnight, listed as having taken a drug overdose. The following morning when I visited him he was distraught. 'You have to get me out of here, Byron,' he said. I explained that the Mother Superior had already told me he could not be discharged without the authority of the Registrar. 'Make a large donation to her favourite charity,' Jimmy instructed. 'That'll change her mind.' He was right. The money produced an immediate reversal of her medical opinion and I spirited Jimmy out of a side entrance, avoiding the waiting reporters who by now were sniffing around intent on having a suicide attempt confirmed.

This was only one of a series of unhappy incidents that plagued this particular film. Henry Hathaway, the veteran director, disliked Kim Novak and treated her shamefully. Kim confided that early in her career she had been told by Harry Cohn, 'All you are is a piece of meat in a butcher's shop,' and that is how Hathaway regarded her. At one point his language was so gross that Laurence Harvey and I left the set and refused to continue until he had apologised. Hathaway then fought to have Kim replaced but in the end he was the one who took a walk. I can't pretend that anybody shed any tears at his departure, for he was unpleasant to underlings and lacked any subtlety as a director. The production went into hiatus, Kim fled to London to escape the press and in order to avoid a permanent closure I was persuaded to relinquish my acting role and take over as director until a replacement could be found. For ten days or so I directed sequences involving Larry and Siobhan McKenna while waiting for Ken Hughes to arrive and complete the film.

Nanette and me with Lord Delfont on the Embankment outside the Savoy Hotel on the day my appointment as Head of Production at Elstree Studios was announced.

First week in the new job at Elstree. My office left much to be desired. The piles of scripts on my desk were but the tip of the iceberg.

Nanette in the title role
of *Jessie* which I wrote
from her original idea.

George Courtney Ward
shot this picture at the
exact moment I was
telling Nanette that I
was stopping production
of the ill-fated *A Fine
and Private Place*.

Nanette and me talking to Bette Davis in the parking lot at Pinewood Studios.

Graham Greene visited the set while we were shooting *Menage a Trois*. This shot was taken an Antibes railway station, a short distance from the simple apartment he lived in for many years.

My sorely missed friend George Hillsden, a man everybody liked, for he had the
true Cockney outlook on life.

My perennial sound man and chess partner, Gus Lloyd.

BRYAN FORBES

With Margaret Thatcher in the garden at Seven Pines while shooting a Party Political. We appear to be about to do a number from *Chorus Line*!

With Katherine Ross on the set of *The Stepford Wives*, in Westport, Connecticut.

Lord Linley, Her Majesty Queen Elizabeth, The Queen Mother, Naim Attallah,
John Asprey (the two executive producers of the film) me, HRH The Princess
Margaret, Bill Daniels (my sound mixer) Lady Sarah Armstrong Jones, and our two
daughters, Emma and Sarah. They were all watching the shooting of one of the
musical numbers, *The Slipper and the Rose*, at Pinewood Studios.

A young Elton John by the lake at Seven Pines with Sarah and Emma.

A shot of the tragic Sharon Tate I took
for the cover of *Queen* long before she was well known.

Before he departed Hathaway had cast Nanette in the role of Roger Livesey's daughter. It was at a time when anything connected with the Profumo affair caused frantic press activity. When Nanette flew from London to Dublin to begin shooting, some misguided journalist at Heathrow decided she was Christine Keeler. By the time she arrived in Dublin a posse of photographers were waiting; and despite her protestations that she was not who they thought she was, shots of Nanette duly appeared under the headline 'Keeler makes mystery trip to Dublin'. It was a curious footnote to a production that was never lacking in unscripted dramatic incidents.

After *L-Shaped* and *Of Human Bondage* I completed my mammoth and ultimately unrealised *Churchill* script, then wrote and directed the second of our Beaver films, *Seance on a Wet Afternoon*. Part of the kidnapping sequence was shot in the garden at Seven Pines and required a dawn shot. I was discussing the scene with Dickie who was made up complete with an altered nose. Engrossed with the problems ahead I suddenly became conscious that he had not answered my last question. I looked around and he was lying on the ground, unconscious. A doctor was called and it was discovered that he had kidney stones. The pain was such that he could not possibly shoot that day; he was given a shot of morphine and put to bed. There was no fat on our budget, so there was nothing else for it: I donned his clothes and our make-up man applied the nose putty. For that one sequence it is me, not Dickie, carrying the child.

When we finished *Seance* I became convinced that I had turned out a turkey, as we name flops in the cinema. My editor Derek Yorke and I slaved over the cut for weeks, but the more I studied the film the more depressed I became, so much so that I decided to leave the country before it opened and sailed off on the *Queen Mary*. Jimmy had offered me *King Rat* to script and direct and I was moving the family to a rented house on Laurel Way in Beverly Hills where we were to stay for the best part of a year. On arrival in New York I was handed a cable from Dickie saying that we had a critical triumph. Curiously, the American distribution rights in the film were acquired by the band leader, Artie Shaw, one time husband of Ava Gardner. In America at least, the film became a cult and is still frequently shown on television there.

Jimmy was his usual pillar of strength during the pre-production period when we were casting *King Rat*, supporting me against the studio front office who were adamant that we should employ a variety of middle-aged Americans. James Clavell's compelling novel had been written about the young men who had been taken prisoner by the Japanese the moment they stepped off the troop ships in Singapore. Most of them, like James, were in their early twenties when captured and it would have been a travesty had we given in to the studio's ludicrous suggestions. Jimmy fought a running battle over many anxious weeks with the Screen Actors' Guild to get them to allow a dozen or so British actors to act the roles the story demanded. Eventually a workable compromise was reached: in return for employing every resident British actor in Hollywood on the SAG list, we were allowed to import a quota from England. John Mills was no problem because of his international status, but some of the others were less well known at the time and were closely scrutinised both by SAG and the US Immigration authorities. Eventually the last piece of red tape was severed and I finally had the cast of my choice: James Donald, Tom Courtenay, Alan Webb, Leonard Rossiter, James Fox, John Standing, Michael Lees and Denholm Elliott. They were selected for their slimness as well as their acting talents and asked to stay on a strict diet until their roles were completed. John Standing, now one of my sons-in-law, always maintains that at one point he fainted from malnutrition. In the interest of realism, before every take the ragged uniforms they wore were drenched in a mixture of oil and water. One Australian actor, Reg Lye, actually went native and set up home in the huts on our enormous fifty-acre set, at the time one of the largest ever built in Hollywood.

The major problem was the casting of the central role. At various times I was asked to accept Frank Sinatra, Robert Mitchum, James Garner and Burt Lancaster, all admirable and sought-after actors, but to have accepted any one of them would have made nonsense of Clavell's novel. With Jimmy's blessing I stuck out for the then unknown George Segal and together we finally wore down the studio's resistance. The King was the plum role for a young actor that year and began George's distinguished career.

I also fought and won a separate battle to have the film shot in black and white instead of the preferred Technicolor. Colour would have detracted from the newsreel quality I was seeking. Without in any way wishing to compare my film with David Lean's masterpiece *The Bridge on the River Kwai*, I was always conscious that his cast looked too clean, too well turned out, the whole film given a gloss that I wanted to avoid.

I remember how immediately impressed I was by the efficiency and knowhow of the Hollywood crew. Burney Guffey's camera crew were all in their sixties, the focus puller, for example, had never had another job and prided himself on the fact that he never took tape measurements but did it all by eye. Raoul Walsh had guided me towards a superb First Assistant, Russ Saunders, an ex-All American quarterback. 'He's a good man to have around when things get rough,' Raoul had said and on the very first day I was given a startling demonstration of the truth of this statement. We had a permanent crowd of some seven hundred extras, called every day to people the make-believe Changi prison, and they proved to be a dedicated and invaluable complement to the main body of actors. Without them I could not have achieved the degree of authenticity that distinguished the finished film. To look at they were a tough and formidable bunch; I was an unknown quantity to them and had to prove myself. On the first day of shooting I called them together and made a short speech, impressing upon them that their individual contributions would be vital to the film. Maybe they took this to be so much British bullshit, since I suspect they were mostly accustomed to being treated as background fodder. A particularly fearsome character in the front row decided he would make a wisecrack at my expense. That was enough for Russ. He stepped forward and decked the man with a single blow. 'Anybody else want to be a comedian?' Russ asked. 'For your information only one guy makes the jokes on this set, and that's the governor here, so listen to what he has to say and keep your mouths shut.' The unfortunate extra was taken away on a stretcher and that was the single untoward happening during the ensuing twelve weeks.

Jimmy only visited the desert location once, still attired in his tweed suit despite the hundred degree heat. He took lunch with the cast then said to me: 'I shan't be coming again. You all get on too well. I like films that have some dissension.' Jimmy was right, there were no holdups caused by temperament, everything went smoothly. I had as good a cast as any director could and throughout the long, punishing schedule in the frequently debilitating heat and despite the grim subject matter we were a remarkably happy band.

Sadly, the aftermath followed a familiar, depressing pattern. Some of the sequences were judged too stark. It was made during the period when the Vietnam war had not become a dirty word, and the depiction of an American soldier as an anti-hero alarmed the studio's distribution arm. Warning bells sounded in my head when I was shown the first posters, which seemed to be based on *King Kong* for they showed George Segal astride a mountain of men and the accompanying text gave the impression that this was an all-action adventure story of the type that John Wayne usually appeared in. THE FIGHTING STORY OF THE MEN OF FOUR NATIONS was one of the first suggestions for a logo. I remonstrated with Mike Frankovitch, pointing out that the only physical action in the entire film was when Segal slapped James Fox's face during their quasi-homosexual relationship. He conceded on that issue, but insisted that another sequence involving a transvestite be deleted and the anti-religious passages toned down. It was then that a panic decision was taken to hold a preview in San Diego, *King Rat* being slipped into a programme normally showing a Jack Lemmon comedy. Such a switch was hardly likely to endear itself to an audience who had come expecting a laugh and instead were given a stark black and white drama with a cast of virtual British unknowns. The response was predictably awful. Then followed a long post-mortem with the assembled studio yes-men profferring alarming solutions –

recast, reshoot, change this, cut that, edit so that a different emphasis is given. Had we agreed to what was demanded the film would have been degutted and meaningless.

Once again Jimmy stood firm. 'Let them talk themselves out, Byron. Give them a few points to make them happy, then we'll take the film back to England and edit it there away from this lunatic asylum. The next time we show it to them they'll be convinced we've done everything they asked for. Believe me, I've been through this too many times.'

I was happy to follow his advice although I will always regret what had to be lost in the final version. The film was premiered in London and proved to be a success everywhere but in America, at one time playing in four cinemas simultaneously on the Champs-Elysées. It wasn't until much later, in the sullen aftermath of the Vietnam war, that the film was rediscovered and became very popular viewing on the American university campuses.

I followed *King Rat* with *The Wrong Box*, another subject that Jimmy found for me, but this time he did not produce it. I believe that, had he lived, my subsequent career would have been totally different. He was a midwife for talent and smacked many of us into life. 'It's more blessed to give than receive,' was another of his favourite sayings, smiling at his own words behind the inevitable cigar, hand always held to his mouth, anxious to conceal his blemished lip that few were aware of. He had a quick mind that panned and found the nuggets before other prospectors on the same trail had even arrived at the mine. I know that he protected me against others and against myself, for I am not the best judge of character and often taken in by the carpetbaggers who abound in our industry. Jimmy was a shield, quite fearless when tackling the front offices. He knew everybody and he was rich enough in his own right not to have to depend on the largesse of others when it came to getting a project off the ground. He had taste, taste in actors, taste in subject matter. The friendship he extended so freely to Nanette and me is something we will always be grateful for. There was a sadness about him at times, for he had demons to fight, and in the end he died alone. Alas there was no Sarah around to rescue him on this occasion, and he was found dead in his room at the Beverly Hills Hotel, the novel he had been reading still clutched in his hand, his generous heart finally succumbing to the variety of painkillers he so depended upon.

TWENTY-SEVEN

I sometimes think what a long journey it has been. So many words written in anonymous rooms, so many hours spent in what is euphemistically called a 'script conference' (actually a post-mortem on a body not yet dead conducted by amateur surgeons), so many rejections, the waste paper basket full of stillborn ideas, the midnight oil burnt low.

The first time I was asked to write for the screen was in Hollywood in 1952 when another Jimmy played a major role in my life – Stewart 'Jimmy' Granger. My short-lived marriage to an Irish actress named Constance Smith was breaking up in spectacular, not to say sordid, fashion and I passed many empty days in a rented house on West Knoll Drive, perhaps not the most fashionable area of Beverly Hills. The only highlights were when I was invited to the house Jimmy Granger and Jean Simmons had in Bel Air, that Shangri-La of the very rich where, during the drought season, multi-million dollar homes explode like firecrackers when fires race through the heavily forested canyons.

On Sundays Jimmy liked to demonstrate his culinary skills and usually cooked an enormous English roast. It was the only time I ever ate well; my life in those days consisted of violent contrasts, more or less constant solitary poverty interrupted once a week by Jimmy's generous hospitality and friendship. After the very British Sunday lunch complete with Yorkshire pudding, we would watch old films; Jimmy had a collection of vintage boxing bouts starting with the bare-knuckle marathons and progressing from Dempsey to Joe Louis. There was no reason, other than kindness, for Jimmy to befriend me, but befriend me he did and together he and Jean saved my sanity. I never thought Jimmy totally enjoyed Hollywood; he was often at loggerheads with MGM about the films they put him into. But he was always a film star, larger than life, stylishly dressed and prepared to speak his mind whatever the consequences. It was he who conquered my fear of water and taught me to swim – his was the first private pool I had ever seen. Jean I had known from the time when we were both starting out in the business; I used to cadge a lift from Pinewood in her first car, a Hillman Minx, and we would sometimes stop on the way and eat fish and chips – a mixture of the mundane and the sublime, for of course I fell in love with her, enchanting creature that she was, full of laughs and always good company.

Elizabeth Taylor, Mike Wilding and Noel Willman were usually fellow guests and it was impossible not to be startled by seeing Jean and Elizabeth together: they seemed to have a monopoly of beauty. On one occasion the five of us made a trip to Palm Springs, in those days a small, unreal oasis in the desert populated by the very rich. One drove there from Los Angeles through orchards of orange trees lining either side of the road for miles; you could buy a large sack of oranges for seventy-five cents and the smog-free sunlight blinded you with its intensity.

It was during this trip that I struck up a friendship with the improbably named Cubby Broccoli. Unbelievably, Cubby had read my collection of short stories. I say 'unbelievably' because it had only been published in a very small edition in England. (Last year I was gratified to see that a copy of this rarity now commands the princely sum of seventy-five dollars from collectors.) It was a chance encounter that was later to have a profound influence on my future career.

Another strange encounter took place in Jean and Jimmy's Bel Air mansion. There I met the elusive Howard Hughes several times. Afterwards, when I related the experience, few people believed I had clapped eyes on him, for he was already showing signs of the paranoia that marked his final years and was seldom seen by anybody other than his closest associates who must have been well paid to endure his grotesque life-style. He usually kept appointments on street corners in the middle of the night, never set foot in the RKO studios he owned, and was constantly being subpoena'd by the US government to appear before a Congressional Committee to explain his latest transgression.

He came to Jimmy's house accompanied by silent bodyguards who wore identical black suits; my first glimpse of the sinister side of America. Hughes, I remember, was always shabbily dressed and would sit gazing fixedly at Jean as though poised to make an offer for her which only Jimmy's presence prevented. If anybody could be said to epitomise Oscar Wilde's epigram – 'He knew the price of everything but the value of nothing' – it was Hughes. Jean was under contract to him at the time and had wasted the best part of a year waiting for shooting to commence on Shaw's *Androcles and the Lion*, a strange choice for her talents, and the hiatus frustrated her.

Hughes' well-documented fetish about dirt and disease was evident even then. He offended Jimmy by never touching a door handle in the house without first wrapping a Kleenex around it. Whenever he went to the bathroom and carried out this procedure Jimmy was understandably angered and would shout after him: 'What sort of house d'you think this is? You're not going to catch the clap off my toilet seat,' but Hughes took no notice. One of the bodyguards would move to stand by the open bathroom door – legend had it that when Hughes was entertaining one of his numerous lady friends a goon was always stationed outside in case the lady cried 'Rape' and tried to blackmail him. It was fascinating stuff for me as a mere spectator. He had a fixation about Jean and his fixations were always charged with danger for he wielded such power and used it ruthlessly. While he wanted something from you, you were relatively safe; once he decided he had no further use for you, watch out was the maxim. I had never been close to somebody who could and did buy his way out of everything. America seems to specialise in this particular breed and since those early days in Bel Air I have met quite a few

Hughes clones who have a total disregard for any law or person standing in their path. The studios were adept at buying their stars out of trouble and most of the major scandals were (and still are) taken care of by fancy lawyers who know every which way to bend and get around the law. I had reason to know this from first-hand experience. My then wife was under contract to Fox, but they did not take kindly to the news that she was pregnant. So they loaned her $3000 to obtain an abortion a few days before Christmas, thus irrevocably dooming a marriage that was already faltering.

I remember a piece of advice Raoul Walsh gave me when I first arrived in town. 'Listen, kid,' he said, 'take a tip. If you're going through a green light at ten miles an hour and some drunken son of a bitch jumps the red and crashes into you doing eighty, get out and settle on the spot. Otherwise the bastard'll take you to the cleaners. Ain't no way you're ever gonna win.'

It was during this arid period in my life that I was suddenly asked to write a screenplay treatment for Anthony Quinn and Jimmy Wong Howe, the innovative cameraman, who had just formed a partnership. I was handed a reproduction of Ben Shahn's painting, *Vacant Lot,* and told to devise a story commencing with Shahn's imagery and from there take it any way I chose. They offered me $150, for me big bucks, which I could live on for a month. I borrowed a typewriter from Jimmy and worked like a maniac. At such far remove I have no memory of the script I turned in, though I am sure it was pedestrian. I have a sneaking suspicion that, like Jimmy Granger, Tony only offered me the assignment out of kindness. The film was never made, but I mistakenly felt that I was on my way. Alas, I wasn't; instead I left Hollywood shortly afterwards to journey home with only a broken marriage and failure as my excess luggage.

It's a funny business, writing for films, because in a sense it is a complete negation of the writer's traditional role as an isolated human being. In the beginning, when the commission comes, you are pampered, treated like an honoured guest, your every whim catered for. Greeted at the airport, your hotel room stocked with baskets of fruit and booze, you are given a stack of yellow legal pads and enough sharpened pencils to keep the average British classroom going for a month, a courtesy car and a secretary. (In my experience American secretaries can make a good cup of coffee, but are not so hot when it comes to dictation, typing or spelling and appear to suffer from chronic hay-fever the year round. They give great telephone, though.) In the beginning your opinions are listened to, your ideas enthusiastically received. The honeymoon lasts until the vice president in charge of creative affairs that week gets somebody else to read what you have written and reduce it down to the couple of pages that constitute his or her interest span.

Films cost so much money these days that everybody is terrified of making a decision that will let Hollywood's spending monster out of the cage. The studios have surrendered control of their product to the largest talent agencies, who now call the shots and often insist on 'packaging' films, a system whereby they provide the writers, producers, directors and stars from their list of clients on their terms, take it or leave it. Studio executives appear unwilling to challenge the immense power of agents like Michael Ovitz of the Creative Artists Agency who in the past has boasted of sending his 'foot soldiers' into battle when his demands are not met. The average cost to the major studios of producing a feature film in 1990 was $26.8 million; to this had to be added marketing and distribution costs reckoned to be an additional $11.6 million per film. Ludicrous sums of money by any standards, the totals concealing hidden and undetectable charges often allied to questionable accounting practices. Moderate profits such as would satisfy any other industry are derided as failures; a film either has to prove to be a gigantic earner within the first few weeks, or else it is junked. There are no half measures simply because the marketing costs to keep it alive are too exorbitant. By this reckoning if the average film costs in the region of $38 million, it has to take a minimum of $100 million at the box office just to break even. When one places such astronomical figures against the money made available in England, it is easy to see why we no longer have a viable film industry of our own. The money expended on a single American blockbuster would more than take care of the entire British output over a year. Our Government's latest handout of £5 million spread over three years is like giving a man with no legs the down payment on a unicycle.

However in the days when I was under contract to Columbia, costs were not out of control; a film like *King Rat* could be made and made well for $3 million and, even if it did not set the world on fire, everybody lived to fight another day. It would have been inconceivable for a single film to put an entire studio out of business, as was the case with *Heaven's Gate* which materially brought about the demise of United Artists, a major force in the industry from the time when Chaplin, Mary Pickford, Douglas Fairbanks and D.W. Griffith first formed it. For all its faults, the old studio system turned out a variety of films that have stood the test of time, many of which are now regarded as classics and form the staple diet of late-night television viewing.

One of my favourite memories of being a studio writer goes back to the days when I was under contract on the old Columbia lot in Gower Street. Sent for by a veteran producer one afternoon I duly took the elevator to his domain. When I was ushered into his office I found he was dwarfed behind an enormous, totally bare desk: to reach him I had to wade through thirty feet of wall-to-wall carpet which came up to my ankles.

He pressed a button and an acolyte came in carrying a script the size of a telephone directory.

'Mr Forbes,' the producer said with disturbing politeness, 'I'd like to have you read this over the weekend. It's a project I inherited from the great Cecil B. De Mille and it concerns the life of your very own, your very considerable, the Lord Baden-Powell. It's nearly there, but it needs a little dialogue polish. I believe you're the man to do it.'

I thanked him and, risking a pulled muscle from the weight of the script, staggered back through the thick undergrowth to the door. Just as I got there he spoke again. 'Mr Forbes! I'd like to leave you with one thought. When you read it you'll see we've played down the Boy Scout angle.'

I read the first hundred pages out of curiosity, and there was no question about it – nobody rubbed even two sticks together in that script, dib dib.

I suppose that in the course of my screenwriting career I devoted a total of three years working on biographical scripts, none of which ever brought me any fame for my efforts. Apart from my early experience writing the life of Churchill, I was next asked to tackle Henry Ford and, more recently, Chaplin. Churchill I wrote in the Gresham Hotel in Dublin, Ford was researched and completed in Detroit where I was incarcerated in a hotel room overlooking a riot-trashed ghetto, and Chaplin took shape in Arizona.

Detroit was the worst experience. The hotel itself, a vast circular edifice, reminded me of a Kafka nightmare. All the rooms had triple security bolts on the doors and there was a warning notice pinned in the bathroom urging guests not to order room service. This I found particularly sinister. There was a machine in the room which operated a dumb waiter; you put your money in and pressed various buttons and eventually a double Scotch and a packet of stale crackers found their way to you from the bowels of the building. On arrival, the Bell Captain had volunteered the information that it wasn't a good idea to take a walk anywhere and for my entire stay I had the feeling that I would never escape. Apart from myself, the hotel appeared to cater exclusively for convention parties. At night the barren corridors echoed to the animal cries of demented middle-aged men wearing comic hats – *Death of a Salesman* with a cast of hundreds. In the morning the elevators would be crammed with these jaundiced unfortunates, now sober and wearing large identification badges on their lapels as they mustered to attend pep talks on how to widen their horizons. None of them ever spoke to me: I had no badge, I was a non-person, and indeed I felt like one.

There was cable television piped to all the rooms which screened something called The Playboy Fantasy Hour, the fantasy being that anybody would pay to watch it. This and the lack of any real news from the outside world contributed to my sense of being divorced from reality.

I worked hard on the Ford script, spent many long hours researching in the Ford archives, where I was eyed suspiciously by two other authors both writing weighty biographies of Mr Ford. I was given a tour of the plant, visited the vast museum and recreated model village that Ford built, and was shown over Edsel Ford's estate on the prestigious North Shore of Lake Forest. Compared to his father's mausoleum of a home, Edsel's house was elegantly luxurious, but I was intrigued to find that only reproductions of his famous Impressionist art collection hung on the walls. His father, I discovered, never wasted his money on art. During the course of my research I unearthed an amusing story of Ford Snr's run-in with Duveen during the Depression. In collaboration with a dozen of the major galleries, Duveen prepared a sumptuous portfolio illustrated with coloured reproductions of the finest paintings then available for purchase. The portfolio was beautifully bound and in due course Duveen took it to Ford. Old Henry admired it and Duveen told him it was a gift for him to keep. Ford showed it to his wife – 'Look, mother, what we've been given, isn't this something?' It was then that Duveen made his pitch. 'Now that you've seen them, Mr Ford, which ones would you like to buy?'

'Why would I buy them?' Ford replied. 'I've got the book.' Duveen went away empty handed.

What drew me to the Ford project was the challenge of dramatising the life of a man who, uneducated, devoid of any academic technical knowledge and lacking funds, built an extraordinary empire from scratch, and by producing the Model T, irrevocably freed the people from being chained to one spot, changed the look of cities and the countryside, scorned the normal trappings of wealth, and lived a life of paradox. On the one hand he destroyed the past, yet his abiding passion was to recreate it, and to this end he collected, housed and exhibited the memorabilia of the world he, more than any other man, had worked to obliterate. He never had an office, sketched most of his ideas on a blackboard, elevated, then emasculated, and finally hastened the death of his only son, Edsel; he treated his workers to a company health scheme, raised their wages during the

Depression, for which he was abused and called a communist by his rivals, yet at the same time employed a thug as his right-hand man and did not hesitate ruthlessly to stamp out any who challenged him. He consistently lowered the price of his product and invented the production line, at one time turning out a new car every forty seconds. He was accused of being anti-Semitic, though I formed the opinion that his attitude towards the Jews was ritualistic rather than sinister. A pacifist, during World War I he gathered together a bizarre collection of people and set sail for Europe in what came to be known as a Ship of Fools, convinced that he and he alone could bring about a peace settlement. When ignored by England and France, the mission petered out in utter failure; he faked an illness and returned home alone, leaving the rest of his companions to fend for themselves. He had revolutionary views about diet, entertained all manner of quack medical theories, stayed married to the same woman all his life, but was almost certainly the father of another son, borne by the wife of his chauffeur, on whom he lavished more affection than on Edsel, but never publicly acknowledged.

When he died all they found on his person was a comb, a pocketknife and a Jew's harp. The day they buried him the entire State of Michigan came to a halt. All Ford factories closed for half a day. He was mourned in the way that great kings were once mourned. But when Edsel died he gave orders that every Ford factory should shut off the power . . . for five minutes.

After nearly a year's work the producer of the Ford project, Dick Cusack, was forced to abandon it: a very inaccurate mini-series had beaten him to the post and so, like my Churchill assignment, my long effort had been in vain.

The Chaplin script also proved to be a tragedy of good intentions. It was the first time Dickie Attenborough and I had been reunited since the days of *Seance on a Wet Afternoon* and I was delighted when he asked me to write the screenplay for him. The project formed part of a very lucrative production deal he then had with Universal Studios, but immediately after I had delivered my second draft, the dead hand of a young script reader, fronting for the chief executive, fell upon it. He delivered a lengthy screed listing all his objections, but, since I was barred from meeting him and since most of his comments bore little or no relation to the craft of screenwriting, the exercise did not advance my cause. I was to write no less than a further three drafts and worked many months in the false belief that I was satisfying everybody's requirements. Sadly, this was not the case. I later found out that I had been a loser from day one, Dickie confessing that Universal had always been unwilling to employ me and had only been reluctantly persuaded at his insistence. He finally revealed that their first choice had been an American writer, though when my contract was terminated they first employed William Boyd and then Tom Stoppard – distinguished company indeed. At which point the Universal top brass disagreed with the casting Dickie preferred and put the project into 'turnaround', a euphemism for we-don't-want-it-so-take-it-elsewhere-but-make-sure-we-get-our-money-back-plus-interest. It was eventually made for another company and a fourth, American, writer was brought in to rehash yet again my original screenplay. The role of Chaplin, that quintessential Englishman, was given to an American actor. So Mammon was eventually satisfied, one presumes.

The saddest part of my dismissal from the project was that, for a time, it blighted one of my oldest and most valued friendships. The greatest hurts always come from those we respect, and although Dickie doubtless acted out of consideration for me in the first instance, the fact that I had never received a hint of Universal's initial and sustained objection to me compounded the hurt. All we ever have to sell in the last analysis is time and at the age of sixty-four I resented squandering a year of my life on a subject doomed to abort. Had I known from the outset that whatever I wrote was never going to find favour, I would have refused the assignment.

Some experience in these matters tells me I wrote a superior, penetrating screenplay, warts and all. By his own admission Dickie considered it my best work, but who or what caused such an abrupt change of mind has never been completely revealed.

Chaplin, himself, was never taken to Hollywood's heart, partly from his sexual predilections, but also because from an early age he never *needed* Hollywood. He financed his own films, consulted nobody about them, edited and scored them, and drove a hard bargain when they were exhibited. On one occasion he had a fight with Mayer outside a restaurant; Mayer struck the first blow and scored a technical knockout. Chaplin was widely regarded as a radical with leanings towards the Soviet Union by the authorities and incurred the vindictive interest of J. Edgar Hoover. He was kept under surveillance, his phone was tapped and there is evidence to suggest that in one instance he was deliberately framed in a sexual scam. Politically he was very naïve and the case brought against him was largely fabricated by Hoover, but Chaplin's marital adventures, including the notorious paternity suit, ensured that his reputation was tarnished. He was denied re-entry into the United States after he went with his last wife, Oona O'Neill, for a holiday in Europe. Thereafter he made his home in Switzerland and was not forgiven until many years later, then allowed back to receive an honorary Oscar. Although he was undoubtedly a pioneering genius in the cinema, I have to confess that during the course of my research I did not find him an entirely likeable character. This was borne out in conversations with some of my regular film crew who worked for him on *The Countess from Hong Kong*, made at Pinewood, where I met him for the first and only time. They were not impressed by his behaviour, especially the humiliations he meted out to his son, Sidney. Obviously it is dangerous to base a character judgement purely on research, but Chaplin's life is so exhaustively docu- mented and so many of the unflattering stories about him dovetail that I believe the portrait I painted was not deliberately biased or exaggerated. Personally I always preferred Laurel and Hardy to the later Chaplin, for he began to take himself too seriously and his talkies had a stilted air to them; the technique creaked and the stories were banal. In killing off the Tramp, he also succeeded in stifling the comic genius that at the height of his fame made him literally the most famous man in the world. Even in death the fame did not leave him: I began my screenplay with the bizarre event of his coffin being stolen and held to ransom by two of the most incompetent thieves in the annals of crime – an incident that in his day Chaplin might have made use of, for it was the very stuff of macabre comedy and a gift to the maker of *Monsieur Verdoux*.

Being rewritten is nothing new to me, or to any other screenwriter who has ever picked up a pen. We all hate it, but we all half-expect it, and the bottom line is I guess we shouldn't accept the money and the perks if we want to remain virgins who are never interfered with. Often we don't know of the existence of other writers until we see the finished film in the cinema, and this can be painful, but that is the way the industry has always operated, despite efforts by the Writers' Guilds to obtain justice and I personally doubt it will ever change.

Although for months after my involvement with the Chaplin project was terminated I felt betrayed and resentful, I decided that friendship was worth more than just another screen credit. I have had my fair share of those, but a partnership such as Dickie and I have cherished over three score years does not come one's way very often and I took the first steps to heal a rift that I hope will never occur again.

TWENTY-EIGHT

There is a moment in any love affair when a man has to make a choice. When that moment came for me I did not hesitate: rather than risk losing Nanette I became a girl named Patricia Fenton, but, before anybody concludes that I was a closet transvestite, let me explain.

Picture if you will Marylebone shunting yards. It is a cold February night and a film unit is at work on a British 'B' picture called, rather fortuitously as it turned out, *Wheel of Fate*. The stars of this long-forgotten epic are Patrick Doonan, Sandra Dorne and yours truly. I play the villain. It is the last night of shooting and the final shot is being lined up. This calls for an apprehensive Bryan Forbes to commit suicide under a train. Since it is a 'B' movie the budget does not run to a stunt double, but I have been assured that the shot will not endanger my life. I am not too sure about this, but being ambitious and not wishing to appear a wimp, I go along, fingers crossed. At the given moment I will be required to run across the tracks in the path of the oncoming train and throw myself onto a wire platform fixed to the front of the engine. The engine driver has been primed to release a burst of steam at that moment, thus blotting out my intact or dead body. In theory nothing could be simpler, except perhaps the idiot foolish enough to believe all will be well on the night. I am keyed up to a point beyond which few actors seldom venture in their right minds. But I am ambitious et cetera.

Now given absolute freedom of choice I doubt whether any young swain would choose Marylebone shunting yards as the ideal location for selecting his future wife, but on that February night God, British Rail and the film industry moved in mysterious ways.

The preparations completed, the First Assistant beckoned me and the producer smiled for the first time in three weeks having just checked his insurance policy. I walked to my start mark trying hard to look like Jean Gabin in *Le Jour se Lève*. The clapper board went before the camera and I heard somebody say, 'This is the last shot, so let's get it right.' It was not a totally encouraging remark.

'Mark it!'

The sound of the clapper reminded me of the fall of the guillotine blade.

'Speed.'

'Give the go-ahead to the train. Let him get under way. Okay? Right! Action, Bryan.'

I ran across the tracks to meet the oncoming train and miraculously timed my jump onto the makeshift cowcatcher to perfection. On cue, steam enveloped me and I was carried forward like some broiler chicken. From far away I heard the word 'Cut' but it was not followed by the expected chorus of congratulation. Instead I made out the figure of the director coming towards me in the semi-gloom.

'That was *great!*' he said. 'Do it like that every time and we've got a winner.'

'What d'you mean, "every time"?' I said. 'Didn't you get it?'

'Yeah, we got it, but Harry thinks the train ought to go faster.'

'Weren't you under-cranking?'

'No, that always looks phoney. Do it again for me exactly like before, except this time give yourself more space. Hit the track about five yards in front of the train so that you turn and we see your terrified face.'

'Didn't you see it before?'

'Not enough. Don't forget this is the moment people are going to remember you by.'

I didn't care for his use of the word 'remember'.

'So you *don't* want it as before?'

'Yeah, as before, but different.'

He went back to the engine driver to explain the details of my demise.

It was then that I spotted the hitherto unknown Miss Newman standing under a lamp post a short distance from the camera. I wondered if this delectable creature realised she was in the presence of a hero. I gave her my Cary Grant smile, lit what I hoped was not my last cigarette, and strolled over to her. It was amazing how a new audience gives an actor an injection of bravado. To die in front of a bored film crew had never been an attractive proposition, but to expire within sight of a beautiful girl at least had romantic compensations. I felt it vital that I exchanged a few words with her before my career and life ended.

'Good evening, Mr Forbes,' were her first words to me.

'Were you watching that take?' I asked.

'Yes, it looked very realistic.'

'Not realistic enough apparently, I've got to do it again . . . Please use my chair.' It didn't have my name on it, just the word 'actor'. 'Have you seen any filming before?'

'Yes. I've acted in one or two myself, but only children's films.'

'Oh, you're an actress, are you?'

'Trying to be . . . There's just a chance I might get a small part in this, in your film.'

I liked the use of the possessive 'your film', but, like Leslie Banks in *Sanders of the River*, I heard those old jungle drums and was immediately alerted to foul play.

'In *this* film?' I said. The cigarette stuck painfully to my upper lip, which never happened to Jean Gabin. Miss Newman looked so very innocent.

'Yes,' she said. 'I gave a reading for the producer this morning and he said if I came here tonight and met the director there was a chance he would cast me.'

'You read for him? Which part?'

'The secretary.'

I inhaled like Bogart. I sensed I was on the brink of greatness.

It isn't everyday that a man has a chance to save a young girl's honour in Marylebone shunting yards before he dies.

'The secretary, huh?' I wanted this to sound casual, but it came out like Peter Lorre in *The Maltese Falcon*. The role of the secretary had already been shot two weeks before, played by a blonde ex-nude model.

'I'm sorry,' I said, 'I don't know your name.'

'Nanette Newman.'

'Look, Miss Newman ... Nanette ... I hate to say this, but you've been brought here under false pretences. The part you're talking about doesn't exist. That's to say, it did exist, but it was shot some weeks ago by another actress. The scene I'm about to do again is the last scene in the picture. When they get it, it's all over. I'm afraid the producer conned you.' By now I had become Lewis Stone telling Andy Hardy the facts of life. I felt so sorry for her. To her credit Miss Newman, aged seventeen, impossibly beautiful, did not cry. She stared at me with wide open eyes.

'What d'you think I should do?' she asked. 'My father will be furious. He'll want to kill him when he finds out.'

I carefully filed that last piece of information, since I had the feeling it might have some pertinence for me in the future. Her father, I was later to discover, was a handsome, magnificently built man who had an adagio act wherein he lifted bodies high in the air with one hand. Nanette was his only daughter and he rightly suspected any young man who had his eye on her.

'How did you get here?'

'I took the Tube and a bus.'

'Right! Go and wait in my car. I'll make sure you get home safely,' I said, gesturing towards a modest Austin, loaned to me by Roger Machell for the duration of the film.

Miss Newman looked dubious. 'What shall I tell the producer?'

'Say I'm a friend of the family and your father asked me to drive you home.'

'D'you think he'll believe that?'

'Don't worry about him,' I said, 'he'd no right to ask you to come here. If he gives you any grief I'll deal with him.' Now it was John Wayne talking.

At that moment I was called to perform again.

'Make it real,' the director shouted. As I walked away from one destiny to another I heard him add, 'Don't cut unless there's an accident,' as a parting example of his unique sense of humour.

I performed like Errol Flynn, careless of life and limb, gave my celebrated frightened expression, flung myself onto the cowcatcher and was obliterated by steam. I lay there for a long time and thought about driving Miss Newman home.

I heard the director say: 'That's a take. Print that. If the gate's clear, it's a wrap,' before adding, 'See if he's okay.' I rolled off my wire mat hoping for a compliment but at mention of the word 'wrap' the crew were already packing the gear.

'Gate's clear,' the focus puller shouted. (This is a procedure carried out every time the director pronounces himself happy. The object is to see if the film gate in the camera is free of foreign bodies which could mar the print.)

'See you at the première,' the director said by way of goodbye. There was never going to be a première, of course, but he had to keep up appearances.

I looked around for Miss Newman. With relief I saw that she was waiting by my car. There was no sign of the producer.

'Did you tell him?'

'Yes.'

'What happened?'

'He said I'm making a big mistake.'

(Much later Nanette confessed that she had asked a member of the crew whether she was safe in allowing me to drive her home. No fool her. To his everlasting credit, the unknown chippy or electrician gave me a good reference.)

I drove Nanette to Streatham, to her flat in Pullman Court. During the drive I decided that immediate honesty was the best course and confessed I was married but had not seen my wife in nearly two years and was in the process of divorcing her. 'So, I haven't got much to offer at the moment,' I said. 'And I'll quite understand if in the circumstances you don't want to see me again. But I want to see you, and if that means waiting, then I'll wait.' I don't know why Nanette accepted me at face value; the evening had already given her one shock, and now I had added another. It was a tough pill for somebody, only seventeen, to swallow, but in my case it truly was love at first sight, and I risked all to convince her that our chance meeting was likely to change my life. Amazingly, she agreed to meet me the following day.

In those days divorce was not a simple matter. The grounds one could cite were all fairly depressing: good old adultery, mental cruelty or desertion were the choices in the lottery. It was still considered the gentlemanly thing for husbands, even when the innocent party, to spare their wives. Many cases came before the courts in which the husband admitted adultery 'with a woman unknown'. The scenario for this farcical charade entailed a firm of private investigators providing a professional lady, often of irreproachable character who, for a fee, spent a chaste night in a hotel with the husband. In the morning a hotel maid, also paid a fee, took breakfast to the room and later gave evidence that she had found them in bed together. Q.E.D. It was a typical example of British hypocrisy in matters sexual since the judges must have been fully aware of the standard deceptions. No matter how the divorce was finally granted, there was a second act to endure between the decree *nisi* and the decree *absolute*. During this fraught period you had to be on your best behaviour because somebody called The Queen's Proctor – did he exist? Was there more than one? – supposedly ran around making sure that those desperate to be torn asunder did not commit the heinous crime of collusion. I did not fancy, nor could I afford, a woman unknown and I therefore opted for a plea of desertion. The snag about desertion was that the court required to be convinced that three whole years had elasped from the date when the husband asked his wife to return to him. I still had two years to go before my case could come to court.

Apparently the moment Nanette returned home that night she told her parents the events of the evening. Her father reacted with wholly understandable dismay. 'You are never to see that man again,' he commanded. His paternal anger was not directed against the producer, but against me. 'He's an actor, he's married and he's Jewish.' He was right on two counts, though I never quite understood the ethnic objection. He went on to warn her that 'actors only want one thing'.

It is a cautionary tale that many years later, having often heard the story, our two daughters often threw back at me when, giving a pale imitation of Nanette's father, I questioned their own choice of escorts. It's a curious thing, having daughters.

Nanette risked the paternal wrath and met me as arranged the following afternoon. Cunning sod that I was, I first impressed her with a visit to the Tate Gallery and then took her to see one of my films which was showing at the Leicester Square Theatre. When the film was over I casually suggested we go back to my Albany chambers. They weren't mine, they were Roger Machell's, but I was out to impress. When Nanette finally met Roger a few days later she innocently said, 'Isn't Bryan lucky to have such a wonderful flat?' Roger sweetly agreed, but when I felt more secure I confessed the truth. I know why I fell hook line and sinker for Nanette, but because of all the difficulties we encountered I was hard put to understand why she returned my infatuation. Not only was she very young, but going out with a married man still carried a social stigma before the permissive age. I was very conscious of this, although once I had found her I had no intention of ever losing her.

Her father remained a problem however and I had to think of a long-term strategy. That is how Patricia Fenton and subsequently 'her' fictitious family came into being. It began as a simple subterfuge. Whenever I telephoned Nanette at home she would answer in one of two ways. If she said, 'Hello, Pat,' I knew that her parents (and more critically her father) were within earshot and therefore intimate conversation was ruled out. If, on the other hand, she responded with some endearment then I knew the coast was clear and we could talk freely. Even the most casual crime compounds like interest and before long we were forced into a more complicated deception. Patricia's 'parents' would invite Nanette to spend an evening with them. Mr Fenton, we decided, was well heeled and insisted on treating Nanette as he did his own daughter, thus enabling me to buy Nanette gifts as the fancy took me. The Fentons even sent Christmas cards to the Newmans. We were drawn further and further into the vortex of our own making as the months went by, but miraculously escaped detection. Then came the moment when Nanette's father felt he had to return the Fentons' kindness and asked to meet them. We had to think quickly. The solution we came up with was to have the Fentons emigrate abroad. Thereafter Patricia rang less often, and always long distance. We breathed again.

I suppose lovers never count the consequences of their acts and certainly we took appalling risks on occasion, for not only did we have to deceive her parents, we also had to be careful that our relationship did not prejudice my chances of divorce. We were forced to haunt unfashionable restaurants whenever I took her out for a meal and we never went to any public functions together in case we were photographed. Roger Machell was in on the secret from the beginning and proved to be our most stalwart ally, and when eventually my divorce came through he was the best man at our wedding. Without his understanding and friendship I doubt whether we could have carried it off.

Mr Newman's professional engagements often took him abroad and it was during one such absence that Nanette and I felt we could no longer deceive her mother. We had been seeing each other for over a year and my intentions were as honourable as the situation allowed. Soberly dressed for the occasion I was taken to meet Mrs Newman. Although we did not reveal the secret of Patricia Fenton I explained that I was in the process of obtaining a divorce and that as soon as I was free I intended to marry Nanette. Her mother was a sweet woman, sadly destined to die before Nanette became my wife, and she accepted my assurances. Ironically, it was her death that brought about the *rapprochement* with Nanette's father. He was in Germany in the middle of a contract he could not break when his wife was diagnosed as having terminal cancer and I took my courage in my hands and wrote him a long letter revealing my feelings for Nanette and promising to look after her. Perhaps I struck the right note or perhaps his distress was such that it came as a relief to know that Nanette was not alone at such a time. Her mother had a hideous end – my last memory of her was seeing somebody who looked like an experiment in some mad scientist's laboratory, for she had undergone three major operations and was now merely the receptacle for a mass of tubes, kept alive for no purpose other than to prove a medical point. Had I had access to the right drug, I am sure I would have found a way to end her suffering, for nobody should be forced to die as she did. Nanette amazed me, visiting the hospital twice a day and somehow never letting her mother glimpse her own agony. But then she has always amazed me in a crisis.

My divorce finally came through and we were married immediately. By then I had made peace with her father, and even he came round to accepting me. Looking back, I still retain a soft spot for Patricia Fenton, for she helped decide the course of the rest of my life. Mr Newman lived to see us married, but died within a year of his wife, both of them aged fifty. I dare say he would be alive today had heart surgery been as advanced as it now is, but within a very short time after our marriage Nanette found herself orphaned. I have always felt the loss for her, especially since neither of her parents ever saw our children or survived long enough to enjoy Nanette's successes in so many fields.

We honeymooned in Tripoli, not from choice but because I had a role in a film called *The Black Tent*. I was under contract to the Rank Organisation as a writer at the time, earning one hundred pounds a week and had just purchased my first new car, a flash two-tone Ford Zodiac with white-wall tyres which I thought was the cat's whiskers. The producer of the film, an urbanely intelligent man named William MacQuitty, had asked me to rewrite Robin Maugham's first draft screenplay and at the same time provide myself with a secondary role as in the film. Learning of my impending marriage he was then generous enough to suggest that I combine business with pleasure and bring my new wife along for the trip. The film was being directed by Brian Desmond Hurst, an amiable but wicked old queen who did not take kindly to my employment. Bill MacQuitty had forewarned me that I would meet with a hostile reception and urged me to answer in kind. Sure enough when I encountered Brian for the first time, he immediately went on the attack. 'Why have they given me a third-rate writer like you?'he said in his thick Irish brogue. Thanks to Bill, I was prepared for this.

'Probably because you're a third-rate director,' I said.

From that moment onwards we got on famously. He took a particular liking to Nanette and would take her for walks in the desert, regaling her with outrageous tales of his life and times for he had a long and not undistinguished career.

The film starred Anthony Steele, then the latest heart-throb and somebody I had acted with before in *The Wooden Horse*. The female star was a young Italian actress called Anna Maria Sandri who was enchanting to look at but spoke next to no English and was heavily chaperoned by a formidable mother. She learned her role parrot fashion and, I suspect, with no comprehension whatsoever and eventually when the film was complete Nanette revoiced her. The rest of the cast included Donald Sinden, André Morell, Michael Craig and Donald Pleasence. The film was shot entirely in the desert, mostly in and around the superb Roman ruins at Sabratha and Leptis Magna. It was at Sabratha that we saw a performance of *Aida* played against the backcloth of the Mediterranean. Nanette had never been out of Europe before and to her the entire experience was a wondrous novelty. I was not so enamoured of the experience having never been drawn to the so-called mystique of the desert. This undoubtedly stems from a particularly unpleasant period when I was posted to Egypt during the war. The stark contrast between the undoubted grandeur and the appalling poverty and degradation I witnessed then blunted my appetite for the Middle East.

The Quaddan Hotel where the majority of us were accommodated was reputed to be three star, but I doubt whether the Michelin Guide would have awarded any knives and forks for the food served. Within hours everybody had been struck down with the Libyan equivalent of Montezuma's Revenge. They would present a large local fish on the trolley on a Monday and it would still be around, black with flies, on Friday. Packs of skeleton-thin wild cats roamed below the terrace where we ate. From time to time an old woman appeared to feed them; it was no surprise to learn that she was English and had made their survival her life's work. It was left to André Morell to come up with a solution for our survival: after experimenting he persuaded us all that a diet of peeled peaches dipped in champagne was the answer, claiming that the combination provided sufficient nutrition and was delicious into the bargain. We went along and, whether by luck or brilliant research on his part, our general condition improved. Curiously, or perhaps not so curiously given the British character, the only occasions we ever had a decent meal was when we all drove fifty miles out into the desert to a crazy one-man restaurant. There on a coastal peninsula, in the middle of the sandy nowhere, was a ramshackle building calling itself The Underwater Club. It was run by an ex-RAF type who had gone native and decided to stay on when the war ended. Visibly fortified by a few cocktails, and still looking every inch the gung-ho airman, he served a passable steak and fresh vegetables. It was certainly manna compared to the fare offered by the Quaddan kitchens. Even the menu at the Quaddan was off-putting. I remember one classic item which read: 'Our English guests can eat the salads with impunity. All the watercress served in the restaurant is grown in water *personally* passed by the Minister of Health.' The mental picture this conjured ensured that we gave the watercress a wide berth. Another culinary first was an obligatory visit to the actual black tents where our Bedouin hosts invited us to partake of a small mountain of couscous topped by the proverbial sheep's eye. George Provis, our estimable art director, was sufficiently drunk that night to sample the delicacy, though in the cold aftermath he swore off food for a month.

When I was out on the desert location Nanette often terrified me by wandering off alone into the souk. It was just about the end of the period when Westerners were treated as welcome guests and I feared for her safety though mercifully she always returned from these excursions unscathed – innocence on these occasions provided its own protection. Then there was the time when she nearly acquired a small ready-made son. Greatly affected as we all were by the relentless poverty and the pitiful state of the many small children, she naïvely gave one mother some money. In return the mother offered her one of her brood. The child was thrust into Nanette's arms and it took a prolonged effort on the part of our interpreter to persuade the woman to take back the child.

The role I played was that of a dying German soldier whom Tony Steele encountered in the desert. In blazing heat I duly delivered my protracted sandy death scene for the cameras and then it was decided to shoot an alternative version for the Italian market. So I changed uniforms and this time gave my Italian death scene. There was absolutely no difference between them and in any case the sequence was deleted from the finished film. Two sterling performances were thus lost to posterity.

Every night before going to bed I took my shoe and killed an army of cockroaches the size of mice which exploded when hit. There was no air conditioning and our fetid bedroom remained at furnace heat day and night. I once made the mistake of giving Nanette some flowers and within minutes the room was infested with a variety of avaricious bugs. It was certainly a honeymoon to remember.

Returning home to a minute flat in East Sheen that I had taken prior to our marriage, we lived a joyous, carefree life, for both our careers were flourishing and we made many new friends, notably John and Mary Mills who lived in a magnificent Georgian house called The Wick on nearby Richmond Hill. They also had a farm in Kent where we spent many an enjoyable weekend, for they entertained on the grand scale. I acted with John in *The Colditz Story* that year and it was on that film that I first met Lionel Jeffries. It is curious how many prisoner of war films were made around this period and I once calculated that I had spent the best part of two years behind fake barbed wire. *The Wooden Horse*, for example, started out as a ten-week schedule, but due to a series of disasters I obtained nearly eleven months' work from it. I not only acted in prisoner of war films, I wrote one – *Danger Within* – and it seemed that the cinema-going public's appetite for this genre and the film industry's willingness to satisfy that appetite were endless. Perhaps it stemmed from the fact that post-war Britain still endured austerity and the general public wanted to be reminded of our finest hours. I'm not complaining, I didn't complain, actors never complain at being constantly in work.

In the early days of our marriage Nanette will freely admit that she was capable of burning a boiled egg and since my own prowess in the kitchen was and still is confined to making minestrone soup, we ate out most of the time. Over the years she taught herself to become a superb and inventive cook and because she never had any formal training her cooking comes from the heart and is never conventional or boring. It has resulted in half a dozen bestselling cookbooks and a deserved reputation as a hostess. I can, without exaggeration or undue prejudice, say that I would rather eat at home than in any restaurant. She has the gift of making food look good (a delicate art) as well as taste good. My meagre contribution to the festive table is that I have taught myself to understand a little about wines, though there was one notable occasion when Nanette was filming and I decided to surprise her by cooking dinner for her return. Armed with a dozen cookbooks I chanced my arm on *Langoustine Flambée* which in the final stages resembled a marine Molotov cocktail – I used a whole bottle of brandy and nearly immolated myself and the kitchen. After that I decided to rest on my laurels for ever.

TWENTY-NINE

Recently I have been thinking about the films I would have liked to have made, those I could have made and those I never made. There is a certain distinction I suppose in having turned down the first Bond film, though many would call it stupidity. (Now I come to think of it, I turned down *two* Bond movies, and I'll get to the second one in due course.) As with my EMI appointment, the initial offer came while we were dining at the White Elephant Club, a propitious watering hole for me, it seems. Cubby Broccoli came up to my table and asked if I would be free to direct *Dr No*. At that point I had never read anything of Ian Fleming's, but from the way Cubby described the book it appeared to be a bang-bang, run-of-the-mill caper movie. I thanked him and said I would think about it. I thought about it and passed. I had no idea that it would become a cult – I doubt if anybody did – and would have made me a millionaire. Do I regret it? No, almost certainly my logical approach would have worked against the material. I made the films I wanted to make, and the films I wanted to make had to have a basis of reality. That is not to say I haven't enjoyed the Bond films as an ordinary cinemagoer, but I know I could not have brought the necessary commitment to direct them. As the series progressed I felt the scripts lost much of the tongue-in-cheek wit of the early films, relying more and more on elaborate, imaginative sets and brilliantly devised action sequences, which were mostly shot by stunt men working with a second unit. As a spectator I can enjoy the spectacle of a ten-car pile-up, but my enthusiasms wane at the prospect of shooting such sequences myself. They are purely mechanical exercises no matter how brilliantly executed and in many films have become a boring cliché for my money. Only when violent action is integrated with a character in a believable story, as in *The French Connection*, do I watch in envy.

History repeated itself with a second Bond. It was just after I had directed *King Rat*. For the first time in my life I was, in the jargon, a 'hot property', being offered deals left, right and centre. After due consideration I accepted a multi-picture contract from the three Mirisch Brothers, then the most respected independent producers in town and noted for their generosity. Harold Mirisch, in particular, was a kindly man who liked to keep his stable of artists and directors smiling. I sealed the contract with him while he was being shaved in his own barber's chair at his Beverly Hills home. I thought that was a nice touch, in keeping with the general air of relaxed goodwill that prevailed.

My contract allowed me to write, produce and direct films of my choice with the Mirisch company providing all the finance. I asked them to buy the rights to *The Egyptologists*, Kingsley Amis' novel, written in collaboration with Robert Conquest, which I visualised as a perfect vehicle for Peter Sellers who was also under the Mirisch umbrella.

Immediately I got back to England to edit *King Rat* I started work on a first draft of the script, and the future seemed rosy. Nanette was pregnant with Emma, who had been conceived in Beverly Hills, for the first time in our lives we seemed to be financially secure, I had a finished film in the can and Hollywood was beckoning me back.

Enter one Charles Feldman into my life.

Charlie was one of the most engaging people I have ever met. An ex-lawyer turned agent turned film producer, he had a charm that was difficult to resist, plus he didn't seem to give a damn about anything. He had demonstrated this early on in his career by marrying a girlfriend of Louis B. Mayer, Jean Howard. Mayer, the purveyor of family entertainment, who liked to give the impression that he alone upheld the traditional moral values, was also not averse to a bit on the side. Mayer had Charlie barred from the MGM lot as a result, but this didn't faze Charlie; he was a superb agent with a roster of top stars as clients and the pudgy hand of Mayer could not reach far enough to cramp his style. Life, for Charlie, was one long party and he liked his friends to share his pleasures.

He came into my life like a whirlwind, brandishing a copy of *Casino Royale*, and commenced to lay siege. Never the one to do things by half measures, he told me that he wanted to have five separate James Bonds in the movie and would guarantee me an all-star cast – Peter Sellers was mentioned, together with David Niven and Orson Welles. The more he pressed the more I found myself resisting the idea. My instincts as well as experience had taught me you cannot parody a parody. Then he applied a different tactic. 'You can write it wherever you want,' he said. 'D'you like the South of France? I'll take a suite of rooms for you at Eden Roc. Move there with your whole family.' Then as now the Hotel du Cap at Eden Roc is one of, if not the, most expensive hotels in the world. Despite this, whenever taken there as a guest I have never enjoyed the company of world-weary socialites, burnt to a crisp, who mostly form its clientele. Anyway I prefer to be a hermit when writing.

Charlie tried again. Gifts started to arrive: half a dozen silk shirts, tickets for the theatre; he treated us to expensive and often hilarious meals. He had a new girlfriend at the time and they alternated between bouts of passion and violent public scenes. Once when we were all four sharing a taxi Charlie unfastened the diamond-encrusted Piaget wristwatch he had just given the lady and flung it out of the taxi window. It was an impressive, if nihilistic, gesture and entirely typical of him. Money, as far as Charlie was concerned, was meant to be spent. He thought little of dropping $100,000 at the gaming tables. And all the time this was going on my then agents were urging me to forget principles and sign. 'What about the Mirisch Brothers contract?' I said. 'Relax. We can get round that. They'll wait. That's just meat and potatoes. What Charlie is offering is serious greenbacks.'

It was true that Charlie was talking Monopoly money to secure my services. Every time I expressed doubts he sweetened the deal. He knew ways and means of putting half of it into a Swiss account, he would pay my tax; if the film proved the success he predicted, I would never have to worry again. His distribution arrangement for the film was with Columbia, and he caused one of their senior officers, Leo Jaffe, to fly to England and add his weight to the argument.

It was at this moment that I had to return to Hollywood and score *King Rat* with John Barry's music. Nanette, heavily pregnant and no longer permitted to fly, went to Heathrow to see me off. Charlie and entourage came too, Charlie talking like a Dutch uncle; his persistence finally wore me down, and just before I walked through into the departure lounge, I said yes. Nanette later told me that as Charlie drove her back to London he promised her a Rolls Royce in any colour she liked to choose.

During the long flight to Los Angeles I had plenty of time to think over my decision. Arriving at the Beverly Hills Hotel I took a long bath before crashing out with jet lag. I thought about the $500,000 I would receive, and then I thought about the basic idiocies of the script Charlie wanted me to write. *Five James Bonds*! That meant departing from Ian Fleming's novel and devising a piece of *brouhaha* which could accommodate the talents of Sellers, Niven, Welles and God knows who else, for I had no illusions about what lay ahead; Charlie had a reputation for frequent changes of mind and Peter Sellers had told me of the chaos that had accompanied Charlie's last success, *What's New Pussycat?*. I lay in the bath until my skin wrinkled, and came to another decision: I would turn it down. I slept on it, but first thing the following morning my convictions were the same. I conveyed the news to Leo Jaffe at Columbia, who went into a conniption fit on the phone, even threatening to sue me for changing my mind. I had never been so wanted. But I stuck to my guns and let the screaming and ranting pass over me. It's funny to think of now, and I'm sorry that I never worked with Charlie on something that captured my imagination. He was a character made for and by Hollywood.

As for *The Egyptologists*, well, that never got made. Harold Mirisch sadly died and I did not enjoy the same relationship with his two brothers. Charlie went on to make *Casino Royale* with his five James Bonds and five different directors, including John Huston, who shot his segment in Ireland, because he wanted the film company to renovate the house he had there. It was not, I gather, altogether a happy picture. Peter did one of his celebrated walkouts and in order to complete his role they were forced to use a double. It never achieved the success of the more conventional Bond films.

I gave the same answer when Elliott Kastner offered me *Where Eagles Dare*, which proved another big winner. Again it was the preposterous plot that daunted me. (The team of heroes parachuted into Germany carrying only small packs. Curiously they never ran out of ammunition and were blazing away regardless to the very end. It's a quirk of mine, but I can't buy that sort of fantasy.)

Years before, I had been commissioned to write the screenplay for a true wartime story, *I Was Monty's Double*; this was based on the real-life exploits of an unknown actor, Clifton James, then serving in the Army Pay Corps, who bore a striking resemblance to the General. Shortly before D-Day, as one of many deceptions, he was carefully rehearsed and then flown to Gibraltar, the idea being that if the commander of the British invasion forces was known to be in Gibraltar the Germans would assume that the invasion was not imminent. What fascinated me was the thought that for three or four days Clifton James held destiny in his hands. Once the plan had been put into operation there could be no turning back. Monty himself was incarcerated in a hideaway; Clifton James had the stage, he wore the badges of rank, he had the authority. Had he botched it, or had he suddenly let the glamour of the role go to his head, all would have been lost. This seemed to me the heart of the matter. Amazingly, he pulled it off, the Germans were taken in and, as with *The Man Who Never Was*, strategically fooled as to the site and timing of the invasion.

The true irony of the tale was that Clifton James went back to the Pay Corps and obscurity. Apart from the book he was permitted to write a few years later, he received little by way of recognition, contracted tuberculosis and shortly afterwards died.

To my mind his story fell into three perfect acts – obscurity, a few moments of fame, then a return to obscurity, my favoured unhappy end again. The director of the film had other ideas and insisted on tagging on a phoney kidnapping by German commandos, reducing the whole to a formula movie. I resisted his demands as far as I could, but was finally overruled. Nanette and I were broke at the time and, having slaved through the screenplay, I could not afford to relinquish it for another writer to garner whatever credit might come its way. Clifton James played himself in the film and proved to be a shy and unassuming man, the antithesis of his real-life counterpart.

Shortly afterwards I was asked to write an original screenplay around D-Day itself and in the course of my research uncovered what I felt was a fascinating piece of history, namely that amongst the very first airborne to land in occupied France was a medical team composed of conscientious objectors. The plot I devised was a simple one. I wanted to reduce the enormity of the day down to human proportions, and the fact that some 20,000 French civilians died *being liberated* held its quota of irony for me. What triggered my invention was one of the codes used by us as a signal to the Resistance that the day had finally dawned. British intelligence did not go in for cryptology, but instead broadcast a mass of unrelated sentences – a scrap of Dickens, an item from a local paper, then something from the *Farmers' Gazette*, say, delivered without pause and I imagine totally baffling to the German monitoring service who would have been looking for a pattern. Into this conglomeration we dropped the vital messages, one of which was, 'The children get bored on Sundays.' It was the word 'children' that set me on the road. In my screenplay I envisaged a small French child wounded during the opening aerial bombardment. In the ensuing twenty-four hours the film spanned, the farmhouse where the child lived changed hands three times: initially captured by the Americans, it was retaken by the Germans and subsequently stormed again by the British. All three nationalities did their best to save the child's life and it was the British team of conscientious objectors who finally got her flown back to England and safety after her leg had been amputated in a field hospital. The last words in my script were, 'Poor little sod, she'll remember being liberated,' and I felt that at the very least my conception had the merit of being different.

Sadly the British company that had commissioned me lacked the resources to get into a race to the post against Daryl Zanuck, who of course went on to make his all-star version employing vast resources. So once again my script hit the dust and still gathers it in my library.

I know that when I started as a director I was influenced by the classic French films – there are sacred and profane echoes of Clement's *Les Jeux Interdits*, for example, in *Whistle Down The Wind*. Most directors will admit that they borrow, consciously or sub-consciously, from films that have impressed them. Equally, a bad film also has its effect; one tries to avoid the worst excesses of others. A critic once pointed out that all of my films deal with aspects of love, something I was never really aware of during the making of them but which I think has more than a grain of truth in it. The vulnerability of my characters always fascinates me and perhaps what I do best is to inject emotion into my films. If I can move an audience, whether it be to laughter or tears, then I feel I have done my job. As a paying customer I like nothing better than to have my own emotions stirred and I love unhappy endings. Films such as *Dr Zhivago*, *The Go-Between*, *The Railway Children*, *Adele H* and *Jean de Florette* never fail to affect me no matter how many times I watch them. Obviously I cannot help being influenced by the technique and craftsmanship as well as the performances, because I admire the art with which my colleagues overcome the many difficulties inherent in every film. There are so many layers of collaboration that go into the whole, some humble, some vital, and on the floor the director has to marry them, making many instantaneous decisions. If an actor does not trust the director's taste, then the fabric of the film can disintegrate, for in the last analysis it is the performance of the actors that makes or breaks any film of content. My own two decades as an actor armed me with certain advantages when I began directing: I knew how exposed and vulnerable all actors

318

feel in front of the camera. In order to draw the best out of an actor, the director has always to be aware of this vulnerability. Of course many a hot chestnut can be pulled out of the fire in the editing stages and with the able assistance of my editors I have sometimes salvaged a mediocre performance in the cutting rooms.

The obituary for David Lean in the *New York Times* stated that he was one of the few directors to edit his own films. This was written in ignorance, for David worked with a superb editor, Anne Coates, and in any case I know of few directors who don't spend long hours in the cutting room alongside their editing team. To deny oneself a role in this final stage would be akin to a painter mixing the colours but never putting them on the canvas. It is in the cutting room that one seeks the nuance of a performance, the look that conveys more than a page of expository dialogue and the juxtaposition of two contrasting images to produce an effect that was never apparent in the script. Lean learned his craft in the cutting rooms and he was a master of the long dissolve, an honourable technique which, when executed with his unerring judgement, produced some memorable images, but which is often shunned by the new generation of film-makers, influenced I have no doubt by the demands of television. Since most programmes on American television are maddeningly interrupted every few minutes by the commercials, everything has to be fragmented into short segments and it is seldom that a director is allowed the luxury of exploring characters in depth. In Arizona where part of this book was written, there is a choice of sixty-four channels, but even so it is difficult to find one programme that isn't ruined by the commercial interruptions. It makes one grateful for the British system. Because exposure on television after a theatrical release is a prerequisite, the cry is for pace, pace and more pace. Lean was wrongly called old fashioned for telling good stories in a straightforward way and having the courage to take his time. It was shameful that a man of his immense talents was forced into retirement for fourteen years after the battering he received for

Ryan's Daughter, and this says a great deal about the savagery of our industry when anybody falls out of favour. I like Billy Wilder's reply to this sort of treatment. When his own notable career suffered an eclipse he responded to the old Hollywood adage that you are only as good as your last picture: 'No,' he said, 'you're as good as your *best* picture.' Even a great director cannot lick a bad script; he may patch it up, employ all his technical skill with the visuals, but in the end unless the blueprint is there on the page it will defeat his efforts.

In his pungent autobiography Arthur Miller states his prejudice against screenwriting as an art, contending that it is produced by the will, not the soul. I take his point, but I think he errs in generalising. Although few screenwriters escape being sucked dry at some point in their careers, the wonder is that masterful scripts continue to find their way through the maze. Miller's excursions into the world of films were unhappy, so his prejudice is understandable, and he also fell foul of the Un-American Activities Committee when many Hollywood writers of note were sacrificed by the studios cravenly operating a black list.

I was in Hollywood when the sessions were actually televised and I witnessed the hideous charade being played out. It so happened that two of my closest friends at the time were Betty Garrett and Larry Parks. Larry was at the peak of his career, having scored an enormous success in the Jolson films, but even this did not save him. I remember that I was warned not to continue the friendship for my own good, a warning I ignored. Driven by God knows what fears for his family and future, Larry appeared before his persecutors as a 'friendly witness' and for this his career was destroyed overnight. I will always believe that the anguish he went through shortened his life. In the few years remaining to him he made a couple of B movies in Europe (one, curiously, with my ex-wife) but as far as Hollywood was concerned he was a leper and he died of a heart attack at an early age.

Arthur Miller was one of those who escaped being sent to jail for contempt and he describes in chilling detail the efforts made by the aged Spyros Skouras, then President of 20th Century Fox, to dissuade his jewel, Monroe, from marriage to a suspect fellow traveller. So many good actors and writers were broken on the rack of bigotry as surely as heretics were broken during the Inquisition. Now the hysteria seems inexplicable, for there was no threat, it was all the work of a few third-rate politicians anxious to put their names on the map. For a time they made a mockery of American justice as surely as the Nazi People's Courts traduced German justice. Nor can all the guilt be directed at those who controlled Hollywood: the whole of America watched and for the most part approved or turned a blind eye. Nobody it seemed, not even in the White House, knew how to tame the monster in their midst. Finally, it took the courage of one man, Ed Murrow, to skewer the junior Senator from Wisconsin with his own words in the memorable CBS television programme of 9 March 1954. Cold, reserved, he methodically reached for the words that would hammer nails into McCarthy's political coffin. 'The unwarranted interference of a demagogue ... The line must be drawn or McCarthy will become the government. We will not be driven by fear into an age of unreason.' Like many a sea-green incorruptible before him, McCarthy was toppled by his own insatiable need for power, but for some the damage was never undone. McCarthy was pivoted towards the downward slope into debt and alcoholism, destined to die alone and unattended at forty-nine (why did he appear so much older?) but the blacklist lived on. J. Edgar Hoover, the *éminence grise* who manipulated so much that was questionable in the so-called defence of democracy and who knew where every single body was buried, kept other witch hunts alive. Murrow himself was later denied a renewal of his passport until he had submitted an affidavit denying he had ever been a member of the Communist Party. Sponsorship of his long-running programme *See it Now* was withdrawn following pressure from the stockholder – not even the most popular television commentator in America was immune from investigation. What had at first seemed a local Hollywood problem now embraced all sections of the media; there was an outbreak of book burning in Los

Angeles; everybody was running scared. (It is often overlooked that Nixon, then a lawyer, played a role alongside McCarthy and the revolting Roy Cohn in trampling on many reputations. Cohn died of Aids a couple of years back and, while I would never wish anybody that sad end, there was a sort of poetic justice in his death.) Writers and directors like Joe Losey and Carl Foreman went into exile in Europe; a few were lucky enough to work under pseudonyms, others left the industry for good, and ten went to jail for their beliefs. The image of America as the home of liberty had a tarnished look.

Perhaps the attack on Hollywood writers had something to do with the fact that few screenwriters through the ages have been given the critical respect accorded to playwrights, even though their work often reaches more people in a single night than a successful play does in six months. Maybe they were regarded with suspicion for the very reason that they were capable of reaching such a vast audience. Tolerated by the studios rather than welcomed, screenwriters have never enjoyed the acclaim so lavishly bestowed on actors and directors. The *auteur* theory which first took hold during the French *Nouvelle Vague* period continues to cause contention in the ranks. It is manifestly absurd to proclaim a director is the author of a film unless he has also written the screenplay, but today any first-time novice director claims and receives the possessive credit. For required reading on the subject I commend the series of articles that Raymond Chandler wrote on the studio system rather than the more vaunted writings of William Goldman. Or, if your taste runs to the scatological, the recent bestseller by Julia Phillips with the stirring title *You'll Never Eat Lunch in This Town Again* describes in bar-room language a world I would be happy never to visit again. There is something so shallow and tawdry about today's hip Hollywood scene that Ms Phillips chronicles in an endless stream of four-letter words. I noted that amongst the acknowledgements she lists one to her cats, Raps and Romona, 'for hanging tough and hanging tight'. Hanging tough is the password for success amongst the Rodeo Drive set, the Guccied-up eighties' guys with heart, designer stubble and armour plus a plentiful supply of crack. It is the age of expensive illusions, often drug-induced, the age of success at any price and never mind the dead bodies along the way. My own two novels about the world of films were said by some to be exaggerated, but in fact Hollywood is beyond parody.

Horror stories about the fate of writers who made the journey west abound, but I am particularly fond of one concerning F. Hugh Herbert which seems to me to sum up the whole scene.

In pre-war days Mr Herbert was a struggling, would-be playwright in New York and anxious to make his mark in films. He prevailed upon a more influential friend to get him a few introductions in tinseltown. The friend said he could not guarantee to get him work, but if Herbert paid his own fare to Los Angeles he would see to it that Herbert met Irving Thalberg. On such a promise young Mr Herbert duly took the train and, true to his word, the friend secured him an invitation to a party where Thalberg and his wife, Norma Shearer, were on the guest list. During the course of the evening he got to shake hands with Thalberg and they exchanged perfunctory greetings. And that was that.

Herbert had taken a small apartment on the wrong side of the tracks and there sweated out a meagre existence while waiting for the main chance that never came. Down to his last few dollars, he was on the verge of packing up and returning to New York when one night he had an unexpected visit. Answering the doorbell he found himself confronted by none other than the great Thalberg. Both men stared at each other in some amazement, then Herbert recovered sufficiently to ask his visitor to step inside. Hastily kicking a few empty beer bottles under the bed, he offered Thalberg the one decent chair. They sat together and conducted a desultory conversation until Thalberg asked him what he was doing. Herbert had a writer's sure instinct for self-preservation and ad-libbed about a play he was working on. When Thalberg got up to go he said, 'Why don't you come to the studio tomorrow? I'll see if we can't find you something.' Then he walked out into the night, leaving Herbert stunned but elated.

The next morning he presented himself at the MGM security

gate. The policeman on duty checked his list and handed Herbert a pass. 'If you'd like to go to the writers' block, Mr Herbert, I'll have somebody meet you there.'

Herbert did as directed and sure enough was welcomed by one of Thalberg's assistants. He was taken to an office where his name was on the door. Inside he found a secretary had been put at his disposal.

'What am I supposed to do?' he asked.

'Just make yourself at home and in due course I'm sure Mr Thalberg will decide what project he's assigning you to.'

'You mean I'm under contract?'

'Absolutely. Mr Thalberg has given instructions for you to be paid a thousand dollars a week for eight weeks.'

Herbert could not believe the transformation of his fortunes. But it was real enough. He was on the payroll at MGM, he had his name on the door, a desk, a typewriter, a ream of paper, pencils and pads, a secretary who made his coffee. He had arrived. He sat there for the first week and spent his time working out ideas against the moment when Thalberg asked to see him. That call did not come, but his first pay cheque was handed to him on Friday. He sought out the same assistant.

'Look,' he said, 'don't think I'm complaining, far from it, but I haven't been given anything to do. I want to earn my keep.'

'Don't worry about it. Mr Thalberg's a very busy man, but I'm sure he'll get round to you in time.'

The second week came and went, a second pay cheque was there on the dot, but still no word from Thalberg. It wasn't until the middle of the third idle week that he saw the assistant again.

'Good news,' the assistant said. 'Mr Thalberg would like you to think up a treatment based around the itinerant potato workers in Idaho.'

Herbert swallowed hard. It wasn't the most thrilling assignment, but who was he to question Mr Thalberg's taste? He immediately applied himself to the task, researching the subject in depth and devising what he believed was a poignant saga with social undertones. At the end of the sixth week he turned in an eighty-page treatment. Every day he rang the assistant to ask what Thalberg's reaction had been and every day he was given the same answer: 'Mr Thalberg hasn't been able to get to it yet.'

On the Friday of the eighth week which marked the end of his contract the assistant came to his office. 'Hugh, I've got good news and bad news. Mr Thalberg has decided not to proceed with the Idaho story. That's the bad news. However, he's so pleased with all the hard work you devoted to it, he wants you to have a bonus. The contract's at an end, but here's a cheque for an extra two big ones.'

The money helped mask Herbert's disappointment at the fate of his treatment; he walked away with $10,000 for his eight-week stint on the hallowed MGM lot, and could now not only afford to move into a decent apartment, but was also able to say he had written a script for Thalberg. Such a reference was enough to open other doors and he never looked back.

Dissolve.

Subsequently he became a successful playwright with a string of Broadway hits to his credit. Many years later he was at a swish New York party when he was approached by a middle-aged blonde who gave the impression that in her younger days she had been quite a beauty. They chatted for a few minutes and then she asked him if he had once lived in an apartment between Olympic and Pico in Beverly Hills.

Herbert confessed he had.

'Do you remember what number?'

Herbert gave the number.

'I lived in the next apartment,' the blonde said. 'In those days I was moonlighting as a fifty-dollar hooker.' She made the admission without embarrassment. 'Let me ask you something else. Did you once have a visit from Irving Thalberg while you were living there?'

'Yes, as a matter of fact. It changed my whole life.'

The blonde nodded. 'Yeah, he told me. He was one of my regulars. That night he knocked on the wrong door by mistake.'

THIRTY

Tom Wolfe called it the age of The Kandy Kolored Tangerine Flake Streamline Baby, those mad Sixties when the grouse-shooting son of a crofter told us we had never had it so good and Beatlemania and the Stones splattered the eardrums of most teenagers. I strolled along the fringe of the hysteria somewhat bemused as our elder daughter sought to indoctrinate me into the new millennium and the house reverberated to the cacophony of strange sounds. As an act of contrition for my lack of faith I converted the garages into a playroom-cum-disco where Sarah held pyjama parties; hordes of nubile pubescent squealies ostensibly 'slept over' though nobody slept and the favoured record of the week was played at a level beyond the threshold of pain until it wore out.

I did have one close encounter of the third kind with this new genus of teen when, unannounced, two of the Rolling Stones arrived at Seven Pines one summer afternoon, stepping from a Rolls Phantom dressed, strangely enough, in furs and accompanied by their manager Allen Klein and his sidekick, an erstwhile pop singer, Andrew Oldham. Klein informed me that I had been selected to direct Mick Jagger in *When the Kissing Had to Stop* and that money was no object. It was more a verbal rape than a proposition and every time I attempted to deflect Klein's nauseating conceits, he became increasingly aggressive. How could I possibly turn down such an offer? Didn't I realise I was being given the opportunity to become an overnight millionaire? He was handing me the chance of immortality, plus a way to

326

outfox the Inland Revenue. 'You get to keep all the loot,' he kept repeating.

The serious novel he had chosen somehow did not seem the ideal vehicle for Mick Jagger's screen début.

'How about Jagger?' I asked. 'Does he want to act, and more importantly, *can* he act?'

'Who cares whether he can act? That's your problem. I'm talking about making money.'

As I recall, the two Stones (Jagger himself was absent) listened to his tirade without comment, and betrayed not the slightest interest in the proceedings. Perhaps they were so conditioned to being manipulated by this fast-talking little guy who controlled their destinies that they found nothing strange in his efforts to manipulate a complete stranger – wasn't that the way the world turned? They looked absurdly young – the dissipation was yet to come – sitting on a sofa still swathed in fur while Nanette served them tea.

'You'll do it,' Klein said, walking me in the garden while pressing his rapacious philosophy. 'I've yet to meet anybody who doesn't have a price. Don't be bashful, tell me what you want. You name it, I'll provide it. I don't take no for an answer.'

I didn't doubt him, but his rancid, devil's advocate voice grated and I distrusted him on sight.

Pleading other commitments, I managed to stall him and they all trooped back into the monolithic Rolls with its darkened windows without a word. I was left bewildered by the strange encounter.

Shortly after this meeting Nanette and I had to make another trip to Hollywood. We were pursued there by Andrew Oldham bearing further blandishments from Klein and so many red roses for Nanette that the bouquet had to be dismantled before it would go through the doorway of our Beverly Hills Hotel bungalow. He was dressed like the head of the school, I remember, a blazer and tie, polite and deferential. I think he and Klein were genuinely amazed that I resisted; it was something they had not come up against before and it became a matter of pride for them to try and wear me down. Though I had nothing against Mick Jagger, and indeed admired his phenomenal nerve on stage, they did not succeed in persuading me and so for the second time in my life I passed up the opportunity of becoming an instant millionaire. Klein later moved in on the Beatles, since all pop groups seem to attract his breed, usually to their cost.

I had no further contact with the pop world until Elton John became a near neighbour. This was during the early Seventies, a time when my two daughters determined to prevent me lapsing into middle-age. Under their influence I grew my hair longer and for a time wore bell-bottomed jeans and hobbled about in cowboy boots which I could never prise loose unaided. Photographs taken at the time confirm that such devotion to filial influence was misguided. In fact I looked a complete prat.

I chalked up an enormous black in Sarah's eyes by failing to recognise Elton John the first time I met him in my bookshop. Having heard on the local grapevine that a pop singer had become a near neighbour, for some reason I had it fixed in my mind that it was a member of the Bee Gees group. So when Elton first appeared in the shop I carried on a conversation that must have baffled him. It so happened that later that same day I was attending a concert at the Shaw Theatre to raise money for the National Youth Theatre, and mentioned this to Elton. 'Princess Margaret is coming and we're hoping to raise some much-needed funds because Elton John has generously donated his services.'

He gave me an odd look before replying: 'Yes, I know. I'll be there.'

'Good,' I said, with unflattering ignorance, 'well perhaps we'll see each other.'

My embarrassment was considerable when the curtain went up and Elton appeared on stage with his original band. I rushed backstage afterwards to apologise for my stupidity and, to make amends, invited him to join us for dinner with Princess Margaret. And that is how our friendship began.

He was indeed a neighbour, living but a few hundred yards away in a new house he had named Hercules. Never having been exposed to the pop world before, Nanette and I found ourselves swept up into a circle of young people who had a refreshingly different approach to life, and who made us question certain attitudes which, with ill-informed prejudice, we had assumed typified the pop scene. Through them we got to know such diverse exponents as Kiki Dee, Long John Baldry, Alice Cooper, Ray Cooper and the ultimately tragic lead singer for T Rex, Marc Bolan. We saw no evidence of drugs, they were all just naïve young people bewildered by the fame and money they were generating. Even before he became successful, Elton had always had expensive tastes and now he was in a position to indulge himself, shopping at Cartier as though he was in Tesco's. He wore outlandish clothes and dyed his hair every other week like Joseph's multi-coloured dreamcoat and wore custom-made spectacles that often gave him the look of a demented alien. His house was crammed with pets, toys, books, pin tables and *objets d'art*, bought helter-skelter fashion as the whim took him. It was not unusual for him to visit my bookshop and buy everything in the window – he seemed parched for experience of all kinds, gave lavish gifts to his friends as though he could not believe his good fortune and wanted to share it before it dried up. 'I want to be a legend,' he said, and it did not seem an absurd ambition.

Both Elton and his gifted partner and lyricist, Bernie Taupin, are extremely intelligent and well read; Elton in particular has one of the quickest and keenest wits I have ever come across, with a gift for verbal as well as musical mimicry. On peak form he can be devastatingly funny and I remember one afternoon when he improvised a complete comic operetta based around the character of our village grocer, Mr Batty. I only wish I had thought to tape it.

At the time our friendship began he was on the threshold of his extraordinary international fame. After a conventional and fairly pedestrian entry into the world he and Bernie were later to conquer, their talents seemed to blossom overnight with the first album they jointly produced. Like many before them, they had to go West to be recognised and it was an unheralded appearance in a small Los Angeles theatre that set them on the road to a Beatles-type notoriety.

I have many times witnessed at first hand the unique way in

which their collaboration works. Bernie writes difficult, poetic lyrics, a far cry from the moon-in-June school. Married to a keen awareness of what the youth of today is tuned into, they frequently have a thread of mature nostalgia running through them, which was also a characteristic of the Beatles. Few, other than Elton, can get their tongues around the moving complicated lyrics or emulate Elton's unique phrasing. Until I got to know them better I had always imagined that composer and lyricist worked in close proximity, but that is not their method. Both totally different in temperament, life-style and philosophy, they work in isolation. Bernie sends Elton a sheaf of new lyrics without prior consultation. Elton then works his way through them, discarding those that do not immediately fit his musical ear, setting down the key chords, but junking his efforts after fifteen minutes if music and lyric do not coalesce. Elton was not exaggerating or voicing a conceit when he claimed they were the most prolific songwriters around in the early Seventies, for album followed album, always breaking new ground and appealing both to teeny-boppers and my own generation.

Intrigued by the pop scene, I persuaded Elton to allow me to shoot a documentary charting the genesis of a number from the moment when Bernie handed him the lyric to the moment when he performed it in public. Financing the project myself, I began to film the birth of a soon-to-be-famous song, *Candle in the Wind*, which derived from Bernie's homage to the legend of Marilyn Monroe. At that time many of Elton's albums were recorded in the semi-derelict Château d'Hierouville outside Paris, the centuries meeting at an electronic crossroads – crumbling stone housing the computerised gadgetry of pop. I followed him there, just as subsequently I followed him to Los Angeles for a live performance in the famous Hollywood Bowl. The shooting took place over several months and the footage obtained included extensive interviews with the other members of his original group together with his manager, John Reid. Elton knew that I was not out to score cheap points at his expense, but had an impartial interest in putting onto film a modern-day phenomenon, for I was educating myself in the process.

The close friendship which quickly developed between us helped sharpen my perceptions of the changing sexual scene at a time in my life when I might easily have slumped into a lazy, reactionary pose: nothing is easier when one passes the forty mark: not only the stomach grows slack, we are in danger of looking back and seeing nothing but halcyon days. It is an illusion, of course, and I was lucky in that I had a wife and two vibrant daughters who made sure that my mind was not closed to new ideas.

There was much that was changing forever in the world, some good, some bad, but all of it challenging. Public opinion on the subject of bisexuality was ambiguous: now it was hailed as a breakthrough, now it was viewed as nauseous, a threat to the stability of the society. Gone were the days when the dear old *News of the World* had achieved an eight million sale on such riveting headlines as 'Vicar on Grave Charge'. Likewise public acceptance of full frontal nudity had travelled a long way from the Windmill Theatre's frozen 'artistic' poses of my youth; the mackintosh brigade could now readily avail themselves of more explicit pleasures in every newsagent, on display cheek by jowl with *The Lady*. While Jennifer's Diary continued to record the doings of the great, the good and the mainly snobbish other scribes were detailing wife swapping in suburbia and a spot of S and M in Mayfair. The F-word first used on television by Kenneth Tynan was frequently beamed into the living room, and every other filmed drama featured a bout of heavy-breathing and simulated fornication, Mary Whitehouse notwithstanding. Yet despite the barriers tumbling in all directions, the British retained a prurient streak, they wanted their sexual cake at the same time as they were clucking disapproval at its flavour. Pop stars in particular were always fair game since they blatantly displayed their sexual drives. At the same time as up-market glossies such as *Vogue* commissioned the latest trendy photographers to present the Jaggers, Bowies and their groupie companions as the new purveyors of taste, tabloids such as the *Sun* concentrated on the jugular, forever reaching for new lows in journalism. Elton was later to become one of their victims in a particularly foul campaign.

I am not being naïve or unobservant in saying that, at the outset of our friendship, I detected no hint of the drug scene, I am merely stating a fact. Elton drank expensive champagne, but did not smoke and always swore that he would never provide the tabloids with their staple diet where pop stars are concerned. He was equally emphatic that he would not allow himself to be ripped off as the Beatles and the Stones had been ripped off. This conviction was proved false in years to come as the size of his empire attracted the inevitable quota of freeloaders. Nor did he make any secret of his emotional life, he was more concerned with the excitement of achieving his ambitions and enjoying the material rewards. After six years of grind, touring England and playing obscure gigs, he had been catapulted into a world where the sky was the limit. To somebody of Elton's ebullient character suddenly being let loose in the toy shop meant that he could indulge his every fantasy, but, whereas he deliberately projected a public image that was finely calculated to outrage (he enjoyed sending himself up, stating that in one year he had made it into the lists of 'the top ten best-dressed men and the top ten worst-dressed women'), in private life his taste ran to collecting the best art and furniture. He had money to burn and he spent it on a heroic scale, transforming his modest bungalow home overnight.

Rerunning my documentary film recently, I believe I did capture certain aspects of this transitionary stage in his develop-ment, for, in the process of being discovered, he was also discovering himself and the image on the screen was that of an extraordinary young man, fully aware of his emerging talents, wary, not entirely sure of where life would take him, yet at the same time revealing a steely determination to push himself to the limit.

The narration I wrote also proved to have a certain prophetic quality in that it anticipated events to come as well as pinpointing the chameleon quality of Elton's personality.

Always ruthlessly honest about himself, street-wise about the hype, he often startled those surrounding him by his sudden changes of mood. What was never in question was his enormous will-power. When on the road during one of his annual marathon tours he worked himself to exhaustion, but it was a matter of pride with him never to short-change his audiences. 'I have to give them a hundred per cent of myself. Even if I had a broken leg, I'd hop around on it for two and a half hours.' What is equally unique about his performances is the absolute command he holds over vast audiences. 'I go out there and get every person in the building quiet when I sing a slow song and get them shouting their heads off when I do a fast one.' I have seen him do this to a crowd of 80,000 in the Dodger Stadium, going on stage mid-afternoon and not coming off until dusk – his fingertips bleeding from the pounding he gave the keys, drenched in sweat, sagging like a ragdoll. At the height of his fame, in addition to writing and recording a new album, he made a world tour every year with all the attendant razzmatazz and it was perhaps inevitable that such pressures would eventually tell, pushing him to sample the instant panacea that was so readily available. As a lifelong smoker I can hardly criticise somebody else's journey into the drug scene; although I have steered clear of that particular vice I am not in a position to assume a holier-than-thou attitude. Together with the pressures, the temptation to boost the diminishing adrenalin every night is understandable if not commendable. Elton was intelligent enough to realise what he was doing to his health, but he was on a roller-coaster that seldom stopped long enough for him to get off. In addition to his professional commitments he was also heavily involved with Watford Football Club, taking them from being a near-insolvent Fourth Division team to the First Division and a Cup Final at Wembley within the space of a few seasons. He also found time to help save the National Youth Theatre which was also struggling to stay afloat, having been refused any grant from the Arts Council.

Success on such a scale inevitably brings a number of worms out of the woodwork and by now he had become a virtual one-man industry and considered an easy target by those sorry arbiters of common taste who increasingly think it their duty to seek out and destroy the famous. With some courage Elton attempted to spike their guns by openly admitting his bisexuality, but this did not satisfy the truffle hounds snapping at his heels. His much publicised marriage to a gentle German girl merely whetted their appetite. He was accorded a brief honeymoon in print, but once the happy wedding snaps had faded, he was once again their prey. Renate, his wife, had been a recording engineer and was therefore no stranger to the foibles of the pop world, but I doubt if she could ever have imagined the extent to which her hitherto private life would now be exposed. Like Elton she was subjected to intense media scrutiny, her every action or chance remark picked up by the columnists; paparazzi lay in wait whenever she paid a visit to a restaurant; the way she dressed, what jewellery she wore or didn't wear, was commented upon, and for somebody who was basically a shy person totally unaccustomed to publicity it was an ordeal that Elton could not shield her from – she was trapped in a no-win situation. If she accompanied Elton on tour she was inevitably a bystander; if she stayed behind to make a home for him to return to, then the tabloids speculated about a rift. Nanette and I saw a great deal of them both during this period whenever they were back at Windsor; Nanette especially formed a friendship with Renate which gave Renate somebody she could confide in and relate to who was not part of the pop world. Nobody can ever truly speculate about other marriages, but there is no doubt in our minds that Elton was in love with his wife and she with him. The fact that the marriage eventually failed was cause for sorrow to their friends, but the breakup, when it came, doubtless disappointed those who were longing for a fresh spate of scurrilous revelations. They separated with dignity and without recriminations, which was entirely typical of both of them. Far from being the predatory, wronged wife the tabloids would have preferred, Renate had not married Elton for the spoils, but out of genuine affection for him.

The collapse of the marriage came during a time when Elton was being buffeted on all sides. He had to overcome a cancer scare which at one time he felt would put an end to his singing career, but which, happily, proved to be a non-malignant condition. Then he was the victim of a particularly evil campaign in the *Sun* that claimed front-page, banner headlines for several days. With considerable courage he took the decision to clear his name in the courts, an act which many others in the same position would have thought twice about, for the perils were many and the opposition formidable. Although the burden of it blighted his life for nearly a year, during which time he became a virtual recluse, mentally and physically worn out by the worry of it, he never wavered in his resolve to obtain justice. I was in a position to know that many of the accusations made against him were total fabrications, a fact subsequently proved when the tabloid's main witness admitted his entire story was a complete falsehood and that he had been paid a large sum of money to invent it. There was also a secondary accusation, the product of poisoned minds determined to get Elton at any cost, that claimed he had removed the voice boxes from his two dogs because their barking disturbed him at night. It is difficult to imagine what drives certain sections of our press to pursue such revolting vendettas against somebody so gifted, and so inoffensive as Elton, when there are other major issues that should properly command the headlines. It can only be put down to the prevailing climate of envy that seems to surround those who find themselves in the public spotlight. Make a success of your life, bring pleasure to others through your work, and you are considered fair game; but commit a really hideous crime and your memoirs will be prominently splashed in bold type, not as a warning to others, but with implied sympathy. It is the perpetrators of crimes, not the victims, who are given the maximum understanding and benefit of the doubt in our enlightened age. What a diet of dangerous pap many newspapers now serve up day after day, hastening the rot that infects the society we live in.

It was entirely typical of Elton's character that once he had determined to change the course of his life, he went the whole hog. He stripped out the entire contents of his Windsor home which had begun to closely resemble the Museum of Modern Art and Memorabilia (in some of the rooms it was scarcely possible to walk without destroying some valuable object). Everything he had collected so avidly went under the hammer during a much publicised Sotheby's auction, including as it happens a small needlepoint cushion which our Sarah had made for him one Christmas. This fetched, I believe, the princely sum of £250. Once denuded of its previous treasures, the house was vacated and degutted and now awaits Elton's return after three years of intensive remodelling on a scale not seen since the days of the Sun King at Versailles. In addition he relinquished his position as Chairman of Watford FC and sold his investment. Everywhere, the decks were cleared; he intended to start afresh, producing a new album in collaboration with Bernie Taupin that to many presented a collection of new songs as good as, if not better than, anything they had done before. The iron will he was so proud of demonstrating had been put to work, the old eccentricities muted: he seemed to have begun shaping his life all over again.

Over the past two decades during which our friendship has flourished, I have often been in awe of his talents, for I have always admired those who stand apart from the crowd. The world he inhabits throws up a goodly quota of the mediocre, since the lure of the riches that flow to those who make it attracts an untalented multitude. Elton's gifts place him amongst the sparse band of composer-performers likely to survive changing fashions. His twenty years at the top did not happen by chance, and he continues to demonstrate that he does not follow trends, but makes them. In addition to the dozen or so standard songs he and Bernie have produced, his non-vocal compositions are equally impressive, for his infallible musical ear enables him to inject an emotional quality into his work that bridges the generation gap, converting people like myself to an understanding of what the pop scene is all about.

When our younger daughter Emma announced she was engaged to be married she produced a guest list for the wedding that 'just includes my closest friends'. The list numbered over eighty such fortunates. I said to her: 'Darling, I'm over sixty and I count myself lucky that I have a dozen closest friends – how come you have managed to acquire such an army by age twenty-two?'

Amongst the twelve, I count Elton, because his friendship has enriched my life.

THIRTY-ONE

Like many before me, from the start of my career I have kept scrap albums, using the services of Messrs Durrant's estimable press-cutting agency to search out and send me references flattering and unflattering. I often conjecture about the anonymous ladies who have spent years snipping out the lives of strangers. For over forty years somebody has been scanning innumerable papers and magazines for mention of my name, and I have never had any personal contact with whoever performs this task. Durrant's employees must learn of our failures and triumphs before we do; they can detect early warning signs of a marriage that is on the rocks, predict the start of a romance, the slide into obscurity as the once proliferate cuttings dwindle.

It is a conceit, of course, to wish to preserve the minutiae of one's life in this fashion, but perhaps my grandchildren will take a more charitable view and the many volumes that now rest on my shelves will give them a blow-by-blow account of the life Nanette and I forged for ourselves, providing the newsprint does not self-destruct before they are old enough to show interest. I have been going through them while writing this book, seeking to authenticate certain dates and verify names, and I have been amazed by the diversity of the fifty years spent in the pursuit of – what? Studying these yellowing tombstones, I have frequently been hard put to recognise the man they depict. Was that really me at that moment in time, did I really say all those things, was that praise deserved, that damning put-down justified or is the truth sleeping somewhere in between? There are vicious reviews from critics long since dead whose passing I did not mourn, interviews I have forgotten giving, ill-judged opinions I long to revise, articles I cannot recall having written. In later volumes the obituaries I have composed for lost contemporaries appear with depressing regularity; there are years when I seem to have made a career from giving the address at memorial services – the list includes Eric Portman, Cicely Courtneidge, Kenneth More, Dame Edith, David Niven, Jack Hawkins. Yet, apart from all the memory aids, perhaps these Dead Sea Scrolls do give all the important map references to the long journey that, in Graham Greene's memorable title, constitute 'a sort of life'.

Sometimes they pull me up with a jolt. After more than twenty years I have all but blotted out memories of my one and only venture into publishing. It was Peter Sellers who persuaded me to take a modest stake in a new magazine called *King*, a would-be serious monthly with a nod towards the *Playboy* market, for it included a few chaste nudes from time to time. We had some distinguished contributors and cartoonists, I remember, and for two years the venture made headway, although publisher and staff lived dangerously. I got sucked in deeper and deeper until in the end, all the other investors having sensibly withdrawn, I was left payrolling the entire operation. I also was forced to write part of it, since we could ill afford to commission outsiders. I fought to save it, but when our paper suppliers cut our credit from three months to thirty days overnight, the point of no return had been reached. We went out of business with a circulation approaching 75,000 copies. I lost some £27,000, but I don't regret it; while it lasted it was quite exciting and there is nothing like losing one's own money to strengthen the resolve to rise again. The title was the only remaining asset and this was sold on for £5000 to help pay off the creditors and for a time was incorporated into the immensely successful, increasingly soft-porn, *Mayfair*.

I suppose I could loosely describe my entire life as a gamble. Being self-employed from age sixteen automatically precludes believing that the world owes you a living. I have a weakness for roulette which first claimed me during a holiday Nanette and I

339

took in the South of France shortly after we were married. We were staying, full *pension*, in a small hotel on the Plage de la Garoupe where, legend has it, Scott and Zelda and the Murphys fashioned the beach by importing sand. It was a modest establishment, boasting only one toilet, and the room we occupied backed onto a chicken run which meant that we were dive-bombed by mosquitoes throughout the fetid nights. However, the food was excellent and plentiful, and we paid eight pounds a day, and arrived with enough funds to last a fortnight with care. Then one evening we ventured into the Palm Beach Casino in Cannes and promptly lost our meagre stake. On the sober drive back to Cap d'Antibes Nanette suddenly announced that she had worked out an infallible system to beat the wheel. She described it to me. I was immediately convinced. We turned the car around and headed back to the fleshpots. Nanette's system was simple but required great patience. It was based on the theory of shortening the odds by using five chips, covering thirty out of the thirty-seven numbers. If you won you came out with six chips per spin of the wheel and by staying at the tables for an average of three tortuous hours we could usually win enough to stay an extra day. By this scheme we extended our holiday a further week, although exhausting ourselves in the process.

Since when I have frequently chanced my arm in my favourite London casino, the Ritz. On home ground the punter does not have to suffer surly croupiers who in France frequently dispute a win and pass it to one of those aged local harpies, permanent features of every table, with whom they undoubtedly have an arrangement. While I have never thrown in the deeds of the plantation, I admit that, as with *King* magazine, I am prone to ventures with a high risk factor. Gambling in this fashion seems a natural extension of life in the film business where every new project is like playing *en plein* with a single chip.

As with scrap books, so with photo albums. From the time when I was a member of the occupation forces in Germany and Austria immediately after the war, I have been obsessed with cameras. The first one I ever possessed was purchased on the black market. In those days virtually anything could be acquired for cigarettes, soap or coffee and the vintage Kodak Retina became mine for a tin of Players. Since when I have worked my way through a variety of cameras from an old Soho reflex and a Rolleiflex through Leicas, Nikons, Hasselblads to the latest auto-focusing masterpieces. Much of my early photographic gear was acquired from Sellers, who changed cameras and cars more frequently than he changed wives. At one period I had my own darkroom, but sensibly gave this up when I went to Elstree studios: there the experts in the labs took over from my own amateur efforts.

I think it is important for a novelist as well as a film director to develop a photographic eye, for a writer should miss nothing, and a director must train himself to seek out the best angles from which to tell his story. Time and time again my photographs have later been transferred to the written word – the bloated, dead cow washed up on the beach in Barbados, and extensively recorded by my camera, surfaced again in my novel *Familiar Strangers*. Hotels have always provided me with good copy especially as each island paradise succumbs to the necessary degradations of the package-tourist trade.

Combining photographs and journal entries I used this description in another novel:

The Holiday Inn, Bridgetown, was like a set for an early Gainsborough film about the Huggets. Amazingly overweight children leaping into the crowded pool; boys of thirteen with flabby breasts watched by parents perched on little bandstands reading out-of-date English newspapers and sipping diluted rum punches through twisted straws. A young man wearing nothing but his Y-fronts and a gold ankle bracelet. Several Stanley Kowalski's with tattoos and sagging bellies, a bearded man buying *Penthouse* the moment his obese wife's back was turned. Coffee made from boiled cricket pads costing sixteen Barbados dollars, served by a hostess who looks like Mrs Simpson. Obvious examples of *Les Anglais* talking in loud, strident voice – 'Yas, we live just outside Auksford now, a little plaice near Henlay' – their weedy, complaining children like sticks of white asparagus. Very curious notice pinned up in

341

nearby beach bar, owned and run by a native Bajan – JOSEPH BROOME ALSO KNOWN AS NIGGER CHARLIE IS NOT ALLOWED ON THESE PREMISES.

Returning to the scrap books, I find that I once wrote an article about a bookseller named Carol Stoll, another addition to the roster of remarkable women I have known and admired.

I went to Chicago for the first time to direct a film called *The Naked Face* and for over six months occupied a suite on the twenty-third floor of the Ritz Carlton, possibly the best hotel in the world, and somewhere I would happily return to. I had been primed with various horror stories about the Second City, mostly by natives of the Big Apple, and expected the worst, only to become a total fan of that windy metropolis. Unlike New York, the inhabitants of Chicago don't push you off the sidewalks in their frenetic hurry to go nowhere. The city not only boasts spectacular architecture but one can see air between the skyscrapers – there is not the feeling of living at the bottom of some concrete and steel Grand Canyon as in New York. In addition one is very conscious of being surrounded by water. In ignorance I had imagined Lake Michigan to be just that, a lake one could see across, not a sea that takes twenty minutes to traverse by modern jet. From my high-rise hotel window I could look down on crowded sandy beaches during the summer season: one might have been on the Mediterranean. The natives boast that if you hang around for fifteen minutes the weather in Chicago will change, but maybe I was lucky that year and it wasn't until near the end of the filming schedule in December that the famed winds blew off the lake with hurricane force and the temperature fell sub-zero. By then the suburbs looked like an old-time Currier and Ives Christmas print, for there are some splendidly preserved houses that by American standards constitute old.

My cast for the film included Rod Steiger, Ann Archer, the inimitable Art Carney, Elliot Gould and Roger Moore, and most nights we ate in Eli's, an old-time steak house that seemed to belong to the age of Capone, where the prime cuts overlapped the plate and the speciality of the house was a cheesecake that added pounds just by looking at it.

Once established, I wandered through the unknown city and chanced upon the Oak Street Bookshop, just off the elegance of Michigan Avenue and tucked away between a cinema and a restaurant. The unprepossessing façade concealed many treasures within, not the least of which was the owner. It was run single-handed, seven days a week, fifty-two weeks a year, by a lady who triumphantly proved that the spirit of youth has nothing to do with age. This was Carol Stoll and she was a local legend.

From the moment I stepped inside her cramped quarters where Carol sat perched behind the till, a mug of coffee in one hand, a cigarette in the other, I sensed I had struck gold. This was not the kind of bookshop where *The Secret Diary of Adrian Mole* is filed in the pet section, for Carol's stock, though eclectic, contained many titles for the discerning customer that the multiples studiously avoided. While I was ferreting through her stock she must have decided that I was the type of customer who gladdens a bookseller's heart. She offered me a cup of coffee and a chocolate chip cookie, I told her that I was a fellow bookseller and our friendship began. Elegantly dressed, always surrounded by fresh flowers, in those days constantly wreathed in cigarette smoke (she has since kicked the habit), she dispensed trenchant wit and wisdom to all comers, though I was soon to discover that she did not suffer fools too gladly. (I was once present in the shop when a woman entered and asked if Carol had a copy of *Do It Yourself Brain Surgery*. Without any discernible sarcasm Carol replied in her smoke-stained voice: 'Sorry, there's been a run on that one, I'm clean out of it. Best not to get involved with an enquiry like that,' she added when the shop was empty, 'I can't fool around with all the polite noises.')

A widow, Carol had turned herself into a bookseller on her husband's death in order, as she put it, to avoid becoming a couch potato. 'I had one last spree,' she told me, 'I took all of my friends on a sea cruise before settling down here, blowing most of the money he left me. So then I had to earn my own living,

343

learning as I went along. An active mind takes your thoughts off sadness. Now in the nightcap of my life, I love working. I don't think I was ever so wonderful before.' She also confided she had been held at gunpoint, locked in her washroom and robbed – incidents she related with amazing nonchalance – that she suffered from a particularly rapacious landlord who constantly raised her rent, and that it was a struggle to survive against her main-street competitors who could afford to heavily discount bestsellers, the bread and butter of the bookseller.

Never one to pass up a busman's holiday, I got into the habit of serving in the shop on my days off, a welcome respite from the demands of the film. I quickly discovered that the small oasis in Oak Street was the village pump. She had a faithful band of regular customers who visited her daily, and who were accorded their own coffee mugs with their names engraved on them. In due course I got my own mug, Carol's accolade. One particularly favoured customer, Warren, the local cop on the beat, made a breakfast call and was provided with fresh croissant as well as coffee. She kept track of all the reviews, read voraciously and passed on her opinions to customers. 'I not only read their books for them first, but I giftwrap and deliver. I do everything but sit next to them while they read and point out the good paragraphs.'

To me Carol symbolised the love and lunacy of the bookselling trade, a small pocket of resistance against the ever encroaching menace of the book *trader*, that impersonal entity who has no real feeling for literature. Carol was passionate about the books she sold, fighting a rearguard action for a quality of life always under attack from the yahoos. She used to say 'I love the mornings, sitting around drinking a pot of coffee and watching the sun come up. I think, "By God, you're going to do a huge amount of business today." Then when I get home at night I think, "something went wrong." But I'm always hopeful.'

Alas, it was to prove a losing battle. We kept in close touch after I left Chicago and do so to this day, but the time came, as both she and I knew it would, when she rang to tell me that she had finally been forced out: the latest demands from her landlord proved too much for even her indomitable spirit. Now she writes to tell me that she feels like a stateless person with no aim in life, but her letters still echo that spunky quality which for two score years, at an age when most people would have been content to put their feet up, compelled her to be in her shop at seven o'clock every morning. We authors are the losers as well as the good citizens of Chicago.

THIRTY-TWO

Few of us escape being touched from afar by some inexplicable tragedy and I am still haunted by the memory of the murder of Sharon Tate and Jay Sebring, both of whom were friends.

I first chanced upon Sharon before she became known, finding myself sitting next to her on a flight from New York to Los Angeles in the early Sixties. She had just been discovered and put under contract by Marty Ransahoff, a producer who came to fame and fortune with a television series called *The Beverly Hillbillies*, and later progressed to feature films. She seemed a pleasant, beautiful girl, possessed of more personality than others like her who still swarmed to Hollywood like pilgrims to Mecca, and during the flight I remember I tried to alert her to some of the more obvious dangers that awaited her, though nothing I described could possibly have anticipated her hideous end.

Jay Sebring was already a friend, and my hairdresser. In many ways he typified the American success story, for he clawed his way out of obscurity, starting in a humble way giving five-dollar haircuts in a small salon off Santa Monica Boulevard. He made a living, but that was about all, and he had bigger ideas. Borrowing some capital, he took new premises and when he reopened hiked his charges to a then outrageous fifty dollars, rightly judging that if he was to attract a clientele in Beverly Hills he needed to make them feel exclusive. The ploy succeeded and he never looked back, subsequently launching his own range of hair products which sold across America. No fake at his own job, he happened to be a superb stylist with revolutionary ideas about hair care, as I can personally attest.

I always made a beeline to his salon the moment I got into town, for I enjoyed his company as well as his expertise. It was during one of these reunions that he confided he had fallen in love with and was living with Sharon. I had not seen her since that chance meeting on the 'plane and she had still to make any real progress with her career; at that point in her life she was comparatively unknown, but strikingly attractive. Jay told me that they had rented the house originally owned by Jean Harlow where in 1932 her husband, Paul Bern, had committed suicide. I spent some time with them both at the house and in fact photographed Sharon there for the cover of *Queen* magazine. The house still carried an aura of disquiet, difficult to rationalise, and doubtless the atmosphere owed much to the Harlow-Bern legend, but Jay and Sharon seemed oblivious to it.

Later they visited London and Nanette and I made our small town house off the Fulham Road available to them during their stay. Jay was proud of his prowess as a Black Belt in judo and the success he had made of his life. A wiry little character with a great sense of humour, his fortunes seemed set fair at that time. He had great plans for enlarging his empire and setting up a chain of franchised hairdressing salons across America bearing his name. I did not see him again, because my film commitments kept me in Europe for two years, and during this period Sharon and he parted, though remaining close friends; she married Roman Polanski and was carrying his child when she was murdered.

Her death and that of Jay's still defy description and were all the more horrific for being motiveless. I still have a copy of my cover photograph of Sharon and it never ceases to remind me of two young people who did not merit such an end. I am not over-superstitious, but in remembering them both it sometimes crosses my mind that they did not choose the Harlow house by accident, but were drawn to it just as on the fateful night when they both met their deaths they were drawn to another appointment in Samarra.

DEATH SPEAKS: There was a merchant in Baghdad who sent his servant to market to buy provisions and in a little while the servant came back, white and trembling, and said, Master, just now when I was in the market-place I was jostled by a woman in the crowd and when I turned I saw it was Death that jostled me. She looked at me and made a threatening gesture; now, lend me your horse, and I will ride away from this city and avoid my fate. I will go to Samarra and there Death will not find me. The merchant lent his horse, and the servant mounted it, and he dug his spurs into its flanks and as fast as the horse could gallop he went. Then the merchant went down to the market-place and he saw me standing in the crowd and he came to me and said, Why did you make a threatening gesture to my servant when you saw him this morning? That was not a threatening gesture, I said, it was only a start of surprise. I was astonished to see him in Baghdad, for I had an appointment with him tonight in Samarra.

W. Somerset Maugham

THIRTY-THREE

For many years before Soviet communism started to rot from within I corresponded with a pen pal in Leningrad to whom I was compelled to write guarded letters. Igor Stupnikov counts himself a privileged person in that he was an author allowed to publish, subject to censorship. He is married to an ex-Kirov ballet dancer who now teaches. Even so for most of their married life they never had an apartment to themselves, were not permitted to travel outside Russia and the books Igor wrote (innocent studies of aspects of the theatre, including a study of Dame Edith Evans' career, which is what had initially prompted him to contact me) sometimes took four years before they were printed, since they had to pass the scrutiny of the Union of Soviet Writers and were edited according to the dictates of that disgraced body. (After the Twentieth Party Congress, Solzhenitsyn spoke of at least six hundred writers betrayed by this same union and obediently handed over to their fate in the camps.) Although our remote friendship went back fifteen years it wasn't until quite recently that we met. I suddenly received a phone call from Igor one evening and at first thought he had miraculously managed to obtain permission to call me from Leningrad. Much to my astonishment he said he was ringing from South Kensington! Less than twenty-four hours before, without prior warning, he had been ordered to accompany the Kirov Ballet to London to act as interpreter. His wife had been refused permission to come with him. I immediately drove to Covent Garden and there we came face to face for the first time. I brought him to Seven Pines for a meal and I remember that, despite the advent of *glasnost*, his caution was so ingrained that during our excited conversations around the dining table he several times prefaced his answers to my questions about his life with the words 'even though I would deny ever saying this' before venturing a mildly critical opinion of conditions in Russia. I assured him that our house was not bugged and that he could speak freely on any subject under the sun and criticise whomsoever he wished, but he remained careful. It was revealing that one of his first questions was to ask Nanette the location of the nearest Marks and Spencer store – he had come armed with a shopping list from his wife and relatives.

I told him that during the period when there had been a limited easing of the Cold War I had become involved with a group of ordinary Jewish women working in North London to free some of the dissidents, at one point helping to solicit Mrs Thatcher's aid by getting a smuggled film to her. Due to their efforts a number of dissident Jews were able to reach Israel, though it was always a tortuous process with many setbacks in the cat-and-mouse game then played with innocent human lives. Igor seemed genuinely surprised that I should have concerned myself with such a cause. 'There was no danger to you in that?' he asked, as though such an admission at my own dining table represented a threat that might incriminate him at a later date. I loaded him with gifts of books before he left, but was careful not to give him copies of my spy novels. His delight at experiencing this small taste of freedom brought home to me the vast chasm between our two societies.

I had of course read Solzhenitsyn's definitive indictment of the Gulag camps and many of the clandestine accounts that had long been suppressed but began to surface in the West following Khrushchev's attempt to discredit the Stalin myth when the *literati* could only grind their teeth and 'make fists in their pockets' to quote Karahuzhin's memorable phrase. I made it my business to obtain and read everything I could lay my hands on, not only for the purposes of research, but because I was obsessed to penetrate the written iron curtain. One short story I shall never forget was a frightening account of the relentless executions carried out by the Cheka in the immediate aftermath of the revolution. Written by Vladimir Zazubrin it is now openly available in English translation under the title *The Chip*. I can never read such accounts without a profound sense of shame at having bitched about the trivial dissatisfactions of our own lot which from time to time we all voice.

As I write this in the momentous week of 19 August 1991, I am conscious that all our fictions have been overtaken ... 'Tomorrow, and tomorrow, and tomorrow,' comes to mind. Seeing the icons toppled, the amazed faces of the crowds in Red Square and outside the KGB headquarters, my thoughts hark back to the Philbys and Blunts who refused to acknowledge that the god they worshipped had failed. I thought, too, of the squalid little men whole nations had followed into the abyss: Honecker, that Crippen-like figure who would have passed unnoticed in a bus queue; the appalling Ceauşescu; the waxwork figures who yearly stood on the Kremlin ramparts, grotesquely bemedalled, solidified with menace; all seemingly pressed from the same mould – the Dzerzhinskys, Yagodas, Yezhovs, Berias, Abakumors and Brezhnevs. The Western mind can just encompass the magnetism of a Hitler, for he was a diabolically inspired demagogue appealing to a defeated nation, but these grey shadows who successfully enslaved half of Europe issued only credit cards of fear to remain in power; they lacked even the rudiments of oratory, their utterances an offence in any language. Where are the apologists for them now, the fellow travellers who found justification for their every act?

Now, the events of the past seven days defy a novelist's imagination; how could any of us have devised such a scenario or plotted, within such a short time-scale, the surprise ending, the fact that Soviet communism now withers on the stalk like last year's nettles? The genre of the modern spy novel with the Russians as the prime villains gave rise to a vastly popular cottage industry, and in the case of Le Carré and Deighton many superior works, but even as the rest of us struggled to give credence to our narratives, there was always a still small

351

voice within that questioned our inventions. My devious plots for *The Endless Game* and *A Song at Twilight* were questioned by certain critics as being too far-fetched, but now they appear tame indeed. Nobody had the nerve to fictionalise a story whereby the slumbering Russian bear rose up and, almost overnight, began the dismantling of seventy-two years of repression. When the Berlin Wall was breached we lost one set of villains; now we are being asked to accept the instant conversion of the KGB from bad guys to boy scouts. Only Castro, Gadaffi and Saddam remain to fill the necessary roles of villains, but given the pace of events, we must be chary of depicting them thus. Even so madmen breed as fast as rabbits and often seem to live charmed lives – witness the monster of yesterday, Idi Amin. Our books, unlike Igor's, don't take four years to reach the printers, but Wilson's famous remark that 'a week is a long time in politics' was never more true. Perhaps, where Russia is concerned, we should be looking to depict the restoration of the Tsar, a new king on the shaky throne of Albania. Have we not already heard German voices raised in support of a Kaiser and seen the reappearance of Neo-Nazism's hideous face?

I thought of Igor many times during this momentous week, hoping that he and his wife were amongst the crowds gathered outside the town hall in Leningrad savouring the sweet smell of freedom that we, the lucky ones, have treated so lightly.

One sober thought remains: in the midst of all the chaos whose finger is now on the nuclear trigger?

THIRTY-FOUR

Graham Greene once wrote in a letter to me that a writer's success is only a delayed failure. If I understand him, I think he meant that our ambitions are seldom matched by the execution, that there is always room for improvement. This is particularly true of an autobiography, for the mirror of the past we stare into is mottled in places and the self-portrait it throws back is inevitably incomplete. I have lived a life of amazement, sorrows and good fortune, doing what I wanted to do, sometimes succeeding, sometimes failing and with more than my fair share of luck. My happiness I owe to my wife and children, sex, books, music, being with friends, food, wine, my garden; the unhappiness to vanity, which sucks all of us down like the law of gravity, and failing to realise the flux of things as imagination presented them. This book has been an attempt to reflect the person I once was and the person by chance I became, but I am sure that others, friends as well as enemies, would paint a different picture, and I must leave final judgements to them.

In seeking out the influences which have shaped me, I have little doubt that the sustaining forces have been two women – my mother who gave me her energy and a respect for morality – and of course Nanette. It is difficult to write of a marriage without invading the privacy of one's partner and Nanette is an intensely private person despite her public image; indeed she is the most self-effacing person I know. She will not thank me for writing about her in this fashion, but I must take the risk because I know only too well that had I not chanced upon her that February night

353

so long ago, my life would have been immeasurably impoverished and not to acknowledge that debt would be a cowardly exit from this book. After thirty-six years of marriage I still find her the most exciting, fascinating and funniest woman who has ever come within my orbit, for her wit and the way in which she deals with life still have the knack of taking me by surprise. I cannot be an easy person to live with. I am untidy, frequently disorganised, irritatingly vague, difficult and faddy about what I eat, with a squirrel-like tendency to hoard trivia, secretive about unimportant matters, blunt where she is placatory, ambitious whereas she is genuinely indifferent to fame, lacking to my cost her intuitions about people and often a prophet of gloom. All these characteristics bear out her often repeated observation that the reason our relationship has endured is because we are complete opposites. Perhaps the Polyfilla that cements the cracks is our shared sense of humour, the fact that even during the direst periods we have been able to see the funny side of our dilemmas. So many times she has prevented me from taking the wrong turning, for a man who does not have somebody to tell him the truth when he puts his head on the pillow at night is somebody to be pitied.

Given that she has always denigrated her beauty, I need have no such reticence, for I never look at her without discovering it anew. She is a feminist without feeling the need to burn her bra or deny the fact that she enjoys being a mother, and more recently a grandmother. In an age where many of our contemporaries bemoan the fact that they have no relationship with their children, we have been blessed with two daughters of widely differing characters, who remain close and affectionate and a constant source of pleasure to us both. In Sarah's and Emma's eyes I was cast as the slightly remote, slightly dotty figure, once described with some justification by a young Sarah as an 'erector' and a 'typewriter'. I may have supplied some useful genes, but Nanette gave them their looks (as the photographs confirm), their character and uncynical attitude towards the world – they have never, to my knowledge, been bored with life. We also scored with our two sons-in-law who, in their differing ways and personalities, share Sarah's and Emma's inherent sense of adventure, of living life to the full. John Standing, Sarah's husband, is of course the stylish and highly acclaimed actor who has sired a trio of extraordinary children, about whom we have no future fears. Emma, who in her early years was the more introverted of the two, blossomed late, but has since made up for lost time. She married out of the profession to Graham Clempson, a brilliant young banker, some hundred Porsche-lengths from being a yuppie.

I seem to have come a long way from the cautionary words I chose to preface my first published book. Then, twenty-one and just returned from the war, uncertain, hollowed by a first love affair, I quoted Flaubert's 'We shall find life tolerable once we have consented to be always ill at ease'. At the time I thought it a philosophy for all my seasons, a sliver of wisdom taken off the shelf. I had said my farewell to arms, lived amongst the defeated in ruined cities, slept with the enemy, and now I had fresh mistakes to make and made them. All except one.

This book then, these further 'notes for a life', is dedicated to she who made it possible.

Appendix One

SCREENWRITING CAREER

1.	*Vacant Lot*	Never made
2.	*The Black Knight*	Additional scenes
3.	*Cockleshell Heroes*	Original screenplay
4.	*An Alligator Named Daisy*	Additional scenes
5.	*The Small Victory*	An original, never made
6.	*A Matter of Room Numbers*	An original, never made
7.	*House of Secrets*	Rewrite
8.	*The Captain's Table*	Shared credit
9.	*No Cover for Harry*	Original, never made
10.	*The Children Get Bored on Sunday*	Original, never made
11.	*SOS Sahara*	Full screenplay
12.	*Danger Within*	Full screenplay
13.	*Passage Home*	Rewrite
14.	*Bus Story*	Original, never made
15.	*The Black Tent*	Rewrite, shared credit
16.	*The Baby and the Battleship*	Shared credit
17.	*Wrong Arm of the Law*	Additional scenes
18.	*SOS Pacific*	Rewrite, full screenplay
19.	*I Was Monty's Double*	Full screenplay
20.	*Paranoiac*	Never made
21.	*The Angry Silence*	Original, full screenplay

22.	*Five Heads Are Better Than One*	Full screenplay, never used
23.	*The League of Gentlemen*	Full screenplay
24.	*Only Two Can Play*	Full screenplay
25.	*The L-Shaped Room*	Full screenplay
26.	*Of Human Bondage*	Full screenplay
27.	*Seance on a Wet Afternoon*	Full screenplay
28.	*The Lion*	Full screenplay, my script never used
29.	*The High Bright Sun*	Full screenplay, no credit
30.	*The Love Ban*	Full screenplay, no credit
31.	*The Man in the Moon*	Full screenplay, shared credit
32.	*The Young Mr Churchill*	Full screenplay, my script never used
33.	*King Rat*	Full screenplay
34.	*The Wrong Box*	Rewrite, no credit taken
35.	*The Egyptologists*	Full screenplay, never made
36.	*The Whisperers*	Full screenplay
37.	*Deadfall*	Full screenplay
38.	*The Madwoman of Chaillot*	Rewrite, no credit
39.	*Eyewitness*	Full screenplay, using pseudonym
40.	*The Man Who Haunted Himself*	Full screenplay, no credit taken
41.	*A Fine and Private Place*	Rewrite, never made
42.	*Conduct Unbecoming*	Full screenplay, my script never used
43.	*Mr and Mrs Attila*	Original, never made
44.	*Triple Echo*	Never finished
45.	*11 Harrowhouse*	Full screenplay, not used
46.	*Hopscotch*	Full screenplay, shared credit
47.	*The Stepford Wives*	Full screenplay, no credit
48.	*The Slipper and the Rose*	Original, full screenplay

49. *International Velvet*	Original, full screenplay
50. *Jessie*	Original, full screenplay
51. *The Seventh Secret*	Full screenplay, never used
52. *Ménage à Trois*	Full screenplay
53. *The Naked Face*	Full screenplay
54. *Henry*	Full screenplay, never made
55. *The Rewrite Man*	Full screenplay, still to be filmed
56. *Nessie*	Full screenplay, never made
57. *The Endless Game*	Full screenplay
58. *Chaplin*	Full screenplay, my script not used

Appendix Two

Telephone:
GERRARD 2677/8.

Telegrams:
"CENSOFILM, PHONE, LONDON."

BRITISH BOARD OF FILM CENSORS

President: THE RT. HON. LORD MORRISON OF LAMBETH. C.H.
Secretary: JOHN TREVELYAN. O.B.E.

3, SOHO SQUARE,

LONDON, W.1

JT/MAB   CONFIDENTIAL   11th April, 1962

Bryan Forbes, Esq.,
Shepperton Studios,
Shepperton, Middx.

Dear Bryan,

"THE L-SHAPED ROOM"

As I told you on the telephone we have now read your script entitled "THE L-SHAPED ROOM". This is a fine piece of writing and it should make a sincere and moving film. It will of course need sensitivity and care in treatment, but I know enough of your work to be sure that it will get it.

The film can of course only be considered in terms of the "X" category. For this category the theme is acceptable and the only things that require comment are points of detail. These are as follows:-

Page 16 Scene 55	The word "Christ!" should be altered. We do not object to "God", "God Almighty" or "My God" as expletives, but always ask for the omission of "Christ" or "Jesus" which are regarded by many people as offensive expletives.
alter	
Page 23 Scene 84	In this scene Toby, whose speech is a little direct in places, refers to "the poor old sod". We keep the word "sod" out of films also. I would like you to alter this. We do not prohibit "arse" in an "X" film, but I suggest the line would be better if it were partially thrown away since it is probably the way in which Toby would use this phrase.
alternative	
alter **Page 24 Scene 86**	Here we get the phrase "Jesus wept!". See my previous comments.
Page 28 Scene 100	This amusing dialogue between Mavis and Sonia is a bit tricky but should be all right if played as light comedy. I do however think that you might omit Mavis's words "I heard" which suggests that

the/

the "goings-on" on the bed were audible all round.

Page 41 Scene 144

While we keep references to contraceptives out of
films unless there is full justification for them, I
think that this might be acceptable here since it is
a talk between a doctor and patient.

alt

Page 55 Scene 168
Page 59 Scene 185

Here "Jesus" is used again.   Previous comments apply.
The dialogue between Jane and Toby in this scene may
pass as light comedy, but if it were serious dialogue
about aphrodisiacs and conception we would be worried
about it.   Perhaps you can shoot the scene in such a
way as to enable the references to be removed later
if they come out in a way that is not acceptable to us.

Ignore

Page 61 Scene 186

We would not be too happy about the broad comedy of
a tart and her customers.   This is purely a question
of treatment and you may do this scene in a fully
acceptable way.   Since it is a separate intercut
scene, it could doubtless be removed if necessary, but
I hope it will not be necessary.

Ignore

Page 62 Scene 188

It is our experence that a fair number of people, both
men and women, get a physical reaction to the sight
and sound of other people being sick. I suggest
therefore in your own interests that you should be
discreet about this.

Ignore

Page 71 Scene 206

I am not sure about Toby's expression "...we were just
about to have it off here in the grass", but I think
it may pass.   Perhaps you could consider an alternative
line to use if necessary.

Ignore

*alternative
or omit*

Page 77 Scene 209

I think we are most unlikely to pass "That's the sort
of thing that makes me want to fornicate right in the
middle of Westminster Abbey during a Royal Wedding".
A lot of people would consider this going a bit too far!
We are not sure about Toby's lines "..I won't be able
to stop.   I do love you, you see... That's why I can
stop". This is rather direct dialogue.   It may pass
in its context, but might present us with a problem.
Perhaps you could have an alternative available if
necessary.

Ignore

Ignore

We are worried also about the reactions of John to
what he hears through the thin partion wall.   This
kind of thing is going to need extreme care and
delicacy if it is not to be offensive.   We know that
he gets no pleasure from what he hears, but even so
the situation is a tricky one and I think you should
play it down as far as possible.

Page 83 Scene 226

Jane's lines are pretty direct. They may pass in the
context, but there is the possibility of their creating
a problem when we see the picture.   I think perhaps
"...in the end, I decided my virginity was becoming

Ignore

rather/

Ignore

rather cumbersome" is a bit too direct. I do not
suggest that you should alter this dialogue now, but
I think that you should have some alternative in mind
in case it is unacceptable.

Page 86-9 Scene 237-49 Care should be taken with the visuals of couples
fondling each other. Some of these as described in
the script are likely to be troublesome. We would
not want breast-rubbing or thigh-rubbing; nor would
we want copulatory-dancing. This kind of shot
presents special difficulties since the boys and girls
are young.

Ignore

Page 90 Scene 253 I think you should omit Toby's line "Can I hold you
there? You're so beautiful there" and end the scene
before then. This goes further than we would want
even for the "X" category.

Ignore

Page 92-3 Scene 256-64 Great care will have to be taken with these scenes.
They present a greater problem than most sex scenes
since the audience knows that the girl is pregnant.
Nudity and semi-nudity should certainly be avoided
and we would like you to avoid erotic visuals.

Ignore

Page 97-8 Scene 291 Here we have emphasis again on what John has heard
from next door. This again needs great care and
discretion. I would prefer the removal of the
emphasis on the fact that he had been listening to
their making love and heard it, even though this was
unavoidable in the situation.   I should think
that in this context the word "whore" would pass,
but if it turned out offensive no doubt you could
re-dub as "tart".

Ignore

Page 105 Scene 321 The fact that John makes it clear that he has heard
her being sick is an entirely different matter, and
causes no trouble.

Page 107-9 Scene 324-34   We are usually anxious to avoid references to
possible sources of abortion. In this case it should
be all right since the nature of the pill is not
specified and since that are not effective.

Page 118 Scene 396 Jane's line "Did you think I was a virgin when you made
love to me?" is rather direct and you might possibly
have a softer alternative available.

Ignore

Page 119 Scene 396 The same applies to Jane's lines on this page about
her previous sexual relations with men.

Ignore

Page 122 Scene 400 Here Jane "sits up and starts to dress herself"
Presumably we shall not have any censorable visuals
especially in view of her pregnant condition.

Ignore

Page 125 Scene 404 When Mavis talks about the love of her life, we learn
from the photograph that this love was for another
woman.   This may well pass especially since Mavis
is talking about love and not about sex, and it will
be helpful in your casting of Mavis, but I suggest

that/

4.

Page 127 Scene 408

Page 129 Scene 411

Page 135 Scene 421

Page 135 Scene 423

Page 142 Scene 437

Ignore

alternative

Ignore

Ignore

Ignore

Ignor.

that you shoot the scene in such a way as to make the omission of the photograph, if considered desirable, something which could be done without spoiling the scene.

Here we get "sod" again.   Please see my previous comments.

I think that Jane's line "I'm up to here with milk" should pass, but we would not want any visuals which made the line offensive.

I think that you should be very careful about the shots in which John and Toby touch Jane in her very pregnant condition.   I think that this could be done sensitively and movingly, but I believe that some people are very sensitive about this kind of thing, so I suggest in your own interests that you take care with it.   It might be as well to shoot this scene in a way which will enable cuts to be made if necessary.   Incidentally, we would be rather unhappy if you showed Jane in an ungainly pregnant condition, but I imagine that you would be equally unhappy about this.

I expect the ribaldry about getting the bird in the oven will be all right, but you should be prepared for cuts if it comes out in an offensive way.

I think we should see as little as possible of the doctor's examination of Jane.   Apart from anything else, as you will know from experience, the actual and real situation of pregnancy is inclined to be somewhat degrading for a woman - degrading is not exactly the right word but I think you will know what I mean.   Fortunately all this is quickly forgotten when the baby arrives.

I hope that these comments will be helpful to you.   If you want further advice at any stage of production please do not hesitate to let me know.   In the meantime I hope that the picture goes well.

I return your script herewith.

Yours sincerely,

Secretary.

363

Appendix Three

To
Peter O'Toole
The Old Vic Theatre   September 8, 1980

My Dear Peter,

   Before leaving I am dictating these notes to be typed up by my
secretary and sent to you.

   Now that most of the captains and the kings have departed and
we can start to build upon what we have, I am most anxious that
certain areas of the production be re-examined in the cold light of
experience and whenever possible my convictions acted upon for the
general good. If you would be my go-between and find time to
discuss these with the members of the cast in my absence I would be
most grateful.

   Some we have already discussed, but they yet bear repeating.
None of them are offered in malice or in recrimination, but only as
valid experiments which I think are worth trying.

   Let me commence with you. Several times in rehearsal I drew
attention to what I rudely called your 'drunken sailor' stance and
walk. I still find this most noticeable in your first two or three scenes
and I think it does you no great service. Fools and vagabonds put
the wrong interpretation on it, believing it to be the result of too
much mead!

   I also find the reactions you do to the witches when they announce
you will be King and the reaction you do to the 1st murderer when
he tells you that Fleance escaped are too broad and need toning
down.

   We have discussed the murderers scene being sing-song and
lacking in menace – and I think that the key to this lies in your
playing of the soliloquy that precedes it. I saw you do this brilliantly

in rehearsal but it has never come up to that since. You play too much out front for one thing – it should be broodingly introspective.

Likewise I never think you prepare yourself sufficiently for the Dagger speech – it seems to be a path to a lighting mark rather than a move which stems from your own dark thoughts.

Now that you have found the pitch of the house I do assure you that you can be heard everywhere and that you will not do your performance any harm if you bring it down in sheer volume and play with the nuances more.

THE BANQUET SCENE: this improves but we are still getting several very unwelcome laughs which must be stamped out. I think this can be achieved by:

1. Considerably less blood from Brian, so that his face is not a mask and the front of his chest does not represent an abattoir. I also think that stillness in the Ghost is more effective than a lot of gestures and movement. He could also try something I previously asked for and that is to wear some form of white stocking over his face which might give a more ghostly look and prevent the blood running into his eyes.

2. Jump to kill not to embrace – we have discussed this.

3. Frances should try to take more time and use a more forbidding tone when she steps on her lines – if you jump straight in, tell her, you invariably get a laugh, because of what Harry Lauder has just done.

4. The general note for Frances is that she has gone back to very swift, ballet-like movements which I have always felt was wrong for the character. This is now very noticeable in the sleep-walking scene and in the entrance 'That which hath made them bold' – take it all much slower as far as movement is concerned.

5. I still believe you are using too much blood for your entrance after the murder of the grooms – especially by covering ALL your hands so that it looks as though painted on. Leave it in streaks if you can – more realistic. The same applies to Frances.

6. Frances' reaction to the knocking – it must have more fear because it looks too casual from the front. I know what she is trying to convey but it just isn't coming over believe me and should be looked at most carefully.

7. Banquo: 'Too cruel anywhere' should be said with more compassion – his naked hatred of Lady M is too subtle and unfortunately does not come over as Brian intended. Likewise when

he throws her John Hugg we get a bad laugh which could easily be avoided.

8. Banquo's murder – once his throat is cut he should never get entirely to his feet – it is wrong and again evinces a laugh we could well do without.

9. Do 'Duncan's in his grave' straight at your wife, not away from her. In general you play too much of this in isolation and it has begun to ruin your marvellous 'light thickens' speech at the end.

10. Make the bridge between 'Be innocent of the deed dearest Chuck' and 'Come seeling night etc.' This is another note as per 9 above.

11. As to the London scene and Macduff's Horror, Horror, I felt that the last time I saw it that we had again moved backwards towards a mere recitation of lines without any discernible real feeling. I know that Dudley never did believe what I had to say in rehearsals and has chosen to go his own route, though it would appear that his route has not given him salvation for he is still changing backwards and forwards. He nearly had Horror, Horror right and then totally regressed back to shouting in a flat monotone – this was especially true on Monday night. Unless he moves the audience with his London speeches then the scene has no point and drags the play down to a level from whence it can never totally recover. He quite obviously does not want to listen to me but perhaps he will take notice of you.

I hope these points are of some creative use to you all and that at least you will do me the courtesy of trying them for I believe that they will materially help the play. We must try and kill the remaining laughs whenever possible.

Fondest love to you all from your absent but never unfaithful director.

dictated by Mr Forbes and signed in his absence.

INDEX

370

373